THE LAW

RELATING TO

THE HINDU WIDOW

THE LAW

RELATING TO

THE HINDU WIDOW

TRAILOKYANATH MITRA, M.A., D.L.

GYAN

Published by

Gyan Publishing House
5, Ansari Road
Daryaganj, New Delhi-110002
Phone: 011-47034999, 9811692060
E-mail: books@gyanbooks.com

Distribution Network
gyanbooks.com
India, USA, Canada, UK, Australia, France

ISBN : 978-81-212-9192-7 (PB)
First Published, 1881

2nd Impression 2023

Printed at: Gyan Press, Delhi.

THE LAW RELATING TO THE HINDU WIDOW
Author: TRAILOKYANATH MITRA

TAGORE LAW LECTURES—1879.

Tagore Law Lectures—1879.

THE LAW

RELATING TO

THE HINDU WIDOW

BY

TRAILOKYANATH MITRA, M.A., D.L.,
LAW LECTURER, PRESIDENCY COLLEGE,
TAGORE LAW PROFESSOR.

CALCUTTA:
THACKER, SPINK, AND CO.,
Publishers to the Calcutta University.
BOMBAY: THACKER & Co., LIMITED. MADRAS: HIGGINBOTHAM & Co.
LONDON: W. THACKER AND CO.

1881.

TABLE OF CONTENTS.

LECTURE I.

LECTURE III.

The Widow's Right of Succession.

Page

LECTURE IV.

The Obligations of the Widow as an Heiress.

LECTURE V.

The Remarriage of Widows.

LECTURE VIII.

THE ALIENATIONS BY THE WIDOW.

LECTURE IX.

THE ALIENATIONS BY THE WIDOW.—*(Continued)*.

LECTURE X.

THE RIGHTS OF THE REVERSIONERS.

LECTURE XI.

SUITS BY REVERSIONERS.

LECTURE XII.

THE MAINTENANCE OF THE WIDOW.

TABLE OF CASES CITED.

I.

J.

K.

L.

S.

LECTURE I.

INTRODUCTION : THE SOURCES OF HINDU LAW.

Conception of law in the jurisprudence of the Hindus—It is of divine origin—Origin of Menu's Code—Summary of the seventh and the eighth chapters of the Code—No trace of the king's power of legislation—Creation of a king — His powers — According to Menu legislation is no part of the king's duties—How cases unprovided for in the Code to be disposed of—Sources of law according to Menu—The duties of a king according to Yajnawalkya—According to Narada—Legislation inconsistent with the fundamental notion of Hindu law that it is immutable—According to Prosonno Kumar Tagore the Kshetryas were the original legislators, afterwards the Brahmins—Reference to the legendary wars of Parusuram to support this view—Value of hypothesis in Sanscrit literature extremely small—Reference to so-called legislative assemblies—This might refer to the ancient custom of teaching the sacred laws—Conclusion—The sources of law according to Menu are four :—(1) The Sruti ; (2) The Smriti ; (3) Approved usage ; (4) Self-satisfaction—Sources of law according to Yajnawalkya—Self-satisfaction as a source of law — Approved usage defined — It consists of customs preserved in Brahmaverta—Their efficacy—Customs not recorded, nor preserved—The Sruti defined—They are three according to Menu—They chiefly contain religious matter—The Smritis defined—Their character—Their division into three parts :—(1) Sruta Sutras ; (2) Grihya Sutras ; (3) Dharma Sutras—Their classification :—(I) Dharma or Samayacharika Sutras ; (II) Metrical versions of the same—Instances—List of the authors of the Smritis from Yajnawalkya—Vijnaneswara's interpretation of the passage—Parasara's enumeration—Enumeration in the Padma Purana—Mr. Borradaile's enumeration—Enumeration by Mr. Stokes—By West and Bühler—Mr. Steele's list—The word Smriti seems to have a definite and restricted meaning—The nature of the Smritis—The opinion regarding them that they never were positive law—Controverted—The mode of reasoning by which the above opinion was arrived at—Fallacy in the same pointed out—It is opposed to the Hindu notion on the subject—Exception to the binding nature of the Smritis—

LECTURE I.

Remarkable agreement among the Smritis—The Smritis constitute one body of law—The Smritis do not exist in their integrity—Variations between them accounted for—Another cause of these variations stated—According to Yajnawalkya the Smritis were actual codes of law—Ethical codes distinct from the sacred code—That the Smritis were positive law maintained by Sir W. Jones—By Mr. Burnell—By Dr. Jolly — Menu-Smriti—Mode of promulgation—A different tradition regarding its promulgation stated—The Smritis originally preserved in memory—According to Parasara particular Smritis applicable to particular ages—Hypothesis regarding the age of Menu's Code—Not satisfactory—The Code divided into twelve chapters—The first chapter contains a history of the creation—The second chapter contains the duties of a Brahmachari—The third chapter relates to the condition of a house-holder—The fourth chapter relates to the same—The fifth chapter relates to different kinds of food, and cause of impurity—The sixth relates to the third and fourth stages of a man's existence—The seventh relates to the rights and duties of a king—The eighth chapter describes the 18 titles of law—The ninth chapter treats of the law of Inheritance — The tenth chapter contains a description of the mixed classes—The eleventh chapter treats of penance and expiation—The twelfth chapter treates of transmigration and *mukti* — The Smriti of Yajnawalkya—Its division into three parts—Hypothesis regarding the age of Yajnawalkya—Contents of Yajnawalkya's Smriti — Hypothesis regarding the date of Narada-Smriti — The Narada-Smriti an abstract of the ninth chapter of the original Code of Menu—Dr. Jolly controverts the same—Fallacy in his reasoning pointed out—Contents of the Narada-Smriti—First part treats of judicature—The second part describes the 18 titles of law—Present condition of the Smritis—Except Menu's Code none of them exists in its integrity—Facility for literary forgeries in India—The Code called Laghu Menu is entire—Other Smritis exist in mere quotations—The Digests—Their influence on Hindu law—The distinction between the digests and the commentaries—The digests give rise to the different schools of Hindu law—Their interpretations of the same text—Illustration—Another illustration, the sister—Another illustration, the widow—The character of these digests—Practically they constitute the positive law of the Hindus—In ancient India, secular learning spread very slowly—Two modes of publication—By teaching—By public recitation—The Mitacshara: its authority—Its date—The Dharmaratna—The Dayabhaga only a part of it—The book was promulgated long after the Mitacshara—The Vivada Chintamani, leading authority in Mithila—The Vyavahara Mayukha, the leading authority in the Maharashtra school—The Parasara Madhavya and the Smriti Chandrica, the leading authorities in the South—The Smriti Chandrica—Other authorities of the Bengal school—Of the Mithila school—Of the Benares school—

Of the Maharashtra school—Of the Daravida school—The judicial decisions—They have modified original Hindu law—Limitations to the proposition that Hindu law has remained unaltered for many thousands of years — Stationary and progressive societies distinguished—The Hindu society has changed, though slowly—The law changes as society changes—Law changed by authentic interpretation and by judge-made law—The Hindu law changed by indirect methods — The Hindu law changed by judicial decision — Illustration—The law of wills and testaments—The alienation of family property opposed to the provisions of Hindu law—How far modified by the Mitacshara—Jimutavahana went a step further—The testamentary law deduced by the Courts from an erroneous view of the law of the Bengal school—The law of wills repugnant to the notions of a Hindu—Another illustration—Suits by reversioners to set aside widow's alienations—An illustration from the Mitacshara—Power of the father to alienate family property—Denied in the Mitacshara—Recognized by the Privy Council — Another illustration—The joint Hindu family of Bengal—Decisions of Courts have created to some extent uncertainty in Hindu law—Illustration—Brother's daughter's sons are heirs or not?—Another illustration of uncertainty created by judicial decisions—The value of standard works—Mischief of disregarding standard authorities — The difficulties of administering Hindu law—Partially removed by translations of standard works—The pundits the interpreters of law—Sometimes disregarded by the Judges — Natural growth of law arrested—Judicial decisions often based upon incomplete materials—Present uncertain condition of Hindu law—Injurious to the interests of the community—Its remedy—By judicial decisions, or by codification — Considerable aid to the Courts by translations of the principal Digests, and the collection of customs—A code of Hindu law is not likely to succeed at present.

THE modern or European conception of law is, that it is the *wish* or *command* of the sovereign individual or sovereign body; and that, beyond this, *positive law* has no other source or origin. This conception does not obtain in Hindu law. There is no trace in Hindu law literature of the notion that law is a matter of *human* institution, ordained by *mere human* rulers; that kings have powers of legislation and also powers of abrogating existing laws. On

Conception of law in the jurisprudence of the Hindus.

LECTURE I.

the contrary, there are numerous texts to be found in the writings of the ancient *Rishis*, to the effect that law is sacred,—that it is of divine origin,—that it is the revealed word of God,—and that it is eternal and immutable. There is a passage in the Vedas, which, as translated by Sir W. Jones according to the gloss of Sankara, reads thus:—"God, having created the four classes, had not yet completed his work; but, in addition to it, lest the Royal and Military Class should become insupportable through their power and ferocity, he produced the transcendent body of law; since law is the king of kings, far more powerful and rigid than they: nothing can be mightier than law, by whose aid, as by that of the highest monarch, even the weak may prevail over the strong."[1] This is the true conception of law according to the Hindus: it is not a mere fiction to aid the purposes of interpretation, but is an article of belief among nearly 150 millions of human beings that dwell in Hindustan.

It is of divine origin.

Regarding the origin of Menu's Code, the highest and most respected of all the Smritis, it is declared in the Code itself, that "He (the Immutable Power), having enacted this Code of laws, himself taught it fully to me in the beginning: afterwards I taught it to Marichi and the nine other holy sages;"[2] thus clearly expressing the divine origin of this Code.

Origin of Menu's Code.

---

[1] Digest, Intro., xi.

[2] Chap. I, v. 58.

Summary of the seventh and the eighth chapters of the Code.

The seventh and the eighth chapters of the Institutes of Menu treat of Government and Public Law, or on the Military Class; and on Judicature, and on Law, "private and criminal." The first verse of the seventh chapter states: "I will fully declare the *duty of kings*; and show how a ruler of men should conduct himself, in what manner he was framed, and how his ultimate reward may be attained by him." In these two chapters, minute rules are laid down for the guidance of the king; his chief duty is described to be the administration of justice according to local usage and to *written codes*;[1] to inflict punishment on all those who act unjustly;[2] the mischievous consequences of indolence on the part of the king in not punishing the guilty are then pointed out.[3] Then we have rules for the selection of ministers and other public officers;[4] the appointment of ambassadors and their duties.[5] Then minute rules are laid down for the selection of a proper site for his capital;[6] for constructing a fortress in the mountains;[7] and the modes of supplying the same with weapons and commissariat stores.[8] Rules for carrying on war and negotiations with enemies, and the conduct towards enemies in battle; what are prizes of war, are next discussed with great

[1] Chap. VIII, vv. 1-3.
[2] Chap. VII, v. 16.
[3] Chap. VII, vv. 20-23.
[4] Chap. VII, v. 54 *et seq.*
[5] Chap. VII, v. 63 *et seq.*
[6] Chap. VII, v. 70.
[7] Chap. VII, v. 71 *et seq.*
[8] Chap. VII, v. 87 *et seq.*, and v. 160 *et seq.*

LECTURE I. minuteness. Then follow rules for the internal management of his kingdom:[1] the appointment of lords or governors of towns and districts: the modes of remunerating those officers of Government: the amount of daily wages to be paid to menial servants in the royal household.[2] Then we find directions for levying taxes and the modes of raising revenue: the king's share in the various kinds of produce.[3] Then follow rules to guide his daily habits of life:[4] what sort of food he is to take, and by whom it is to be prepared; musical recreations and dalliance with females of the royal household.[5] Next we find elaborate regulations[6] on military matters: enlistment of soldiers: modes of arranging the army in the battle-field: the proper time of the year for going out on military expeditions: negotiations for peace and alliance: the treatment of allies and confederates in war: the treatment of princes vanquished in war, and the mode of governing a conquered country.

No trace of the king's power of legislation.

In this most minute and elaborate description of a king's duties—minute even to trivialness—there is not the slightest trace of, or the least allusion to, that most important function of a king,—*viz.*, legislation. On the contrary, he is directed to govern his kingdom, and to decide the disputes of his subjects,

[1] Chap. VII, v. 113 *et seq.*
[2] Chap. VII, v. 128 *et seq.*
[3] Chap. VII, v. 145.
[4] Chap. VII, v. 217.
[5] Chap. VII, vv. 221 and 225.
[6] Chap. VII, v. 160 *et seq.*

according to "rules drawn from local usages and from written codes."[1]

Creation of a king.

Menu describes a king as created by "the ruler of this universe," "forming him of eternal particles drawn from the substance of Indra, Pavana, Yama, Surya, of Agni and Varuna, of Chandra and Cuvera."[2] "And since a king was composed of particles drawn from those chief guardian deities, he consequently surpasses all mortals in glory."[3] He is fire and air: he, both sun and moon: he, the god of criminal justice: he, the genius of wealth: he, the regent of waters: he, the lord of the firmament."[4] "A king, even though a child, must not be treated lightly from an idea that he is a mere mortal: no: he is a powerful divinity who appears in a human shape."[5] Amid this extravagant description of the superhuman—nay divine—origin of kings, there is no power reserved to them of enacting or altering the law, which exists independent of them, and has an origin superior to them.

His powers.

According to Menu legislation is no part of the king's duties.

There is another passage in the Institutes which establishes, beyond doubt, the proposition that legislation formed no part of the duties of a king according to the Hindu Sastras. The Code of Menu assumes this position, which is generally accepted by the Hindus, that it is a *complete* code of duties for *all* classes of people constituting the Hindu

[1] Chap. VIII, v. 3. [2] Chap. VIII, v. 4. [3] Chap. VIII, v. 5. [4] Chap. VIII, v. 7. [5] Chap. VIII, v. 8.

LECTURE I.

society: and that it is not a code intended for only one class of people or one class of duties. In fact, universality is its great merit and its chief pride. The great legislator, however, anticipating that cases might arise which may not have been provided for in his Code, declares that, in particular cases which are not comprised in any of the general rules, the law shall be ascertained by the opinion of the well-instructed Brahmins, which shall be held to be incontestable law:[1] and well-instructed Brahmins are declared to be those "who can adduce ocular proof from the Scripture itself, having studied, as the law ordains, the Vedas and their extended branches," which are, according to Kulluka Bhatta, "the Vedangas Mimansa, Nyaya, Dharma Sastra, Puranas;"[2] and further, "a point of law before not expressly revealed, which shall be decided by an assembly of ten such virtuous Brahmins under one chief, or, if ten be not procurable, of three such, under one president, let no man controvert."[3] It is clear that even in these exceptional cases, which the Code considers must be of rare occurrence, express legislative powers of the king are not recognised; but that the law is to be declared from the analogy of existing rules to be determined by Brahmins learned in the law.

How cases unprovided for in the Code to be disposed of.

In another place Menu, speaking of the sources of law, declares there are only four,—*viz.*, the Scriptures,

Sources of law according to Menu.

[1] Chap. XII, v. 108. [2] Chap. XII, v. 109. [3] Chap. XII, v. 100.

the codes of law, approved usage, and self-satisfaction;[1] and does not mention legislation among the sources of law. This subject will be considered more fully hereafter.

In the Institutes of Yajnawalkya, we find the duties of a king laid down in a similar manner, though with more brevity, and his chief duty is described to be the "daily investigation of judicial proceedings, being aided by assessors." **The duties of a king according to Yajnawalkya.**

It is again laid down, that "the king, divested of anger and avarice, and associated with learned Brahmins, should investigate judicial proceedings conformably to the *sacred code of laws.*"[2] It is clear that the king's decision must be based upon the *sacred code of laws*, and not upon any laws enacted or ordained by him. And nowhere, in the whole of these Institutes, do we find any reference to any sort of legislative functions to be exercised by the king.

In the Narada Smriti we find the same notion prevailing. Narada describes the eight constituent parts of a judicial proceeding to be "the king, his officer, the assessors, the *law book*, the accountant and scribe, gold and fire for ordeals, and water for refreshment."[3] **According to Narada.**

Justice is to be administered by the king by "taking the *law code* for his guide, and abiding by the opinion pronounced by the chief judge."[4] The

---

[1] Chap. II, v. 12. [2] Yajnawalkya, cited in the Mitacshara, Chap. I.
[3] Chap. I, v. 16. [4] Chap. I, v. 31.

LECTURE I. chapter closes by a sort of summing up of the king's duties in these words:—"A king, thus constantly paying attention to the trial of law-suits, here acquires brilliant glory, and hereafter reaches the abode of the sun."[1] From these passages it is clear that the *law code* is something *pre-existing*, which the king is directed to follow and in no way to transgress.

Legislation inconsistent with the fundamental notion of Hindu law that it is immutable.

Again, the universally accepted conception that Hindu law is Revelation, immutable and eternal, cannot be consistently maintained if it is once admitted that there is a power in kings to alter or abrogate those laws, and to substitute other laws in their stead; and the fact is incontrovertible that this law has remained unchanged, theoretically as well as practically, from the very earliest times of which we have any historical record. And there is no evidence to show that this system of law was ever touched, or in any manner interfered with, by any body of *human beings after* the date of its first promulgation. Legislative power, if existing anywhere, would most certainly have tampered with its integrity at some period of its immensely long existence.

According to Prosonno Kumar Tagore, the Kshetryas were the original legislators.

Babu Prosonno Kumar Tagore, in the preface to his translation of the Vivada Chintamani, has hinted an opinion that the legislative functions originally belonged to the Kshetryas, or the second of the four original classes: that, on account of their despotic

[1] Chap. I, v. 68.

and arbitrary measures, the other classes revolted against their authority, snatched the legislative powers from their hands, and entrusted the same into the hands of the Brahmins. From that time the Brahmins became the legislators, and the Kshetryas the repository of executive authority in the country.

afterwards the Brahmins.

This view is attempted to be supported by a reference to the legendary wars of Parasuram, which have a very doubtful signification; and the learned translator has quoted no other authority in support of his opinion. This opinion, therefore, rests upon mere conjecture; and the value of hypothesis, unsupported by positive data, in laying the historic basis of changes or revolutions in Hindu law or religion is now generally admitted to be extremely small: opinions thus formed may be historically true or historically false; but true or false, they are as easily formed as they are exploded.

Reference to the legendary wars of Parasuram to support this view.

Value of hypothesis in Sanscrit literature extremely small.

Unfortunately, Sanscrit literature has been oftentimes made the subject of crude and hasty generalisations. In it general conclusions have been boldly drawn from the most scanty materials, and the most questionable and spurious authorities have been employed to support them without the least historical investigation or the exercise of that critical ingenuity which, from its peculiar character, Sanscrit literature requires more than any other.

The learned translator further talks of Bhrigu being appointed president of the *supreme legislative*

Reference to so-called legislative assemblies.

LECTURE I.

assembly, and "presidents were likewise appointed to all the other legislative assemblies as they became established in the various parts of the land."[1] For this there is no historic evidence, and there is no authority in support of this position in the ancient texts. It is true, in the Code of Menu it is stated that Bhrigu recited this code to the *Rishis*, who came to learn it from him:[2] and that Yajnawalkya delivered his texts to the sages who had assembled to hear him.

This might refer to the ancient custom of teaching the sacred laws.

Might not this refer to the most ancient and laudable practice (mentioned by Menu) of teaching the sacred laws to disciples, who afterwards expounded and disseminated the doctrines of their great master, rather than to the formation of legislative assemblies presided over by learned sages (a purely modern notion)?

Conclusion.

I think it is clear, from the ancient texts and the universally accepted notions on the subject, that, according to Hindu authorities, Law had a pre-existing entity, and was promulgated by the divine power himself; that there was no necessity or room for the exercise of legislative functions by human kings. The unaltered state of the law for so many thousands of years, in theory and also in practice, can alone be explained on the theory that Law is Revealed. The *Rishivakya* constitutes the Hindu law; but one *Rishi* has never been held to contradict or override another *Rishi*; and it is the great object of the

[1] Preface, vi.

[2] Chap. I, v. 59.

Digest-writers or commentators to explain or reconcile the *apparent* contradictions. I say apparent, because the theory is, there is no *real* conflict between two *Rishivakyas*, and that they are all reconcilable with each other, as being derived from the same source.

Lecture I.

Such being the origin of Hindu law, the next question that presents itself is,—where are we to get this law ; in what documents are they embodied, or in what books are they contained ?

The sources of law according to Menu are four:—

To this question the learned Pundits return an unanimous answer,—*viz.*, that the Law is contained—

(1.) In the Sruti.

(1) The Sruti.

(2.) In the Smriti.

(2) The Smriti.

And Menu adds a third and fourth source of law, *viz.*, *approved usage* and *self-satisfaction.*

(3) Approved usage.

(4) Self-satisfaction.

" The Scripture, the codes of law, approved usage, and, in all indifferent cases, self-satisfaction, the wise have openly declared to be the quadruple description of the juridical system."[1] In another place Menu lays down " the roots of law are the whole *Veda*, the ordinances and moral practices of such as perfectly understand it, the immemorial customs of good men, and, in cases quite indifferent, self-satisfaction." [2]

According to Yajnawalkya, the sources or root of law are "the Sruti, the Smriti, the practice of good men, what seems good to one's self, and a desire maturely considered."[3] If the two *slokas* of Menu refer to the same

Sources of law according to Yajnawalkya.

---

[1] Chap. II, v. 12. [2] Chap. II, v. 6.

[3] Bk. I, v. 7, p. 3, Röer and Montriou's Translation.

LECTURE I.

objects, as evidently they do, *the ordinances and moral practices of such as understand the Veda*, mentioned in the latter *sloka*, would be identical with *the codes of law* mentioned in the former, a rather difficult identity, looking to the import of the two expressions. But the most difficult part in the two *slokas* is, that self-satisfaction is mentioned as a source of law. What the great lawgiver meant by *self-satisfaction* as a root or source of law, is very difficult at this distance of time to determine. Probably he meant, as his great commentator Kulluka Bhatta indicates by using as a comment the words "in cases quite indifferent" that in insignificant matters not provided for in the other sources of law, the man's own ideas of right and wrong ought to be the test of his conduct. Is it the elementary conception of the doctrine of the liberty of private judgment, which is the foundation of some of the modern systems of religion and morality, but of which hardly any trace is to be found in the Hindu religion?

Self-satisfaction as a source of law.

Approved usage defined.

Approved usage, as a source of law, is declared to be a body of customs which have sprung up and been preserved in that tract of country which is styled *Brahmaverta*, situated between the two divine rivers *Saraswati* and *Drishadwati*, a tract of country frequented by the gods.[1] This is the tract of country which is believed by oriental scholars to be the first settlement or home in India of the first Aryan inva-

It consists of customs preserved in Brahmaverta.

[1] Chap. II, v. 17.

ders or immigrants in that country. "The custom preserved by immemorial tradition in that country, among the four pure classes and among those which are mixed, is called approved usage."[1] The efficacy or validity of these customs is declared in another part of the Code. "Immemorial custom is transcendent law approved in the sacred Scriptures and in the codes of the divine legislators: let every man, therefore, of the three principal classes, who has a due reverence for the supreme spirit which dwells in him, diligently and constantly observe immemorial custom."[2] And punishment is ordained for those who deviate from such immemorial usage. "A man of the priestly, military, or commercial class, who deviates from immemorial usage tastes not the fruit of the *Vedas*, but by an exact observance of it he gathers that fruit in perfection."[3] "Thus have holy sages, well knowing that law is grounded on immemorial custom, embraced, as the root of all piety, good usages long established."[4] This is evidence of the growth of a large body of what European jurists call customary laws: and it is clear that the *Aryans* must have been settled in India for many centuries before a large body of customs could have sprung up, and been preserved by immemorial tradition to which transcendental efficacy could be ascribed.

Their efficacy.

Though we have in the above passages a clear

Customs not recorded, nor preserved.

---

[1] Chap. II, v. 18.

[2] Chap. I, v. 108.

[3] Chap. I, v. 109.

[4] Chap. I, v. 110.

LECTURE I. recognition of immemorial custom as a source of positive law, it is well known, however, that these customs have not been preserved. They have never been collected or embodied in a book and handed down from generation to generation, except isolated and obscure references to some individual custom occurring in some Digest or Commentary. I do not think there is any authentic or complete record of these ancient customs.

The administration of justice in this country has also the effect of ignoring these customs. Our Courts have never recognised them, and have never attempted to resuscitate them or enquire into their existance. An ancient text, promulgated many thousand years ago, is given an inflexible interpretation, and made applicable to diverse nationalities of Hindus, without considering the immense change that long standing custom has introduced upon that text among the several populations of Hindus to whom it is made applicable. Take for instance the case of adoption. It has been held by the Bengal High Court, in the case of *Behary Lal Mullic* v. *Indurmonee Chowdrain*,[1] that, among Sudras in Bengal, no ceremonies are necessary to make a valid adoption in addition to the giving and taking of the child in adoption. The parties to the suit belonged to a class of *Kayasthas* of Bengal, who are generally admitted

[1] 21 W. R., 285.

to belong to the class of Sudras, though some scholars have maintained a contrary opinion. Now, among the *Kayasthas* of Bengal, it is notorious that all religious ceremonies are performed in the same way as among the twiceborn classes, with this exception that a Brahmin performs for them those parts of the ceremonies which they themselves are precluded from performing,—*i.e.*, the performance of the *homa*. This has been the custom with the *Kayasthas* from time immemorial, and in cases of adoption among them the religious ceremonies, including the *datta homam*, have been invariably performed from very ancient times. The existence of this custom was never made the subject of enquiry in the above case. If it was, the Court would certainly have come to the conclusion that an adoption among *Kayasthas* of Bengal cannot be valid unless the religious ceremonies, including the *datta homam*, were performed. The Court, however, neglecting that enquiry, came to the conclusion, on the authority of ancient texts, which, however, have been modified by long-standing custom, that the religious ceremonies were not necessary to the validity of the adoption—a conclusion directly opposed to the customary law of the caste to which it was held applicable.

The non-preservation of the customary law of the several classes of Hindus, and the mode in which they have been disregarded by our Courts, have been a source of serious loss to Hindu law, in the absence of

LECTURE I.

which the several stages of its development can now be hardly explained.

The Sruti or the Veda is considered in theory the ultimate source of all law. All the Smritis are supposed to be contained in or evolved out of the Sruti. Menu's Code is said to be fully contained in the Veda. "Whatever law has been ordained for any person by Menu, that law is fully declared in the Veda."[1] The *Sruti* is thus defined by Menu: "By Sruti, or what was heard from above, is meant the Veda,"[2] and the Vedas are said to have existed before the creation. "He too (the Great Power) first assigned to all creatures distinct names, distinct acts, and distinct occupations: as they had been revealed in the pre-existing Veda;"[3] and the Vedas are said to have been formed by the Great Power in the following manner:—"From fire, from air, and from the sun, he milked out as it were the three primordial Vedas,—named Rich, Yajush, and Saman,—for the due performances of the sacrifice."[4] I may mention here in passing, that, in the Code of Menu, the fourth, or the Atharvan Veda, is never mentioned; but that wherever the Vedas are referred to, only the above three Vedas are either expressly mentioned or referred to by implication. This, probably, will account for the belief prevalent among the Pundits and orthodox Hindus that the Atharvan Veda is heterodox in its doctrines.

The Sruti defined.

They are three according to Menu.

[1] Chap. II, v. 7.
[2] Chap. II, v. 10.
[3] Chap. I, v. 21.
[4] Chap. I, v. 23.

The Vedas, however, contain more of religious ordinances, and texts bearing upon law are very rare: hence the Smritis are usually referred to as containing a complete exposition of the legal duties. LECTURE I. They chiefly contain religious matters.

THE SMRITIS.

The Smritis are the codes of law. Their authority is thus described by Menu:—"By Smriti, or what was remembered from the beginning, the body of law; those two (Sruti and Smriti) must not be oppugned by heterodox arguments: since from those two proceeds the whole system of duties."[1] The Smritis are considered to be revealed law, proclaimed or promulgated by certain sages or Rishis (*inspired men*). The Mimansists say these works partake of the *human* character on account of their origin, and are, therefore, distinguished from the *Sruti*, the texts of which are supposed to exist in the very words of the Revelation. "The word 'Smriti' means literally 'recollection,' and is used to denote a work or body of works in which the Rishis or sages of antiquity, who saw or received the revelation of the Vedas, set down *their recollections* regarding the performance of sacrifices, initiatory and daily rites, and the duty of man generally. The aphorisms on Vedic sacrifices (Sruta Sutras); the aphorisms on ceremonies for the performance of which the domestic fire kindled at the time of marriage is required (Grihya Sutras); and the works treating of

The Smritis defined.

Their character.

Their division into three parts.

1. Sruta Sutras.

2. Grihya Sutras.

---

[1] Chap. II, v. 10.

LECTURE I. — 3. Dharma Sutras. the duties of men in their various relations (Dharma Sutras) are all comprised by the term Smriti. In the common parlance of our days, however, the term has a narrower meaning, and is restricted to the last kind of works."[1]

Their classification. Oriental scholars maintain an opinion that these law books may be divided into two principal classes.

I—Dharma, or Samayacharika Sutras. I.—*Dharma, or Samayacharika Sutras,*

i.e., literally "Aphorisms on law or established custom" written partly in prose, partly in mixed prose and verse.

II—Metrical versions of the same. II.—*Metrical versions of such works.*

The former class of works is considered to be more Instances. ancient than the latter. Apastamba's Dharma Sutra and Vishnu's Dharma Sutra are considered as specimens of the former class; and the Institutes of Menu, of Yajnawalkya, and of Parasara are considered as belonging to the latter class. This opinion originated with Professor Max Müller, and was subsequently followed by West and Bühler in their Introduction to the Digest of Hindu law. The reasoning by which this view is supported will be found in Max Müller's History of Ancient Sanscrit Literature, pp. 61, 132, 199, 206-208, and his letter printed in Morley's Digest, Introduction, p. cxcvi.

---

[1] West and Bühler, Intro., xi.

The sages, or Rishis, who are considered as the reputed authors of the *Smritis*, are the following :— LECTURE I.

List of the authors of the Smritis from Yajnawalkya.

1. Menu.	11. Katyayana.
2. Atri.	12. Vrihaspati.
3. Vishnu.	13. Parasara.
4. Harita.	14. Vyasa.
5. Yajnawalkya.	15. Sankha.
6. Usanas.	16. Likhita.
7. Angira.	17. Daksha.
8. Yama.	18. Gotama.
9. Apastamba.	19. Satatapa.
10. Sambarta.	20. Vasishtha.

These are the names of the twenty Rishis as given by Yajnawalkya.[1] The author of the Mitacshara, commenting upon the text which contains the above enumeration, says (*Mitacshara Acharakanda*):— "The meaning of this verse is, that the Institutes of Law, composed by Yajnawalkya, ought to be studied. The enumeration (of authors of Smritis given in this verse) is not intended to be exhaustive, but merely to give examples. Therefore, this verse does not exclude the works of Baudhayana and the rest (who are not mentioned) from the Institutes of Law; as each of these Smritis possesses authority, the points left doubtful by the one may be decided from the other. If one set of Institutes contradicts the other, then there is an option."

Vijnaneswara's interpretation of the passage.

[1] Bk. I, vv. 4, 5, p. 2, Roer and Montriou's Translation.

LECTURE I.

Parasara's enumeration.

Parasara, who is one of the twenty Rishis in Yajnawalkya's list, names also twenty sages whose works are entitled to be called Smritis: his list[1] agrees generally with Yajnawalkya's, except in these names: instead of Yama, Vrihaspati, and Vyasa, he substitutes, Kasyapa, Gargya, and Prachetas.

Enumeration in the Padma Purana.

The Padma Purana, however, extends the list to thirty-six sages, which is made up, by excluding Atri's name in Yajnawalkya's list, by the following additional names:—

20. Marichi.	29. Gargya.
21. Pulastya.	30. Baudhayana.
22. Prachetas.	31. Paithinasi.
23. Bhrigu.	32. Jabali.
24. Narada.	33. Sumantu.
25. Kasyapa.	34. Parascara.
26. Viswamitra.	35. Locacshi.
27. Devala.	36. Kuthumi.[2]
28. Rishyasringa.	

Mr. Borradaile's enumeration.

Mr. Borradaile, in his preface to the translation of Vyavahara Mayukha, enumerates forty-seven Rishis, twenty-seven of whom are considered as authors of *Upa Smritis*, or works inferior in authority to the Smritis. Mr. Stokes, in a note on the above passage, gives fifty-one names. Messrs. West and Bühler, in the Introduction[3] to the Digest of Hindu Law, give the names of seventy-eight sages, who are the

Enumeration by Mr. Stokes.

By West and Bühler.

[1] Chap. I, vv. 12—15.

[2] Colebrooke's Digest, Pref., xiv.

[3] P. xiii.

authors of one hundred and thirteen distinct works; some of them being reputed to be the authors of more than one work. But the most singular list is furnished by Mr. Steele in his Summary of the Law and Custom of Hindu Castes. He gives the names of eighteen Smritis and eleven Upa Smritis, and among the Upa Smritis curiously enough is the Code of Menu placed. This list was furnished to him by persons assembled in Khandesh.

LECTURE I.

Mr. Steele's list.

The word 'Smriti' does not seem to be so flexible as the European scholars seem to think. It had a certain definite meaning attached to it in Hindu law, and it seems that the term applied to the writings of certain well-known sages and to no other. The European scholars have arrived at this enormous list of names by extracting the name of every author quoted or referred to in some work or other on Hindu law; that everyone of such personages is entitled to the honor of being styled the author of a Smriti seems very questionable: and there is no authority in the writings of the ancient sages for such an indiscriminate use of the term.

The word Smriti seems to have a definite and restricted meaning.

The nature or character of the Smritis must be next considered; an opinion has grown up among European scholars, that these Smritis never embodied the *actual* laws current among the Hindus at any time; that all of them were not *positive laws* in the modern sense of the term; they rather consisted of actual laws and hypothetical laws according to the

The nature of the Smritis.

The opinion regarding them that they never were positive law.

LECTURE I.

notions of the author as to what perfect laws ought to be in a Brahmin community: they at best resemble the modern treatises on Jurisprudence embodying the ideal of laws than actual laws themselves. This opinion it is necessary to examine in detail, as it affects the authority of those writings, and contradicts the universally accepted *Hindu* notion on the subject. The opinion, I believe, originated with Mr. Elphinstone. In his History of India, speaking of Menu's Code, he says :—"I have adhered to the usual phraseology in speaking of this compilation: but though early adopted as an unquestionable authority for the law, I should scarcely venture to regard it as a code drawn up for the regulation of a particular state under the sanction of a Government. It seems rather to be the work of a learned man designed to set forth his idea of a perfect commonwealth under Hindu institutions."[1] This is Mr. Elphinstone's "supposition," and he thought Menu's Code, like Plato's Republic, represented an ideal commonwealth. Sir Henry Maine, deriving his notion probably from Mr. Elphinstone's remark, says as follows of Menu's Code: "The Hindu Code, called the laws of Menu, which is certainly a Brahmin compilation, undoubtedly enshrines many genuine observances of the Hindu race, but the opinion of the best contemporary Orientalists is, that it does not, as a whole, represent a set of

---

[1] 4th ed., p. 11.

rules ever actually administered in Hindoostan. It is in great part an ideal picture of that which in the view of the Brahmins *ought* to be the law."[1] Messrs. West and Bühler, in the Introduction to their Digest of Hindu Law, say as follows :—"The older Smritis and the originals of the rest are not codes, but simply manuals for the instruction of the students of the *Charanas*, or schools. Hence it is not to be expected that each of these works should treat its subject in all its details. It was enough to give certain general principles, and only those details which appeared particularly interesting to each individual teacher. It is, therefore, unreasonable to charge the Smriti 'codes' with a want of precision and of discrimination between moral and legal maxims, etc. Such strictures would only be justified if they were really 'codes' intended from the first to settle the law between man and man."[2] And Justice Jackson, in his judgment in the Unchastity case, has maintained the same opinion.[3] He has quoted the above authorities and some others, except Mr. Elphinstone, and has given his adherence to the opinion expressed by them. LECTURE I.

With due deference to the opinion of the above authorities, I venture to say that the result of my readings and enquiries has been to come to a different conclusion. In the first place, the above authorities Controverted. The mode of reasoning, by

[1] Ancient Law, p. 17, ed. of 1863.

[2] Intro., p. xxxvi.

[3] 19 W. R., 403.

LECTURE I.

which the above opinion was arrived at.

seemed to have arrived at the conclusion by a sort of argument from *analogy*. Examining the Codes themselves, they found that they contained rules—some of them very harsh, some very light, considering the nature of the offences, some provisions were very puerile, some only rules of morality, and some apparently self-contradictory ; some favored one class, and some pressed very hard upon another class. From this picture of incongruities and self-contradictions, the modern critics arrived at the conclusion that the Codes never constituted an actual body of positive law for the government of a living community.

Fallacy in the same pointed out.

Now, reasoning of this kind is liable to some peculiar errors. We are apt to forget that, although the Code has to a certain extent come down intact, the state of society, for which it was intended, has long since passed away ; that far from having a living model to represent it, it is difficult even in imagination to correctly conceive it. Again, we are apt to make our present notions of law, morality, government, etc., as our standard of comparison, and arrive at the grotesque picture described above. Add to this the circumstance, which is of considerable significance in this discussion, that perhaps none of the Codes has come down to our times in its integrity, and that certainly most of them exist in a very fragmentary or mutilated shape ; and the so-called incongruities or self-contradictions could, probably, have been explained away if we had the benefit of seeing the *whole* Code. Supposing the Indian Penal Code in a fragmentary state was to come down to a people that would exist 2,000 years hence, and who differed from us as much as the Greeks of Homer differed from the modern subjects of the Porte. What would that society think of our Penal Code: would they not think somewhat in the same way that the European scholars named above consider the Smritis?' This reminds one of Lord Macaulay's famous story of the New Zealander.

It must also be remembered that the harshness and incongruities of a code are very much toned down by the mode in which its several provisions are administered. The Code, probably, prescribed the maximum penalty, or embodied the extreme views on a particular question: but the Judge, who had to administer the law, taking into consideration all the circumstances, passed sentences or decrees which were very far from the actual provisions of the Code itself. We do not know how far the rigours of ancient law were mitigated by the Judges who administered that law, and, in the absence of that evidence, we have only one side of the picture from which to draw our conclusions.

It is opposed to the Hindu notion on the subject.

In the second place, the opinion is directly opposed to the Hindu notion of the authority of these Smritis. Ask any Pundit or native scholar, well-read in the Sastras, in any part of India, and he will at once answer that the Smritis contain *binding* rules of con-

LECTURE I.

duct, and he will be surprised by the opinion that they are like treatises on Ethics or Jurisprudence. This is the traditional opinion; and, in India, traditions have a remarkable continuity embodying truth which is oftentimes disguised. Now this traditional opinion must have had some factitious basis, though it is impossible, at this distance of time, to identify or determine it, which would lead to the conclusion that these Smritis, or a Smriti, must have been the actual code of law governing the Hindu society at some stage of its existence.

Exception to the binding nature of the Smritis.

Of course, there is one exception to the binding nature of the rules in the Smritis. It is in the case of certain of their provisions which are declared not applicable to the present, or Kali Age. For this there is authority in the Smritis themselves, which expressly declare that certain rules are not to be observed in the present age. Such as the practice of Niyoga, the several descriptions of sons, and so forth. These provisions will be similar to what would be now styled as laws repealed.

Remarkable agreement among the Smritis.

There is another singular circumstance about all these Smritis. If carefully examined, it will appear that all these Smritis agree most remarkably in all important or principal points. The eight forms of marriage, the eighteen titles of law, the twelve descriptions of sons, the practice of Niyoga, or permission to raise up issue, the mode of administering justice, the several duties of the four primary classes, the rules about expiation, and, in such principal points, all the Smritis generally agree. Now whence is this agreement derived? Probably the Smritis embody *one* body of laws which obtained among the Aryans in their first home in Hindoostan, or in their ancient home outside the limits of Hindoostan. The latter seems to be the likelier hypothesis. The Smritis, being considered *remembered* law, remembered from time *immemorial*, and as there is no written record of the Aryan people in their home beyond the Hindu Kush mountains, whereas there is a faint trace of their gradual settlements in Hindoostan, in Menu,[1] it is more likely that the Smritis embodied the laws or rules that were remembered and brought with them by the Hindus from their ancient home beyond the Hindu Kush mountains.

The Smritis constitute one body of law.

That the Smritis constitute *one* body of law, supplementing each other, is universally maintained by all the Pundits of modern as well as of ancient times; and there is authority for it in Menu, where it is stated that, "when there are two sacred texts, apparently inconsistent, both are held to be law: for both are pronounced by the wise to be valid and reconcilable."[2] This may be the traditional embodiment of an archaic fact referring to the unity of this body of law.

Our examination of the Smritis for the purpose of tracing the agreement between them is very much

---

[1] Chap. II, v. 17 *et seq.*

[2] Chap. II, v. 14.

LECTURE I.

impaired by the fact of the mutilated condition in which they at present exist, coupled with the circumstance of many interpolations existing among them, and the suspicion of the existence of many more.

The Smritis do not exist in their integrity.

If we had a genuine body of Smritis existing in its integrity, our enquiries on this head would have been attended with signal success; as it is, we must be satisfied with the defective materials that we possess, and work upon them as best we can. The difference in the provisions that exist in the several Smritis in matters of detail, is probably accounted for by the import of local customs influencing their provisions. We have evidence in Menu's Code that, at the time of its promulgation, the Aryans had occupied the whole or nearly the whole of Hindoostan Proper.

Variations between them accounted for.

They had occupied the country called *Brahmavarta* situated between the rivers *Saraswati* and *Drishadwati* in the Punjab.[1] They had occupied the country called *Brahmarshi*, consisting of *Kurukshetra*, *Matsya*, *Panchala* or *Kanyacubja*, and *Surasena* or *Mathura*, including the modern Doab and the adjacent territories.[2] They had occupied "the country which lies between *Himawat* and *Vindhya* to the east of *Vinasana* and to the west of *Prayaga* (Allahabad), celebrated by the title of *Madhya Desa*, or the central region."[3] And they had occupied the country which is situated "as far as the eastern and as far as the western oceans

---

[1] Chap. II, v. 17. [2] Chap. II, v. 19. [3] Chap. II, v. 21.

between the two mountains just mentioned, which the wise have named *Aryavarta*, or inhabited by respectable men."[1] Among the ancient Aryans who had occupied such various parts of the country, local customs must have arisen which varied from the provisions of ancient law; and as custom is authoritatively respected, its silent influence exerted upon the provisions of ancient law may probably have caused the variations that are now observable among the several Smritis.

Another cause of these variations stated.

Another circumstance may have contributed to create the variations. The ancient law must have existed at one time as unwritten law, before writing was invented; it existed as part of the spoken literature of the country before written literature came into use. This body of law was handed down by tradition by the ancient and approved custom of the country from teachers to disciples in succession. We find Menu's Code promulgated to an assembly of *Rishis* who came to be instructed in it by Bhrigu, the son of Menu.[2] We find the Institutes of Yajnawalkya in a similar manner declared before an assembly of Rishis in ancient Mithila. And it is still the custom among the Pundits of this country for each one to teach a number of disciples in some branch of law or ritual. I shall afterwards show that this is one of the two modes by which new tenets or doctrines

---

[1] Chap. II, v. 22.

[2] Chap. I, vv. 59 & 60.

LECTURE I.

were *published* among the ancient Hindus. Now, this body of law must have existed in memory for a considerable length of time, probably for some centuries. In the course of its devolution in this manner, the traditional body of law must have received accretions, either by accident or by design, till it was reduced into writing, when it obtained a fixedness, and was for the first time, what may be called, stereotyped. The accretions to the traditions must have been various according to the parts of the country where they were severally current, and the variations among the several Smritis will, probably, be thus accounted for.

According to Yajnawalkya the Smritis were actual codes of law.

That the Smritis were codes of *law*, and not treatises on *morality*, will appear clearly from two remarkable passages in the Smriti of Yajnawalkya:—"The King should investigate judicial proceedings conformably to the *sacred code* of *laws*." This passage has been quoted before, and the *sacred code* of *laws* here refer to the *Smritis*. Vijnaneswara in his commentary upon the passage "conformably to the sacred code of laws," says "not according to *ethical law*," thereby clearly showing that the *sacred code of laws* or *Smritis* are something different from *ethical law*: and the king is enjoined not to decide cases according to codes on ethics, but according to the sacred code of laws. The next passage of Yajnawalkya, to which I shall refer, occurs in the 2nd chapter of Mitacshara (Grish Tarkalankar's edition, p. 52). The sage declares: "It is a fixed rule that the *sacred code* is of greater authority than the *rule* of *ethics*," and the commentary upon this passage mentions "ethical codes, such as those compiled by Usanas and others;" and further lays down, that "where the sacred and ethical codes are at variance, the former is more authoritative than the latter: this is the established rule or definition." Then the commentary gives some instances of moral rules and also of rules of law, and points out the apparent contradiction between them, and tries to reconcile it. The chapter closes with an anathema against those who prefer the ethical code. "Here then the sacred code is more authoritative than the ethical code; and Apastamba has propounded a heavy penance, where ethical and sacred rules interfere with each other, for the person who inclines to the ethical. The penance endures twelve years."

Ethical codes distinct from the sacred codes.

This, I think, is almost conclusive. It shows that, apart from the sacred codes, ethical codes were well known; that the provisions of the ethical codes were, to a great measure, derived from the sacred code; and from this fact the ethical rules became binding rules of conduct; but that when there was a conflict between the sacred code and the ethical code, the former was authoritative, and he who followed the latter nevertheless was doomed to severe punishment. Of course, at this distance of time, it is impossible correctly to enumerate which are the sacred codes of law, and which are the codes on ethics; but I think the distinction was perfectly well known to the

LECTURE I. ancient writers on law and religion, and the sacred codes were probably confined to the writings of the select twenty as named by Yajnawalkya, or the select thirty-six as enumerated in the Padma Purana, as I have already pointed out. The enormous list of authors of Smriti given by European scholars (Messrs. Borradaile, Stokes, West, and Bühler) probably arose from the confusion between the authors of *Smriti*, strictly so called, and the authors of ethical codes. The great distinction between codes of law and codes of morality is observable in the actual application of the rules in the government of the society; but where that test is wanting, and where none is positive law except a small portion, by courtesy, the difficulty of distinguishing between them becomes almost insurmountable. Of the present English law, for instance, there is no difficulty in distinguishing between a treatise on positive law and a treatise on jurisprudence; but I think there is considerable difficulty in distinguishing between a rule of positive law and a mere opinion of a *juris consult* in the body of law called the *Corpus Juris Civilis*.

That the Smritis were positive law maintained by Sir W. Jones.

As regards the opinion of European scholars that the Smritis are not actual codes of law, I think there is a conflict. Sir W. Jones, in his preface to the translation of Menu, seems to incline to the opposite opinion.

By Mr. Burnell.

Mr. Burnell, in the introduction to his translation of the Dayavibhaga, speaking of the Smritis, says—

" A great difference between the original Smritis is apparent . . . . ; but there is no reason to believe that these works do not represent the actual laws which were administered."[1] Justice Jackson, in his judgment referred to above, has quoted from Burnell in support of his own view ; but the passage quoted refers to the " modern so-called digests," and *not* to the *Smritis* ; and between the digests or commentaries and the original Smritis there is, I think, a wide difference, as I shall hereafter show. Mr. Burnell speaks of the *Smritis* in the passage quoted above ; but he refers to the *digests* in the very next sentence in the following words:—" On the other hand, the case of the modern so-called digests is very different. They are based on the principle that one Smriti is to be supplemented by another. . . . . The digests, however, were never intended to be actual codes of law," &c.[2]

By Dr. Jolly.

Dr. Jolly, in the preface to his translation of the Narada Smriti, states as follows:—" But that which is perhaps the highest encomium that can be bestowed upon a Hindu law book, is deserved by the civil laws of the Narada Smriti, in that they are not mere theoretical rules and precepts, but such as have doubtless been actually administered."[3]

Menu Smriti.

According to the opinion of the Hindus, Menu Smriti, or, as it is otherwise called, the *Manava Dharma*

---

[1] Intro., xiii. [2] Intro., xiii. [3] Intro., xxvii.

LECTURE I.

Mode of promulgation.

Sastras, is in point of authority the highest and most respected. The mode of its promulgation is thus described in the Code itself: Menu sat reclined with his attention fixed on the Supreme God, when the divine sages approaching him requested to be informed of the sacred laws and duties of the four classes and of the mixed classes.[1] To which the great legislator returned a comprehensive answer, saying "Be it heard."[2] Then follow the recital of the Code. At first Menu, desirous of giving birth to a race of men, produced ten lords of created beings eminent in holiness.[3] They are:

1. Marichi.	6. Kratu.
2. Atri.	7. Prachetas or Dacsha.
3. Angira.	8. Vasishtha.
4. Pulastya.	9. Bhrigu.
5. Pulaha.	10. Narada.[4]

Of these, Atri, Angira, Dacsha, and Vasishtha are four of the twenty sages named by Yajnawalkya as authors of the Smritis: and all of them, except Pulaha and Kratu, are mentioned in the list occurring in the Padma Purana. It will appear, however, from the enumerations that Prachetas and Dacsha are two different Rishis, and not one as Menu declares. The "Immutable Power" enacted this code of laws, and himself taught it fully to Menu in the beginning, who afterwards taught it to Marichi and the nine other holy sages

[1] Chap. I, vv. 1 & 2.
[2] Chap. I, v. 4.
[3] Chap. I, v. 34.
[4] Chap. I, v. 35.

mentioned above.[1] Then Menu is said to have directed his son Bhrigu to repeat the divine code to the Rishis who formed his audience,[2] and the code, as recited by Bhrigu, is said to have come down to our times in its integrity. This Menu, be it observed, is the first of a series of seven Menus—all descendants of the first, who is the most exalted of all, and is therefore styled the *Swayambhuva*, or sprung from the self-existing.[3]

A different tradition regarding its promulgation stated.

There is a different tradition regarding the promulgation of the existing code, which is thus described in the introduction to the Institutes of Narada, and of which a free translation is given by Sir W. Jones in the preface[4] to his translation of Menu. The code, as originally composed by Menu Prajapati, consisted of twenty-four divisions, or parts, and contained one hundred thousand *slokas*, arranged in a thousand chapters. It was in that condition delivered to Narada, who, after perusing it, thought it was too long for human comprehension, and accordingly abridged it in twelve thousand *slokas*. The abridgment was then made over to Sumati, the son of Bhrigu; who again abridged it for similar reasons, and reduced it to four thousand *slokas*. It is this *second* abridgment by Sumati that mortals read, whereas the original code of one hundred thousand *slokas* is read by gods, *gandharvas*, and other similar beings. Of Narada's

---

[1] Chap. I, v. 58. [2] Chap. I, v. 60. [3] Chap. I, v. 61. [4] P. xiii.

LECTURE I. abridgment, it is said, nothing exists except an abstract of the ninth chapter of the original Code, which was headed "On Judicial Procedure," made in the form of short rules, or *sutras*.[1] What is at present called the Institutes of Narada is said to be this abstract of the ninth chapter of the original Code of Menu. The Code of Menu, which at present exists, consists of two thousand six hundred and eighty-five verses; from which Sir W. Jones infers that this could not be the abridgment of Sumati, "which is, probably, distinguished by the name of the *Vriddha*, or ancient *Manava*, which cannot be found entire; though several passages from it which have been preserved by tradition are occasionally cited in the new digest," and the present Code, he thinks, is a subsequent abridgment of Sumati's work.[2]

The Smritis originally preserved in memory.

I think it is clear from internal evidence contained in the body of the Code itself, that Menu's Code, like the other Smritis which followed it in point of time, was originally preserved in the memory of the sages, or Rishis, before writing was invented; and that it must have been reduced into writing a considerable length of time (which cannot be precisely determined) after its first promulgation. There is no trace in the Code itself of its having been reduced into writing, or existing as a piece of writing; on the contrary, the Code itself declares that Brahma

[1] Intro. Jolly's Narada. [2] Pref., xiv.

taught it to Menu, who taught it to the ten sages, Bhrigu included; and that Bhrigu again recited the Code to the Rishis who came to be instructed in it from him. It may seem somewhat extraordinary to *us* that such a bulky Code could be so accurately preserved in memory and handed down in that condition through several generations of sages; but if we remember the habits of the Pundits of this country, who have got by heart whole *Puthis*, or volumes, and still teach their pupils from memory without the aid of written books or manuscripts, the mode of preservation of the Code will not at all surprise us. It was owing partly to the rareness of the manuscripts; and we are apt *now* to derogate from the powers of memory by the facility of access to books arising from the introduction of printing.

According to Parasara particular Smritis applicable to particular ages.

There is a passage in the Parasara Smriti,[1] which lays down that the Institutes of Menu apply to the *Krita Yuga*, or the first age; the ordinances of Gotama to the *Treta Yuga*, or the second age; the Institutes of Sankha and Likhita to the *Dwapara Yuga*, or the third age; and the Smriti of Parasara is exclusively applicable to the *Kali Yuga*, or the fourth age. This distinction is not usually observed, and as a matter of fact the texts of all the sages are equally respected in this age. With this exception that certain portions of the ancient law are declared not binding in

[1] Chap. I, v. 23.

LECTURE I. — the present age, such as the practice of Niyoga, the intermarriage among the four classes, the twelve descriptions of sons, and some other like provisions. As regards the Parasara Smriti it is observed that the Vyavahara Kanda in it is entirely wanting. Hence it can hardly be supposed to have formed a complete code for the fourth, or the *Kali Yuga*.

Hypothesis regarding the age of Menu's Code.

As regards the age of Menu's Code, we are completely at sea: the original Hindu authorities furnish us no aid beyond giving a mysterious immensity of time that is said to have elapsed between the date of its promulgation and the present times. Sir W. Jones, in the preface[1] to his translation of the Code, has fixed the time when it was reduced into writing to be 880 B. C.,—*i. e.*, three hundred years after Parasara, whose age he has determined to be the end of the twelfth century before Christ, by a comparison of the position of the equinoctial point at the time of Parasara and the position it occupied in the year of Christ 499. The age of Parasara being thus determined, that of his son Vyasa, the compiler of the Vedas, and therefore of the compilation, is fixed at the twelfth century before Christ. Sir W. Jones further supposes, that between the language of the Vedas, the language of Menu's Code, and the language of the Puranas, the same difference is observable as is to be found between the Latin of Numa, the Latin of Appius, as seen in the

[1] P. viii.

Twelve Tables, and the Latin of Cicero; and as nearly 300 years elapsed between each of the latter intervals, he concludes, the same period must have elapsed between the former intervals; and thus he places the compilation of Menu's Code at 300 years after that of the Vedas. LECTURE I.

This conjectural reasoning is certainly remarkable for its originality; but it did not fully satisfy its author, and has not certainly satisfied the later scholars who have examined this question.[1] There are so many premises in this process of reasoning, which are based upon pure conjecture, that it is impossible to be satisfied with the result of this reasoning as being at all accurate. One fact need be mentioned here, which is this, *viz.*, that the authorship of the Puranas and the compilation of the Vedas are both ascribed by the *same* authorities to Vyasa, whereas by Sir W. Jones's reasoning these events are said to have happened *six hundred years* apart. Besides, the Vedas and the Code of Menu were never *written*, at the periods mentioned by Sir W. Jones, in the *current* language of the times; but were simply reduced into writing in the ancient dialects in which they were preserved unaltered in language; and Sir W. Jones[2] is of opinion that the laws of Menu might have been *promulgated* contemporaneously with the establish- Not satisfactory.

[1] See Morley's Digest, Intro., p. cxcv. Max Müller's History of Ancient Sanscrit Literature, p. 61.

[2] Pref., vi.

LECTURE I.

ment of the first monarchies in Egypt or Asia,—*i. e.*, 1500—1700 B. C.

Comparison of language is hardly in this matter a safe guide. Two languages spoken by two different people, living under different circumstances, and subject to different influences, physical, political, and social, can never be developed uniformly; and consequently changes in the style and form of the languages can never take place in the same intervals of time in both of them. This circumstance considerably takes away from the argument derived from the analogy of the Latin language. All speculations regarding the probable age of these ancient writings must be more or less unsatisfactory, and can seldom be accurate; the absence of chronological data in ancient Sanscrit literature being the chief reason. Arguments are based upon analogies which are very slender. Facts are relied upon which are either misunderstood, or to which undue importance is attached; and Hindu traditions are totally disregarded, which oftentimes contain truth more or less disguised. It must, however, be observed that nothing new has been added to the subject since Sir W. Jones expressed his views nearly a century ago.

The Code divided into twelve chapters.

The Code is divided into twelve chapters.[1] The first chapter[2] contains an account of the creation of this world and of all creatures, animate as well as

[1] NOTE.—The page references are to the Edition of 1794. [2] Pp. 1—16.

inanimate; the creation of the four primary orders or classes, and a short account of their respective duties; and closes with a general summary of the contents of the whole Code.

LECTURE I. — The first chapter contains a history of the creation.

The second chapter[1] opens with the geography of the countries which the Aryans have occupied; then follow a description of the ceremonies to be performed from the conception of a child to his investiture with the holy thread; rules to be observed by a *Brahmachări*, or student (being the first of the four stages in the life of every man), in receiving instructions in the sacred texts, and the mode of education generally, including the conduct of the student towards his *Acharya*, or *Upadhaya*, and other people generally, together with rules governing his mode of life.

The second chapter contains the duties of a Brahmachari.

The third chapter[2] relates to the condition of a *Grihasta*, or householder; the prohibited degrees in marriage are mentioned; the eight forms of marriage are described: then the duties of a householder are minutely described; then follow a curious description of people who are not to be invited at the Sradh ceremony on account of their low occupations, with a somewhat detailed account of the ceremony itself.

The third chapter relates to the condition of a householder.

The fourth chapter[3] gives in greater detail the duties of a householder, the approved modes of obtaining a livelihood, and other matters which relate to the subject of private morals and domestic economy.

The fourth chapter relates to the same.

---

[1] Pp. 17—50. [2] Pp. 51—88. [3] Pp 89—122.

LECTURE I.

The fifth chapter relates to different kinds of food, and causes of impurity.

The fifth chapter[1] describes in detail the food that is lawful and the food that is prohibited, with a description of the various kinds of flesh meat that may be eaten or should be avoided. Then follow a description of the causes of impurity on account of birth, death, and contact with persons or things; the modes of purification prescribed for human beings and for things rendered impure: then follow the duties of women towards their husbands; and the duties of the widow, with the special injunction to remain chaste.

The sixth relates to the third and fourth stages of a man's existence.

The sixth chapter[2] describes the condition of men in the third and fourth stages of their existence when they become severally *Ban prastha* and a *Yati;* an enumeration of their several duties and their mode of living, together with rules for devotion.

The seventh relates to the rights and duties of a king.

The seventh chapter[3] refers to the rights and duties of a king, which I have described in some detail before.

The eighth chapter describes the 18 titles of law.

The eighth chapter[4] opens with an enumeration of the eighteen titles of law ; and the details of each title follow in order. The eighteen titles are the following:—

I.—Debt or loans for consumption.
II.—Deposits and loans for use.
III.—Sale without ownership.
IV.—Concerns among partners.
V.—Subtraction of what has been given.

---

[1] Pp. 123—144.
[2] Pp. 145—158.
[3] Pp. 159—188.
[4] Pp. 189—244.

VI.—Nonpayment of wages or hire.
VII.—Nonperformance of agreements.
VIII.—Rescission of sale and purchase.
IX.—Disputes between master and servant.
X.—Contests on boundaries.
XI & XII.—Assault and slander.
XIII.—Larceny or theft.
XIV.—Robbery and other violence.
XV.—Adultery.
XVI.—Altercation between man and wife.
XVII.—The law of inheritance.
XVIII.—Gaming with dice and with living creatures.

The ninth chapter[1] commences with a description of the reciprocal duties of the husband and wife towards each other. The law of inheritance is next considered; then the eighteenth title of law is discussed, followed by a further description of the duties of the king.

The ninth chapter treats of the law of Inheritance.

The tenth chapter[2] contains a description of the mixed classes or castes that have sprung up by the intermarriage between the four primary classes, together with a description of the occupations that these classes must severally follow. These are the approved modes of living; and the chapter closes with a description of low or inferior occupations that these classes may pursue in times of distress.

The tenth chapter contains a description of the mixed classes.

---

[1] Pp. 245—288.

[2] Pp. 289—306.

LECTURE I.

The eleventh chapter treats of penance and expiation.

The eleventh chapter[1] treats of penance and expiation. It describes the various kinds of offences and sins, and the acts of expiation proper for each.

The twelfth chapter treats of transmigration and *mukti*.

The twelfth chapter[2] contains the doctrine of transmigration and *mukti;* the various kinds of transmigrations to which souls will be subjected according to their different degrees of merit.

Such is a short epitome of the contents of the whole Code.

The Smriti of Yajnawalkya.

The Smriti of Yajnawalkya claims a place probably next after that of Menu, both on account of its importance as well as on account of the complete form in which it is preserved in the writings of one of its ancient and most famous commentators, Vijnaneswara. The book is divided into three parts,—*viz.*, *Achara*, *Vyavahara*, and *Prayaschitta;* and I think this triple division of Dharma Sastra first originates in this law tract, which has been followed afterwards in all the succeeding law literature.

Its division into three parts.

Hypothesis regarding the age of Yajnawalkya.

The age of Yajnawalkya cannot be ascertained with any degree of certainty. He is the grandson of Viswamitra, and is described in the Introduction of his own Institutes as delivering his precepts to an assembly of sages who had come to hear him, in the province of Mithila.[3] From the evidence derived from the subjects of which he treats, and the mode of treatment of those subjects, it is believed that his

---

[1] Pp. 307—344. [2] Pp. 345—362. [3] Digest, Intro., p. xii.

work must have been composed after the Smriti of Menu and before that of Narada.[1] The arrangement is more systematic than in Menu, but it is less developed than is found in Narada; consequently this Smriti is supposed to occupy an intermediate position in point of time between that of Menu on the one hand and that of Narada on the other.

LECTURE I.

Contents of Yajnawalkya's Smriti.

Yajnawalkya's Smriti is divided into three chapters, and contains one thousand and twenty-three couplets. The first chapter treats of moral conduct and the rules regarding the performance of ceremonies, and contains a very full and elaborate description of the duties of the four classes. The second chapter treats of law and the administration of justice. It contains rules of procedure and the law of evidence; the law relating to pledges and other securities and the rates of interest; the law relating to the five kinds of ordeals; the law of inheritance and partition; and the law relating to boundaries. The book closes with a description of all sorts of offences, and the punishments that are prescribed for them. The third chapter is devoted exclusively to the law relating to penances and the several modes of expiation; and the doctrine of final beatitude, or *mukti*.

Hypothesis regarding the date of Narada Smriti.

The Narada Smriti is supposed to be a later composition than Yajnawalkya Smriti. Dr. Jolly thinks[2] that this work must have been composed after the

---

[1] Jolly, Pref. to Narada, p. xviii. [2] Pref., p. xix.

LECTURE I. — beginning of the Brahminical reaction against Buddhism, and consequently the earliest possible date of the work may be put at about 400 or 500 A.D. The only fact on which this conclusion is attempted to be based is that Buddhism is nowhere mentioned in this Smriti, and therefore the work must be later than the time when Buddhism succumbed to Brahminical attacks. The process of reasoning does not seem to be very convincing.

The Narada Smriti an abstract of the ninth chapter of the original Code of Menu.

In this Smriti there is an introduction which states that Menu's first Code of one hundred thousand *slokas* was abridged by Narada into a shorter work of twelve thousand *slokas* for the benefit of the human race. The ninth chapter of this abridgment was headed "On Judicial Procedure;" and a general abstract of it was made by Narada himself in the form of short rules or *sutras*. This abstract of the ninth chapter has come down to us, and is called the Narada Smriti; no other portion of the writings of this sage is believed to be extant.

Dr. Jolly controverts the same.

This is the Hindu tradition regarding the authorship of the present Smriti. Dr. Jolly[1] is, however, of opinion, that this Hindu tradition is not authentic, because, he says, "this author has but a very limited number of *slokas* in common with Menu." There is not much force in this reasoning, because if we remember the tradition, it says that the present

Fallacy in his reasoning pointed out.

---

[1] Pref., pp. xi–xiii.

Narada Smriti is an abstract of one chapter only of the code of twelve thousand verses, and the present Code of Menu is a second abridgment by different authors from the same Code ; consequently one can see there must be very little of *language* common between the two, though there must be, as there is actually, much the same *substance* or *purport* in both. Besides, there is nothing to show that the 'Introduction' is a recent or modern addition to the Smriti itself. Whether it is contemporaneous with the Smriti itself, may be doubted ; but this seems probable that the 'Introduction' was added shortly after the Smriti was promulgated ; at least within such time of its promulgation that the traditions regarding its origin was fresh in the memory of the people at the time. In the absence of any evidence to the contrary, we must take it that the 'Introduction' embodies an authentic fact.

Contents of the Narada Smriti.

The Narada Smriti contains, besides the introduction, two parts. The first part treats of judicature. It describes the duties of the king and the constitution of courts of justice ; recovery of debts and the several kinds of evidence by writing and by witnesses ; and it lastly describes the five kinds of ordeals,—*viz.*, ordeal by balance, ordeal by fire, ordeal by water, ordeal by poison, and the ordeal by sacred libation.

First part treats of judicature.

The second part

The second part is devoted to the discussion of

LECTURE I. — describes the 18 titles of law.

the eighteen titles of law, or heads of dispute. They are enumerated as follows:—

I. The recovery of a debt.
II. On deposits.
III. Concerns among partners.
IV. Recovery of a gift.
V. Breach of promised obedience.
VI. Nonpayment of wages.
VII. Sale without ownership.
VIII. Nondelivery of a thing sold.
IX. Rescission of purchase.
X. Breach of order.
XI. Contests regarding boundaries.
XII. Duties of man and wife.
XIII. Partition of heritage.
XIV. Violence.
XV. & XVI. Abuse and assault.
XVII. Gambling with dice and living creatures.
XVIII. Miscellaneous disputes.

You will observe from the above enumeration of the eighteen titles of law, as given by Narada, that it differs somewhat from that given by Menu.[1]

Present condition of the Smritis.

Some of the Smritis have come down to our times as separate and independent books, and it is believed that they have existed in that shape from a very long time; others, however, are totally lost, save

[1] See *ante*, pp. 44, 45.

and except isolated *slokas*, which are preserved as quotations in the writings of later authors. LECTURE I.

Except Menu's Code none of them exists in its integrity.

Regarding those that exist as separate books, the opinion of the Pundits is, that, with the exception of Menu's Code, none of the other Smritis has come down to us in its integrity or in a complete form: they have come down in a fragmentary form, the parts that now exist having been put together from scattered materials by some scholar, considerably after the time when the whole Code was first delivered, and when portions of it have been irretrievably lost. There is considerable truth in this assertion, because, as a matter of fact, we find numerous instances of *slokas*, quoted from particular Smritis, in works of admitted authority, which are not to be found in the copies of those *Smritis* as they exist now. One of two conclusions is inevitable from this state of things: either the quotation is false, or the Smriti is fragmentary. In particular instances it becomes very difficult to determine whether the quotation is wrong or the Smriti is defective. If the *sloka*, however, is quoted by more than one *contemporaneous* author, which is wanting in the Smriti, in that case we might safely assert that the copy of the Smriti is fragmentary. Unless the quotations are from *contemporaneous* authors, this test would be wanting, because subsequent writers, often quoting from earlier authors, perpetuate the error, and do not by any means add to the authenticity of the original

LECTURE I. quotation. Manuscripts in India have been always very rare. And the facilities of verifying quotations were always wanting; the consequence is, that writers were obliged to accept quotations second-hand. Errors, if once committed, were thus often-times perpetuated, and very seldom refuted.

Facility for literary forgeries in India.

From circumstances like these, literary forgeries became rather common in India, both of isolated passages and sometimes of whole books. The motives or inducements for such attempts were always great, because the subjects which were thus tampered with being either religion or law, exercised immense influence over the destinies of the people. A particular book is known to have existed, but no copy of it is found entire except occasional quotations here and there. A clever scholar writes a book in an archaic style, and puts it forward before the world as the work of the ancient sage, which is supposed to have been lost, but which he has fortunately discovered under some peculiar circumstances. The Pundits are very credulous in these matters, the book is subjected to very ordinary criticism, and it stands the test. From that time the book is accepted as the production of the ancient sage whose name it bears. How many books in Sanscrit literature have this sort of pretended authorship it is impossible to say. In the case of isolated texts the facilities of forgery are greater still: the whole book from which the quotation is supposed to be made is seldom studied or even known, and the false quotation is rarely detected.

The Code called Laghu Menu is entire.

In the case of Menu's Code, which is supposed by the Pundits to have come down entire, it is only the Code called *Laghu Menu* that exists in that shape. There were two or one of such codes which existed, but which have not come down to us entire. I refer to *Vrihat Menu*, or *Vriddha Menu*, *slokas* from which are frequently quoted in approved works of authority, but the original Code, it is well known, is not in existence.

Other Smritis exist in mere quotations.

As regards the other Smritis which exist only in isolated quotations, their condition is still more unfortunate. They have no independent existence; they live in a very doubtful form in the writings of later authors. In the case of these Smritis facilities for forging texts were great, and it is impossible *now* to say whether a particular text ascribed to a particular Rishi is the genuine production of that Rishi. This must, however, be said with reference to such quotations, that they have been quoted for so many centuries as the texts of particular Rishis that we cannot now with any show of reason object to their genuineness. They have obtained a sort of authorized and recognized existence; they live as if petrified among living matter, not themselves lifeless, but have acquired a sort of derivative life from animated matter that surrounds them. It is not possible now for a scholar or pundit to forge a text and to pass it

LECTURE I. — as the text of some ancient Rishi. He will at once be asked the question—where does he find it? If the *Sanhita* is extant, he will have to point out its place there, or if the *Sanhita* is not extant, he will have to say by what authority or authorities has this text been before quoted? If he cannot answer either of these questions, the text will not be accepted as genuine, and the forgery will be apparent.

The Digests or Commentaries.

The Digests. Their influence on Hindu law.

No branch of Sanscrit literature has exercised a greater influence on Hindu law than the digests or the commentaries on the Smritis. These writings have been composed in historic times in different parts of India, and their utmost limit may be safely placed within one thousand years from the present times. Their authority is various, and they are held absolutely binding in some cases, and in others they are merely treated as opinions of learned pundits or scholars.

The distinction between the digests and the commentaries.

They are usually commentaries on particular Smritis; they expound the text and amplify its narrow provisions very considerably by large additions of relevant matter. Sometimes they take the shape of general digests on all topics of Achara, Vyavahara, and Prayaschitta. A commentary, as it purports to be, is a gloss on some particular Smriti: adopting that as its text, it explains and enlarges upon its positions. The Mitacshara may be cited as an instance of a commentary, being one on the

Institutes of Yajnawalkya. A digest, on the other hand, does not adopt any particular text. It is a general treatise on a particular subject or topic of Hindu law. As an instance of a digest may be cited the Dayabhaga of Jimutavahana and the Vyavahara Mayukha of Nilkantha.

The digests give rise to the different schools of Hindu law.

With these writings originate the five different schools of Hindu law—the Gourya, the Mithila, the Benares, the Maharashtra, and the Dravira schools. The Smritis, or, as they are usually called, *Rishibakyani* (the sayings of the sages), are universally binding in every part of Hindoostan. The different commentators, however, expound the same text very differently, and according to this difference of interpretation arise the different doctrines of the several schools. One such commentary held in esteem in a particular part of the country becomes the authority for that school; its doctrines are followed there in total disregard of the doctrines contained in another commentary, which may be equally respected in another part of the country. To take one instance: the word *pitarau* in the text of Yajṇawalkya. "The wife, daughters also, &c.," has been variously interpreted. The Bengal school[1] interprets it so as to make the *father* succeed *before* the *mother*. The interpretation by the Mitacshara[2] places the *mother before* the *father*; the Vivada

Their interpretations of the same text.

Illustration.

[1] Dayabhaga, Chap. XI, Sec. iii, para. 4.

[2] Chap. II, Sec. iii, para. 2.

LECTURE I. — Chintamani,[1] the recognised authority for the Mithila school, agrees with the Mitacshara.

The Vyavahara Mayukha,[2] the recognized authority for the Mahrashtra school, agrees with the Bengal school in this respect. The Parasara Madhavya, a leading authority in the Dravira school, leaves the question undecided,[3] and the Smriti Chandrica, another authority for the South, agrees[4] with the Bengal school.

Another illustration—the sister.

Another instance is the case of the *sister*. According to all the authorities in the different schools, except the Maharashtra, the *sister* does *not* at all succeed. The *Vyavahara Mayukha*, however, makes the sister an *heir*,[5] and places her after the paternal grandmother. This is on the authority of two well-known texts: one of Menu,—"To the nearest *sapinda*, male or female, &c.;" and another of Vrihaspati, "where many claim the inheritance of a childless man, &c." Now both these texts are quoted by other commentators, and by none of them have they been interpreted in such a manner as to be authority for the sister's title to succeed.

Another illustration—the widow.

The case of the *widow* is another instance in point. In the Bengal school she succeeds *in all cases;* in the other schools she succeeds *only* when her husband was living, after partition, separate from his other co-parceners; and instances of this kind may be multiplied.

---

[1] P. 294.

[2] Chap. IV, Sec. viii, para. 14.

[3] Burnell, p. 27, para. 38.

[4] Chap. XI, Sec. iii, para. 9.

[5] Chap. IV, Sec. viii, para. 19.

Now this remarkable diversity in the interpretation of the same texts is very singular; the more so when it is remembered that all of them profess to proceed according to the same rules of interpretation,—*viz.*, the Mimansa. I think this diversity is attributable to the influence of local customs or customary laws, which have sprung up in different parts of the country. A pundit or scholar, writing a treatise on a particular topic, interprets the texts according to local customs, and that which is in consonance with the altered social feelings, is accepted as the correct interpretation of the text. The local customs are respected; no violence is done to the altered social feelings, and a sort of foregone conclusion is established on the authority of ancient texts. As these customs are various, and, according to the Smritis, they are to be respected, the interpretations of the ancient texts may have silently taken their impression from these customary laws.

These commentaries stand on a footing essentially different from the Smritis themselves. These latter are binding on all Hindus as being the sacred law promulgated by the sages or Rishis; the former, however, as being the interpretations of learned men only, are wanting in the *binding* character which the others possess. They are analogous to commentaries on modern statute law, the binding nature of which is never even asserted. *Practically*, however, these commentaries have a very large influence, and con- The character of these digests. Practically they constitute the

LECTURE I.

Positive law of the Hindus.

stitute the positive law of the Hindus. The Smritis are generally admitted to contain the substance of human duties; they are brief, and are expressed in a language so ancient that, but for these continued series of commentaries, they would be unintelligible. Hence, these commentaries are considered as the *authoritative* exposition of the Smritis, and are accepted as such in the different parts of the country where each has a local application. Mr. Burnell, speaking of these commentaries, says:—"There is not a particle of evidence to show that these works were ever even used by the Judges of ancient India as authoritative guides; they were, it is certain, considered as merely speculative treatises, and bore the same relation to the actual practice of the Courts as in Europe treatises on jurisprudence to the law which is actually administered."[1] Whatever may have been the case in *ancient India*, a term somewhat indefinite, this is certain that, from the time when the several schools of law came into existence, these commentaries have been accepted as the authoritative expositions, and formed guides for the determination of the duties of men in the territories where their doctrines prevailed.

In ancient India, secular learning spread very slowly.

In ancient times in India printing was not known, and writing was not frequently practised even by those who knew how to write. They would rather

[1] Intro., p. xiv.

preserve a new text or *sloka* in memory, rather than make a memorandum of it in writing; the consequence was, that new doctrines in law and literature (mere secular learning) were published and disseminated rather slowly: a treatise on law which has been generally studied for a considerable length of time in a particular part of the country is seldom known in a neighbouring tract of the country. The religious doctrines, however, stand on a different footing; they would be promulgated not by writings, but by itinerant preachers or missionaries, who would go about the country, and whose extraordinary zeal and energy would contribute to the propagation of the new doctrines with remarkable rapidity.

LECTURE I.

There are two modes by which mere secular learning would be published: By teaching and by public recitation, or discussion on some festive occasion. According to the *sastras*, teaching is one of the six approved and honorable occupations for a Brahmin,[1] and until lately, perhaps, the only occupation of learned Brahmins in India. In proportion to the reputation of a teacher will be the number of pupils that will come from different parts of the country to receive instructions from him in his *Chutuspathi*.[2]

Two modes of publication:

By teaching.

By public recitation.

[1] Menu, Chap. I, v. 88, and Chap. X, v. 75. Narada, p. 116, v. 49.

[2] *Chutuspathi* means, literally, a place where four sorts of learning are taught; in other words, where the four Vedas are taught. *Now* it means a place where instruction is given by a Pundit to his pupils.

LECTURE I. New doctrines, or ideas, that originate with the teacher will be communicated to his pupils or disciples in the course of his teaching, before the teacher himself had thought fit to reduce his ideas in the form of a new treatise or book. The pupils, after finishing their education, will go and establish their own *Chutuspathis* in different parts of the country, where they will teach the new doctrines of their master; and in this way these new doctrines will be propagated. The second mode of publication is by public recitation followed by a discussion, which is called *vichara*, in which the correctness of the doctrine is tested by scholars or *pundits* assembled on the occasion. On festive occasions, *pundits*, among others, are, as a rule, invited: the author of a new doctrine recites his production in the midst of that assembly, or *sabha*, that forms the topic of discussion, and the assembled pundits, who are usually the advocates of established doctrines, maintain their own view in this controversy, till it happens that the author of the new doctrine silences all opposition by his arguments, and his doctrines from that time obtain currency. In some cases the new doctrinaire is refuted. The conclusion, however, is not always so decisive; but in either case it has the effect of giving the new doctrine publicity. I believe the doctrines of the Mitacshara, which at one time were current in Bengal, were exploded from this country by the joint operation of the two methods that I have described, which at the same time gave currency to the doctrines of the Dayabhaga. LECTURE I.

The Mitacshara: its authority.

Among these digests or commentaries, the Mitacshara is pre-eminently entitled to the first place, both on account of its inherent merits as well as on account of the range of its authority. It professes to be a commentary on the Institutes of Yajnawalkya; but really is a comprehensive digest on all the topics that are usually discussed under the three heads of Achara, Vyavahara, and Prayaschitta. Its author is Vijnaneswara, or Vijnana Yogi. Mr. Colebrooke[1] is of opinion that he was an ascetic belonging to one of the orders of *Sanyasis* said to have been founded by *Sankara Acharya*. The probable date of the work he assigns to be between 500 and 1,000 years ago. The authority of this work is extensive: at one time, it appears, it was the leading authority in every part of India, till the introduction of the works of later authors of local renown has considerably displaced its authority. It is still the paramount authority in all the schools of law except Bengal; and in the Maharashtra country its authority is disputed by the writings of Nilkantha Bhatta. Even in Bengal, where its authority is least respected, it is recognized as an authority in all matters in which it does not contradict the Dayabhaga.

Its date.

The Dharmaratna.

The Dharmaratna, a digest of law composed by

[1] Preface to his translation of the Mitacshara and Dayabhaga, p. xiii.

LECTURE I.

The Dayabhaga only a part of it.

Jimutavahana, is of paramount authority in Bengal.[1] The whole of this work is not extant; only a portion of it, which is called the Dayabhaga, has come down to us.[2] The Dayabhaga treats of inheritance and partition. Bengal was formed into a new school of law by following the doctrines contained in this book, which, in all disputed points, differs from the Mitacshara. Nothing is known about Jimutavahana. Mr. Colebrooke[3] thinks the name belongs to a prince of the house of Silara, under whose direction the book may have been composed, and the authorship has accordingly been ascribed to him. The opinion of the Pundits of Bengal is, however, different; they think the real author bore that name; that he was a celebrated lawyer of Bengal, who performed the functions of judge and law-adviser to one of the Hindu kings of Bengal. All this is mere conjecture. This, however, is certain that the book was promulgated a considerable time after the Mitacshara was written. The book is essentially a controversial one, engaged in refuting certain doctrines or opinions; whose opinions they are, the book nowhere mentions; but a perusal of the Mitacshara will convince everyone that the Dayabhaga is

The book was promulgated long after the Mitacshara.

---

[1] Dayabhaga, Chap. XV, para. 3.

[2] It is remarkable that a large portion of this digest should be totally lost within the course of a very few centuries, showing how unsafe was the tradition of even written literature within recent times in India.

[3] Preface to his translation of the Dayabhaga and the Mitacshara, p. xiii.

controverting the doctrines of the Mitacshara. It is clear, therefore, that the doctrines of the Mitacshara were prevalent in Bengal at that time, and Jimutavahana was engaged in controverting those well-known doctrines. Remembering the slow mode in which doctrines were propagated in those times, it must have taken some considerable time before the doctrines of the Mitacshara could have been so well established in Bengal. Jimutavahana has the credit, so far as Bengal is concerned, of refuting those doctrines, and displacing their authority by his own. He has the rare merit of being the founder of that school, and in Bengal no other lawyer has ventured to dispute his authority with any degree of success. Both the Mitacshara and the Dayabhaga have been translated into English by Mr. Colebrooke.

The Vivada Chintamani, leading authority in Mithila.

In the Mithila school the leading authority is the digest called Vivada Chintamani, by Vachaspati Misra, a native lawyer of Mithila. This work is founded on the earlier treatise of Chandeswara, called Vivada Ratnakara, which is much respected in the Mithila country. The Vivada Chintamani treats of all the eighteen titles of law with brevity but clearness, and quotes nearly all the texts of the Smritis under their appropriate heads, followed by short but relevant commentaries by the author himself. This work has been translated into English by Babu Prosonno Kumar Tagore.

The Vyavahara

The authority that is most respected in the Maha-

LECTURE I.

Mayukha, the leading authority in the Maharashtra school.

rashtra country (which includes the Bombay Presidency) and probably next only to the Mitacshara, is Nilkantha Bhatta. He is the author of Bhagvanta Bhaskara, an encyclopædic writing, divided into twelve parts, or mayukhas, which mean the "rays" of the sun; and which embrace all the topics that are usually discussed under the three heads of *Achara*, *Vyavahara*, and *Prayaschitta*. Nilkantha[1] is said, by one of his descendants, who was living at Puna at the time when Mr. Borradaile wrote (1827), to have lived about 1600 A.D., and that his writings came into repute about 1700 A.D. He was a Maharashtra Brahmin, born at Benares. The Bhagvanta Bhaskara was compiled by him in the court of Bhagvant Deva, king of Bhoreha, a small town situated at the confluence of the Jamna and the Chambal. The prince belonged to the Sungur dynasty of kings, and in return for the protection afforded to him by the prince, Nilkantha styled his work Bhagvanta Bhaskara, the sun composed by the permission of Bhagvanta Deva.[2] The sixth chapter or division of this work is called the Vyavahara Mayukha, a treatise which bears upon law directly. Like other digests, it discusses the eighteen titles of law with clearness and with appropriate quotations from the Smritis. It generally follows the Mitacshara, but it is found

---

[1] For an account of Nilkantha and his writings, see Stokes's Hindu Law Books, p. 7.

[2] See Vyavahara Mayukha, conclusion.

sometimes to dispute the authority of Vijnaneswara; and the reputation of the author in the Maharashtra country is such, that in points where he differs from the Mitacshara his opinion is followed in preference to the Mitacshara. Nilkantha enjoys in the Maharashtra country a reputation similar to that which Raghunandana enjoys in Bengal, and the encyclopædic work of the former, consisting of the twelve Mayukhas, embracing almost all the topics of the Dharmasastras, resembles the twenty-eight *tatwas* of the latter.

The Parasara Madhavya and the Smriti Chandrica, the leading authorities in the south.

In the southern or Dravira school, which embraces the territories under the Madras Government, two authorities enjoy almost equal reputation next after the Mitacshara. They are the Madhavya, commentary on the Parasara Smriti and the Smriti Chandrica.

The former was composed by Madhavacharya, prime minister of the King of Vijayanagor, a kingdom in the south of India. He flourished during the last half of the fourteenth century. His brother was the famous Sayanacharya, who is otherwise styled Vidyaranya Swami, and who is the author of the celebrated commentaries on the Vedas, which are now-a-days usually referred to. The two brothers were the authors of numerous works on philosophy, law, vedic ritual, astrology, and many other kindred subjects.[1] It is doubtful, however, whether all the

[1] Burnell, Intro., p. x.

LECTURE I. works popularly ascribed to the two brothers were actually composed by them; and there is reason to believe that some of the works, written by other authors, were, for the purpose of obtaining authority, falsely ascribed to the two brothers, a practice rather common in India in former times. The commentary on the Parasara Smriti was commenced, says Mr. Burnell,[1] "after the commentaries on the Vedas. It is an immense work in three sections, and the part now translated (the Dayavibhaga) is a small portion of the last section, which is rather an appendix, as the text of the Parasara Smriti only extends to the end of the second section, leaving jurisprudence unnoticed. The first two sections are diffuse to a degree, and the writer seems to have tried rather to display his learning than to illustrate the text before him. The third section is much more concise, and has less original matter in it." The author follows the Mitacshara very closely, though the style is very concise, in imitation rather of the Sutras. Mr. Burnell thinks the Dayavibhaga of the Madhavya commentary "is little more than an abridgment of the Mitacshara, except in some of the last sections."[2] This work is also studied in the Maharashtra and in the Benares schools, and is therefore referred to as an authority of some consequence. The Dayavibhaga, or that portion of the work which relates

---

[1] Intro., p. xii.

[2] Intro., p. xii.

to inheritance, has been translated into English by Mr. Burnell of the Madras Civil Service. LECTURE I.

The Smriti Chandrica.

The Smriti Chandrica is generally followed as a work of great and almost paramount authority in the south of India. Its author, Devanda Bhatta, is also the author of the famous treatise on the law of adoption, called Dattaca Chandrica, which in matters of adoption is exclusively followed in Bengal and in the Deccan. The author is supposed to have lived some time between the time of Vijnaneswara and that of Madhavacharya; and Mr. Burnell would place him a century and a half later than the Mitacshara.[1] The author follows to a great extent the doctrines of the Mitacshara, and the book is remarkable for its good common sense and the soundness of its criticisms.

These are the principal digests or commentaries which are accepted as authorities in the different schools. Besides the above there are other works of inferior authority in all the schools; and I shall here only mention those which are most frequently quoted.

Other authorities of the Bengal school.

In Bengal the commentaries on the Dayabhaga, which are four in number, *viz.*—

By Srinatha Acharya Chudamani,
By Achyuta Chakravarti,
By Maheswara,
By Srikrishna Tarkalankara;

[1] Intro., p. ix.

LECTURE I.

and—

Dayatatwa, by Raghunandana;

Dayakrama Sangraha, by Srikrishna Tarkalankara;

Vivadarnava Setu;

Vivada Sararnava, by Sarvaru Tribedi;

Vivada Bhangarnava, by Jagganatha Tarkpanchanana,—

are authorities next in importance to the Dayabhaga itself.

Of the Mithila school.

In the Mithila school, the following works are frequently quoted as next in authority to the Mitacshara:—

Vivada Ratnakara.
Vivada Chintamani.
Vyavahara Chintamani.
Dwaita Parisishta.
Vivada Chandra.
Smriti Sara.
Madana Parijata.

Of the Benares school.

In the Benares school, next in authority to the Mitacshara are the following:—

Viramitrodaya. Madhavya.
Vivada Tandava. Nirnaya Sindhu.

Of the Maharashtra school.

In the Maharashtra school, besides the Mitacshara and the Vyavahara Mayukha, the following works are also respected as authorities:—

Nirnaya Sindhu. Smriti Kaustubha.
Hemadri. Madhavya.

In the Southern school, besides the Mitacshara, the following works are usually quoted as authorities :— Of the Dravida school.

Madhavya. Saraswati Vilasa.
Smriti Chandrica. Varadarajya.[1]

I omit to consider in this place as sources of law the writings of European scholars, such as those of the two Macnaghtens, of Strange, &c. Though valuable in themselves, but as they are mainly based upon the original authorities which I have mentioned, and upon reported cases, and being at best mere compilations, they are not entitled to be classed with, or named as, sources of Hindu law.

The subject that has exercised immense influence on the development of Hindu law is the case-law of the country; and the chapter on the sources of Hindu law will be incomplete if I were not to devote a portion of it to the consideration of this topic. Though in theory the decisions of our Courts are supposed to be based on the Hindu law *as it is*, yet, practically, as I shall show afterwards, the case-law has effected a considerable modification on the original stock of Hindu law—a change which, in some cases, has had a beneficial effect, but in other cases its influence for good upon Hindu society has been very questionable. The judicial decisions. They have modified original Hindu law.

I have told you before that Hindu law has remained unaltered for many thousands of years. That Limitations to the proposition that Hindu law has remained

[1] Morley's Digest, Intro., p. ccxxi.

LECTURE I. — proposition you must accept with some limitations. No system of rules for the government of a living society, and for the conduct of its members, can remain unchanged for a very long time. A society, however stationary in its character and traditions, must move, however slowly that motion may be effected; and it is now an axiom in Sociology that all societies do move, and that no society is *absolutely* stationary. The difference between a society that is *stationary* and a society that is *progressive* is not that any society is absolutely stationary, but that all societies move; the one moving more slowly is called a stationary society, whereas a society that moves more rapidly than another is called a progressive society.

unaltered for many thousands of years.

Stationary and progressive societies distinguished.

The Hindu society has changed, though slowly.

The Hindu society is no exception to this universal law of social movements. The Hindu society does change, and has changed; of this there is abundant evidence. With the change in the society the law of that society must change; the law must adapt itself to the altered social phenomena, and to the altered requirements of that society. In some societies the law is changed by express legislation, the sovereign exercising his legitimate function to make the law and the society harmonious; in other societies the law is changed by indirect methods, by authentic interpretation and by judge-made law, which latter, however, is only a mode of interpretation. The commentators, or Judges, purporting to *interpret* the law, do oftentimes, in

The law changes as society changes.

Law changed by authentic interpretation and by judge-made law.

substance *modify* that law; though the *form* of the law remains unaltered, a material change in the *substance* of it is effected, which the altered state of the society rendered imperatively necessary. If law and society are not kept in harmony, the necessary consequence is a social revolution followed by a political revolution, which sweeps away in its fury the existing fabric of law, bringing in its train great deal of misery and suffering upon the whole community. The French Revolution of 1788 may be quoted as a standing evidence of this law.

The Hindu law changed by indirect methods.

The Hindu law has been changed by these indirect methods, by the interpretation of commentators and by judicial interpretation. I have pointed out to you that the law of the commentators and of the digest-writers is *not* the law of the ancient Rishis; if it were so, how could there be a diversity of opinion on important points between the different schools.

The *one* law of the Smritis has been *variously* interpreted by the commentators; and these various interpretations called *authentic* interpretations have been accepted as law in different parts of India.

The Hindu law changed by judicial decisions.

I shall now try to explain to you the influence of judicial decisions in modifying or developing the existing Hindu law. The English rulers, when they assumed the reins of Government in this country, declared that they shall not alter the Hindu law, and that disputes relating to "inheritance, succession to lands, rents and goods, and all matters of contract

LECTURE I. — and dealing between party and party," between Hindus, shall be determined by the laws and usages of the Hindus.[1] The consequence of this declaration was to arrest the natural development of Hindu law by the aid of the writings of commentators. The English Government accepted the existing Hindu law, and accepted also the theory that it is unchangeable; consequently there was no inducement to pundits and native scholars to write treatises on any of the branches of law. This will account for the fact that, since the advent of the British rule, excepting Jaggannatha's Digest, which was written under the patronage of Government, no work of any reputation or importance has been written in any part of India bearing upon any of the branches of law. Another reason which may, probably, be assigned for this fact, is the general decay of Sanscrit learning owing to the want of encouragement from the ruling power.

Illustration—the law of wills and testaments.

The first and one of the most important illustrations of the development of Hindu law by judicial decisions is afforded by the law of wills and testaments. You may, probably, have heard it said, that the law of wills and testaments is unknown to the original Hindu law. That statement is strictly correct. Examine the authorities on Hindu law, and you will find that the power of a dying man to dispose of his property in any manner he thought

---

[1] Section 17, Declaratory Act of 1781, passed by Parliament.

proper is never recognised in any of the schools. The Hindu law notion is, that property is for the *family*, and not for the *individual*. That property shall be preserved for the *deceased* members of the family, for the *present* members, and for the *future* members of that family. That the spiritual welfare of the deceased members, as well as of the present and future members, of the family depends upon the maintenance of certain religious ceremonies, for which the family property must be preserved. If then this family property is alienated, how is the performance of these religious rites secured, on which the happiness of all the members so materially depends. Hence the power of one member of the family to alienate the family property either during his lifetime or to take effect after his death, is, in Hindu law, so strenuously denied. Every member of the family has a sort of usufructuary right over the family property, a right of enjoyment of the profits, subject to the performance of certain duties. On his death the property shall go to the other members of the family, unalienated and inalienable. A sort of perpetuity in the family property was thus secured.

The alienation of family property opposed to the provisions of Hindu law.

This is the strict ancient doctrine, and we find it considerably modified by the author of the Mitacshara, who admits the power of the owner to alienate property during his lifetime if he has no son, grandson or great-grandson, living at the time of aliena-

How far modified by the Mitacshara.

LECTURE I.

tion. But his power of alienation is otherwise denied, and his testamentary power is never recognised.

Jimutavahana went a step further.

The founder of the Bengal school, Jimutavahana, went a step further. He admitted the power of the present holder of the property to make an unequal distribution of the property among his sons. The law of *factum valet* was introduced; and the right of the Bengal owner to alienate his property in any manner during his lifetime was deduced as a consequence by the decisions of the Courts during the latter part of the eighteenth and the beginning of the nineteenth century; though it must be here stated that there is no direct authority for such an unqualified proposition in the Dayabhaga itself.

The testamentary law deduced by the Courts from an erroneous view of the law of the Bengal school.

The English lawyers who came to administer justice in this country in the latter end of the eighteenth century, found that, in the Dayabhaga, the son's right did not accrue till after the death of his father, and that the father could alienate the property during his lifetime. From this they thought that the Bengal father has, by the law, the power of making a testamentary disposition of his property, and accordingly, in the administration of justice, they came to recognise the power of making wills. In Calcutta, wills were for the first time made by the native inhabitants; and they were upheld by the late Supreme Court. The example was gradually followed in the mofussil, and the Courts there also followed the decisions of the Supreme Court in this respect.

To an Englishman, and to an English lawyer, nothing could be more natural than the right of making wills. He was accustomed to it in his own country, and all his social and political predilections tended in the same direction. To a Hindu of the eighteenth century, however, nothing could be more repugnant to his social instincts and to his religious education. That a man on his deathbed should have the power of giving away the whole family property to an absolute stranger, and thereby extinguish the family worship and the observance of religious rites on which the spiritual welfare of the family depends, is an idea totally abhorrent to all Hindu feelings. Yet this is exactly the innovation which judicial decisions have engrafted on the original stock of Hindu law.

The law of wills repugnant to the notions of a Hindu.

Another instance I shall quote here. Suits by reversioners to set aside alienations by the Hindu widow, and similar suits to remove the widow from possession of her husband's estate, are very common in our Courts. Now, it may be pointed out here, that there is no direct authority in the text-books to warrant suits of that description. But the Judges administering the law found that the widow's alienations were voidable, and that they are bound to protect the contingent interest of the reversioners. From considerations like these, they came to allow suits of the description before pointed out.

Another illustration. Suits by reversioners to set aside widow's alienations.

To take an instance from the Mitacshara law.

An illustration

LECTURE I.

from the Mitacshara.

According to that authority, no member of the family can validly encumber the family property for his own necessities. The subordinate members of the family cannot do it on any account. The father, or head of the family, however, can encumber the estate for the necessities of the *family*; but for his own extravagance he would be personally liable, and not the family estate. This is the correct law according to the Mitacshara. The Privy Council,[1] however, has held that the interest of a co-sharer in the joint family property can be sold in execution of a decree obtained against him personally, and the purchaser in that sale can insist on being put in possession of the share of the family property by partition. This is the extent of the innovation that judicial decisions have brought about. This is a recognition of individual rights against corporate or joint rights. Whether this is beneficial or injurious to the interests of Hindu society, I do not pretend to determine. All I say is, that the law on this subject has been considerably modified by judicial decisions.

Power of the father to alienate family property.

Denied in the Mitacshara.

Recognised by the Privy Council.

Another illustration: The joint Hindu family of Bengal.

Take again the instance of the joint Hindu family in Bengal. The decisions of Courts on this head have been marked by a uniform tendency to show a greater consideration for the rights of the earning member; and for this purpose our Judges have created

[1] Deendyal v. Jugdeep Narain, I. L. R., 3 Calc., 198; see also I. L. R., 4 Calc., 809.

several presumptions. This desire on the part of our Judges may be a thing just in itself; it may be in keeping with the progress of times and with the laws of society; but it is a change nevertheless—a change on the primitive doctrine of Hindu law brought about by judicial legislation. Without multiplying instances, I may say that, in almost every branch of Hindu law, the effect of judicial decisions in changing the law is apparent.

LECTURE I.

Decisions of Courts have created to some extent uncertainty in Hindu law.

Another effect of the decisions of Courts on Hindu law has been, unfortunately, to create a certain amount of uncertainty and want of fixedness in that law. To take a particular instance. Whether the brother's daughter's son is an heir according to the Bengal school? On the authority of Srikrishna Tarkalankara, he was recognised as an heir. That was the state of the law before 1864. In 1864 the Bengal High Court, after an elaborate argument, held,[1] that he cannot inherit, and that the passage in the Dayakrama Sangraha, on which his title to inherit is based, is an interpolation. The law continued in that state till 1870, when a Full Bench of the Bengal High Court,[2] deliberately sat to consider the correctness of the law laid down in the case of 1864. The Judges who referred the question to the Full Bench were of opinion that the passage[3] in the Dayakrama Sangraha is

Illustration. Brother's daughter's sons are heirs or not?

[1] Gobind Hureekur v. Womesh Chunder Roy, W. R., Sp. No., p. 176.

[2] Goorogobind Shaha v. Anund Lal Ghosh, 13 W. R., 49, F. B.

[3] Chap. I, Sec. X, v. 2.

LECTURE I. not an interpolation. The Chief Justice (Sir Barnes Peacock) was of the same opinion, for he held on the authority of the passages in the Dayakrama Sangraha, that the father's brother's daughter's son is an heir. Justice Mitter, who delivered the judgment of the Full Bench, came to the same conclusion as to the point of law, without any reference however to the passages in the Dayakrama Sangraha. He held, that the father's brother's daughter's son is an heir, because he is a *sapinda* according to the doctrine of Jimutavahana, and satisfies the crucial text of heirship proposed by that author. In the course of six years we have the law differently interpreted on three different occasions, and one might hope that the law is finally settled by this last decision of the Bengal High Court, and that the brother's daughter's son is not going to be disturbed again for purposes of judicial interpretation.

Another illustration of uncertainty created by judicial decisions.

Another case of uncertainty created by judicial legislation I will cite here. Srikrishna Tarkalankara's Dayakrama Sangraha has been held by our Courts as a work of high authority for the doctrines of the Bengal school; and according to this authority cases have been decided in this country for nearly three quarters of a century. On the authority of this book the brother's daughter's son, as the descendant of the *father*, is entitled to succeed in preference to the descendants of the *grandfather* (e. g.), the grandfather's great-grandson. The Bengal High Court has, how-

LECTURE I.

ever, held[1] that the grandfather's great-grandson succeeds in preference to the brother's daughter's son. The error in this decision I have tried to point out elsewhere. But apart from the error which may be said to involve a particular case only, the mischief committed by this decision is immense. It has the effect of questioning the authority of the Dayakrama Sangraha, which, long before this, was considered as settled. It unsettles the whole list of heirs as given by Srikrishna. No one, after this, will feel confident in basing his conclusions upon the authority of this book, seeing that it may be disregarded by our Courts, without the least ceremony.

The value of standard works.

The value of having a standard work on a particular branch of law, which is accepted as an authority on all hands, is immense. The country gains by it; unnecessary litigation is at once put a stop to by an appeal to its authority. Every man, the litigant as well as the lawyer, feels himself on firm ground when he can refer to this authority in support of his contention. The uncertainty of a system of law is its great reproach; its certainty, on the other hand, is its chief merit; nothing more tends to create uncertainty in law than by disregarding current authorities, and by deposing a standard authority from the high position which it has justly attained. To make standard authorities the sport of chance, and subject

Mischief of disregarding standard authorities.

[1] Gobindpersaud Talookdar *v.* Mohesh Chunder Surmah, 23 W. R., 117.

LECTURE I. — to the caprice of Judges, whose knowledge of Hindu law is derived from very slender, sometimes very doubtful, sources, is the just complaint of those who take an interest in the proper administration of Hindu law.

The difficulties of administering Hindu law.

The difficulties, however, which the early English Judges had to encounter in administering the Hindu law must not be overlooked—difficulties which, considering the circumstances, were almost insurmountable. In the first place, the very name of the Hindu law was probably unknown to Englishmen before the middle of the eighteenth century, and it is only after the establishment of Courts in British India in the latter part of that century, that the English Judges began first to direct their attention to that subject. They found, however, that the law was written in a very ancient language, a knowledge of which could, with very great difficulty and application, be acquired. They also found that there was an extreme disinclination on the part of the Brahmins, the accepted repositories of that law, to teach them this system of law. Attention was directed to translations as the only mode of acquiring a knowledge of this law, and the eighteenth century closed with the English translations of only two Sanscrit law books. Five more treatises were translated in the course of the next twenty years; and the numerous other treatises bearing upon the same subject remained untranslated. With the incomplete materials thus avail-

Partially removed by translations of standard works.

able, which were however hardly used, the English Judges went to work; and they were by law and necessity compelled to avail themselves of the assistance of the Pundits attached to their Courts. The early Hindu law of our Courts was, therefore, the law as delivered by the Pundits; and be it said to the credit of these much-abused officers, that they, with few exceptions, interpreted the law according to their own lights.

The pundits the interpreters of law.

Sometimes, however, the Judges did not accept the Pundit's version of the law. That the law had outgrown the authorities was recognised by the Pundits, and this fact tended to modify their opinions. The Judges, however, could not appreciate or recognize the fact; the progress of Hindu society, and the consequent change of its laws by the introduction of customs, were ignored by them. The effect of this sort of administration of justice was to arrest the natural development of the law. Nothing was accepted by the Judges as an authority, but what was very old; and customs, which had stood the test of several centuries, were totally disregarded. It must be said to the credit of the Judges, that they accepted the fundamental maxim of Hindu law, and acted upon it. The mischief, which was committed, was the want of appreciation that by thus crystallising the law, they were checking its natural growth.

Sometimes disregarded by the Judges.

Natural growth of law arrested.

Another defect of judicial legislation was the incomplete materials on which the conclusions were

Judicial decisions of ten

LECTURE I.

based upon incomplete materials.

often based. All the approved commentaries and digests had not been, nor yet have they been, translated. The Judges had not placed before them the latest views of the commentators or the digest-writers. In the countries governed by the Mitacshara the later authorities being unknown, the Judges accepted the views of the Mitacshara unmodified by the writings of later authorities. In Bengal the authorities after the Dayabhaga being unknown were not recognized. The consequence is, that cases were really decided, throughout India, almost on the authority of these two books ; and earlier decisions being followed generally in later cases, a sort of consensus of judicial authorities was the result. The difficulties began to be felt when later authorities began to be studied and placed before the Courts. The Judges found that later writers had considerably modified the earlier authorities of the Mitacshara and the Dayabhaga. If the later authorities are followed, a long course of decisions will have to be overruled ; if they are disregarded, the changes in the Hindu law by its natural and recognized exponents will have to be ignored. In the present times, the Judges found themselves in this dilemma ; but their action has not been uniform. Sometimes they overruled the case-law, and sometimes they ignored the later authorities. A considerable uncertainty was the result. Professional men could not advise with any degree of certainty whether the earlier case-law will be followed or the authorities recently brought to light. LECTURE I.

Such is the present condition of Hindu law. Questions frequently arise in our Courts on which "much might be said on both sides," and they are not finally settled until they come up before the Court of last resort. Even then the question seems to be settled for the purposes of that case only; for we not unfrequently find the same question disposed of differently in another case which may arise a few years later. Present uncertain condition of Hindu law.

This state of the law is very injurious to the interests of the community at large. People do not know what their rights are until they have spent large sums of money in litigating the questions through all the Courts; a mode of solution of the difficulty which is to be very much deprecated. Injurious to the interests of the community.

The remedy for this state of the law is very difficult to prescribe. Whether the law should be allowed to settle itself in the way in which it has been doing, *viz.*, by the action of the Courts in interpreting the original authorities, with the occasional introduction of foreign conceptions into the body of this law, or whether the law should be settled by a *Code*, is a very difficult question to determine. Of course, considerable aid will be afforded to the Courts by the translations of all or at least of most of the principal Digests or Commentaries, so that the Judges might have the whole law placed before them. Another Its remedy. By judicial decisions, or by codification. Considerable aid to the Courts by translations of the principal Digests,

LECTURE I. important element which has been so often overlooked by our Courts is the consideration of customs of the people in determining the law to be applicable to each case. Dry bones of ancient law, unless viewed in connection with the customs which have grown out of them, and, in some cases, have supplanted them, can never correctly represent the conditions or feelings of the people. I have already pointed out the great want in this direction, the total absence of any record or collection of these customs. Something must be done in this direction, to collect and generalise local as well as tribal or caste customs, to supplement the written law and to co-operate in the administration of justice. Until this is done, and the chief Digests are translated, I do not think it is possible to codify the Hindu law with any degree of success. With the materials that are at present available, a code drawn up must be a very imperfect production. It will not give satisfaction to the various tribes of Hindus and semi-Hindus that dwell in different parts of Hindoostan. The law reform in the present times must, I venture to think, be confined to the translations of the Digests and to a complete and correct record of the customary laws throughout the country.

and the collection of customs.

A code of Hindu law is not likely to succeed at present.

LECTURE II.

THE CONDITION OF WOMEN AND THE OBLIGATIONS OF WIDOWS.

Condition of women in ancient India—Females must be treated with consideration and respect—Their persons adorned—Undue liberty not to be given to females—They must be always dependent—Household management their chief duty—They must be devoted to their husbands—Vices of women described—The strict life of a Hindu widow described—Her obligation to burn—Called *sahamarana*—Who are exempted from it—Abolition of the practice of *sati*—By Reg. XVII of 1829—Reasons for its abolition—Practice rendered penal—The practice still prevalent in the Native States—The antiquity of this custom admitted—According to Colebrooke it is enjoined in the Rig Veda—Professor Wilson denies its Vedic origin—Text of the Rig Veda as read by Wilson—The Custom known in Vedic times—Raghunandana's discussion on the subject—Authorities quoted by him—His conclusion—The two readings of the text of the Rig Veda—Raja Radhakant's interpretation of the 8th hymn—Raja Radhakant's opinion that the rite is enjoined in the Vedas—Text of Black Yajush quoted as authority—Its authenticity doubted by Wilson—*Brahmacharya* next alternative for a widow—*Brahmacharya* described—The practice of Niyoga, or appointment to raise issue—Reprobated by Menu—Yama on the same subject—Conflict of opinion among the Rishis on this subject—Practice authorized by Narada—By Yama—By Yajnawalkya—Condemned by Menu—Attempts to reconcile these conflicting texts—Reconciliation by Vrihaspati—Accepted as authority for the prohibition in the present age—Text of Menu condemning the practice considered an interpolation—No authority for this opinion—Ascetic life of a widow, matter of religious observance, not of legal obligation.

Condition of women in ancient India.

EUROPEAN scholars are apt to describe the condition of women in ancient India as something very

LECTURE II. — object. This description is not exactly accurate, as the authorities to which we have access give us a different picture. No doubt, the materials are somewhat meagre; still, with the help of those that we possess, we have a rather fair picture of their condition.

Females must be treated with consideration and respect.

In the *Shasters* we find repeated injunctions to treat the females with the utmost consideration, and punishment is enjoined as the share of those who treat them with neglect or cruelty. "Married women must be honored and adorned by their fathers and brethren; by their husbands and by the brethren of their husbands if they seek abundant prosperity."[1] "Where females are honored there the deities are pleased; but where they are dishonored, there all religious acts become fruitless."[2] "Where female relations are made miserable, the family of him who makes them so, very soon perishes; but where they are not unhappy, the family always increases."[3] "On whatever houses the women of a family, not being duly honored, pronounce an imprecation, those houses, with all that belong to them, utterly perish as if destroyed by a sacrifice for the death of an enemy."[4] "Let those women, therefore, be continually supplied with ornaments, apparel, and food at festivals and at jubilees by men desirous of wealth."[5] "In

---

[1] Menu, Chap. III, v. 55.
[2] Menu, Chap. III, v. 56.
[3] Menu, Chap. III, v. 57.
[4] Menu, Chap. III, v. 58.
[5] Menu, Chap. III, v. 59.

whatever family the husband is contented with his wife, and the wife with her husband, in that house will fortune be assuredly permanent."[1] LECTURE II.

The ancient legislator was not regardless of the personal appearance of women; for he ordains, "certainly, if the wife be not elegantly attired, she will not exhilarate her husband; and if her lord want hilarity, offspring will not be produced."[2] Again, "a wife being gaily adorned, her whole house is embellished; but if she be destitute of ornament, all will be deprived of decoration."[3]

Their persons adorned.

The spirit of the Hindu law and customs is not to give undue liberty to women, whatever be their age or condition in life; and this traditional morality so often inculcated in the *Shashters* is still the abiding rule governing the conduct and behaviour of females throughout Hindoostan. No doubt, these rules are somewhat repugnant to the advanced notions of the western nations on the subject of female rights, but the Hindus are instructed from the earliest, almost pre-historic, times in a system of rules entirely different. We find Menu ordaining that "by a girl or by a young woman, or by a woman advanced in years, nothing must be done even in her own dwelling-place, according to her mere pleasure."[4] "In childhood must a female be dependent on her father; in youth, on her husband; her lord being dead, on

Undue liberty not to be given to females.

They must be always dependent.

---

[1] Menu, Chap. III, v. 60.
[2] Menu, Chap. III, v. 61.
[3] Menu, Chap. III, v. 62.
[4] Chap. V, v. 147.

LECTURE II. her sons; if she have no sons, on the near kinsmen of her husband; if he left no kinsmen, on those of her father; if she have no paternal kinsmen, on the sovereign; a woman must never seek independence."[1] "Never let her wish to separate herself from her father, her husband, or her sons: for, by a separation from them, she exposes both families to contempt."[2] And in another place, the same authority has ordained thus: "Day and night must women be held by their protectors in a state of dependence: but in lawful and innocent recreations, though rather addicted to them, they may be left at their own disposal."[3] "Their fathers protect them in childhood; their husbands protect them in youth; their sons protect them in age; a woman is never fit for independence."[4] "Women must, above all, be restrained from the smallest illicit gratification; for not being thus restrained, they bring sorrow on both families."[5] "Let husbands consider this as the supreme law ordained for all classes; and let them, how weak soever, diligently keep their wives under lawful restrictions."[6] "For he who preserves his wife from vice, preserves his offspring from suspicions of bastardy, his ancient usages from neglect, his family from disgrace, himself from anguish, and his duty from violation."[7] "By confinement at home,

---

[1] Chap. V, v. 148. [2] Chap. V, v. 149. [3] Chap. IX, v. 2.
[4] Chap. IX, v. 3. [5] Chap. IX, v. 5. [6] Chap. IX, v. 6.
[7] Chap. IX, v. 7.

even under affectionate and observant guardians, they are not secure: but those women are truly secure who are guarded by their own good inclinations." [1]

Household management their chief duty.

Her chief duty consists in the management of household affairs. "She must always live with a cheerful temper, with good management in the affairs of the house, with great care of the household furniture, and with a frugal hand in all her expenses." [2] Again: "Let the husband keep his wife employed in the collection and expenditure of wealth, in purification and female duty, in the preparation of daily food, and the superintendence of household utensils." [3] "The production of children, the nurture of them when produced, and the daily superintendence of domestic affairs,—are peculiar to the wife." [4] "From the wife alone proceed offspring, good household management, most exquisite caresses, and that heavenly beatitude which she obtains for the manes of ancestors and for the husband himself." [5]

They must be devoted to their husbands.

But that for which a woman lives, her mission in this world, and the cause of her *mukti* hereafter, is devotion to her husband. "Him to whom her father has given her, or her brother with the paternal assent, let her obsequiously honor while he lives; and, when he dies, let her never neglect him." [6] "When the husband has performed the nuptial rites with the texts of the Vedas, he gives bliss conti-

[1] Chap. IX, v. 12. [2] Chap. V, v. 150. [3] Chap. IX, v. 11.
[4] Chap. IX, v. 27. [5] Chap. IX, v. 28. [6] Chap. V, v. 151.

LECTURE II. nually to his wife here below, both in season and out of season, and he will give her happiness in the next world."[1] "To a wife her husband is like a god. Though inobservant of approved usages, or enamoured of another woman, or devoid of good qualities, yet a husband must constantly be revered as a god by a virtuous wife."[2] "No sacrifice is allowed to women apart from their husbands; no religious rite, no fasting; as far only as a wife honors her lord, so far she is exalted in heaven."[3] "A faithful wife who wishes to attain in heaven the mansion of her husband, must do nothing unkind to him, be he living or dead."[4] "She who deserts not her lord, but keeps in subjection to him her heart, her speech, and her body, shall attain his mansion in heaven, and by the virtuous in this world be called *Sádhwí*, or good and faithful;"[5] and punishment here and hereafter is declared to be the lot of those women who slight their husbands. "But a wife, by disloyalty to her husband, shall incur disgrace in this life, and be born in the next from the womb of a jackal, or be tormented with horrible diseases that punish vice."[6]

Vices of women described.

There is another side of this picture which describes the vices of women, and which they are enjoined to avoid. "Drinking spirituous liquor, associating with evil persons, absence from her husband, rambling

[1] Chap. V, v. 153.
[2] Chap. V, v. 154.
[3] Chap. V, v. 155.
[4] Chap. V, v. 156.
[5] Chap. IX, v. 29.
[6] Chap. IX, v. 30.

abroad, unseasonable sleep, and dwelling in the house of another,—are six faults which bring infamy on a married woman."[1] It is impossible to say whether these are not some of the vices that were rather common among the women of the time, and which the great legislator was so anxious to check, and he has, accordingly, stigmatised such conduct in very strong language. "Such women examine not beauty, nor pay attention to age; whether their lover be handsome or ugly, they think it is enough that he is a man, and pursue their pleasures."[2] "Through their passion for men, their mutable temper, their want of settled affection, and their perverse nature (let them be guarded in this world ever so well), they soon become alienated from their husbands."[3] "Yet, should their husbands be diligently careful in guarding them; though they well know the disposition with which the lord of creation formed them."[4] "Menu allotted to such women a love of their bed, of their seat and of ornament, impure appetites, wrath, weak flexibility, desire of mischief, and bad conduct."[5]

The strict life of a Hindu widow described.

The above observations apply to the condition of females generally and to married women in particular. The Hindu widow, however, was subjected to a more strict and severe discipline. On the death of her husband, her obligation was to ascend the funeral pile

Her obligation to burn.

---

[1] Chap. IX, v. 13. [2] Chap. IX, v. 14. [3] Chap. IX, v. 15.
[4] Chap. IX, v. 16. [5] Chap. IX, v. 17.

LECTURE II.

of her husband, and there to burn herself to death: for, by such an act, she would be exalted to heaven; this will secure her residence in another world in a region of joy for thirty-five million of years, and shall expiate the sins of her husband's family, which have accrued during three generations. She will also have the great merit of removing her husband from a region of torment: and expiate all his sins, although they may be of the most heinous description. If the widow declined to burn herself, she is subject to be born again in this world in the body of some female animal, and this penalty will attach to her in all successive transmigrations.[1]

Called *sahamarana.*

This practice was called *sahamarana*, which means literally *dying with* the husband. This was possible when the husband died where the wife was living, and she could, therefore, be burned with the dead body of her husband. If he, however, died in another part of the country, and there his cremation took place, and the information of his death was brought to his widow living at his home or elsewhere, in such a case *sahamarana* was not possible, and *anumarana* was prescribed, which meant dying *after* her husband on a subsequent day. The merits of this were equal to *sahamarana*, and the obligation is the same.[2] The faithful wife in this case is to enter the fire,

---

[1] Angiras, quoted in the Digest, Bk. IV, Chap. III, Sec. I, v. cxxiii.

[2] Vyasa quoted in the Digest, Bk. IV, Chap. III, Sec. I, v. cxxv.

placing the sandals, or something belonging to her husband, on her breast.[1]

LECTURE II.

Who are exempted from it.

This obligation to burn was enjoined upon every female except mothers of infant children, pregnant women, young girls, and women who are actually unclean after childbirth or from other cause.[2] This exception was admitted in consideration of other lives being at stake, or the extreme youth of the person who is to suffer, for, among the commentators, Raghunandana[3] in particular observes:—That, if the infant can be nurtured by any other person, then the mother is entitled to follow her deceased husband. It was further held, that all the wives of a man are entitled to die with or after him; and the cremation of the husband may be postponed by one day (a serious departure from the strict injunction on the subject) to allow the absent wife to come and die with her husband;[4] and facilities were so far afforded for the purpose, that if, on account of any uncleanness, a woman is prevented from dying *with* her husband, she will be entitled to all the benefit of *sahamarana*, if she followed her husband within one month after the impurity had ceased.[5]

Abolition of the practice of *sati*

This practice of what is popularly called *becoming sati*, was observed in British India within recent

---

[1] Brahma Puran, quoted in the Digest, Bk. IV, Chap. III, Sec. I, v. cxxvi.

[2] Vrihat Naradiya Puran, *ibid*, v. cxxvii.

[3] Quoted in the Digest under v. cxxviii.

[4] Vyasa, *ibid*, v. cxxxi.

[5] Commentary on v. cxxviii.

LECTURE II. — times, when it was abolished during the government of Lord William Bentinck by legislative enactment, and the observance of it was declared penal within British territories.

By Reg. XVII of 1829.

The Statute by which the practice of *satí* was declared penal is Reg. XVII of 1829. The preamble of this Regulation, which embodies the reasons, which induced, as well as justified, the Government in abolishing this ancient practice, stated as follows :—

Reasons for its abolition.

"The practice of *sati*, or of burning or burying alive the widows of Hindus, is revolting to the feelings of human nature; it is nowhere enjoined by the religion of the Hindus as an imperative duty; on the contrary, a life of purity and retirement on the part of the widow is more especially and preferably inculcated, and by a vast majority of that people throughout India the practice is not kept up, nor observed. In some extensive districts it does not exist. In those in which it has been most frequent, it is notorious that, in many instances, acts of atrocity have been perpetrated, which have been shocking to the Hindus themselves and in their eyes unlawful and wicked. The measures hitherto adopted to discourage and prevent such acts have failed of success, and the Governor-General in Council is deeply impressed with the conviction that the abuses in question cannot be effectually put an end to without abolishing the practice altogether. Actuated by these considerations, the Goveror-General in Council—without intending to depart from one of the first and most important principles of the system of British Government in India, that all classes of the people be secure in the observance of their religious usages, so long as that system can be adhered to without violation of the paramount dictates of justice and humanity—has deemed it right to establish the following rules, which are hereby enacted to be in force from the time of their promulgation throughout the territories immediately subject to the Presidency of Fort William."

Practice rendered penal.

This Statute, therefore, rendered the practice of *sati*, or of burning or burying alive the widows of Hindus, illegal and punishable by the criminal courts,[1] and every person aiding and abetting the same was declared liable to punishment.

It was further ordained,[2] that all zemindars, talookdars, and other proprietors of land are responsible for the immediate communication to the officers of the nearest police stations of any intended case of *sati*, and in case of neglect they were declared liable to a fine.

You will see from the Regulations that the practice of burying alive the widows of Hindus is mentioned in it: which also was suppressed by the Statute. I am not aware in what part of India this custom of burying alive the widows of Hindus

---

[1] Sec. II. [2] Sec. III.

LECTURE II. was prevalent. The *Shasters* explicitly mention the case of burning only, and not of burying, though by the generic expression *sahamarana*, or *dying with the husband*, any other mode of death than by burning may be inferred. I believe, by the evidences before the Government in 1829, the practice of burying was also found to be locally prevalent as a custom in certain parts of the country, or among certain castes or tribes of Hindus; and hence the legislature thought it necessary to declare that practice also as penal.

The practice still prevalent in the Native States.

After its abolition in British India, the custom was still observed in the Native States. When Maharajah Runjeet Sing died in 1839, some of his wives became *sati*;[1] and recently, when Maharajah Jung Bahadur of Nepal died, his widow became *sati*.

The antiquity of this custom admitted.

The antiquity of this custom is beyond question. Professor Wilson says, that "it is of long standing is not to be disputed;" and the Pundits of this country maintain that it was observed in Vedic times, and has a direct Vedic origin. The question excited a good deal of political as well as literary and antiquarian discussion, at the time when the Indian Government suppressed it by legislative enactment.

According to Colebrooke it is enjoined in the Rig Veda.

Mr. Colebrooke, in his Essay[2] upon the "Duties of a *sati*, or faithful widow," was of opinion, that the custom was enjoined by a text of the Rig Veda,

---

[1] Up the Country, by E. Eden, Vol. II, pp. 138, 139; see Cunningham's History of the Sikhs, p. 230, *note*. [2] Asiatic Researches, Vol. IV, p. 213.

of which he gave the following translation :—" Om : Let these women not to be widowed, good wives adorned with *collyrium*, holding clarified butter, consign themselves to the fire. Immortal, not childless, nor husbandless, excellent ; let them pass into fire whose original element is water."

LECTURE II.

The discussion was resumed by Professor Wilson in 1854 in his paper " On the supposed Vaidic authority for the Burning of Hindu Widows," which was printed in the 16th Volume of the Journal of the Royal Asiatic Society ; and he maintained, " that the text of the Rig Veda, cited as authority for the burning of widows, enjoins the very contrary, and directs them to remain in the world." Professor Wilson has given a literal translation of the whole súkta, or hymn, in which this passage occurs.[1] The

Professor Wilson denies its Vedic origin.

[1] The following is the translation of the hymn by Professor Wilson :—

1. Depart, Mrityu, by a different path, by that which is thine own, different from the path of the Gods. I speak to thee who hast eyes, who hast ears. Injure not our female progeny, harm not our male.

2. Ye who approach the path of death, but are possessed of prolonged existence, ye who are entitled to reverence, prosperous with offspring and wealth, may ye be pure and sanctified.

3. May those who are living be kept distinct from the dead ; may the offering we present this day to the gods be propitious. Let us go with our faces to the east, to dance and be merry ; for we are in the enjoyment of prolonged life.

4. I place this circle [of stones] for the living, on this account, that no other may go beyond it. May they live a hundred years ; keeping death at a distance by this heap.

5. As days follow days in succession, and seasons are succeeded by seasons, as one man follows another, so, Dhátri, do thou prolong the lives of these [my kinsmen].

6. Reaching to old age with still-ascending life, and following active in succession as many as may be, may Twashtri, being propitiated, grant you prolonged life.

LECTURE II. — verse of which Mr. Colebrooke has given the translation is thus rendered by Mr. Wilson; it is the seventh verse in that hymn:—"May these women who are not widows, who have good husbands, who are mothers, enter with unguents and clarified butter, without tears, without sorrow: let them first go up into the dwelling." Eighth verse:—"Rise up, woman, come to the world of living beings; thou sleepest nigh unto the lifeless, come; thou hast been associated with maternity through the husband by whom thy hand was formerly taken."

Text of the Rig Veda as read by Wilson.

The learned Professor points out the difference between the text translated by him and that trans-

---

7. May these women, who are not widows, who have good husbands, who are mothers, enter with unguents and clarified butter: without tears, without sorrow, let them first go up into the dwelling.

8. Rise up, woman, come to the world of living beings, thou sleepest nigh unto the lifeless. Come; thou hast been associated with maternity through the husband by whom thy hand was formerly taken.

9. Taking his bow from the hand of the dead, that it may be to us for help, for strength, for fame, [I say] here verily art thou, and here are we: accompanied by our valiant descendants, may we overcome all arrogant adversaries.

10. Go to the mother earth, this wide-spread blessed earth; to the liberal man she is a maiden soft as wool; may she protect thee from the proximity of the evil being.

11. Lie up [lightly] earth, oppress him not, be bounteous to him, treat him kindly, cover him, earth, as a mother covers an infant with the skirts of her garment.

12. May earth lying lightly up, stay well; may thousands of particles [of soil] rest upon it; may these abodes be ever sprinkled with clarified butter, and may they, day by day, be to him an asylum.

13. I heap up the earth above thee, and placing this clod of clay, may I not hurt thee; may the Manes protect this thy monument, and Yama ever grant thee here an abode.

14. New days sustain me, as the feather upholds the shaft, but I restrain my voice now grown old, as the reins hold in a horse.

lated by Mr. Colebrooke. His reading of the most important part is *arohantu yonim agre*, literally "let them go up into the dwelling first;" and Mr. Colebrooke's reading is *arohantu yonim agneh*, "let them go up to the place of the fire;"[1] and he is of opinion that his reading is the correct one, "not only by the concurrence of the manuscripts, but also by the explanation given by the commentator Sayanacharya, who explains it *sarvesham prathamato griham agachchhantu*, 'let them come home first of all,' the phrase having reference, therefore, to some procession, one possibly accompanying the corpse and having nothing whatever to do with consigning themselves to the fire."

Mr. Colebrooke obtained his reading from Raghunandana as the text is given by him in his Suddhitattwa.

The question ultimately settles itself into one of disputed readings; and the question is one of considerable difficulty, whether the reading as given by Professor Wilson is the correct one.

The custom known in Vedic times.

Whether that passage contains any *injunctions* for the widow to burn, may be doubtful: but it is almost certain that the practice was *known* in Vedic times.

Raghunandana's discussion on the subject.

The subject of *sahamarana* is discussed by Raghunandana in his Suddhitattwa. It forms the first chapter of that treatise; all the provisions of law

---

[1] See *post*, p. 101.

LECTURE II. — bearing upon that topic are collected there, and the disputed points are discussed with the author's characteristic ability, clearness, and research. The chapter opens with a discussion as to whether *sahamarana* is lawful. For this purpose the author first quotes a text[1] of Angira, which has been quoted before :—

Authorities quoted by him.

> "That woman who, on the death of her husband, ascends the *same* burning pile with him, is exalted to heaven as equal in virtue to Arundhati," &c. &c.

Then the following passage[2] from the Mahabharata is quoted :—

> "Those who have slighted their former lord, through an evil disposition, or have remained at all times averse from their husbands, if they follow their lords at the proper time in such a mode, are all purified from lust, wrath, fear, and avarice."

Then the well-known passage[3] from the Brahma Purana is quoted :—

> "If her lord die in another country, let the faithful wife place his sandals on her breast and, pure, enter the fire."

---

[1] मृते भर्त्तरि या नारी समारोहेद्धुताशनं।
सारुन्धतीसमाचारा स्वर्गलोके महीयते॥
&c., &c., &c.

[2] अवमत्य च याः पूर्व्वं पतिं दुष्टेन चेतसा।
वर्त्तन्ते याश्च सततं भर्त्तृणां प्रतिकूलतः॥
&c., &c., &c.

[3] देशान्तरमृते पत्यौ साध्वी तत्पादुकाद्वयं।
निधायोरसि संशुद्धा प्रविशेज्जातवेदसं॥
See *ante*, p. 92-93.

And the subject is here concluded by a reference to the famous passage from the Rig Veda, which is in fact a *sahamarana mantra*.

LECTURE II.

इमा नारी रविधवा, &c.

His conclusion.

On these authorities Raghunandana comes to the conclusion, "that the wives of Brahmins and of others desirous of enjoying the rewards of their own acts, and of their husband's acts, are entitled to *sahamarana* and *anumarana*, except women who are pregnant and those who have infant children."

The two readings of the text of the Rig Veda.

The famous passage in the Rig Veda on which the whole discussion turns is quoted by Raghunandana as follows :—

ओम् इमा नारी रविधवाः सपत्नीरञ्जनेन सर्पिषा संविशन्तु ।
अनश्वरोऽनमीवा सुरत्ना आरोहन्तु जल योनिमग्ने ॥

This text was accepted by Mr. Colebrooke[1] as correct.

Professor Wilson's reading of this text is as follows :—

इमा नारी रविधवाः सुपत्नीरांजनेन सर्पिषा संविशन्तु ।
अनश्रवोऽनमीवाः सुरत्ना आरोहन्तु जनयो योनिमग्ने ॥

On the material part the difference between the two readings is, as has been pointed out by Professor Wilson. If Raghunandana's reading is incorrect, an assertion regarding which there are doubts, it is difficult to say where he could have got this false reading,

[1] Asiatic Researches, Vol. IV.

LECTURE II. and how it is that Professor Wilson succeeded in obtaining the correct reading of the text. Be it observed here, that Raghunandana's reading had passed unchallenged for nearly three centuries.

The passage from the Brahma Purana is also quoted by Jaggannatha,[1] where he discusses the question, whether a widow by burning herself incurs the sin of suicide; and comes to the conclusion that she does not. Besides, if, as the learned Professor says, the text of the Rig Veda, instead of being "an authority for the burning of widows, enjoins the very contrary,"—*i. e.*, contains a *prohibition* against the practice, it is clear that the custom must have been *known* or *observed* at the time before it can be *prohibited;* and he was himself very much pressed by this argument, and tried to get over it by saying that "the *prohibition which would imply the existence of the rite* is matter of inference only; the direction that the widow is to be led away from the proximity of her deceased husband, does not necessarily imply that she was to depart from his funeral pile, and there is no term in the text that indicates such a position."[2]

Raja Radhakant's interpretation of the 8th hymn.

Further, the eighth verse of the hymn quoted above, as translated by Professor Wilson, refers, as it has been well observed by Raja Radhakant Deb, to the address by the relatives "to the widow lying on the

[1] Digest, Bk. IV, Chap. III, Sec. I, v. cxxvi.

[2] The italics are given by me.

funeral pile of her husband." The Raja observes: "The Sutrakaras upon the Vaidic authorities direct that the widow, as well as the sacrificial utensils of the deceased Brahmin, should be placed upon his funeral pile; but as the widow has a will of her own, she cannot be disposed of like the inert utensils. The Rig Veda, therefore, gives her the option of sacrificing herself or not according as she may or may not have her courage screwed up to the sticking place. When the *sati* lies on the funeral pile, it is presumed she is inclined to immolate herself; and the eighth verse is addressed to her, as the author of the *sahamarana bidhi* explains, only to test her resolution, and to induce her to retire if she be not sufficiently firm in her purpose. The necessity of giving her this option, and trying her fortitude beforehand, appears the more strong when we find it declared that the *sati* who becomes *chitabhrasta*, who retires from the funeral pile after the conclusion of the rites, commits a highly sinful act."[1]

The Raja further observes:—"Our own personal observation of the actual practice, when it prevailed in British India, confirms this view; from the moment a *sati* expressed a desire to follow her lord, up to the time she ascended the funeral pile, every persuasive language was used to induce her to continue in the family and to discharge her proper duties

[1] Journal of the Royal Asiatic Society, Vol. XVII, p. 209.

LECTURE II. there, and it was not until she was found inflexible that she was allowed to sacrifice herself; this was perfectly in keeping with the Udirshwa, &c., Mantra."[1]

It is clear, therefore, that the rite was certainly *known* in the Vedic times, and that it is distinctly referred to in the hymn quoted above. Professor Wilson, therefore, it seems, is not strictly accurate when he maintained that the origin of the practice is later than the Sanhita or primary Vedic period.

Rajah Radhakant's opinion that the rite is enjoined in the Vedas.

The essay contributed by Professor Wilson to the Journal of the Royal Asiatic Society, and which was printed in the sixteenth volume, evoked a rejoinder from a Hindu scholar of great learning, who occupied "a foremost place among Sanscrit scholars,"—Raja Radhakant Deb of Calcutta. It was a letter addressed to Professor Wilson, and was, with the writer's permission, printed in the seventeenth volume of the Journal of the Royal Asiatic Society, and from which passages have already been quoted. The Raja observed, that there was the most explicit authority for the burning of a widow with her deceased husband: and the text is to be found in the "two verses of the Aukhya Sakha of the Taittiriya Sanhita quoted in the eighty-fourth Anuvaka of the Narayaniya Upanishad,"—*i. e.*, the verses will be found in the Taittiriya Sanhita of the Black Yajush quoted in the Narayaniya Upanishad.

[1] Journal of the Royal Asiatic Society, Vol. XVII, pp. 209-20.

The two verses as translated by the Raja, read thus :—

LECTURE II.

Text of Black Yajush quoted as authority.

(1.) "Oh Agni, of all *vratas* thou art the Vratapati, I will observe the vow (*vrata*) of following the husband. Do thou enable me to accomplish it!

(2.) "Here (in this rite) to thee, Oh Agni, I offer salutation, to join the heavenly mansion. I enter into thee; (wherefore) Oh Jatavedah,[1] this day satisfied with the clarified butter (offered by me) inspire me with courage (for *sahagamana*) and take me to my lord."

The Raja then quoted texts from the Sutras of Bharadwaja and Aswalayana, and came to the conclusion, that the rules and directions contained in the Smritis and the Puranas for the burning of the *sati* are derived from "these Vaidic and Sautric injunctions," thus establishing that the burning of the widow was explicitly authorised by the Vedas.

The Raja, however, admitted that the seventh verse of the súkta from the Rig Veda, as translated by Professor Wilson, may be correct, and that his (Wilson's) reading may be genuine; but he pointed out, on the authority of the Sutras of Bharadwaja and Aswalayana, "that the verse in question had nothing to do with the concremation of a *sati*; it is directed to be chaunted on the tenth day after the burning of the dead, when the relatives of the deceased assemble on the *smasána* to perform certain ceremonies, on the conclusion of which, the *adhwaryu*

[1] Source of the Vedas.

LECTURE II. takes butter with a new blade of *kusa* grass or clarified butter between the thumb and ring-finger, and applying it as *collyrium* to the eyes of *Sadhavas*, recites the seventh hymn in question the moment they are directed to depart towards the east."

Its authenticity doubted by Wilson. Referring to the two verses of the Black Yajush, quoted by the Raja, the learned Professor seemed to doubt the correctness of the quotation. He was obliged, however, to admit that he had not examined the Taittiriya Sanhita of the Black Yajush himself; and, therefore, could not positively deny whether the verses actually occur there or not.

In justice to the Professor it must be observed that the Raja has quoted from the Upanishad, which again is a quotation from the Taittiriya Sanhita itself. But, in the absence of any evidence to the contrary, we have no reason to suppose that the author of the Upanishad wrongly quoted from the Sanhita itself.

This subject of the *sati* rite has now no longer any practical or political interest; it has become matter of history. To the historian and the Indian antiquary, therefore, it still affords matter of considerable interest.

Brahmacharya next alternative for a widow. If the widow did not burn herself with her deceased husband, but chose to survive him, then a very strict discipline[1] was prescribed to her as

[1] There is a difference of opinion as to whether *Brahmacharya* was the *first* or the *second* alternative prescribed for a widow. Some authorities

regards her mode of life. She must observe *Brahmacharya*,—*i.e.*, the duties observed by a *Brahmachari*, or a Vedic student. She must practise austerities.[1] She must not take betel leaf, nor rub herself with oil, nor eat or drink from vessels of zinc.[2] She must take one meal daily, and on no account shall she take a second repast; she must not sleep on a bed, nor use perfumed substances. In the months of Baisack, Kartic, and Magh, she must observe special fasts, perform ablutions, make gifts, travel to places of pilgrimage, and repeatedly utter the name of Vishnu. She must daily make offerings for her husband with *kusa* grass, *tila*, and water.[3]

LECTURE II.

Brahmacharya described.

She is required to leave the favorite abode of her husband, to keep her tongue, hands, feet, and other organs in subjection; strict in her conduct, all day mourning for her husband, with harsh duties, devotion, and fasts, she must live to the end of her life; and the reward for such austerities is declared to be the acquisition by the widow of the mansion of her husband in the next world, and the cancelment of all her sins.[4] Although the woman may have no son, a condition generally considered unfortunate for

maintain that *Brahmacharya* is the *first* alternative for a widow. If she thought herself *incapable* of observing *Brahmacharya* with strictness, she was allowed, as the *second* or the inferior alternative, to burn herself with her husband. See Vishnu quoted by Raghunandana in his Suddhitattwa, p. 426, Calcutta Edition. See also Parasara, Chap. IV, vv. 28 and 29.

[1] Vishnu quoted in Digest, Bk. IV, Chap. III, Sec. II, v. cxxxiii.

[2] Prachetas in *ibid*, v. cxxxiv.

[3] Smriti in *ibid*, v. cxxxv.

[4] Harita quoted in *ibid*, v. cxxxvii.

LECTURE II. religious purposes, still she will attain heaven, if she is strict in austerities and rigid devotion, firm in avoiding sensuality, and always patient and liberal ;[1] and the necessity for raising up issue by appointed kinsmen is reprobated.

The injunctions of Menu regarding the life to be led by widows are generally followed as the leading authority on the subject : "Let her emaciate her body by living voluntarily on pure flowers, roots, and fruits ; but let her not, when her lord is deceased, even pronounce the name of another man."[2] "Let her continue till death, forgiving all injuries, performing harsh duties, avoiding every sensual pleasure, and cheerfully practising the incomparable rules of virtue which have been followed by such women as were devoted to one only husband."[3] "And like those abstemious men, a virtuous wife ascends to heaven, though she have no child, if, after the decease of her lord, she devote herself to pious austerity."[4]

The practice of Niyoga, or appointment to raise issue,

The practice of raising up issue by appointment or the marriage of the widow is strongly reprobated by Menu. On this subject the ancient legislator thus delivers himself: "A widow who from a wish to bear children slights her deceased husband by marrying again, brings disgrace on herself here below, and shall be excluded from the seat of her lord."[5]

---

[1] Vrihaspati quoted in Digest, Bk. IV, Chap. III, Sec. II, v. cxxxviii.
[2] Menu, Chap. V, v. 157.
[3] Menu, Chap. V. v. 158.
[4] Menu, Chap. V, v. 160.
[5] Menu, Chap. V, v. 161.

Again: "Issue begotten on a woman by any other than her husband, is here declared to be no progeny of hers; no more than a child begotten on the wife of another man belongs to the begetter; nor is a second husband allowed in any part of this code to a virtuous woman."[1]

reprobated by Menu.

On the same subject Yama thus delivers himself:— "Let her continue, as long as she lives, performing austere duties, avoiding every sensual pleasure, and cheerfully practising those rules of virtue which have been followed by such women as were devoted to one only husband." "Neither in the Veda, nor in the sacred code, is religious seclusion allowed to a woman; her own duties practised with a husband of equal class, are indeed her religious rites: this is a settled rule." "Eighty-eight thousand holy sages of the sacerdotal class, superior to sensual pleasures, and having left no issue in their families, have ascended nevertheless to heaven." "Like them a betrothed damsel becomes a widow, and devoting herself to pious austerity, shall attain heaven, though she have no sons: thus Menu, sprung from the self-existent, has declared."[2]

Yama on the same subject.

There is a considerable conflict of opinion among the ancient Smritis as to the validity of the practice of appointment to raise up issue to a deceased person. On this subject Narada ordains, that "a wife duly

Conflict of opinion among the Rishis on this subject.

[1] Menu, Chap. V, v. 162. [2] Digest, Bk. IV, Chap. III, Sec. II, v. cxliv.

LECTURE II.

Practice authorized by Narada.

authorised by her spiritual parents through a wish that male issue should be obtained, may go to her husband's brother; and he may approach her until a son be produced" "But when a son is begotten, he must restrain, otherwise duty is violated." The husband's brother here mentioned may be either an elder or a younger brother, and the object of this is declared to be for the sake of offspring that the family may be perpetuated, and not through amorous desire. The authority for the purpose must be obtained beforehand to render the appointment valid; and the spiritual parents of the woman are declared to be the persons who shall give the authority. If none of the spiritual parents be living, and other members of the family competent to give the authority be also dead, the requisite authority may be obtained from the king; such was the extreme anxiety of the ancient legislators for perpetuating the family. After the woman has conceived, the injunctions of law are obeyed, and the man is forbidden to visit the woman any longer, and is directed to treat her as his daughter-in-law. If the visit is repeated after this, the man and woman shall both be fined by the king for this transgression.[1]

By Yama.

Yama also enjoins or permits the practice, and declares that the appointment may be kept by any kinsman who is so authorised; and that the hus-

[1] Narada quoted in Digest, Bk. IV, Chap. IV, Sec. I, v. cxlvii. There it is quoted from *Smriti*. See Jolly's Narada, pp. 90-91, paras. 80—88.

band's brother is not the only person who is declared competent to keep the appointment. The birth of a son thus begotten is considered an auspicious event. "The king should cause the auspicious ceremony for a happy delivery and all other solemn rites to be performed by those who desire offspring for their brother and obsequies for their ancestors."[1]

LECTURE II.

Yajnawalkya not only sanctions the practice, but explicitly names the relatives who can be authorised for the purpose, and the circle of relatives named by him is wide enough to embrace all kinds of persons, to prevent, probably, a possible failure in keeping the appointment. He declares that "a brother of her husband, a kinsman who offers funeral cakes to the same ancestor, or one who is descended from the same original stock, being authorised by spiritual parents, through a wish that a son may be produced, may approach a woman, who has no son, at the proper season." The son so begotten in this mode is called a *kshetraja* son; and the man who departs from the strict letter of the injunction is threatened with the penalty of degradation from his class.[2]

By Yajnawalkya.

Other Rishis have, in the same manner, and almost in the same words, enjoined this practice. Whether the practice originated in these injunctions, or that the practice pre-existed and was merely sanctioned or authorised by these texts, it is very difficult now to

[1] Yama, quoted in Digest, Bk. IV, Chap. IV, Sec. I, v. cxlviii.
[2] Yajnawalya, *ibid*, v. cxlix.

LECTURE II. determine. But the purpose for which the practice originated, or the texts enjoined it, is not difficult to make out. It is the anxiety to prevent the unfortunate condition of *childlessness* so much deprecated in the Smritis ; and it is a branch of the same law by which eleven descriptions of sons were authorised as substitutes for the natural begotten (*aurasa*) son. This *kshetraja* son is included in the twelve descriptions of sons enumerated by Menu and Yajnawalkya, being the second in the list of Menu and the third in that of Yajnawalkya.

It should be observed here that a modification of the practice also obtained in the case of the husband himself authorising his wife, during his lifetime, to have issue begotten on her by another person. The five heroes of the Mahabharata, the five Pandabs, were children thus begotten on the wives of Pandu by Dharma, Vayu, Indra, and others by his permission.

Condemned by Menu.

On the other hand, we find Menu condemning this practice of appointment in very strong language. The sage declares that, "on failure of issue by the husband, the desired offspring may be procreated, either by his brother or some other sapinda, on the wife who has been duly authorised."[1] This passage, it is now accepted on the authority of his great commentator Kulluka Bhatta, applies to the Sudras only; and the appointment can only be kept by a widow belonging to that class whose husband was also

[1] Menu, Chap. IX, v. 59.

a Sudra. For we find in another place Menu, speaking of this custom, thus delivers himself:— LECTURE II.

"By men of twice-born classes no widow or childless wife must be authorised to conceive by any other than her lord; for they who authorise her to conceive by any other violate the primeval law.[1]

"Such a commission to a brother or other near kinsman is nowhere mentioned in the nuptial texts of the Veda, nor is the marriage of a widow even named in the laws concerning marriages.[2]

"This practice, fit only for cattle, is reprehended by learned Brahmins; yet it is declared to have been the practice even of men while Vena had sovereign power.[3]

"He possessing the whole earth, and thence only called the chief of sage monarchs, gave rise to a confusion of classes when his intellect became weak through lust.[4]

"Since his time the virtuous disapprove of that man who, through delusion of mind, directs a widow to receive the caresses of another for the sake of progeny."[5]

This is clear unmistakable language in which the practice is strongly condemned, and it is difficult to reconcile these texts with the ordinances of the other sages quoted before by which the practice is enjoined

[1] Menu, Chap. IX, v. 64.
[2] *Ibid*, 65.
[3] Menu, Chap. IX, v. 66.
[4] *Ibid*, 67.
[5] Menu, Chap. IX, v. 68.

Attempts to reconcile these conflicting texts.

and approved. Different explanations are proposed; some declare that the practice was either unknown or reprehended by learned men conversant in the Vedas before the reign of Vena; and that the practice was introduced during the reign of that monarch by his independent authority slighting revealed law; since his time some few persons follow that practice through delusion of mind, but it is reprehended by the learned. Other commentators again declare that the practice was authorized and approved before the reign of Vena; but that monarch having exhibited a bad practice founded thereon, such a commission even to a brother or near kinsman has been prohibited since his time.[1]

Reconciliation by Vrihaspati.

The sage Vrihaspati has attempted to reconcile these conflicting texts by a reference to the four ages in some of which the practice was allowed, while in the fourth or Kali age it is forbidden. He ordains that "appointments of kinsmen to beget children on widows or married women when the husbands are deceased, or impotent, are mentioned by Menu, but forbidden by himself with a view to the order of the four ages; no such act can be legally done in this age by any other than the husband." The reason assigned for this difference is declared to be, that, in the first three ages, men were endued with true piety and sound knowledge, whereas in the fourth age their intellectual and moral powers have greatly diminish-

[1] Digest, Bk. IV, Chap. IV, Sec. II, commentary on v. clvi.

ed;[1] consequently, what would not, in the first three ages, have led to any abuse, would, it was apprehended, have led to mischievous consequences among a people morally and intellectually inferior, hence it was prohibited for the fourth age by a sort of preordinance.

Accepted as authority for the prohibition in the present age.

This reconciliation is accepted by the Pundits, and is acted upon in the present age as an authority for the prohibition. I am informed, however, that the custom obtains, even to this day, with very little modification, in Orissa. How the native scholars of that country attempt to interpret this text of Vrihaspati I am not informed. How far the limitation proposed by Vrihaspati is warranted by the texts themselves it is difficult to say.

Text of Menu condemning the practice considered an interpolation.

Some European scholars,[2] however, think that the text of Menu which condemns the practice, is a much later interpolation in the ancient Sanhita; they seem to think that the interpolation occurred at a time when the abuses incident to the practice had become so great that it became necessary in the interests of morality to stop it by the authority of Menu, in whose Sanhita the passage was accordingly interpolated. The only argument in support of this hypothesis is, that it explains the supposed conflict between Menu on the one hand, and Yajnawalkya, Yama, Narada, and others on the other hand: for

[1] Digest, Bk. IV, Chap. IV, Sec. II, v. clvii.

[2] Dr. Jolly, Pref. to the Institutes of Nareda, xiii.

LECTURE II.

No authority for this opinion.

on this supposition there is no conflict. On the other hand, it must be admitted that an interpolation of such an important passage in a Smriti, which is so well known and so carefully studied as that of Menu, is almost impossible, as it is almost certain to be detected; and the evidence is, that, in India, the passage was never questioned from the earliest times. The consensus of opinion of native scholars from the earliest times is, that the passage is a genuine text of Menu, no one having ever questioned it. The chances of successful interpolation in a work of such widespread reputation are very slender. It would be possible in the case of some obscure local treatise, the existence of which was known only to a few, and the study of which was confined to a still fewer persons.

Such is the condition of Hindu widows as described in their ancient writings. I may observe that, with very little modifications, the injunctions of the *Shasters* have continued to be respected even to the present times; and that widows belonging to the higher castes of the Hindus are still governed in their habits and modes of life by ordinances which were promulgated more than three or four thousand years ago; a picture of conservative ideas unique in the history of the world.

How far the Hindu widow is obliged in these days to observe the strict mode of life enjoined upon her, was the subject of discussion before the Bengal High

LECTURE II.

Ascetic life of a widow, matter of religious observance, not of legal obligation.

Court.[1] The suit was one for maintenance brought by the stepmother against her stepson; and the defendant pleaded, in diminution of the plaintiff's claim, that by the *Shasters* she is bound to lead a very strict and austere life, and, consequently, the amount claimed was excessive. On this the Court observed as follows:—"As to the life of semi-starvation and wretchedness, in which it is argued that, according to the *Shasters*, a Hindu widow ought to live, that is a matter of religious or ceremonial observance rather than of law. A Hindu widow is in these days at all events entitled to decent food and clothing if the head of the family is in a position to supply them."

No doubt, our Courts will not take cognizance of suits brought by persons, relatives or otherwise, to compel Hindu widows to observe the strict discipline enjoined in the *Shasters*. It will be considered more a matter of positive morality, rather than of positive law, and the interference of the Court will be considered extremely unwarranted. But it is doubtful whether, during the Hindu period, a Hindu king would not have compelled a Hindu widow to conform to the strict discipline or would not have punished her for any gross dereliction of duty on her part.

These are some of the obligations which a Hindu widow is bound to observe according to the *Shasters*. This subject of widow's obligations will be resumed hereafter in another part of these lectures.

---

[1] Hurry Mohun Roy *v.* S. M. Nayantara, 25 W. R., 474.

LECTURE III.

THE WIDOW'S RIGHT OF SUCCESSION.

Five female heirs—The sister, an heir according to the Maharashtra school; but not according to the other schools—Widow's estate a typical one—The widow succeeds after the great grandson—Women incompetent to hold property—The text of Yajnawalkya establishing the widow as an heir—Vrihaspati on the same—Vishnu on the same—Vrihat Menu—Katyayana—Authorities adverse to the widow's rights—Narada—Menu—Sancha—Devala—The widow's right depend upon the appointment to raise up issue—Refuted by Vijnaneswara—Another argument adverse to the widow, refuted by Vijnaneswara—His conclusion—The development of the widow's rights by Jimutavahana—The age of Jimutavahana—The conclusion of Vijnaneswara combated by Jimutavahana—First argument—Second argument—His conclusion—Earlier cases establishing the widow's right of succession—According to the Bengal school—According to the Benares school—The *chaste* widow alone succeeds—All the authorities agree in this proposition, *viz.*, The Mitacshara—The Dayabhaga—The Dayatattwa—The Dayakrama Sangraha—The Digest—The reported cases on the subject—The widow does not represent her husband for purposes of inheritance—The husband's cause of action descends to the widow—The widows of disqualified Hindus do not inherit property from which their husbands were excluded—*Anuloma* and *pratiloma* marriages described—Intermarriage allowed in the first three ages—According to the Mitacshara the widows of different classes succeed together—According to the Dayabhaga, the widow of the highest class alone succeeds—Raghunandana maintains the same opinion.

Five female heirs.

ALMOST all the authorities current in the different schools are agreed in recognising the title of five female relatives to succeed to the property of a Hindu dying without male issue and intestate. These are:

LECTURE III.

1. The widow.
2. The daughter.
3. The mother.
4. The grandmother.
5. The great grandmother.

The sister, an heir according to the Maharashtra school;

The *Maharashtra* school, having accepted the writings of Nilkantha Bhatta as its guide, has recognised the *sister* as an heir in addition to the female relatives named above, except, perhaps, the great grandmother, whom Nilkantha does not expressly name among the heirs.[1] After the father's mother, according to Nilkantha, "comes the sister:" according to this text of Menu "to the nearest *sapinda*, male or female, after him in the third degree, the inheritance next belongs:" and another of Vrihaspati "where many claim the inheritance of a childless man, whether they be paternal or maternal relations (*sakulya*) or more distant kinsmen (*bandhava*), he who is the nearest of them shall take the estate." "And the next rank is hers, both from her being begotten under the brother's family name, and there being no further reservation with respect to the gentile relationship (*gotroja*); it does not particularly specify the same gentile kindred. Neither is she mentioned in the text as the occasion of taking the wealth (but as

---

[1] Vyavahara Mayukha, Chap. IV, Sec. viii, paras. 20 and 21.

LECTURE III. next-of-kin she succeeds)."[1] This is the whole of the argument on which Nilkantha bases his opinion by which the sister is declared to be an heir. It is curious that the passages from the two Smritis, which are quoted in support of the sister's title, are quoted by other commentators for a very different object; and by none of the commentators are the two passages considered as authority declaratory of the sister's title. Accordingly, by none of the schools is the *sister* recognised as an heir. The Courts of Justice in the Bombay Presidency, which is almost co-extensive with the local limits of the *Maharashtra* school, have followed this opinion of Nilkantha, and have conferred the inheritance on the sister in default of preferable heirs.[2] The same view was taken in a case reported in 9 Moore, p. 516.[3]

but not according to the other schools.

The Courts of Justice in the other Presidencies have, however, refused to recognise the sister's title as an heir in accordance with the doctrines of the schools which are severally current in those parts of the country. We find, so far back as 1819, in a case which arose in the Zillah Court of Burdwan, it was declared that the sister is not entitled to succeed, as she does not confer spiritual benefits on her late brother.[4] This was decided on the opinion of the Pundits who were consulted in the case.

[1] Vyavahara Mayukha, Chap. IV, Sec. viii, para. 19.

[2] Bhaskar Trimbak Acharya v. Mahadev Ramji and others, 6 Bomb. H. C. Rep., 1.

[3] Venayeck Anund Row v. Luxumee Bai and others.

[4] Unnupurna Debia v. Gungahuree Seromonee, 2 Macnaghten, p. 80.

Of the five female relatives mentioned before, the widow succeeds first. All the schools agree, as a rule, in regarding the widow's estate as a representative estate, as typical of the estates which the other female heirs have in the property of their male relatives. It will be shown hereafter that the incidents which belong to the widow's estate also attach to the estate of the other female heirs.

LECTURE III.

Widow's estate a typical one.

All the *Smritis* are unanimous in declaring the *son* as the first heir of a Hindu; in his default the grandson, and in default of the grandson, comes the great grandson; so far there is no difference. In default of the great grandson, who shall succeed was a very difficult question. It is now settled law that the *widow* succeeds after the great grandson; and that, on the authority of the great commentators who have expounded the original Smritis so as to bear that interpretation. It is, however, a very difficult question, which it is impossible *now* to answer with certainty, whether the *ancient Smritis* did actually recognise the widow as an heir after the great grandson. That they were not unanimous is certain, and that the widow's title was doubtful is clear from the laborious attempt of the commentators to establish it.

The widow succeeds after the great grandson.

In the ancient Smritis, for purposes of holding property, women generally were treated with dislike or disregard; and there is a general reluctance displayed by the ancient Rishis to allow females to hold property. The origin or cause of this dislike, it is

Women incompetent to hold property.

LECTURE III. difficult now to ascertain. Probably, it has its origin on the following considerations. According to the Smritis, property was intended for the performance of religious ceremonies; the primary obligation of a person holding property was to perform religious rites and ceremonies, and he was considered a sort of trustee for the performance of those rites and ceremonies. Now, as a rule, females are declared by the Smritis to be incompetent to perform religious ceremonies. "Women have no business with the texts of the *Veda;* thus is the law fully settled: having therefore no evidence of law, and no knowledge of expiatory texts, sinful women must be as foul as falsehood itself: and this is a fixed rule." [1]

"To this effect, many texts which show their true disposition are chanted in the Vedas." [2]

On the same subject there is a passage in the Mitacshara,[3] which, though it may not be the opinion of Vijnaneswara himself, certainly embodies the substance of the prevailing opinion against the rights of females. The passage runs thus:—"Moreover, since the wealth of regenerate man is designed for religious uses, the succession of women to such property is unfit: because they are not competent to the performance of religious rites. Accordingly it has been declared by some author, 'wealth was produced for the sake of solemn sacrifices, and they who are

[1] Menu, Chap. IX, v. 18. [2] *Ibid*, 19.
[3] Chap. II, Sec. i, para. 14.

incompetent to the celebration of those rites do not participate in the property, but are all entitled to food and raiment.' Riches were ordained for sacrifices. Therefore they should be allotted to persons who are concerned with religious duties; and not be assigned to women, to fools, and to people neglectful of holy obligations;" and texts may be quoted from other Smritis which take the same adverse view of the rights of females.

The author of the Mitacshara was probably the first commentator who entered the field in defence of the rights of the widow. The subject is discussed in Sec. i, Chap. II of his commentaries. The whole section purports to be an elaborate commentary on the following well-known text of Yajnawalkya: "The wife and the daughters also, both parents, brothers likewise, and their sons, gentiles, cognates, a pupil, and a fellow student." "On failure of the first among these, the next in order is indeed heir to the estate of one who departed for heaven leaving no male issue. This rule extends to all persons and classes."

The text of Yajnawalkya establishing the widow as an heir.

The author of the Mitacshara quotes this text as the chief authority in support of the widow's right of inheritance; that being the text of the author whose commentary he was writing.

The other Smritis that support the widow's title are the following:—Vrihaspati says: "In scripture and in the code of law, as well as in popular practice, a

Vrihaspati on the same.

LECTURE III.

wife is declared by the wise to be half the body of her husband, equally sharing the fruit of pure and impure acts. Of him whose wife is not deceased, half the body survives. How then should another take his property while half his person is alive? Let the wife of a deceased man who left no male issue take his share, notwithstanding kinsmen, a father, a mother, or uterine brother be present. Dying before her husband, a virtuous wife partakes of his consecrated fire; or if her husband die before her, she shares his wealth; this is a primeval law. Having taken his moveables, and immoveable property, the precious and the base metals, the grains, the liquids, and the clothes, let her duly offer his monthly, half-yearly, and other funeral repasts. With presents offered to his manes and by pious liberality, let her honor the paternal uncle of her husband, his spiritual parents and daughter's son, the children of his sisters, his maternal uncles, and also ancient and unprotected persons and guests and females of the family. Those near or distant kinsmen who become her adversaries, or who injure the woman's property, let the king chastise by inflicting on them the punishment of robbery."[1]

Vishnu on the same.

Vishnu ordains that "the wealth of him who leaves no male issue goes to his wife; on failure of her it devolves on daughters: if there be none, it belongs to the father: if he be dead, it appertains to

[1] Dayabhaga, Chap. XI, Sec. i, para. 2; Mitacshara, Chap. II, Sec. i, para. 6.

the mother; on failure of her it goes to the brothers; after them it descends to the brothers' sons; if none exist, it passes to the kinsmen (*bandhu*); in their default it devolves on relations (*sakulya*); failing them it belongs to the pupil: on failure of these, it comes to the fellow student, and for want of all those heirs it escheats to the king, excepting the wealth of a Brahmana."[1]

LECTURE III.

Vrihat Menu.

Vrihat Menu declares that "the widow of a childless man, keeping unsullied her husband's bed, and persevering in religious observances, shall present his funeral oblation and obtain his entire share."[2]

Katyayana.

Katyayana declares,—"Let the widow succeed to her husband's wealth provided she be chaste, and in default of her the daughter inherits, if unmarried;" and in another place, "the widow being a woman of honest family, or the daughters, or on failure of them the father or the mother or the brother or his sons are pronounced to be the heirs of one who leaves no male issue."[3]

Authorities adverse to the widow's rights.

The authorities that are adverse to the widow's claim are the following:—Thus Narada says: "Among brothers, if any one die without issue, or enter a religious order, let the rest of his brethren divide his wealth, except the wife's separate property. Let them

Narada.

---

[1] This is quoted in the Mitacshara, Chap. II, Sec. i, para. 6, as a passage from Vrihad Vishnu: but in the Dayabhaga, Chap. XI, Sec. i, para. 5, it is quoted as that of Vishnu simply.

[2] Mitacshara, Chap. II, Sec. i. para. 6; Dayabhaga, Chap. XI, Sec. i, para. 7.

[3] Mitacshara, Chap. II, Sec. i, para. 6.

LECTURE III.

allow a maintenance to his women for life, provided these preserve unsullied the bed of their lord. But if they behave otherwise, the brethren may resume that allowance."[1] Menu ordains: "Of him who leaves no son, the father shall take the inheritance, or the brothers;" and again,—"of a son dying childless, the mother shall take the estate; and the mother also being dead, the father's mother shall take the heritage."[2] Also Sancha: "The wealth of a man who departs for heaven leaving no male issue, goes to his brothers. If there be none, his father and mother take it, or his eldest wife."[3] And Devala: "Next let brothers of the whole blood divide the heritage of him who leaves no male issue or daughters equal (*i. e.*) as appertaining to the same tribe, or let the father if he survive, or half-brothers belonging to the same tribe or the mother or the wife inherit in their order. On failure of all these the nearest of the kinsmen succeed."[4]

Menu.

Sancha.

Devala.

When Vijnaneswara wrote his commentary, the ancient doctrine excluding the widow seems to have received considerable relaxation, and a controversy seems to have been going on in favor of the widow's claims. It was, however, maintained that the wife shall take the estate only when she was the widow

The widow's right de-

[1] Mitacshara, Chap. II, Sec. i, para. 7.

[2] *Ibid.*

[3] Quoted in the Mitacshara, Chap. II, Sec. i, para. 7, as a text of Sancha; but in the Dayabhaga, Chap. XI, Sec. i, para. 15, it is quoted as a text of Saucha. Lichita, Paithinisi, and Yama. Probably the same or similar passages occur in the three latter Smritis.

[4] Dayabhaga, Chap. XI, Sec. i, para. 17.

LECTURE III.

of a separated brother; and that *provided she be solicitous of authority for raising up issue to her husband.* The author of the Mitacshara employed himself, it seems, successfully in controverting the proviso by which the widow's rights were made contingent upon the appointment to raise up issue to her deceased husband.

pend upon the appointment to raise up issue.

This ancient custom of *Niyoga*, or authority to raise up issue to one's deceased husband, seems to have been approved of by the majority of the authors of the Smritis, though in some of them it is reprobated as an immoral custom; Menu in particular has expressed himself very strongly against this practice.[1]

Whatever may be the origin of this custom, this is certain that it was generally prevalent at one time in Hindustan. It is a very interesting question to determine whether this practice of *Niyoga* was prevalent simultaneously with the custom or law of adoption, or whether the conception of adoption is a later substitute for the earlier practice of *Niyoga*. This question I do not pretend to determine beyond a mere surmise that, chronologically, the practice of *Niyoga* preceded the law of adoption.

Refuted by Vijnaneswara.

The author of the Mitacshara combated the doctrine by which the widow's right was made contingent upon the appointment by the following process of reasoning:—"That is wrong; for authority to raise up issue to the husband is neither specified in

[1] See *ante*, p. 113.

LECTURE III.

the text (the wife and the daughter also, &c.), nor is it suggested by the premises. Besides it may be here asked—Is the appointment to raise up issue a reason for the widow's succession to the property? or is the issue borne by her the cause of her succession? If the appointment alone be the reason, it follows that she has a right to the estate without having borne a son; and the right of the son subsequently produced by means of the appointment does not ensue. But if the offspring be the sole cause of her claim, the wife should not be recited as a successor; since in that case the son alone has a right to the goods."[1] But the argument which seemed to have carried the greatest weight was derived from the fact of the practice of *Niyoga* having been considered a disreputable one in popular opinion at the time when the Mitacshara was written;[2] and the author fortifies himself by that argument as well as by the prohibition against the practice contained in some of the Smritis.

Another argument adverse to the widow,

Another argument put forward against the widow's claim was derived from the fact that all wealth is intended for religious uses, and females being incompetent to perform religious rites are, therefore, declared incapable of inheriting property. The author of the Mitacshara meets this argument by quoting the following texts, which declare that wealth was not intended for religious uses only, but was intended also

refuted by Vijnaneswara.

[1] Mitacshara, Chap. II, Sec. i, para. 15.

[2] *Ibid*, 18.

LECTURE III.

for lay or human purposes. "Neglect not religious duty, wealth, or pleasure in their proper season."[1] "To the utmost of his power a man should not let morning, noon, or evening be fruitless in respect of virtue, wealth, and pleasure."[2] "The organs cannot so effectually be restrained by avoiding their gratification as by constant knowledge of the ills incident to sensual pleasure."[3] Further there is a passage in the Vedas which ordains that gold should be carefully preserved, not for religious ends, but for human purposes.[4] The author further states that incapacity of females extends to the performance of religious rites strictly considered: but their capacity to perform acts intended for pious or charitable purposes is nowhere denied, and their succession to property for these purposes becomes most proper.[5]

His conclusion.

Vijnaneswara thus disposes of the arguments against the widow's rights which were current in his time: and the conclusion at which he arrives on the subject is thus declared by himself: "Therefore it is a settled rule, that a wedded wife being chaste takes the whole estate of a man who, being separated from his co-heirs, and not subsequently reunited with them, dies leaving no male issue."[6]

This doctrine of the Mitacshara may be considered

---

[1] Yajnawalkya, quoted in the Mitacshara, Chap. II, Sec. i, para. 22.
[2] Gautama, Mitacshara, Chap. II, Sec. i, para. 22.
[3] Menu, Mitacshara, Chap. II, Sec. i, para. 22.
[4] Mitacshara, Chap. II, Sec. i, para. 23.
[5] *Ibid*, 24. [6] *Ibid*, 39.

LECTURE III.

as marking the second epoch in the history of the widow's right of succession. The first epoch may be placed at the earlier period when the widow was declared ineligible for the succession and was simply allowed a maintenance during the period of her natural life; the kinsmen of the husband taking his estate in the order of proximity. The author of the Mitacshara lived at a time when the current of public opinion in favor of the widow's rights had set in: but he also found there was still a considerable amount of authority highly respected arrayed against the widow. In this state of things he took a mediate course: he established the widow's claim, but made the innovation as little felt as possible; he declared the heirship of the widow of a separated parcener; and as in those ancient times joint holding was the rule, and several holding was exceptional, by his doctrine he did the least violence to established authorities.

The development of the widow's rights by Jimutavahana.

The law remained in this condition till the time of Jimutavahana, whose writings may be considered to have given the ultimate development to the widow's rights; a state of law which continues unmodified to the present times in Bengal, where the doctrines of Jimutavahana were accepted as law. That Jimutavahana followed Vijnaneswara in point of time is clear from the Dayabhaga itself. In this work the author combats certain doctrines; but has nowhere named the author whose opinions he has been so earnestly controverting. A perusal of the Mitacshara, however, will convince every reader that the essential doctrines controverted in the Dayabhaga are those contained in the Mitacshara. LECTURE III.

The period that elapsed between the respective ages of the two authors is a much more difficult question, for we have almost absolutely no materials for its determination. If the lapse of time be measured by the progress of doctrines, it may be inferred that the period was not considerable. Now the widow's title does not seem to have been so well established even in Jimutavahana's time, so as to obviate the necessity of trying to establish the same by arguments and authorities, for we find Jimutavahana devoting a *very long* chapter of his work to the establishment of this doctrine, and concluding thus: "Since by these and other passages it is declared that the wife rescues her husband from hell, and since a woman doing improper acts through indigence causes her husband to fall to a region of horror—for they share the fruits of virtue and of vice—therefore the wealth devolving on her is for the benefit of the former owner, and the wife's succession is consequently proper."[1] Of course, Jimutavahana here considers the question with reference to the great doctrine of spiritual benefits which he had the unrivalled merit of establishing as the sole basis of succession in Hindu law. It may, therefore, be The age of Jimutavahana.

[1] Dayabhaga, Chap. XI, Sec. i, para. 44.

LECTURE III.

surmised that the time that elapsed from the date of the Mitacshara to the date of the Dayabhaga may be roughly put at between two to three hundred years.

The conclusion of Vijnaneswara combated by Jimutavahana.

The logical consequence of this position was, that inasmuch as the widow conferred spiritual benefits under all circumstances, her heritable right could not be restricted by the contingencies of separation or reunion. Jimutavahana accordingly employs himself in controverting the conclusion which the author of the Mitacshara had arrived at, *viz.*, that the widow of a separated parcener alone was entitled to succeed to his estate. He thus notices the conclusion arrived at in the Mitacshara: "Some reconcile the contradiction by saying that the preferable right of the brother supposes him either to be not separated or to be reunited, and the widow's right of succession is relative to the estate of one who was separated from his co-heirs, and not reunited with them."[1]

First argument.

He then impeaches this conclusion, first by quoting a text of Vrihaspati, which runs thus: "Among brothers, who become reunited through mutual affection after being separated, there is no right of seniority if partition be again made. Should any one of them die, or in any manner depart by entering into a religious order, his portion is not lost, but devolves on his uterine brother. His sister also is entitled to take a share of it. This law concerns

[1] Dayabhaga, Chap. XI, Sec. i, para. 19.

one who leaves no issue, nor wife, nor parent. If any one of the reunited brethren acquire wealth by science, valour, or the like, with the use of the joint stock, two shares of it must be given to him, and the rest shall have each a share."[1] From this passage Jimutavahana says, that as "this law concerns one who leaves no issue, nor wife, nor parent," it is declaratory of the right of a reunited uterine brother as taking effect on failure of the son, daughter, widow, and parents, and he very pertinently puts this question: "How then does the reunited brother bar the widow's title to the succession?"[2]

Second argument.

In the second place, Jimutavahana says, that the interpretation put upon the texts of Sancha and others (which have been quoted before) as referring to a reunited brother, must be drawn either from the authority of express texts of law or from reasoning. "Now it is not deducible from a text of law, for there is none which bears that meaning expressly, and the passages concerning the succession of the reunited parcener containing special provisions regarding brother's succession, cannot intend generally the right of a brother to inherit to the exclusion of a widow."[3]

The substance of the argument that the position of the Mitacshara is deducible from reasoning is

---

[1] Dayabhaga, Chap. XI, Sec. i, para. 20.

[2] *Ibid*, 21.

[3] *Ibid*, 23.

LECTURE III. stated as follows:—"Thus in the instance of reunion, or in that of a subsisting coparcenary, the same goods which appertain to one brother belong to another likewise. In such case, when the right of one ceases by his demise, those goods belong exclusively to the survivor, since his ownership is not divested. They do not belong to the widow, for her right ceases on demise of her husband in like manner as his property devolves not on her, if sons or other male descendants be left."[1]

The answer to this cannot be put better than in the words of Jimutavahana himself. He says: "That argument is futile. It is not true that, in the instance of reunion and of a subsisting coparcenary, what belongs to one appertains also to the other parcener. But the property is referred severally to unascertained portions of the aggregate. Both parceners have not a proprietary right to the whole, for there is no proof to establish their ownership of the whole, as has been before shown when defining the term partition of heritage. Nor is there any proof of the position that the wife's right in her husband's property accruing to her from her marriage ceases on his demise. But the cessation of the widow's right of property, if there be male issue, appears only from the law ordaining the succession of male issue."[2] He further goes on: "If it be said that the cessation of her right, in

[1] Dayabhaga, Chap. XI, Sec. i, para. 25.
[2] *Ibid*, 26.

this instance also, does appear from the law which ordains the succession of the reunited parcener, the answer is, no; for it is not true that the text relates to reunited parceners, since the law which declares the brother's right of succession may relate to reunited brethren, if it be true that the widow's right of ownership ceases by the demise of her husband, who was reunited with his co-heirs; and the widow's proprietary right does so cease provided the law relate to the case of reunited brethren. Thus the propositions reciprocate."[1]

LECTURE III.

Jimutavahana then employs himself in reconciling the contradictory texts that have been quoted before, and concludes thus: "The assumption of any reference to the condition of the brethren as unseparated or as reunited, not specified in the text, is inadmissible as being burdensome and unnecessary. Therefore the doctrine of Jitendriya, who affirms the right of the wife to inherit the whole property of her husband leaving no male issue, without attention to the circumstance of his being separated from his co-heirs or united with them (for no such distinction is specified) should be respected."[2] And "therefore the interpretation of the law is right as set forth by us."[3]

His conclusion.

This is the ultimate conclusion to which the author

[1] Dayabhaga, Chap. XI, Sec. i, para. 27.

[2] *Ibid*, 46.

[3] *Ibid*, 55.

LECTURE III. of the Dayabhaga has arrived, *viz.*, that a widow succeeds to the estate of her husband under all circumstances—a great innovation upon the law as is laid down in the Mitacshara. This may be considered as the highest development of the widow's rights. This doctrine obtains in Bengal alone, the other schools still adhering to the doctrine of the Mitacshara.

Earlier cases establishing the widow's right of succession. According to the Bengal School.

Soon after the establishment of Courts of Justice in this country by the English Government, questions relating to the widow's rights came on for discussion before the Courts. The earliest reported case on the subject is that of *Radhamonee Dosee* v. *Doorga Dosee*,[1] decided in 1794 by the late Supreme Court. The facts of the case were these. One Lalbehari Dhur died, leaving his son and his widow, who was the defendant in the case. The son died leaving a widow, who was the plaintiff in the case. The question was, whether the widow of the last owner was entitled to succeed to the property or his mother. The opinion of the Pundits was asked: one of them gave in favor of the defendant, the mother; the reasons on which he based his opinion are not reported. The Court, however, gave judgment in favor of the plaintiff, relying upon the Vyavastha of the other Pundit, who is reported to have given his opinion "according to the Vyavastharnava by Raghunath Survabhouma, and according to the Dayatattwa of

[1] Montriou's Cases on Hindu Law, p. 353.

Raghanandana Smarta Bhuttacharjya, and according to the Vivada Ratnakara by Chandeswara, and according to the Vivada Chintamoni by Vachaspati Misra, and according to the comment on Menu by Kulluka Bhatta, and according to the Mitacshara by Bhattaraka Paramahansa and other authorities in use." The first and the last authority mentioned in the above extract do not seem to be well-known. LECTURE III.

The next case in which the widow's right to succeed was raised, was decided by the Sudder Dewany Adawlut in 1796—the case of *Srinath Surma* v. *Radha Kaunt*.[1] The property in suit was situated within the district of Bhagulpore, and it was held in coparcenary, and the profits had been enjoyed in common by the parceners. It appears from a note that the property was probably situated within that part of Bhagulpore to which the doctrines of the Bengal school would apply. The Court gave judgment according to the opinions of the Pundits, which declared that the plaintiff was entitled to one-fifth of the property claimed; the widow of his uncle was entitled to one-fifth, and the descendants of his three uncles were respectively entitled to one-fifth each.

The next case in which this question was raised was decided by the Sudder Dewany Adawlut in

[1] 1 Sel. Rep., p. 19. *Note.* The page-references of the Select Reports are to the new edition of the work by Sreenath Banerjee and Brothers.

LECTURE III. 1801 in the case of *Radha Churn Rai* v. *Kissen Chand Rai and another.*[1] The property in this case was situated within the district of 24-Pergunnahs, and the defendant contended that his brother's widow had no right to the share of her husband, but that she was only entitled to a maintenance. The Court, however, held, on the authority of the opinion of the Pundits, as well as by a reference to the Digest of Hindu Law, that she was entitled to the whole estate of her deceased husband, and directed that the widow should be put into possession of the fourth share belonging to her husband.

Another case in which the same question was raised was decided by the Sudder Dewany Adawlut in 1801. It is the case of *Rajbullub Bhooyan* v. *Mussamut Buneta De.*[2] The property in this case was situated in the district of Mymensing ; and the plaintiff, as heir of her husband, claimed a third share of a zemindary, that being the share of her husband. The defendant, who was one of the three brothers of the plaintiff's husband, denied that the plaintiff had a title to any share of the zemindary claimed ; and alleged that it had been held undivided for many generations, and was not subject to division. The Court, basing its judgment upon the opinion of the Pundit, held, that the widow, as heiress of her husband, was entitled to his share of the zemindary, and gave her a decree accordingly.

[1] 1 Sel. Rep., p. 44.

[2] *Ibid*, p. 59.

In another case,[1] decided by the Sudder Dewany Adawlut in 1802, the widow's right to succeed to her husband's estate was the subject of discussion. The plaintiff, as the widow of her husband, claimed as his heiress a third share of a certain zemindary from her husband's brothers; her husband and the two defendants being three brothers who held the zemindary jointly. The defendant, among other objections, raised the question as to whether the plaintiff as heir of her husband was entitled to a third share of the zemindary, or whether she was only entitled to maintenance. The Sudder Dewany Adawlut, after consulting with the Pundits, declared that the widow was entitled to her husband's share of the property, and gave a decree accordingly. The property in this case was situated within the district of Moorshedabad.

These are some of the earliest cases in which the question regarding the widow's right to succeed was raised; and it seems that it was uniformly held in favor of the widow's claim. So far, therefore, as the Courts are concerned, the point seems to have been well settled in the latter end of the last century and in the commencement of the present century. It does not appear that in any subsequent case the point was ever seriously contested on the broad basis of the Hindu law applicable to the subject.

According to the Benares school.

The cases that have been quoted above are all determined by the doctrines of the Bengal school.

---

[1] Nilkant Rai v. Munee Chowdrain, 1 Sel. Rep., p. 77.

LECTURE III. I propose now to refer to some cases which were determined according to the doctrines of the Benares school.

The earliest reported case on the subject is that of *Duljeet Sing* v. *Sheomunook Sing*,[1] decided in 1802. The suit was originally brought in the City Court of Benares by the plaintiff to recover a moiety of a certain zemindary from his uncle. In the course of the case it appeared that there were living two widows of another uncle of the plaintiff, and the three brothers had formed a joint family. The rights of these two ladies came on for discussion, and the Pundits declared that "the widows were entitled to no share, but had a right to maintenance from the estate; that the estate being undivided, Sheomunook (plaintiff) and Duljeet (defendant) would each take half." The Court held accordingly. The widows, however, obtained a third of the estate according to certain admissions of the plaintiff and the defendant made before, on which the provincial Court gave the ladies a decree.

In another case,[2] decided in 1816 by the Sudder Dewany Adawlut, regarding property situated in the district of Goruckpore, a point was raised as to whether the widow succeeded to a *raj* and zemindary held by her late husband. The Pundits in answer stated the law as follows: "The raj and zemindary

---

[1] 1 Sel. Rep., p. 79.

[2] Raja Shumsere Lal v. Ranee Dilraj Kouwar, 2 Sel. Rep., p. 216.

having descended entire and without partition to Raja Ajeet Mull from his ancestors, his widow can maintain no right to possession of it during her lifetime, because, according to the shasters current in Goruckpore, a widow is only entitled to the portion of the ancestral estate which, on a partition, may have fallen to her husband." The Court held in accordance with this opinion of the Hindu law officers. It may be here observed that although the property in suit was a *raj* and zemindary, the opinion of the law officers was not based upon that circumstance, but rested upon the broad principle of Hindu law applicable to widows generally.

In the case of *Runjeet Sing* v. *Obhoy Narain Sing*,[1] which was originally instituted in the Zillah Court of Tirhoot, and decided by the Sudder Dewany Adawlut in 1817, the following question was put by the Court to the Hindu law officer :—

"Ancestral property being in the possession of three brothers, one dies leaving a widow; who will succeed to his share? his widow or his brothers?"

To this the following answer was submitted by the law officer :—

"In case of undivided property, if the deceased left no issue, the brothers, and not the widow, will succeed to his share. This is according to the doctrine of *Narud Munee* as entered in the Mitacshara

---

[1] 2 Sel. Rep., p. 315.

LECTURE III. — and other tracts." The decree of the Court was given according to this opinion. It will be seen here that this case was governed by the doctrines of the Mithila school, but as regards the point in issue, the Mithila school follows the rule of the Mitacshara.

The *chaste* widow alone succeeds.

The widow, however, who succeeds to the estate of her husband is, according to all authorities, the *chaste* widow; or, in other words, the widow who, during her husband's lifetime, was not guilty of unchastity. The Hindu religion and Hindu law attaches special merit to chastity in females. The chief duty and the highest virtue of a female is to remain chaste, and the Hindu law, accordingly, declares unchastity as a serious disqualification in a female such as to dis-entitle her to succeed to the estate of her late husband. The passages of Hindu law bearing upon this point are all collected in the prefatory part of the order of reference by Justice Mitter in the well-known case of *Kerry Kolitanee* v. *Moniram Kolita*, reported in 19 Weekly Reporter, p. 367 *et seq.*

All the authorities agree in this proposition, viz.—

All the authorities of Hindu law are unanimous on this point, *viz.*, that a chaste widow only succeeds, and that a wife guilty of unchastity during the life-time of her husband, is declared incapable of succession. We find the author of the Mitacshara laying down thus: "Therefore, the right interpretation is this,—when a man who was separated from his co-heirs and not reunited with them dies, leaving no male issue, his widow (if chaste) takes the estate in the first instance."[1] The words '*if chaste*' are the comments of Ballambhatta, and do not occur in the original text: that Vijnaneswara intended to confine his observations to a *chaste* widow, will appear from the concluding sentence in the chapter relating to the right of the widow to succeed: "Therefore, it is a settled rule that a wedded wife *being chaste* takes the whole estate of a man who, being separated from his co-heirs, and not subsequently reunited with them, dies leaving no male issue."[2]

LECTURE III.

The Mitacshara.

The author even proceeds further, so as to declare that a wife suspected of incontinence is incapable of succession. For this purpose the following text of Harita is quoted: "If a woman becoming a widow in her youth be headstrong, a maintenance must, in that case, be given to her for the support of life." This passage is thus interpreted: "This passage of Harita is intended for a denial of the right of a widow suspected of incontinency to take the whole estate. From this very passage it appears that a widow not suspected of misconduct has a right to take the whole property."[3] And again: "With the same view Sancha has said 'or his eldest wife,' being eldest by good qualities, and not supposed likely to be guilty of incontinency, she takes the whole wealth: and like a mother maintains any other headstrong wife of her husband."[4]

[1] Chap. II, Sec. i, para. 30.
[2] *Ibid*, 37.
[3] *Ibid*, 39.
[4] *Ibid*, 38.

LECTURE III.

The Dayabhaga.

There is no separate discussion of this subject in the Dayabhaga. That is owing to the fact that the author of the Dayabhaga did not dissent from this position of the Mitacshara, but accepted it. Hence the rule of the Mitacshara on this subject also obtains in Bengal. The author of the Dayabhaga has indicated his adherence to this doctrine in several passages of his work, where he has attempted to establish the widow's title to inherit.

The Dayatattwa.

The other authorities of the Bengal school have adhered to the same doctrine. Raghunandana, in his Dayatattwa, commenting on the well-known passage of Katyayana relative to the widow's duties, thus delivers himself: "'Keeping unsullied the bed of her husband' intends one who knows no other man than the husband. Accordingly, in that part of the Harivansa which treats of religious observances, it is said: O auspicious Arundhati, of unchaste women, all good acts consisting of gift, fasting, and merits, likewise all religious observances, are fruitless."[1] And in the next paragraph Raghunandana quotes as an authority the following text of Vrihat Menu: "Let the sonless wife, keeping unsullied the bed of her husband, and persevering in religious observances, offer his oblations and take (his) entire share."

The Dayakrama Sangraha.

To the same purport Sreekrishna Tarkalankar, in his Dayakrama Sangraha, quotes the text of Katyayana before-mentioned for the purpose of showing

[1] Chap. XI, para. 17.

that a widow who "*preserves* unsullied the bed of her lord" succeeds to his estate.[1] LECTURE III.

The Digest.

Jagannatha Tarkapanchanana, the author of the Digest, holds the same opinion regarding unchastity in the widow. He has considered the question in several places, particularly in Book V, Chap. VIII, Sec. i, which is devoted to the discussion of the widow's title to succeed to the estate of her husband. The passages of this author bearing upon this point are most of them collected together in the reference order by Justice Mitter in the case of *Kerry Kolitany* v. *Moniram Kolita*, which has been before referred to.

The reported cases on the subject.

The following are some of the reported cases bearing upon this point of Hindu law. In the case of *Radhamoney Raur* v. *Nilmoney Doss*,[2] decided by the late Supreme Court in 1792, it was found that "the plaintiff, after her husband's death, had been incontinent, and had long since voluntarily quitted the house and protection of her husband's family. She was at the time of the action living with her own father and brothers." The Court held, that the widow had forfeited, by her incontinence, her right to her husband's estate. It may be observed that, in this case, the unchastity was *subsequent* to her husband's death, and not during the husband's lifetime; and the Court in this case did not appear to have drawn any distinction between unchastity during the *husband's lifetime* and unchastity *after his death.*

[1] Chap. I, Sec. ii, para. 3.

[2] Montriou's Hindu Law Cases, p. 314.

LECTURE III.

In another case, which arose in the Zillah Court of Hooghly, the questions that were put to the Hindu law officers for their opinion were these :—1*st*, whether a widow, who subsequently to her husband's death became unchaste, succeeded to his estate? 2*nd*, whether a widow, who was guilty of unchastity during her husband's lifetime, and had on that account been expelled from the family, had any right to inherit her husband's estate? The answer of the law officers to both the questions was in the negative. It appears that the law officers seemed to draw no distinction between the two cases; for, in support of their answer, they quoted the same authorities on Hindu law which referred indifferently to the two questions.[1]

In another case, which arose in 1811 in the Zillah Court of the 24-Pergunnahs, it was found that a man died leaving a widow, who had become a prostitute, and the Hindu law officers answered that, in such case, "she has no title to her husband's property, and ought to be expelled from his house."[2] It does not appear from the report whether the unchastity was during the husband's lifetime or subsequent to his death.

The case of *Kerry Kolitany* v. *Moniram Kolita*[3] may be considered as an authority in support of

---

[1] Macnaghten's Hindu Law, Vol. II, p. 19, case iii.
[2] *Ibid*, p. 21, case iv.
[3] 19 W. R., 367.

the above proposition of Hindu law. Although the question directly at issue in that case was different, it was, however, conceded on both sides, and accepted by the Court, on the authorities that were brought to bear upon the question, that a widow who was guilty of unchastity during the husband's lifetime, did not succeed to his estate.

In the case of *Matunginee Debea* v. *Joy Kali Debea*,[1] it was held by Peacock, C. J., delivering the judgment of the Appellate Court, that "there is no doubt that, according to the Hindu law of inheritance, a wife who commits adultery during the lifetime of her husband loses her right to inherit her husband's estate, unless the act is condoned by her husband or expiated by penance." The point, however, that was directly in issue in the case was, whether a widow, who *after* succeeding to the estate of her husband becomes unchaste, is deprived of the estate which has so devolved on her. The Court of Original Jurisdiction held, and so did the Court of Appeal, that the widow would not be deprived of the estate.

The widow does not represent her husband for purposes of inheritance.

The widow succeeds to the property of her husband, (*i. e.*) to the property which her husband possessed at the time of his death, or was entitled to at that time. The widow does not, for the purposes of inheritance, *represent* the husband; (*i. e.*) the widow will not be entitled to any property to which her husband, if living, would have been entitled by

---

[1] 14 W. R., 23, A. O. J.

LECTURE III.

right of inheritance.[1] Thus a man dies leaving a brother and the widow of another brother; in this case the surviving brother will take the whole estate to the exclusion of the widow; but the husband of the widow, if living, would have shared the inheritance with the surviving brother. This point was decided in the case of *Ranee Bhubani Debi and Ranee Mohamaya Debi* v. *Ranee Suroojmoni*.[2] It was held in that case that "the appellants (the widows of the first and second sons) were the persons entitled to succeed to the shares of their husbands respectively, though not to the share of Rubinder Narain, their husband's brother, who died long after their husbands, and to whose property they could have no title." In another case[3] the same point was raised and decided. The question in that case was put very obscurely, but it appears from its purport and the answer to it, that the widow did not succeed to the property to which her husband, if living, would have been entitled; the answer being "that the surviving widow has no title to inherit from her *sapindas*."

The husband's cause of action descends to the widow.

If the husband, however, had been entitled to property of which he did not or could not take possession during his lifetime, then, on his death, his widow, as his heiress, would be entitled to sue, if the law of limitation did not bar her, to recover posses-

[1] Huroosunderee Debee v. Rajessuree Debee, 2 W. R., 321.

[2] 1 Sel. Rep., p. 179.

[3] 2 Macnaghten, p. 29.

sion of the said property, the cause of action in such a case descending to the widow. The widow would also be entitled to succeed to possession of the property in which her husband had a vested interest under a will or deed, the actual enjoyment of the same by her husband having been postponed by an intervening life-estate.[1]

The widows of disqualified Hindus do not inherit property from which their husbands were excluded.

There is a class of persons whom the Hindu law has declared incapable of inheriting. They are as follows:—"Impotent persons, outcasts, persons born blind and deaf, madmen, idiots, dumb persons, and those who have lost a sense or a limb."[2] Other sages[3] include lepers and religious mendicants in this category. These persons are excluded from the inheritance. Their widows, therefore, take nothing, since they themselves took nothing; although their sons, who are free from those defects, would inherit property which they, but for those defects, would have themselves inherited. The widows of such persons however are entitled to maintenance to the end of their lives;[4] and Yajnawalkya adds, on condition of their conducting themselves aright.[5] But if they are unchaste, they should be expelled.

The Hindu law, however, only declares that these persons (impotent, &c.) are incapable of *inheriting*

[1] Hurosunduree Debee *v.* Rajessuree Debee, 2 W. R., 321; Rewan Persad *v.* Mussamut Radha Bebee, 4 Moore's I. A., 137.

[2] Menu, Chap. IX, v. 201.

[3] Devala.

[4] Dayabhaga, Chap. V, para. 19.

[5] Mitacshara, Chap. II, Sec. i, para. 21.

LECTURE III.

property ; there is no authority which declares that they are incapable of *holding* property (like persons attainted in English law). Therefore, a person falling within this category is perfectly competent to acquire property by purchase or gift or the like ; and their widows would succeed to any such property which they might have held during their lifetime.

Anuloma and *pratiloma* marriages described.

I have been up to this time considering the case of widows who belong to the same caste with their husbands. That, however, though a necessary limit of the discussion in the present age (Kali Yuga) was not so during the other three ages, when intermarriages between the four castes were allowed both in the direct order of the castes called *anuloma* marriages, as well as in their inverse order called *pratiloma* marriages. The *anuloma* marriages, however, were considered proper ; and the *pratiloma* marriages, though legal, were considered blameworthy. In the present age (Kali Yuga) intermarriages between the castes have been prohibited,[1] and marriage between persons of the same caste only allowed.

Inter-marriage allowed in the first three ages.

In the first three ages intermarriage between the four classes was allowed. In *anuloma* marriages a Brahmin could legally have four wives, one from each of the four classes ; a Kshetrya could have only three ; a Vaisya two, and a Sudra only one. The

---

[1] Brahma Purana: Vrihat Naradya Purana and Aditya Purana quoted by Raghunandana in his Udvaha Tattwa.

first wife of a man must, however, be from his *own* class;[1] his *dharma patni*, whom he marries from a sense of duty. "For the first marriage of the twice-born classes, a woman of the same tribe is recommended; but for such as are impelled by inclination to marry again, women in the direct order of the classes is to be preferred."[2]

"A Sudra woman only must be the wife of a Sudra; she and a Vaisya, of a Vaisya; those two and a Kshetrya, of a Kshetrya; those three and a Brahmani, of a Brahmana."[3]

On the same subject another ancient Rishi thus ordains: "The most suitable match for every tribe is a wife of the same class. Or four wives may be allowed to a priest in the order of the classes; three to a warrior; two to a merchant; and one to a man of the servile class."[4] Paithinasi in the same way declares: "Four wives may be espoused by a Brahmana, and three, two, and one, by men of other classes respectively."[5]

According to the Mitacshara the widows of different classes succeed together.

As regards the title of the widows of the several classes to succeed simultaneously to the properties of their husbands, there is a difference of opinion among the authorities. The author of the Mitacshara is of opinion that all the widows succeed together although they belong to different classes. It is there

---

[1] Menu, Chap. III, v. 4. [2] *Ibid*, v. 12. [3] *Ibid*, v. 13.
[4] Sancha and Lichita, quoted in Digest, Bk. V, Chap. ii, v. 152.
[5] *Ibid*, v. 151.

LECTURE III.

laid down that, "in the first place, the wife shares the estate. Wife (*patni*) signifies a woman espoused in lawful wedlock, conformably with the etymology of the term as implying a connection with religious rites. Singular number, because the class is denoted. Hence, if there be several, whether of same or different castes, they divide and take the property according to their shares."[1] What the shares of the widows of different castes are, whether equal or unequal, the author does not say; and no inference can be drawn from the text itself.

According to the Dayabhaga, the widow of the highest class alone succeeds.

The author of the Dayabhaga maintains a contrary opinion. He says the word '*patni*' means a wife belonging to the highest tribe, and the *patni* who is entitled to succeed is a wife of that description. If a Brahmin happens to have four wives belonging to the four classes, then, on his death, his Brahmin widow shall succeed to his estate: in her default the Kshetrya wife, but not a Vaisya, nor a Sudra, though married to him. The passage in which this matter is discussed is as follows:—"The rank of wife belongs in the first place to a woman of the highest tribe: for the text [of Sancha, &c.] expresses that the eldest wife takes the wealth, and seniority is reckoned in the order of the tribes. Thus Menu

[1] Mitacshara, Chap. II, Sec. i, para. 5. *Note.*—The last two sentences do not occur in Mr. Colebrooke's translation. But it is now well established, that they occur in the Mitacshara; and Mr. Colebrooke's MS. was in that respect defective. See Jijoyiaumba Bayi *v.* Kamachi Bayi, 3 Mad. Rep., p. 424; Norton's Leading Cases, p. 509.

says, "When regenerate men take wives both of their own class and others, the precedence, honor, and habitation of those wives must be settled according to the order of their classes." Therefore, since seniority is by tribe, a woman of equal class, though youngest in respect of the date of marriage, is deemed eldest. The rank of wife (*patni*) belongs to her, for she alone is competent to assist in the performance of sacrifices and other sacred rites. Accordingly Menu says: "To all such married men the wives of the same class only (not wives of a different class by any means) must perform the duty of personal attendance and the daily business relating to acts of religion. For he who foolishly causes those duties to be performed by any other than his wife of the same class when she is near at hand, has been immemorially considered as a mere *Chandala* begotten on a Brahmini." But on failure of a wife of the same tribe, one of the tribes immediately following may be employed in such duties. Thus Vishnu ordains: "If there be no wife belonging to the same tribe, [he may execute the business relating to acts of religion] with one of the tribes immediately following, in case of distress. But a regenerate man must not do so with a woman of the Sudra class." 'Execute business relating to acts of religion' is understood from the preceding sentence. Therefore, a Brahmini is lawful wife (*patni*) of a Brahmana. On failure of such, a *Kshetrya* may be

LECTURE III. such in case of distress: but not a *Vaisya* nor a *Sudra*, though married to him. A Kshetrya woman is wife of a Khestrya man. In her default a *Vaisya* woman may be so, as belonging to the next following tribe; but not a Sudra woman. A *Vaisya* is the only wife for a Vaisya, since a Sudra wife is denied in respect of the regenerate tribes simply."[1]

The authorities quoted by Jimutavahana in the above passage do not expressly refer to the question of succession to property; they seem rather to express the spiritual superiority of a wife belonging to the same class with the husband. As succession to property, however, is dependent upon considerations of a spiritual nature; the inference from the above authorities is, that a wife whose spiritual superiority is thus declared, is also preferable in matters of succession. Jimutavahana accordingly says, as an inference from the preceding passage, that, "in this manner must be understood the *succession* to property in the order in which the rank of wife is acknowledged. Therefore, since women actually espoused may not have the rank of wives, the following passage of Narada intends such a case: 'Among brothers if any one die without issue, or enter a religious order, let the rest of the brethren divide his wealth, except the wife's separate property. Let them allow a maintenance to his women for life, provided these preserve unsullied the bed of their

[1] Dayabhaga, Chap. XI, Sec. i, para. 47.

lord. But if they behave otherwise, the brethren may resume that allowance.' "[1]

LECTURE III.

" Accordingly, in passages declaratory of the wife's right of succession, the term 'wife' (*patni*) is used; and in those which ordain a maintenance, the terms 'woman' (*stri* or *nari*) or 'spouse' (*bharya*), or other similar word."[2]

Raghunandana maintains the same opinion.

Raghunandana, following Jimutavahana, maintains the same opinion on this subject. He says: " By the term 'wife' (*patni*) is intended the wife of the same class with the husband; since it is expressed (in several texts) that the senior wife (takes the wealth).[3]

" The seniority is described by Menu: 'When regenerate men take wives both of their own class and others, the seniority, honor, and apartment of those wives must be settled according to the order of their classes.' "[4]

" Narada ordains mere maintenance of wives other than those of the same class. Of the brothers, if any one departs without issue, or enters into a religious order, let the rest divide his wealth excepting the wives' separate property. Let them allow a maintenance to his wives (*stri*) for life, provided these preserve unsullied the bed of their lord. But if they behave otherwise, the brethren may resume that allowance."[5]

---

[1] Dayabhaga, Chap. XI, Sec. i, para. 48. [2] *Ibid*, 49.
[3] Dayatattwa, Chap. XI, para. 19. [4] *Ibid*, 20. [5] *Ibid*, 21.

LECTURE III.

"Thus, as there is a distinction between a wife taken from the same class and one who is not so, texts like the following should be interpreted with reference to this distinction."[1]

Raghunandana, therefore, is of opinion that the wife of the same class with the husband succeeds to his property. The wives belonging to the other classes do not inherit property; they are only entitled to maintenance.

---

[1] Dayatattwa, Chap. XI, para. 22.

LECTURE IV.

THE OBLIGATIONS OF THE WIDOW AS AN HEIRESS.

Effect of unchastity after widowhood—Matunginee Debee v. Jay Kal Debee—Justice Markby's conclusion—Judgment in appeal—Interpretation of Act XXI of 1850—Kerry Kolitanee v. Moniram Kolita Justice Mitter's judgment—The judgment of Couch, C.J.—Obligation to reside with the husband's family—Optional—Kasinath Bysack v. Hurrosundery Dossee—Raja Pirthee Sing v. Ranee Raj Kower—Effect of a direction in the husband's will to reside at a particular place—Obligation to perform the husband's *sraddha*—Effect of omission.

I HAVE considered, in a previous lecture, the obligations of widows generally, irrespective of their condition as heiresses or not. I shall now try to explain to you the special obligations which a widow must fulfil when she inherits the property of her husband.

The first obligation of a Hindu widow, after she inherits the property of her husband, is to remain chaste. "Let the childless widow, preserving unsullied the bed of her lord, and abiding with her venerable protector, enjoy with moderation the property until her death;"[1] and similar authorities may be quoted from the other Smritis in which the obligation to continue chaste during widowhood is strictly

[1] Katyayana quoted in the Dayabhaga, Chap. XI, Sec. i, para. 56.

LECTURE IV.

Effect of unchastity after widowhood.

enjoined. The important question, however, arises as to what will be the effect of unchastity during widowhood, on the enjoyment of her husband's property which she had inherited. I have pointed out, in a previous lecture, that unchastity during the husband's lifetime disentitles the widow from succession on his death. The Bengal High Court has maintained that the two questions are not the same; and, consequently, a decision on the latter question does not conclude the previous question. It becomes necessary, therefore, to decide the question independently as to whether unchastity during widowhood will have any prejudicial effect on the widow's enjoyment of her husband's property. In the case of

Matunginee Debee v. Jay Kali Debee.

Matunginee Debee v. *Jay Kali Debee*[1] the point was directly raised. The plaintiff, as the daughter of one Ramgopal Banerjee, sued for possession of the moveable and immoveable property belonging to the said Ramgopal, which was in the possession of the defendant, his widow and heiress, on the ground that the said defendant, who was the widow and heiress of the said Ramgopal, had forfeited her estate of a Hindu widow in the property of her husband, by an act of unchastity; it being proved that, after her husband's death, the defendant had a child by a person in her employ. The plaintiff prayed that the defendant be deprived of the property, and that it be handed over to her as the next heir of her father.

[1] 14 W. R., A. O. J., 23.

Justice Markby, who tried the case in the first instance, held:—

1*st.*—That, according to the authority of Menu (Laghu Menu as he calls it), the widow had "no right of succession whatever to the estate of her husband."

2*nd.*—That, according to the seven texts of Vrihaspati (quoted before[1]), the *virtuous* wife, if her husband die before her, shares his wealth.

3*rd.*—That the words '*virtuous* wife' are a rendering of the words *pati-brota sadhwi* (पतिव्रता साध्वी) in the original Sanscrit, which, according to Jagannatha, "include chastity and many other virtues besides the observance of certain religious practices and austerities."

4*th.*—That, of all the inspired writers whose texts have been referred to, Katyayana and Vrihat Menu are the only two authorities who make conjugal fidelity as a condition to the widow's right of succession.

5*th.*—That, according to the reasoning of Jimutavahana, by which he establishes the widow's title to succession, it seems he was of opinion "that the widow continues to hold the estate only so long as she performs the duties which are the foundation of her right."

6*th.*—That, according to the Mitacshara, "the succession of a chaste widow is expressly declared," and "that the widow may either seek to obtain progeny or may remain chaste."

---

[1] See *ante*, pp. 123-124.

LECTURE IV. 7*th.*—That, according to the Vivada Chintamoni and the Vyavahara Mayukha, "a wife, faithful to her husband, takes his wealth, not if she be unfaithful;" and "faithful to her lord" means "chaste."

8*th.*—That, according to Jagannatha, "what is chiefly enjoined on the widow is the general practice of austerities." No special mention is made of chastity: but "a widow who from a wish to bear children slights her deceased husband by marrying again, brings disgrace on herself here below, and shall be excluded from the seat of her lord."

9*th.*—That, in all the Commentaries there is a chapter on Exclusion from Inheritance; but in none of them is unchastity mentioned as a reason for exclusion.

10*th.*—That, according to the opinion of Mr. Colebrooke quoted by Sir Thomas Strange in his Elements of Hindu Law, "an unchaste wife is excluded from the inheritance; but nothing short of actual infidelity in this respect disqualifies, nor the inheritance once vested in her is liable to be divested unless for loss of caste unexpiated by penance and unredeemed by atonement."

11*th.*—That the cases of *Radhamoney Raur* versus *Nilmoney Doss*,[1] *Moharanee Busunt Kumaree* versus *Moharanee Kumul Kumary*,[2] and *Rajkumaree Dossee* versus *Golabee Dossee*[3] did not decide the point at issue in the present case; and in

[1] Montriou's Hindu Law Cas., p. 314. [2] 7 Sel. Rep., p. 168.
[3] S. D. A. Rep. of 1858, p. 1891.

the first case the facts are "too scantily stated for any very secure inference."

12*th.*—The conclusion arrived at is "that neither for unchastity, nor any other vicious act, is a right forfeited under the Hindu law;" "that it is not the immoral act alone which in any case destroys the right, but the loss of caste or degradation which may follow thereupon;" "that the defendant has not, by the simple act of unchastity proved against her, she not having been degraded or expelled from caste, forfeited her right as widow of Ramgopal to inherit his estate." The suit was, accordingly, dismissed. **Justice Markby's conclusion.**

The plaintiff appealed against the judgment, and the appeal came on for hearing before the Appellate Bench consisting of Peacock, C.J., and Macpherson, J. The judgment of the Appellate Court, which was delivered by the Chief Justice, was generally in affirmance of the judgment of the first Court. Peacock, C.J., says :—"Mr. Justice Markby has stated that adultery is not sufficient to deprive a widow of an estate which she has taken by inheritance from her deceased husband in the absence of degradation or expulsion from caste. I wish to avoid being supposed to express any opinion that if she were degraded or deprived of her caste, her estate would cease to exist." **Judgment in appeal.**

The Chief Justice then expressed his opinion as to the meaning of Act XXI of 1850. He took the same view of it that Sir Lawrence Peel expressed in **Interpretation of Act XXI of 1850.**

LECTURE IV. a case[1] in 2 Taylor and Bell, and he held that the Act was intended to cover all cases of loss of caste consequent upon a change of religion or from any other cause. He dissented from a decision of the Sudder Dewanny Adawlut,[2] which held that the loss of caste in the Act "meant loss of caste by reason of excommunication from religion." And the Chief Justice is reported to have said,—"I, therefore, notwithstanding the decision of the Sudder Court in the case decided in 1858, take the same view of Act XXI of 1850 which was taken by Sir Lawrence Peel in the case to which I have referred; and I, therefore, am of opinion, that the principle of this case is not affected by the fact that the respondent had a child by a Sudra. As far as chastity was concerned, it made no difference whether the father of hte chil dwas a Sudra or a Brahmin. It is only as regards caste that that circumstance would make any difference."

There is one important point which the judgment of the Chief Justice decided, which is this, *viz.*,—that even if the Hindu widow was guilty of adultery of such a nature as led to a loss of caste, it would not still deprive her of the estate which she had inherited from her husband; for the Chief Justice was of opinion that the forfeiture which the Hindu law would entail in such a case would be saved by the operation of Act XXI of 1850. What sort of adul-

[1] Sornomoney Dosee *v.* Nemychurn Doss, p. 300.

[2] Rajkoomaree Dosee *v.* Golabee Dosee, Sudder Decision for 1858, p. 1891.

tery would entail a loss of caste on the adulteress is a mixed question of Hindu religion and Hindu customs. Probably, adultery with a *non-Hindu* will have that effect, or of a high caste Hindu woman with one belonging to the lowest castes of Hindu society. LECTURE IV.

This case of *Matunginee Debee* v. *Jay Kali Debee* was decided by the Appeal Bench in 1869, and the case of *Kerry Kolitanee* v. *Moniram Kolita* came on before a Division Bench of the High Court, presided over by Bayley and Mitter, JJ., in 1872. Their Lordships, dissenting from the judgment in the case of *Matunginee Debee*, referred the following points for the opinion of the Full Bench :—

Kerry Kolitanee v. Moniram Kolita.

1st.—Whether, under the Hindu law as administered in the Bengal school, a widow, who has once inherited the estate of her deceased husband, is liable to forfeit that estate by reason of unchastity?

2nd.—Whether the forfeiture, if any, is barred by Act XXI of 1850 ?

Two judgments in this case need be referred to ; one is the referring order of Justice Mitter, which was accepted by him as his judgment in the case, and which ultimately became the judgment of the minority of the Judges of the Bench, consisting of Kemp, Glover, and Mitter, JJ., and the other is the judgment of Chief Justice Couch, which was the judgment of the majority of the Bench, consisting of Couch, C.J., Jackson, Phear, Macpherson, Markby, Ainslie, and Pontifex, JJ. The latter, as the judg-

LECTURE IV.

ment of the majority, is the judgment of the Court, and in substance affirms the judgment in the case of *Matunginee Debee* v. *Jay Kali Debee.*

Justice Mitter's judgment.

Justice Mitter in his judgment held :—

1. That, according to the ancient sages or *Rishis*, Menu, Narada, Yajnawalkya, Vrihaspati, Paithinasi, Harita, and others, woman must be maintained in a state of perpetual dependence by her husband and relatives.

2. That the widow is a mere trustee for her life for the soul of her deceased husband.

3. That the rules restricting the widow's rights are not mere moral precepts, but are intended to be strictly enforced.

4. That the tendency of Hindu law is to exclude females generally from succession on account of their incapacity to perform the *parbanna sraddha.*

5. That, so far as her mode of enjoyment is concerned, there is no difference between the *corpus* of the estate which she inherits, and its profits.

6. That the reversioner is entitled to take steps to prevent her from using those proceeds for a purpose other than that sanctioned by the Hindu law.

7. Every act done by the widow which renders her incapable of using the estate for the benefit of her deceased husband, operates as a cause of forfeiture.

8. That, according to the original authorities on Hindu law (the texts from the Rishis and the com-

mentators are cited at length), unchastity on the part of the widow renders her incapable of performing acts beneficial to the soul of her deceased husband, and therefore operates as a cause of forfeiture. LECTURE IV.

The judgment of Couch, C.J., which was the judgment of the Full Bench, established the following points :— The judgment of Couch, C.J.

1. The widow is not a *trustee* in the sense which is ordinarily attributed to that word.

2. That as other female heirs, such as the daughter, &c., do not forfeit their estate if they fail to perform duties for which the estate was conferred upon them, there is no reason for declaring, in the case of the widow, that she forfeits her estate for such incapacity. A daughter, who had succeeded as a spinster, would continue to hold the estate even after the death of her childless husband, when she becomes wholly inefficacious to confer benefits for which she was selected.

3. The widow's estate is not conditional upon her using it for the purpose of benefiting her husband.

4. The proposition that, if a trustee is not in a position to fulfil his duties, the trust property must be taken way from him, is not correct either in Hindu or in English law.

5. The text of Katyayana, "let the childless widow preserving unsullied the bed of her lord," &c., is not to be interpreted as making the enjoyment conditional upon her keeping unsullied the bed of her lord.

LECTURE IV.

6. The proposition that an estate once vested cannot afterwards be divested, is unsupported by authorities in Hindu law.

7. There is no analogy between the widow's estate and the widow's maintenance.

8. That the estate once inherited by the widow is not forfeited simply by unchastity.

No opinion was given by the Chief Justice as to the effect of Act XXI of 1850 upon unchastity on the part of the widow: it was considered unnecessary with reference to the answer that was given to the first question.

The judgment[1] in this case is pending in appeal

---

[1] NOTE.—The Privy Council has since delivered its judgment, affirming the judgment of the majority of the Judges of the High Court. Their Lordships' judgment is as follows :—

SIR B. PEACOCK.—This is an appeal from a decision of a Full Bench of the High Court of Judicature at Calcutta. It was admitted by virtue of a special order of Her Majesty in Council, whereby the appellant had leave to appeal in the form of a special case upon the following questions, *viz.* :—

1st.—Whether, under the Hindu law as administered in the Bengal school, a widow who has once inherited the estate of a deceased husband is liable to forfeit that estate by reason of unchastity ; and,

2nd.—Whether the forfeiture, if any, is barred by Act XXI of 1850.

The appeal was admitted on account of the importance of the questions submitted for determination, and the great interest which the Hindu community take in it.

The case came in the first instance upon special appeal before a Division Bench, consisting of Mr. Justice Bayley and Mr. Justice Dwarkanath Mitter, who were of opinion that the defendant had, by reason of unchastity, forfeited her right in her husband's property ; but in consequence of a contrary ruling of the High Court, referred the two questions abovementioned to a Full Bench, with their remarks thereon.

The Full Bench consisted of the Chief Justice and nine other Judges, and the majority held that the widow, having once inherited the estate, did not forfeit it by reason of her subsequent unchastity. Three of the Judges however, *viz.*, Mr. Justice Kemp, Mr. Justice Glover, and Mr.

before Her Majesty's Privy Council; the expenses of the appeal having been met by a public subscription.

Justice Dwarkanath Mitter, dissented from the opinions expressed by the majority of the Court. The case is fully reported in the 13 B. L. R., p. 1.

The subject has been very elaborately discussed by the Chief Justice and the other Judges of the Full Bench, and it has also been fully argued before their Lordships on behalf of the appellant. The respondent did not appear.

The opinion of Mr. Justice Mitter, who was himself a learned and accomplished Hindu lawyer, and those of the other two Judges who were in the minority, are entitled to very great weight; but having considered and weighed all their arguments, their Lordships are unable to concur in the opinions which they expressed.

The earliest case in which the subject was fully discussed in the High Court is the case of *Srimati Matunginee Debee* v. *Srimati Jay Kali Debee* (5 B. L. R, 463), which was the cause of the reference.

That case was originally tried before Mr. Justice Markby, who delivered a judgment, in which he showed much research and great knowledge of the subject. The case was appealed to the High Court, and heard before the then Chief Justice and Mr. Justice Macpherson, who affirmed the judgment of Mr. Justice Markby.

Their Lordships will, in the first instance, advert to the judgments of the dissentient Judges, and in particular to the opinion expressed by Mr. Justice Mitter on referring the case, and to his judgment after the argument in the Full Bench. Reasoning from the general notions of the Hindu commentators, touching the frailty and incapacity of women, and the necessity for their dependence upon and control by some male protector, and from the origin and nature of a widow's interest in the property which she takes in succession to her husband, he arrived at the conclusion that she is, as he expresses it, "a trustee for the benefit of her husband's soul;" that inasmuch as, by reason of unchastity subsequent to her husband's death, she becomes incapable of performing effectually the religious services that are essential to his spiritual welfare, she ceases to be capable of performing her trust, and must therefore be taken to have broken the condition on which she holds the property, and to have incurred the forfeiture of her estate. It may be remarked that the other two dissentient Judges differed from Mr. Justice Mitter's view of the nature of a Hindu widow's estate, and, therefore, from a good deal of the reasoning upon which his conclusion is founded. But, however that may be, their Lordships entirely concur with the Chief Justice and the majority of the Judges in rejecting the somewhat fanciful analogy of trusteeship.

Mr. Justice Glover's judgment is founded upon the express texts, and upon the ground that by reason of unchastity a widow becomes incapable

LECTURE IV.

The judgment of the High Court does not seem to have been approved by the Hindu community.

of performing those religious ceremonies which are for the benefit of her husband's soul. He draws a distinction between a widow and a son, and says (13 B. L. R., p. 55) :—

" The theory of the Hindu law of inheritance is the capability by the heir of performing certain religious ceremonies which do good to the soul of the departed, and he takes who can render most service. The sons down to the third generation could do most, offer most oblations, and confer greatest benefits, therefore they are first in the line of heirship. The *widow comes next, as being able to confer considerable, though less, benefits*, and *it is only because she is able to do this that she is allowed to take her husband's share.*

" It would seem, therefore, to be a condition precedent to her taking that estate, that she should be in a position to perform the ceremonies, and offer the continual funeral oblations, which are to benefit her deceased husband in the other world ; and in this respect her position is very different from that of a son. The son confers benefits upon his father from the mere fact of being born capable of performing certain ceremonies. His birth delivers him from the hell called *put:* and, whether in after-life he offer the funeral oblations or no, *he succeeds to his father's inheritance from the fact of being able to offer them.* With the widow it is not so ; she can only perform ceremonies and offer oblations so long as she continues chaste, and directly she becomes unchaste, from that moment her right to offer the funeral cake ceases."

These reasons do not appear to be sufficient to support the learned Judge's conclusion that a widow forfeits her estate when she ceases to be able to perform the necessary religious ceremonies. It is admitted that she may by law hold the estate without performing them, and that she may give, sell, or transfer the estate to another for her own life. Nor does there appear to be any sufficient reason for the distinction attempted to be drawn between a son or other heirs and a widow with reference to the forfeiture of the estate when the person who has succeeded to it has become incompetent to perform the duties which he or she ought to perform. The proprietary right of a son by inheritance from his father is expressly ordained, because the wealth devolving upon sons benefits the deceased (Dayabhaga, Chap. XI, Sec. I, v. 38), and the right of succession of other heirs to the property is also founded on competence for offering oblations at obsequies (18th verse) ; see also v. 32. But a son, even if by the mere fact of his birth he delivers his father from the hell called *put*, is, according to the Dayabhaga, excluded for certain causes from inheritance in the same manner as other heirs (*see* the Dayabhaga, Chap. V., paras. 4, 5, and 6) ; but, if he once succeeds, the estate is not divested for anything less than degradation, though causes which would have excluded him if they had existed before succession arise

The public subscription got up to contest its validity by an appeal to the Privy Council is evidence of that

---

after the estate has descended. This is admitted by Mr. Justice Mitter (13 B. L. R., p. 7).

Their Lordships will proceed to consider the principal texts upon which the learned Judges who were in the minority founded their judgments.

Mr. Justice Mittter, in his judgment, delivered upon the Full Bench (13 B. L. R., p. 40), says:—

"Of all the authorities above referred to, the Dayabhaga of Jimutavahana, the acknowledged founder of the Bengal school, is undoubtedly the highest; and it is therefore to the Dayabhaga that I shall first direct my attention. I do not wish, however, to go over all the texts quoted and relied upon by the author of that treatise in discussing the widow's right of succession. I will refer to two of those texts only,—namely, the texts of Vrihat Menu, cited in v. 7, Sec. I, Chap. XI of Mr. Colebrooke's translation of the Dayabhaga; and that of Katyayana, cited in v. 56 of the same section and chapter. These two verses are as follows:—

'(1.) The widow of a childless man, keeping unsullied her husband's bed, and persevering in religious observances, shall present his funeral oblation and obtain his entire share.'

'(2.) Let the childless widow, keeping unsullied the bed of her lord and abiding with her venerable protector, enjoy with moderation the property until her death. After her let the heirs take it.'"

With regard to the former of the texts above cited, although the present participle is used, it clearly refers only to the conduct of the widow up to the time of her husband's death, and not to her conduct subsequently. It cannot mean up to the time of her presenting the funeral oblation; for, notwithstanding the order of the words, the meaning of the text is, that having obtained the husband's share, the *patni* or widow should perform those ceremonies conducive to the spiritual benefit of her husband and herself, which can be accomplished by wealth, and which a female is competent to perform. *See* The Viramitrodaya, Chap. III, Part I, s. 2, and the Smriti Chandrika, Chap. XI, Sec. I, vv. 13, 16, and 20. In this view the text would run thus,—"The widow of a childless man having kept unsullied her husband's bed, and persevered in religious observances, shall obtain his entire share, and present his funeral oblation."

Mr. Justice Glover points to the words "persevering in religious observances," to prove that the whole text applies to a period subsequent to the husband's death, and as referring to a continually abiding condition, because he assumes that a wife cannot perform religious observances during her husband's life, and that, therefore, those words must have relation to a period after her husband's death. But the assumption

LECTURE IV.

fact. It appeared to be opposed to the instinctive convictions of the community. How that conviction

---

does not appear to be correct, for in the Smriti Chandrika, Chap. XI, Sec. I, v. 17, the meaning of the words, "persevering in religious observances" are thus explained,—"practising religious ceremonies even during the lifetime of the husband, with the husband's permission," &c., whence the inference is drawn, in v. 18, that a *patni*, to inherit her husband's estate, must be a pious woman. And again in v. 12, a virtuous woman is "one that lives with her husband, associating with him in the performance of rites ordained by Cruti and Smriti, and observing fastings and other religious ceremonies."

The second of the texts relied upon is that of Katyayana.

It is important to see for what purpose the text was cited, and with that view to refer to the verses immediately preceding those in which the text is cited, for there is nothing more likely to mislead than to read a single paragraph from the Dayabhaga or Mitakshara alone without studying the whole chapter, and in some cases, even, without studying several chapters of the same treatise.

In Chap. XI, Sec. I, the author of the Dayabhaga, v. 54, sums up his argument in support of the widow's right to succeed to the entire property of her husband, for which purpose he had cited the text of Vrihat Menu. He says:—

"By the term 'his share' is understood the entire share appertaining to her husband, not a part only," (the translator adds the words "sufficient for her support.")

And then in v. 55 he concludes:—

"Therefore the interpretation of the law is right as set forth by us," *viz.*, that "the widow's right must be affirmed to extend to the whole estate of her husband" (v. 6).

He then proceeds, in v. 56, to deal with the mode of enjoyment, and to show that, notwithstanding a widow takes the entire estate, she is not entitled to make a gift, sale, or mortgage of it, to the exclusion of her husband's heirs. He says:—

"But the wife must only enjoy her husband's estate after his demise; she is not entitled to make a gift, mortgage, or sale of it"

And then, in support of that proposition, he refers to the second text cited, and proceeds:—

"Thus Katyayana says:—'Let the childless widow, preserving unsullied the bed of her lord, and abiding with her venerable protector, 'enjoy with moderation the property until her death. *After her death* 'let the heirs take it.'"

Mr. Justice Mitter, in his judgment, remarks at p. 41 of 13 B. L. R., that the author of the Dayabhaga cited that text, not for the purpose for which he cited that of Vrihat Menu, *viz.*, that of establishing a widow's right to succeed to the entire estate of her deceased husband, but for that

was based, whether upon custom or upon express law, or upon both, it is difficult to say. In the case

---

of defining the nature and extent of the interest which devolves upon her by virtue of that right.

In his remarks made on referring the case, however, he reasons upon it as an isolated text, and says (13 B. L. R., p. 16):—

"This passage shows clearly, not only that the widow's right is a mere right of enjoyment, the word 'enjoyment' being understood in the sense explained above, but that the exercise of that right is absolutely dependent on her 'preserving unsullied the bed of her lord.' *The participial form* of the word 'preserving,' *i.e.*, continually preserving, which is also the form used in the original (*palayanti*), proves conclusively that the injunction is one in the nature of a permanently abiding condition, which the widow is bound at all times, and under all circumstances, to satisfy; and the right of enjoyment conferred upon her being expressly declared *to be subject to such a condition*, every violation of it must necessarily involve a forfeiture of that right."

Mr. Justice Glover also, at page 57 of 13 B. L. R., expresses a similar opinion, and he refers to the present participle "preserving" as denoting continuance, and as referring to the time after the widow has taken the property originally; and he adds besides, if the words "keeping unsullied" refer only to passed time, what is to be made of the other part, which he assumes to import a condition, *viz.*, "living with her venerable protector." "She cannot," he says, "live with him until she is a widow, and "while she lives with him she is to keep unsullied her husband's bed." It is by treating the words "living with her venerable protector" as constituting a condition that he endeavours to add force to his argument that the words "keeping unsullied the bed of her lord" also express a condition. But that argument fails, inasmuch as it has been expressly held by the Privy Council, in the case of *Kashinath Bysack* v. *Hurrosundery Dossee*, Vayavastha Darpana, 97, and 2 Morley's Digest, 198, that the words "abiding with her venerable protector" do not create a condition of forfeiture in case of her refusing to abide with him. Referring to that decision, Mr. Justice Mitter says, that it lends in an indirect way considerable support to his view, inasmuch as that particular case was decided expressly upon the ground that the widow had not changed her residence for unchaste purposes. Their Lordships, however, are of opinion that the words "abiding with her venerable protector" do not, under any circumstances, create a condition or a limitation of a widow's right to enjoy the property of her husband to the period during which she abides with her protector. They agree with the Chief Justice in the opinion which he expressed at p. 82, that neither the words "preserving unsullied the bed of her lord," nor the words "and abiding with her venerable protector," import conditions involving a forfeiture of the widow's

LECTURE IV. itself, there was no enquiry as to the custom, if any, bearing upon the subject; that I think was a serious

---

vested estate; but even if the words were more open to such a construction than they appear to be, their Lordships are of opinion that what they have to consider is not so much what inference can be drawn from the words of Katyayana's text taken by itself, as what are the conclusions which the author of the Dayabhaga has himself drawn from them. It is to that treatise that we must look for the authoritative exposition of the law which governs Lower Bengal, whilst on the other hand nothing is more certain than that, in dealing with the same ancient texts, the Hindu commentators have often drawn opposite conclusions. Now how has Jimutavahana dealt with this particular text? It has been seen for what purpose he cited it; but how does he comment on it in the rest of the section in which it occurs? He comments on the words "venerable protector" (v. 57); he defines who are intended to take after the demise of the widow under the term "the heirs" (vv. 38 and 59); glances at her duty to lead an abstinent, if not an ascetic, life, and to avoid "waste" (vv. 60 and 61), and deals with her power of alienation, and the limitations upon it (vv. 62, 63, and 64). But he nowhere says one word from which it can be inferred that, in his opinion, the text implied continued chastity as a condition for the duration of her estate, or that a breach of chastity subsequent to the death of her husband would operate as a forfeiture of her right. It can scarcely be supposed that a commentator so acute and careful as Jimutavahana, if he had drawn from the text of Katyayana the inference that a widow was to forfeit the estate if she should become unchaste after her husband's death, would not have stated that inference clearly by saying, in v. 57, "let her enjoy her husband's estate during her life, or so long as she continues chaste," instead of using only the words "during her life" and stating that "when she dies" the daughters and others are to succeed.

The right to receive maintenance is very different from a vested estate in property, and therefore what is said as to maintenance cannot be extended to the case of a widow's estate by succession. However, the texts cited in regard to maintenance show that when it was intended to point out that a right was liable to resumption or forfeiture clear and express words to that effect were used. Jimutavahana, in Chap. XI, Sec. I, v. 48, of the Dayabhaga, refers to a text of Narada, in which he says,—"Let them allow a maintenance to his women for life, "provided they keep unsullied the bed of their lord. But if they "behave otherwise, the brother may resume that allowance." How different are those words from those used in the text of Katyayana.

Mr. Justice Mitter, in order to get rid of the argument that a daughter, becoming a sonless widow, or unchaste after having succeeded to the estate of her father, does not forfeit the estate, argues that the

omission. This was pointed out by Jackson, J., in his judgment.[1] As it is the decision in a case

LECTURE IV.

texts to which he refers are applicable to a daughter as well as to a widow, and he refers to v. 31, Sec. II, Chap. XI of the Dayabhaga to show that the text of Katyayana is applicable to all women. (*See* 13 B. L. R., pp. 45 and 46, 48 and 49.)

It seems clear, however, that though an unchaste daughter is excluded from inheriting her father's estate, or an unchaste mother that of her son, it is not by virtue of either of the above-mentioned text of Vrihat Menu or that of Katyayana. Those texts have reference to the bed of the deceased owner of the estate. The words, "his funeral oblation," and "his share," and "the property," have reference to the oblation, the share, and the property of the lord or husband mentioned in the preceding parts of the texts, whose estate is to be inherited, and not to the husband or lord whose estate is not to be inherited, such as the husband or lord of a daughter or mother, as the case may be, of the deceased owner, who, in default of a widow, may be next in succession to inherit his estate.

Verse 31, Sec. II, Chap. XI, only extends to other women the rule applicable to a wife, that a gift, sale, or mortgage of the estate is not to be made, and that after her death the heirs of the deceased owner are to take, and not that part of the rule which is included in the words "keeping unsullied the bed of her lord." This is made clear by s. 30, in which it is said:—

"Since it has been shown by a text cited (Sec. I, v. 56) that on the decease of the widow in whom the succession had vested, the legal heirs of the former owner who would regularly inherit his property if there were no widow in whom the succession vested, namely, the daughters and the rest, succeed to the wealth; therefore, the same rule (*concerning the succession of the former possessors'* next heirs) is inferred *à fortiori* in the case of the daughter and grandson (meaning a daughter's son), whose pretensions are inferior to the wife's."

Then comes s. 31, which is in the words following:—

"The word 'wife' in the text above quoted (Sec. I, v. 56) is employed with a general import, and it implies that the rule" (meaning the rule referred to in Chap. XI, Sec. II, and para. 30) "must be understood as applicable generally to the case of a woman's succession by inheritance."

Their Lordships have dwelt at some length upon the two texts that have been considered, since it is upon them that the arguments of the dissentient Judges are mainly founded. For the reasons above stated, they are of opinion that these texts, neither expressly nor by necessary implication, affirm the doctrine that the estate of a widow, once vested, is liable to forfeiture by reason of unchastity subsequent to the death of her husband.

[1] 19 W. R., 401.

LECTURE IV. among two blacksmiths residing in a corner of Assam, gives the law to the whole of the Hindu community residing in this presidency.[1]

The judgments of the High Court have so exhaustively reviewed the later authorities upon this question, that their Lordships do not think it necessary to go through the same task. It is sufficient to say that, in their opinion, those authorities, though in some degree conflicting, greatly preponderate in favour of the conclusion of the majority of the Judges of the High Court.

In their Lordships' view it has not been established that the estate of a widow forms an exception to what appears to be the general rule of Hindu law, that an estate once vested by succession or inheritance is not divested by any act which, before succession or incapacity, would have formed a ground for exclusion of inheritance.

The general rule is stated in the Viramitrodaya, a book of authority in Southern India (*see* 12 Moore's Indian Appeals, 466 ; and Mr. Colebrooke's Preface to the Dayabhaga), and which may also, like the Mitacshara, be referred to in Bengal in cases where the Dayabhaga is silent. It is there said, in para. 3 of the Chapter on Exclusion from Inheritance (Chap. VIII), " amongst them, however, an outcast (*patita*) and addicted to vice (*upa pátáki*) are excluded if they do not perform penance ;" and then in para. 4 the exclusion again of these takes place if their disqualification occur previously to partition (or succession), but not if subsequently to partition (or succession), for there is no authority for the resumption of allotted shares. In para. 5 it is said that the masculine gender in the word " outcast," &c., is not intended to be expressive of restriction, and that the law of exclusion based upon defects excludes the wife or the daughters, female heirs as well.

Mr. Justice Jackson has ably pointed out the great mischief, uncertainty, and confusion that might follow upon the affirmance of the doctrine that a widow's estate is forfeited for unchastity, particularly in the present constitution of Hindu society, and the relaxation of so many of the precepts relating to Hindu widows. The following consequences may also be pointed out :—

According to the Hindu law, a widow who succeeds to the estate of her husband in default of male issue, whether she succeeds by inheritance or survivorship—as to which *see* the *Shivagunga case*, 9 Moore's I. A., 604—does not take a mere life-estate in the property. The whole estate is for the time vested in her absolutely for some purposes, though in some

[1] The decision of the majority of the Calcutta Judges has been lately followed in two similar cases before the Allahabad High Court :—Nehalo *v.* Kishen Lal, 2 All., 150 ; Bhobani *v.* Mohtab Kuor, 2 All., 171.

Another obligation which the Hindu law imposed upon the widow was the obligation to reside with the

LECTURE IV.

Obligation to reside with the husband's family.

respects for only a qualified interest. Her estate is an anomalous one, and has been compared to that of a tenant-in-tail. It would perhaps be more correct to say that she holds an estate of inheritance to herself and the heirs of her husband. But whatever her estate is, it is clear that, until the termination of it, it is impossible to say who are the persons who will be entitled to succeed as heirs to her husband. The succession does not open to the heirs of the husband until the termination of the widow's estate. Upon the termination of that estate the property descends to those who would have been the heirs of the husband if he had lived up to and died at the moment of her death (Moore's I. A., 400).

If the widow's estate ceases upon her committing an act of unchastity, the period of succession will be accelerated, and the title of the heirs of her husband must accrue at that period. Suppose a husband dies leaving no male issue and no daughter, mother, or father, but leaving a chaste wife, a brother, a nephew, the son of the surviving brother, and other nephews, sons of deceased brothers. The wife succeeds to the estate, and the surviving brother is her protector. (*See* Dayabhaga, Chap. XI, Sec. I, v. 57.) If he survive the widow, he, according to the Bengal school, will take the whole estate, as sole heir to his deceased brother, and the nephews will take no interest therein, for brothers' sons are totally excluded by the existence of a b rother (Dayabhaga, Chap. XI, Sec. I, v. 5 ; *id.*, Chap. XI, Sec VI, vv. 1 and 2). The surviving brother may be advanced in years ; the widow may be young. The probability may be that she will survive him. If her estate were to cease by reason of her unchastity, the benefit which he would derive from her fall would give him an interest in direct conflict with his moral duty of shielding her from temptation. But, further, the widow has a right to sell or mortgage her own interest in the estate, or in case of necessity to sell or mortgage the whole interest in it. (Dayabhaga, Chap. XI, Sec. I, v. 62.) If her estate ceases by an act of unchastity, the purchaser or mortgagee might be deprived of his estate if the surviving brother of the husband should prove that the widow's estate had ceased in consequence of an act of unchastity committed by her prior to the sale or mortgage.

Again, if the surviving brother should die in the lifetime of the widow, all the nephews would succeed as heirs of their deceased uncle ; but if the son of the surviving brother could prove that the widow s estate had ceased, by reason of an act of unchastity committed in the lifetime of his father, and that consequently the estate had descended to his father in his lifetime, he would be entitled to the whole estate as heir to his father, to the exclusion of the other nephews. Thus the period of descent to the reversionary heirs of the husband might be accele-

LECTURE IV. members of her husband's family. On this subject the author of the Dayabhaga has quoted the follow-

---

rated by an act of unchastity committed by the widow; the course of descent might be changed by her act, and persons become entitled to inherit as heirs of the husband, who, if the widow had remained chaste, would never have succeeded to the estate; and others who would otherwise have succeeded would be deprived of the right to inherit.

In the case of *Srimati Matunginee Debee* v. *Srimati Jay Kali Debee*, 5 B. L. R., 490, the following remark was made by the then Chief Justice. He said:—

"In the case of *Katama Natchier* v. *The Rajah of Shivagunga*, 9 Moore's I. A., 539, it was held that a decree in a suit brought by a Hindu widow binds the heirs who claim in succession to her; but that can only be in a suit brought by her so long as she holds a widow's estate. It would cause infinite confusion if a decree in a suit brought by a widow could be avoided, if it could be shown that she had committed an act of unchastity before she commenced the suit. But if the rule contended for is correct, and the estate which a widow takes by inheritance is merely an estate so long as she continues chaste, all the acts which a Hindu widow could do in reference to the estate might be avoided by raking up some act of unchastity against her. Inconvenience would not be a ground for deciding a case like the present, if the law were clear upon the subject; but it is an argument which may be fairly adduced when the authorities in favour of the opposite view are merely the expressions of opinion by Hindu law-officers, or by European or modern text-writers, however eminent, or even decisions of a Court of Justice, when they are in conflict with the decisions of other Courts of equal weight."

Upon the whole, then, their Lordships, after careful consideration of this question, and of the authorities bearing upon it, have come to the conclusion that the decision of the majority of the Judges was the correct one, and it is important to remark that the High Court at Bombay, in the case of *Parvati* v. *Bhiku*, 4 Bom. H. C. R., 25, and the High Court in the North-Western Provinces, in the case of *Nehalo* v. *Kishen Lall*, I. L. R., 2 All., 150, have given judgments to the same effect as that of the Full Bench at Calcutta in the present case.

The widow has never been degraded or deprived of caste. If she had been, the case might have been different, subject to the question as to the construction of Act XXI of 1850; for upon degradation from caste, before that Act, a Hindu, whether male or female, was considered as dead by the Hindu law, so much so that libations were directed to be offered to his manes as though he were naturally dead. *See* Strange's Hindu Law, 160 and 261; Menu, Chap. XI, s. 183. His degradation caused an extinction of all his property, whether acquired by inheritance, succession, or in any other manner. Dayabhaga, Chap. I, paras. 31, 32, and 33.

ing text of Katyayana as authority: "Let the childless widow, preserving unsullied the bed of her lord, *and abiding with her venerable protector*, enjoy with moderation the property until her death." On this Jimutavahana says—"abiding with her venerable protector, that is, with her father-in-law or others of her husband's family, let her enjoy her husband's estate during her life."[1] It would seem from the text of Katyayana that there were two conditions precedent to the widow's enjoyment of the life-estate: first, she must continue chaste; second, she must reside with her husband's family, otherwise her right of enjoyment of the life-estate would cease. It has, however, been held in the case of *Kerry Kolitanee* v. *Moniram Kolita*, which has been quoted before, that chastity is not a permanent abiding condition to the widow's estate; in other words, the widow will not forfeit her estate by becoming unchaste.

Optional.

As regards the second condition it has also been held, on the authority of the answers of the Pundits, that the obligation to reside with the husband's family can be violated by the widow without at all jeopardising her rights of inheritance or other rights.

The opinion of Mr. Colebrooke in the *Trichinopoly case* is founded on the distinction between mere unchastity and degradation.

It is unnecessary to determine what would have been the effect of Act XXI of 1850, if she had been degraded or deprived of her caste in consequence of her unchastity.

Their Lordships, for the above reasons, will humbly advise Her Majesty to affirm the judgment of the High Court.

[1] Dàyabhaga, Chap. XI, Sec. i, para. 57.

LECTURE IV.

No doubt, it is clear that this obligation was founded upon the well-known principles of Hindu law, which declared the continuous dependence of females upon their male relatives: before marriage upon their parents; after marriage upon their husbands; and after the husband's death, upon their sons or other male relatives.[1] But one would suppose that when the ancient sages declared it obligatory upon the widow to reside with her husband's family, that they had some object in view in laying down the injunction so specifically. The interpretation, however, which the Pundits have put upon this passage, and which has been followed by the Courts, has rendered it perfectly optional with the widow to comply with this injunction or not. Whether this was owing to the prevalence of more liberal notions on the subject of family discipline which made an impression upon the otherwise conservative and orthodox Pundits, it is difficult to say.

Kasinath Bysack v. Hurrosundery Dossee.

The first case in which the question was raised for discussion, and upon which all the later cases are based, is that of *Kasinath Bysack* against *Hurrosundery Dossee.* The case came on, in the first instance, before the late Supreme Court, in 1814. The suit was brought by Hurrosundery Dossee, the widow of Biswanath Bysack, to recover, as a Hindu widow, the property belonging to her husband, from the hands of her husband's brothers. The Court having decreed the suit, the defendants applied for a review,

[1] Menu, Chap. V., v. 148.

among other grounds, assigning for error, "that it is not ordered by either of the said decrees that Hurrosundery Dossee should abide or reside with and under the care, protection, and guardianship of the complainants, who, as surviving brothers of Biswanath, are alone entitled by the Hindu law to the care, protection, and guardianship of his widow." Upon this the Court held that "the Pundits have uniformly answered that the widow was not bound to live with her husband's relatives. If a widow, from any other cause than for unchaste purposes, cease to reside in her husband's family, and take up her abode in the family of her parents, her right would not be forfeited. Here there was a good cause at the time, *viz.*, the extreme youth of the widow, and no pretence was made of the prohibited cause." LECTURE IV.

On the case coming up in appeal before the Privy Council in 1826, Lord Gifford, in delivering judgment, is reported to have said as folllows:—"With respect to the last supposed ground of error in this decree, which was assigned by the appellants,—*viz.*, that it was not ordered by either of the decrees that Hurrosundery Dossee should abide or reside with and under the care, protection, and guardianship of the appellants, who, as the surviving brothers of Biswanath Bysack, were alone entitled to have the care, protection, and guardianship of his widow,—the Pundits appear to be unanimous in the opinion 'that a Hindu widow is not bound to live with her husband's rela-

LECTURE IV. tives.' I will read the answer to the eighth question put, which will explain what the Hindu law is upon the subject; and in that, it appears, the other Pundits, who were called in, agreed, or at least they expressed no objection to the opinion pronounced. The question put is this: 'If a widow, for a just cause, ceases to reside with the family of her husband, does she thereby forfeit her right of succession to her deceased husband's estate?' The answer is: 'If a widow, from any cause other than unchaste purposes, ceases to reside with her husband's family, and takes up her abode in the family of her parents, her right would not be forfeited.' Now it was not pretended in the case that she had removed from the protection of her husband's family for unchaste purposes; she was only of the age of fourteen years at the death of her husband; his brothers were young men; and she thought it more prudent and decorous to retire from their protection, and live with her mother and her family, after the husband's death; therefore, it appears quite clear, from the answers given by the Pundits, that she did not forfeit the right of succession to her husband's estate, on account of removing from the brothers of her late husband; that they had no right to insist upon her not withdrawing from them, in order to put herself under the protection of her mother; and, therefore, there appears to be no foundation, to that extent, for the appeal."[1]

[1] Montriou's Cases of Hindu Law, p. 495.

The limitation in this case is important, that the widow must not leave the protection of her husband's family for unchaste purposes. The circumstance which weighed principally with the Pundits in this case was, that the widow had gone to live with her mother, a residence by no means improper. If the question had been put as to whether the widow had a prefect freedom in the choice of her residence, barring, of course, the prohibited case, I think their answer would have been in the negative.

In the case of *Oma Debia and others* v. *Kishen Moni Debia*, the question was raised "whether the plaintiff, the widow of Gobind Persaud Lahory, was debarred from suing for her husband's share of the property, by the fact of her having chosen to reside in the family of her father instead of in that of her husband." The Sudder Dewany Adawlut held: "On this point the decision of the Privy Council in the case of *Kasinath Bysack* v. *Hurrosundery Dossee* is, in the opinion of the Court, quite decisive as to the right of the plaintiff to sue."[1]

Raja Pirthee Sing v. Ranee Raj Kower.

The last case in which this point was raised was decided by the Privy Council in 1873, on appeal from the judgment of the Allahabad High Court. It is the case of *Raja Pirthee Singh* against *Ranee Raj Kower*.[2] The suit was to recover arrears of maintenance, and also to have a decree for future maintenance, by one of the widows of the late Rajah against his adopted

[1] 7 Sel. Rep., p. 323.

[2] 20 W. R., p. 21.

LECTURE IV. son, the appellant. Their Lordships first referred to the case of *Kasinath Bysack* v. *Hurrosundery Dossee*, and came to the conclusion "that a Hindu widow is not bound to reside with the relatives of her husband; that the relatives of her husband have no right to compel her to live with them; and that she does not forfeit her right to property or maintenance merely on account of her going and residing with her family, or leaving her husband's residence from any other cause than unchaste or improper purposes."

The contention was raised in the case that it is obligatory upon the widow to preserve her reputation, and that she preserves her reputation better by living with her husband's family than elsewhere. To this the Privy Council answered: "It has been held that the Hindu law does not require a Hindu widow, for the purpose of maintaining her reputation, necessarily to live with her husband's relatives. She does not injure her reputation by living with her own mother or her own father. It is laid down as a rule of law that she is not bound to live with her husband's relatives."

Effect of a direction in the husband's will to reside at a particular place.

If, however, the husband, by his will or otherwise directs that his widow shall reside in his family dwelling-house, and be maintained there, then non-residence on the part of the widow will deprive her of her claim to maintenance. In the above case it was pleaded in defence "that the plaintiff, disregarding her husband's honor, left for Kotah contrary to the terms of the will and the family custom." On this the Privy Council held, "there was no direction by the husband's will which rendered it necessary for the widow to reside in her husband's house." "The case of a widow is very different from the case of a wife. A wife, of course, cannot leave her husband's house when she chooses, and require him to provide maintenance for her elsewhere; but the case of a widow is different. All that is required of her is, that she is not to leave her husband's house for improper or unchaste purposes, and she is entitled to retain her maintenance unless she is guilty of unchastity or other disreputable practices after she leaves that residence."

In the judgment in the above case, their Lordships referred to the case of *Jadumoni Dasi* v. *Khetra Mohun Sil*,[1] in which it was held that the widow had perfect freedom in her choice of residence, and that by voluntarily quitting the residence of her husband she does not forfeit her right to maintenance. Sir Lawrence Peel, in delivering the judgment of the Court, said, "the question is, whether a Hindu childless widow, who, sometime after the death of her husband uncompelled by cruelty or ill-usage, left the house of the family of her deceased husband to dwell at first in the house of her own father, and subsequently with her aunt, living with her own relations, the

[1] Shama Churn Sircar's Vyavastha Darpana, p. 384.

LECTURE IV. residence being in all respects a proper one and her conduct unimpeached, forfeits her right of maintenance out of the property, which was that of her deceased husband in his life-time, and which had devolved on his heirs."

Referring to the case of *Kasinath Bysack* v. *Hurrosundery Dossee*, Peel, C.J., observed: "In the Privy Council the question was, whether the Hindu heiress forfeited her estate, by selecting without impropriety her father's roof for her residence. But it is to be observed that the opinion of the Pundits was generally expressed as to forfeiture of rights, and the Court expressed in general terms, that the widow had a right, under the circumstance, to select that residence, and could not be compelled to reside under the roof of her husband's family. This freedom of choice had respect to causes as applicable to a widow not an heiress as to one who inherited," meaning to say that the rule which had been laid down was equally applicable to a case of maintenance as it was to the case of property which the widow had inherited; that is to say, that she was entitled to a freedom of choice, and that unless she left the residence of her deceased husband for unchaste purposes, she could not be deprived either of the property which she had inherited from him, or be deprived of maintenance which the Hindu law requires the heirs of her husband to provide for her.[1]

[1] See also Surnomoyee Dossee *v.* Gopal Lal Doss, 1 Marshall, 497.

The result, on an examination of the authorities, may be summed up as follows:

1. The widow is not obliged to reside with her husband's family.

2. That she has a perfect freedom of choice in the matter of her residence, provided the residence be not improper or be not for unchaste purposes.

3. By the voluntary change of residence, or by refusal without any cause to reside with her husband's family, she does not forfeit her right to the property of her husband.

4. Nor does she forfeit her right to maintenance from the heirs of her husband, to whom her husband's property has passed on his death.

It is clear, therefore, on the above authorities, that the obligation of the Hindu widow to reside "with her venerable protector" has become a mere moral obligation, which the widow is at liberty to violate without incurring any forfeiture of her rights whatever.

It is difficult to say what the effect of the ruling in the case of *Kerry Kolitanee* will be upon the claims of widows for maintenance, who may be guilty of unchastity, or who may have left their husband's family for unchaste purposes. The Bengal High Court has ruled, that the widow who has inherited her husband's property does not forfeit the same by subsequent unchastity. It may be said that the right of maintenance being based upon nearly the

LECTURE IV. same considerations as the right of the widow to succeed, the former right will not be forfeited by unchastity, if the latter is not so forfeitable. The only thing, however, which distinguishes a right of maintenance from the widow's inherited property is that, in the case of the former, the person bound to provide for the maintenance of the widow may say that she is guilty of such improper conduct as disentitles her from claiming the same,—that is to say, the heir may be justified in refusing to furnish her maintenance on account of gross impropriety on her part.

The limitation prescribed in the cases of *Kasinath Bysack* v. *Hurrosundery Dossee* and *Jadumoni Dosi* v. *Khetur Mohun Sil*, that the widow shall not change her residence for improper purposes, seems to have been done away with by the recent case of *Kerry Kolitanee*. This last case has ruled, that if the widow is guilty of unchastity after the husband's death, she does not forfeit her estate. Now if actual unchastity does not entail forfeiture, why should a mere change of residence for unchaste purposes entail such a forfeiture. The result of the law now is, that if the widow changes her residence for unchaste purposes, her right of property or of maintenance is not at all prejudiced.

It is singular to trace the development of this branch of the law from the time of the case of *Kasinath Bysack* v. *Hurrosundery Dossee* down to the case of *Kerry Kolitanee*. If the Pundits who gave their opinion in the first case, knew that their opinion would be the foundation of the present doctrines on the subject, they would certainly have expressed themselves more reservedly, and they would have been very much surprised to find that the inferences drawn from their opinions would have led to conclusions so much opposed to their own convictions on the subject. The first case of *Hurrosundery Dossee* simply justified a change of residence by the widow to that of her parents; the next case of *Jadumoni Dosi* went further, it gave her a freedom of choice with one restriction only; and after the case of *Kerry Kolitanee*, that single restriction is also removed.

Obligation to perform the husband's *sraddha*.

Another obligation which the Hindu law imposed upon the widow, is to perform the *sraddha* of her husband. It is the general obligation imposed upon all heirs taking property under the Hindu law by succession to the late owner: the obligation to confer spiritual benefits being the measure as well as the test of succession. On this subject Vrihaspati[1] has thus ordained: "Taking his (husband's) effects, moveable and immoveable, the precious and base metals, the grain, liquids, and clothes, let her (the widow) cause the several *sraddhas* to be offered in each month, in the sixth, and at the close of the year." Jagannatha Tarkapanchanana, in commenting

---

[1] Quoted in the Dayabhaga, Chap. XI, Sec. i, para. 2.

LECTURE IV. upon the passage, says : " 'Let her perform the *sraddhas* in each month, and in the sixth and so forth,' the text should be so supplied. The double set of oblations must not be offered, because women are forbidden to perform this rite; consequently the *sraddha*, and honor shown to paternal uncles and the like being mentioned under the title of inheritance, she is only competent to the performance of those rites which are specified. But Chandeswara remarks,— 'some hold that a woman may offer the double set of oblations ; to forbid that, the legislator enumerates the *sraddhas* 'in each month, in the sixth and so forth.' By the word 'month' are suggested the *sraddhas* offered in twelve *successive* months ; by the term 'sixth' are suggested two *sraddhas* celebrated in the sixth month, one before the expiration of it, the other performed as usual; the term 'and so forth,' includes the first annual obsequies and the anniversary *sraddha* to be performed yearly; hence she must celebrate no other obsequies; else those other *sraddhas* must be authorised by other texts ; and this precept would be unnecessary.' "

Since a double set of oblations is offered in the first annual obsequies, Raghunandana and the rest hold, " that the performance of this rite by a woman must be deduced from a special text expressing that the first annual obsequies by *sapindas* and the anniversary *sraddhas* may also be performed by a woman."[1]

[1] Digest, Bk. V, Chap. VIII, Sec. i, comment on v. cccxcix.

LECTURE IV.

The commentator here was referring to the sixteen *sraddhas* which must be performed for a man recently deceased, *viz.*, the first on the day immediately following the period of mourning, twelve monthly oblations, one additional *sraddha* before the expiration of the sixth month, another before the end of the year, and lastly the *sapindakarana*, or the first annual obsequies performed on the anniversary of his death.

Effect of omission.

The widow is thus obliged by the Hindu law, taking the estate of her husband, to perform his *sraddhas*. Supposing the widow omits or refuses to perform any or all of these *sraddhas*, what will be the consequence? Will she forfeit the property which she has inherited from her husband? Can the next taker of the property, the reversioner, bring an action against the widow to deprive her of the inheritance, on the ground that she has failed in her obligation as a Hindu widow to perform the *sraddhas* of her deceased husband? These are questions which it is very difficult to answer. In the first place, the original authorities on Hindu law are silent on this topic: while they lay down very particularly the widow's obligation on this head, they nowhere lay down the penalty which she incurs by violating these obligations. At the same time it is not clear from the authorities whether the obligation is a mere moral one which the widow is recommended to comply with, or it is a legal one the nonperformance of which will prejudice her

LECTURE IV. legal rights. In the next place, there is no reported case bearing upon this point directly.

The case of *Kerry Kolitanee* v. *Moniram Kolita* may throw some light upon the subject, as being a decision upon a kindred topic. It has been held in that case that a widow guilty of unchastity after the death of her husband, does not forfeit her estate, notwithstanding the repeated injunctions of the *shasters* that the widow must "preserve unsullied the bed of her lord." In the case of a widow the estate vests in her immediately on the death of her husband, provided she is at that time not disqualified; she is enjoined to perform the *sraddhas* of her husband *afterwards*, the first *sraddha* following on the eleventh day, after death, among the Brahmins, and on the thirty-first day among the Sudras; she omits to perform that,—why should she, for that or subsequent omissions forfeit her estate, if subsequent unchastity, which is a violation of another obligation, equally imperative, does not entail such consequences. It cannot be said that the performance of the *sraddhas* is a condition precedent to her taking the estate, for the widow takes the estate immediately on the death of her husband, and the *sraddhas* are required to be performed at some future time; the inheritance does not remain in abeyance till the performance of the *sraddhas*.

Apart from the enjoyment of her husband's estate, which imposes upon her certain obligations, the other obligations of a Hindu widow may be enumerated as follows :— LECTURE IV.

1. The widow is bound to be strictly chaste.

2. She is bound to reside with her husband's family.

3. She is bound to perform her husband's *sraddha.*

The present state of the authorities, as based upon the reported cases on the subject, is, that the widow, by violating any or all these obligations, does not, in any manner, prejudice her legal rights over the property of her husband; that she cannot be deprived of the property which she has inherited from her husband even if she were guilty of violating all these several obligations; and it seems to me doubtful whether the next heir who, taking the property of the husband, is bound to maintain the widow, can refuse to give her maintenance in case of her violating all the three obligations; her right to maintenance is as much a legal right as her right to the property of her husband; and if she cannot be deprived of the latter on account of her violating those obligations, it does not seem reasonable to deprive her of the former on account of such infringement. In the case of *Kerry Kolitanee* the question of maintenance was incidentally raised; but the judgment of Chief Justice Couch, which was the judgment of the Full Bench, did not decide that point at all. Justice Jackson seems, however, to have held, that the "widow receiving maintenance loses her right thereto by subsequent profli-

LECTURE IV. gacy," and he says that the rule "is in accordance with reason and justice; for a man cannot be bound to feed misconduct in his own family, or to recognise a bond of union which the widow herself has trampled under foot."

Such is the present state of the law regarding the violations by the widow of her obligations. It seems probable that the ancient legislators did not contemplate results such as these, and reading the ancient authorities as a whole, it may be fairly observed that the present interpretation of the law is wholly repugnant to its ancient spirit.

LECTURE V.

THE REMARRIAGE OF WIDOWS.

Remarriage of widows believed to be forbidden in the *Kali Yuga*—Ishwar Chunder Vidyasagar's widow marriage tracts—Their effect upon the Hindu society—The text of Parasara authorising marriage of widows—How interpreted—The omission in this controversy—Custom prohibiting widow marriage in force at the time of the Digests—The Dayabhaga clear upon it—How did the custom originate—Act XV of 1856—The preamble—Sec. I—Sec. II—Effect of remarriage before succession opens—Sec. III—Secs. IV and V—Sec. VI—What is her *gotra*—Sec. VII—The Widow Marriage Act has not succeeded—The Hindus have not accepted it—The effect of a change of religion by a Hindu widow—Contradiction between Act XV of 1856 and the case of Kerry Kolitany—Widow marriage sometimes sanctioned by custom—The *Pat* or *Natra* marriage—Effects of a *Pat* marriage—Causes of extinction of title to property—Causes of degradation—Degradation will not extinguish title to property—Sec. 9, Reg. VII of 1832—Act XXI of 1850.

Remarriage of widows believed to be forbidden in the *Kali Yuga*.

ANOTHER obligation which the Hindu law and the Hindu religion imposed upon all widows, is to continue in a state of perpetual widowhood. It was believed by the learned in Hindu law, and by the Pundits, the accepted repositories of Hindu law and religion, that, in the present age (*Kali Yuga*), the marriage of a widow was prohibited in the *Shasters*; that, in the first three ages, there was no such prohibition; but that, in the present age (*Kali Yuga*), the

LECTURE. V. human race having degenerated from its original virtue and purity, the sages of Hindu law, for the benefit of the human race, by a sort of preordinance, declared that the marriage of widows in the present age is forbidden. This was the general belief of all Hindus, whether they belonged to the Pundit class or to the lay portion of the community; and no one ever for a moment thought that there was any error or heresy in such a belief.

Ishwar Chunder Vidyasagar's widow marriage tracts.

Nearly twenty-five years ago, this belief of the Hindu community received a rude shock. Pundit Ishwar Chunder Vidyasagar published his famous tracts on widow marriage, in which he attempted to establish the legality, according to the *Shasters*, of the marriage of widows. He told the Hindu community that their belief that the marriage of widows is prohibited in the *Shasters*, is a mistake and is utterly unfounded. Instead of there being a prohibition, there is a clear warrant in the *Shasters* for such a practice; and that the present practice or custom by which the widows are condemned to perpetual widowhood, is opposed to the direct injunctions of the *Shasters*, and therefore sinful. He thought that the Hindu society has been perpetrating a great wrong on a considerable section of its body for a long time, and he exhorted the Hindu society to do justice to that section of its body by acting according to the *Shasters* and allowing the marriage of widows. This was in substance the conclusion at which that illustrious scholar arrived after a careful examination of the *Shasters*.

LECTURE V.

Their effect upon the Hindu society.

These two tracts ran like wild fire among the orthodox Hindu community, and the Hindu society was as if galvanised. A fierce controversy was the result, which, among mild and low abiding Hindus, manifested itself in social ex-communications and family disunion, rather than in any political disturbance. The whole of the orthodox community arrayed itself against the conclusions of Vidyasagar. The really learned, as well as the pretenders to Sanscrit learning, all thought themselves called upon to refute Vidyasagar's arguments, and to defend Hindu law and Hindu religion, which they thought was seriously imperilled, from his heresy. The really learned were impelled by motives of earnestness and deep conviction, the pretenders with the object of gaining a certain amount of celebrity in having "broken a lance" with such an accomplished scholar as Pundit Ishwar Chunder Vidyasagar. The controversy produced a vast mass of literature in the shape of answers and rejoinders, which furnishes a considerable amount of curious reading. This mass of literature is characterised by shallow reading and puerile observations and arguments, though in some of them you find a good deal of independent research and really valuable learning.

The text of Parasara authorising

Pundit Ishwar Chunder Vidyasagar based his famous argument upon the now well-known text of

LECTURE V. — marriage of widows.

Parasara, which is the 27th verse in the fourth chapter of his Institutes. The verse runs as follows:—

नष्टे मृते प्रव्रजिते क्लीबेच पतिते पतौ ।
पञ्चस्वापत्सु नारीनां पतिरन्यो विधीयते ॥

He pointed out that the Institutes of Parasara was specially ordained, so says the sage,[1] to be the law for the present age (*Kali Yuga*), and that the Institutes of other sages constitute the special law for the other three ages. Consequently he argued, that a text occurring in the Institutes of Parasara must be held to be specially binding in the present age.

How interpreted.

The answers to Vidyasagar's tracts were, as I have said, numerous; some evincing considerable learning and research, while others only indicated superficial criticism. The substance of their arguments was, that the passage in Parasara, quoted by Vidyasagar, has no application to the present age, otherwise there will be a direct conflict between the passages in the other Smritis, by which the marriage of widows is prohibited. Another phase of the argument was, that the passage of Parasara referred not to the marriage of *widows*, but to the marriage of *betrothed* (वागदत्ता), girls whose would-be husbands are dead.

How far Vidyasagar's arguments were satisfactorily answered by his opponents, or he answered their objections, I do not pretend to determine. The

[1] Chap. I, v. 23.

result, however, like other controversies on similar subjects, was not decisive. Each party claimed victory for itself, and remained satisfied with the soundness of its arguments and conclusions.

The omission in this controversy.

There was one important point of enquiry in this controversy, which seems to have been overlooked by both sides, and which would have thrown considerable light over this abstruse discussion, and probably would have afforded a solution of the difficulty. It was admitted on all hands that the existing custom among Hindus prohibited the marriage of widows. Now when did this custom prohibiting the marriage of widows originate, and under what circumstances? If the custom originated *after* the promulgation of Parasara's institutes, I think it is clear that the custom came into vogue in spite of, and in a manner in supersession of, that text of Parasara. If the custom came into vogue *before* the promulgation of Parasara's institutes, then it is clear that the text of Parasara did not, or could not, affect or influence it. In either case the custom continued to exist, or came into existence, in total disregard of the text of Parasara. Then the question arises whether, according to the true interpretation of Hindu law, the text or the custom in contravention of it should be respected. If, however, this custom is entitled to the dignity of being called an *immemorial custom*, then it is "transcendent law, approved in the sacred scripture," and therefore must

LECTURE V.

be respected in spite of the text which is at variance with it.[1]

Custom prohibiting widow marriage in force at the time of the Digests.

That the custom is of long standing is, I believe, undisputed. Without attempting to construe the doubtful and difficult passages in Menu and in the other Smritis relating to the subject in question, I think it is clear that, when the great commentaries on Hindu law were written, the custom prohibiting the marriage of widows was in full force. Let us look at the Mitacshara and the chapters in it relating to the succession of widows and daughters. The discussion there excludes the possibility of the marriage of widows being then in vogue. This is particularly observable in the case of the succession of the daughter, for we find the childless widowed daughter succeeding last. She is postponed in favor of a married daughter.

The Dayabhaga clear upon it.

In the Dayabhaga it is still more clear. In Chap. XI, Sec. ii, which treats of the daughter's right of succession, it is laid down in para. 3 thus: "Therefore the doctrine should be respected which Dicshita maintains, namely:—that a daughter who is mother of male issue, or who is likely to become so, is competent to inherit; not one who is a widow, or is barren, or fails in bringing male issue, as bearing none but daughters, or from some other cause." You see, therefore, a childless widowed daughter is

---

[1] Menu, Chap. I, vv. 108 and 109.

excluded from inheritance by Jimutavahana. If the marriage of a widow was possible, there was no ground for excluding the childless widowed daughter, as by remarrying she might get sons who would benefit the late owner, and would therefore have been placed in the category of daughters who are likely to have male issue.

If the promulgation of the Mitacshara be placed at about 1000 A. D., or 1100 A. D., the custom would certainly be over seven or eight hundred years' standing; a long period certainly, and probably would entitle the custom to be styled *immemorial* according to Menu.

How did the custom originate.

Whether the custom originated in any authorised text in the *Shasters*, or in any approved Commentary or Digest, or whether it sprung up silently and was gradually adopted, remains uncertain. If it had some such origin as the latter, the state of society which could have favored the growth of such a custom must have been somewhat peculiar. There must have been something in the social condition of that society which must have rendered the marriage of widows highly inexpedient, otherwise a custom which is so unnatural, and therefore mischievous, could not have commended itself to the good sense of the society so as to lead to its general adoption. If the custom had a *shastric* origin, the question would be different: the law-abiding Hindus would observe it irrespective of its consequences.

LECTURE V. There is one thing remarkable in this controversy, which is this. The Smriti of Parasara is a well-known Smriti; it is so generally read and so widely known. How it is we do not find a discussion on the subject of widow marriage in any of the numerous writers on law and religion, who wrote after Parasara, attempting to establish the legality of such marriages on the authority of that text of Parasara, which has been quoted by Vidyasagar. As it is, there is a total absence of any such discussion in any subsequent work of authority, and it is not pointed out that that text of Parasara was ever, before this controversy, quoted as an authority to establish the legality of widow marriages in the present age *(Kali Yuga)*. The only author of reputation who has expressly commented upon this passage is the famous Madhub Acharyya, the commentator on Parasara Smriti. His opinion, however, is, that the text in question does not apply to the present (*Kali*) age. Vidyasagar has attempted to show [1] that Madhub Acharyya's interpretation of this text, as applicable to other ages than the present, is fallacious. How far he has succeeded in the attempt I do not pretend to determine.

Such is the state of the controversy, and the conclusions which can be drawn from it. No doubt, a certain state of doubt and uncertainty pervades the

[1] Widow Marriage Tract, 4th ed., pp. 34-47.

whole question. If the question had been attempted to be decided by an appeal to reason, rather than by an appeal to authority, there is no doubt as to what the conclusion would have been. LECTURE V.

The result of the controversy was, that a petition, largely signed by the supporters of Vidyasagar, was presented to Government to remove all legal obstacles to the marriages of widows, and the Legislature, in accordance with the wishes of the memorialists, enacted Act XV of 1856.

Act XV of 1856.

The Act is styled "an Act to remove all legal obstacles to the marriage of Hindu widows:" and the preamble of the statute is in these words :—

The preamble.

"Whereas it is known that, by the law as administered in the Civil Courts established in the Territories in the possession and under the Government of the East India Company, Hindu widows, with certain exceptions, are held to be, by reason of their having been once married, incapable of contracting a second valid marriage, and the offspring of such widows by any second marriage are held to be illegitimate and incapable of inheriting property; and whereas many Hindus believe that this imputed legal incapacity, although it is in accordance with established custom, is not in accordance with a true interpretation of the precepts of their religion, and desire that the civil law administered by the Courts of Justice shall no longer prevent those Hindus who may be so minded from adopting a different custom, in accordance with the dictates of their own conscience; and whereas it is just to relieve all such Hindus from this legal incapacity of which they complain; and the removal of all legal obstacles to the

LECTURE V. marriage of Hindu widows will tend to the promotion of good morals and to the public welfare, it is enacted as follows :"

If the marriage of Hindu widows was, by the existing law invalid, as the preamble declared it was, then the Act altered the existing Hindu law, and in that respect it was a departure from the position of neutrality which the British Government maintained with reference to the Hindu law and Hindu religion. If the marriage of widows was authorised in the *Shasters*, and therefore legal, then the legislation on the subject was superfluous. As it was, the Legislature was not quite satisfied that the marriage of widows was in accordance with the true interpretation of the precepts of Hindu religion, and it accordingly justified the law on the ground that it "will tend to the promotion of good morals and to the public welfare."

The first section of the Act reads in the following words :—

Sec. I. "I. No marriage contracted between Hindus shall be invalid, and the issue of no such marriage shall be illegitimate, by reason of the woman having been previously married or betrothed to another person who was dead at the time of such marriage, any custom and any interpretation of Hindu law to the contrary notwithstanding."

It simply removes the disability, and declares that the marriage of widows shall be valid, and the issue of such marriage shall be legitimate.

The second section of the Act is a very important one. It reads as follows :— Lecture V.

"II. All rights and interests which any widow may have in her deceased husband's property by way of maintenance, or by inheritance to her husband or to his lineal successors, or by virtue of any will or testamentary disposition conferring upon her, without express permission to remarry, only a limited interest in such property with no power of alienating the same, shall, upon her remarriage, cease and determine as if she had then died ; and the next heirs of her deceased husband, or other persons entitled to the property on her death, shall thereupon succeed to the same." Sec. II.

This section contemplates the case of the widow, the mother, the grandmother, and the great grandmother (four out of the five female heirs under the Hindu law) remarrying. Rights of inheritance or of maintenance, which the female heir possesses in the property of the late owner at the time of her remarriage, shall cease and determine upon her remarriage. But a right of property conferred by will, which is larger than the widow's estate under the Hindu law, shall not so determine.

Effect of remarriage before succession opens.

Supposing the widow remarries, and *after* her remarriage her son or other descendant dies, to whom she would be an heir under the Hindu law, would the fact of her previous remarriage preclude her from succeeding to such property? This question was raised in the case of *Okhorah Soot* v. *Bheden Barianee*,[1]

[1] 10 W. R., 34.

LECTURE V. in which the plaintiff claimed to succeed to the property of her son, who had died *after* she had remarried. Kemp, J., held, she was entitled to succeed. He observed that, "at the time of her remarriage, no rights and interests, either in the estate of her deceased husband, or in the estate of his lineal successor, the son, had become vested in the plaintiff; therefore, no estate in which she had any rights and interests ceased and determined upon her remarriage. After the remarriage the son died, and the estate which he inherited from his father devolved on the plaintiff, and under Sec. 5 of the same Act, *viz.*, XV of 1856, she does not by reason of her remarriage forfeit her right thereto." Jackson, J., differed from the judgment of Justice Kemp. He held that the plaintiff was not entitled to succeed, "as the policy of the law seems to be to prevent any further interference by the widow, after her remarriage, in her deceased husband's property, or as stated in the abstract of this section given at the head of that law, that the rights of the widow in her deceased husband's property are to cease on her remarriage."

Owing to this difference of opinion among the Judges, there was an appeal under the Charter. Peacock, C. J., delivering the judgment of the Appellate Bench, observed as follows:—"In the present case, at the time of her remarriage, the property belonged to her son, and she had no right or interest in that property. It came to her by inheritance from her son, who died after her remarriage. If the son had pleased he might have given the property to his mother notwithstanding her remarriage. At the time of her remarriage, she had no interest in her deceased husband's property by inheritance to her husband or to his lineal successors. It could not, therefore, cease or determine upon her remarriage, and if she had died at the time when she had remarried, the property would never have descended to her."[1]

Again, suppose in the Mitacshara country the mother then a *wife* succeeded to the property of her son, and subsequently became a widow and remarried. What will be its effect upon the property which she had inherited from his son? Would she forfeit it, or retain it, is a somewhat difficult question to answer.

As she did not get the property as a widow, it may be said she ought not to be deprived of it. On the other hand, it may be said, she was holding the property as a *widow*, and therefore, on her remarriage, she ought to be deprived of it by this section.

What would be the effect of remarriage upon the property of the widow which she had obtained on a partition among her sons, does not seem to be provided for by the Act. If it is not a right or interest which she has in the property of her husband by inheritance, or by way of maintenance, then she will

---

[1] 11 W. R., 82; *see* also Musst. Rupan *v.* Hukmi Singh, Punjab Customs, 99.

LECTURE V. retain it on her remarriage: but if it is considered as in lieu of maintenance, I think she will be deprived of it.

The third section provides for the guardianship of the children of the deceased husband on remarriage of his widow. It is as follows:—

SEC. III. "III. On the remarriage of a Hindu widow, if neither the widow nor any other person has been expressly constituted by the will or testamentary disposition of the deceased husband the guardian of his children, the father or paternal grandfather, or the mother or paternal grandmother, of the deceased husband, or any male relative of the deceased husband, may petition the highest Court having original jurisdiction in civil cases in the place where the deceased husband was domiciled at the time of his death for the appointment of some proper person to be guardian of the said children, and thereupon it shall be lawful for the said Court, if it shall think fit, to appoint such guardian, who, when appointed, shall be entitled to have the care and custody of the said children, or of any of them, during their minority, in the place of their mother; and in making such appointment the Court shall be guided, so far as may be, by the laws and rules in force touching the guardianship of children who have neither father nor mother. Provided that, when the said children have not property of their own sufficient for their support and proper education whilst minors, no such appointment shall be made otherwise than with the consent of the mother, unless the proposed guardian shall have given security for the support and proper education of the children whilst minors."

The fourth and the fifth sections of the Act are in these words :— LECTURE V.

Secs. IV and V.

"IV. Nothing in this Act contained shall be construed to render any widow, who, at the time of the death of any person leaving any property, is a childless widow, capable of inheriting the whole or any share of such property, if, before the passing of this Act, she would have been incapable of inheriting the same by reason of her being a childless widow."

"V. Except as in the three preceding sections is provided, a widow shall not, by reason of her remarriage, forfeit any property, or any right to which she would otherwise be entitled; and every widow who has remarried shall have the same rights of inheritance as she would have had, had such marriage been her first marriage."

It follows from this, that a daughter, who is a childless widow at the time of her father's death, will not, in Bengal, succeed to her father's property by the operation of this Act: she will not be considered in the light of a daughter who is likely to have male issue. But supposing a childless widowed daughter marries during her father's lifetime, she will, on her father's death, succeed to his property as a daughter likely to have male issue. That will follow from the second part of Sec. 5. It will follow, therefore, that of two childless widowed daughters of a Hindu, one who marries during her father's lifetime will be entitled to succeed to his property in preference to his sister who chooses to remain a widow, thus holding out a direct inducement to remarry and placing

LECTURE V. the daughter who chooses to remain a widow in a disadvantageous position. Why the Legislature should have made this distinction, it is difficult to see.

The real truth is, that this Act is a sort of compromise between the existing Hindu law and the wish of the Legislature not to change that law, but at the same time to legalise the remarriage of widows. The existing Hindu law is based upon the assumption that the marriage of widows is illegal: when such marriages are legalised, and made part of the existing Hindu law, the consequence is, that startling anomalies appear. The Act does not fit into the existing frame-work of Hindu law, in which there is no place for it.

Again, suppose a Hindu dies leaving two daughters, *A*, a childless widow, and *B*, having or likely to have male issue. In this case *B* succeeds to her father's property. Supposing the other daughter *A*, after her father's death, remarries, and has sons, and then *B* dies leaving sons. In this case who will succeed to the property? By Sec. 2 of the Act the sons of *A* are all legitimate, therefore, the correct view will be that the sons of *A* and *B* will both succeed to the property simultaneously. This involves an anomaly that the sons of *A* succeed to her father's property while she herself is *living*. The Hindu law does not allow the daughter's sons to succeed in supersession of their mother, who is living. There is a further anomaly in this, *viz.*, that the sons of *A*, who may be born *after* the death of *B*, do not succeed at all. LECTURE V.

The sixth section of the Act is in these words :—

"VI. Whatever words spoken, ceremonies performed, or engagements made, on the marriage of a Hindu female who has not been previously married, are sufficient to constitute a valid marriage, shall have the same effect if spoken, performed, or made on the marriage of a Hindu widow; and no marriage shall be declared invalid on the ground that such words, ceremonies, or engagements are inapplicable to the case of a widow." Sec. VI.

From this it will appear that the same ceremonies which render the first marriage of a woman valid will also be effectual in making the remarriage of a widow valid. A question might arise as to what is to be *gotra* of the widow at the time of her marriage. Is it the *gotra* of her father, or the *gotra* of her deceased husband? Pundit Ishwar Chunder Vidyasagar has pointed out[1] that, at the time of her remarriage, the father's *gotra* of the widow is to be mentioned as her *gotra*; and that a female, even after her marriage, retains the *gotra* of her father. This latter proposition seems opposed to the weight of authorities which declare that a woman after her marriage passes into the *gotra* of her husband, which from that time becomes her *gotra*. If Vidyasagar's proposition is correct, it will follow that the widow can lawfully remarry a person who belongs to her deceased What is her *gotra*.

[1] Widow Marriage Tract, pp. 165—172.

LECTURE V. husband's *gotra*, he not being her *sagotra;* and consequently she can lawfully marry her deceased husband's elder brother, or even her own father-in-law. There is nothing in the rules of prohibited degrees in marriages which can bar such marriages, if those persons belong to a different *gotra* from the widow. Thus marriages will be sanctioned between persons whose connection according to Hindu law would be considered as *mohapatuck*, great sin.[1] These difficulties are avoided if the widow is treated as still belonging to the *gotra* of her deceased husband.

The seventh section of the Act, which is the last section, is in these words :—

Sec. VII. "VII. If the widow remarrying is a minor whose marriage has not been consummated, she shall not remarry without the consent of her father, or if she has no father, of her paternal grandfather, or if she has no such grandfather, of her mother, or failing all these, of her elder brother, or failing also brothers, of her next male relative. All persons knowingly abetting marriage made contrary to the provisions of this section shall be liable to imprisonment for any term not exceeding one year, or to fine, or to both. And all marriages made contrary to the provisions of this section may be declared void by a Court of law. Provided that, in any question regarding the validity of a marriage made contrary to the provisions of this section, such consent as is aforesaid shall be presumed until the contrary is proved, and that no such marriage shall be

[1] Menu, Chap. XI, v. 59.

declared void after it has been consummated. In the case of a widow who is of full age, or whose marriage had been consummated, her own consent shall be sufficient consent to constitute her remarriage lawful and valid." LECTURE V.

This section enumerates the persons whose consent is necessary to render the marriage of a minor widow valid. In the case of a widow whose marriage has been consummated, her own consent alone will be sufficient. Now, seeing the very early age in which marriages of girls in this country are consummated, the propriety of allowing girls of such tender years to dispose themselves of in marriages, unrestrained by the wishes of their relatives, seems extremely questionable.

The Widow Marriage Act has not succeeded.

This Act, so important in its provisions, has almost remained a dead letter in the statute book, although it is passed nearly a quarter of a century ago. It is still a fact that very few marriages among the high caste Hindus have taken place in accordance with the provisions of this Act, and the consequence is, that questions bearing upon the provisions of this Act have rarely come up before the Courts for adjudication.

The Hindus have not accepted it.

The Hindu community at large has not accepted Pundit Ishwar Chunder Vidyasagar's interpretation of the *Shasters* as correct. It does not seem to be convinced by his arguments, otherwise I take it, widow marriages would have been ere long more frequent, and would have been by this time a well

LECTURE V.

established custom in the country. The movement would, probably, have succeeded better, if, instead of an appeal to the Legislature, which is alien in its constitution, a grand congress of the Hindus learned in the *Shasters* throughout the country, and representing all possible shades of opinion, had been called under the presidency of some of its respected leaders, and the orthodox nature of the measure had been established by the decision of such an assembly. Such a decision would have been, among the Hindus, what the decree of an Æcumenical Council is among the Roman catholics, and would have been accepted by the mass of Hindus as genuine *shaster*, and the social reform would have been carried out most successfully.

The effect of a change of religion by a Hindu widow.

The effect of a change of religion by a Hindu widow upon the property which she holds, becomes sometimes an important question. Act XXI of 1850 will save a forfeiture of her rights, which the Hindu law would otherwise have inflicted upon her.[1] If after her conversion she remarried, will Sec. 2 of Act XV of 1856 deprive her of the estate which she obtained as a Hindu widow ? The Bengal High Court answered this question in the negative.[2] There the Hindu widow had become a Mahomedan, and had *afterwards* married a Mahomedan. The reversionary heir of her Hindu husband sued for

[1] See *ante*, p. 162.

[2] Gopal Singh *v.* Dhungazee, 3 W. R., 206.

possession of the property which she obtained as a Hindu widow. The Court held, " that the Hindu law will not apply to the defendant, as it is found as a fact that, when she remarried, she was not a Hindu, but a Mahomedan. We are equally clearly of opinion, that the real principle to be kept in view is, that of equity and good conscience under Sec. 3, Act XXI of 1850 ; and that, under this principle, and that laid down in Sec. 9, Reg. VII of 1832, conversion should not involve forfeiture of inheritance."

The correctness of this decision is open to question. If the defendant in the case is a Hindu widow, she is subject to the disability of a Hindu widow after remarriage under Sec. 2 of Act XV of 1859. If she is not a Hindu widow, then she cannot continue to hold the property, which is given to her as a Hindu widow.

Contradiction between Act XV of 1856 and the case of Kerry Kolitany.

There is a singular contradiction between Act XV of 1856 and the case of Kerry Kolitany.[1] If a widow remarried she will lose her husband's property by Sec. 2 of the Act, but if she became unchaste, she will continue to hold the property. Therefore, a honest widow who from conviction remarries, is subjected to the forfeiture of her rights ; but a libertine widow is protected from similar forfeiture. Does not the decision in the case of Kerry Kolitany, as compared with Act XV of 1856, hold out induce-

[1] 19 W. R., 367.

LECTURE V.

ments to widows to become unchaste, rather than remarry under the sanction of law and religion ?

Widow marriage sometimes sanctioned by custom.

I have been considering up to this time the marriage of widows as authorized by Act XV of 1856. There are, however, certain classes of Hindus among whom the marriage of a widow was allowed by custom. These, I take it, will be governed by the custom on the subject rather than by the Act of 1856 ; as among them the remarriage of the widow owes its origin to custom, so the incidents connected with that marriage must be governed by the same custom.

I may mention to you, however, that the custom of remarriage of widows obtains only among the very lowest castes of Hindus. In the Bengal Presidency it is extremely doubtful whether a well recognised custom on the subject, at all obtains among any caste of the Hindus. Where instances are met with, they are found among the very lowest castes, and even among them, they are not treated as recognised unions, but as illegitimate and improper connections.

The *Pat* or *Natra* marriage.

In the other Presidencies, however, though still confined among the lower classes only, these marriages have obtained a recognised footing. Such marriages are called *Pat* among the Mahrattas, and *Natra* in Guzerat.[1] I may mention to you, however, that this kind of union is also allowed to women who

[1] Steele, pp. 26, 168 ; *see* Rahi *v.* Gobinda Valad Teja, I. L. R., 1 Bom., 97.

are *wives*, and who are separated from their husbands by a sort of divorce, which is allowed under certain specified circumstances ; as for instance, when the husband is proved to be impotent, or the parties continually quarrel, or where the marriage was irregularly concluded, or where by mutual consent the husband breaks his wife's neck ornament, and gives her a *char chittee*.[1]

Effects of a *Pat* marriage.

Where a widow enters into this form of a *Pat* marriage, she is obliged to give up all she inherited from her first husband to her husband's relations ; she is allowed to retain only what was given to her by her parents.[2] This is in the Bombay Presidency ; and the same principle has been applied by the Madras High Court to the case of the second marriage of a Maraver woman.[3] The custody of the children, except infants, also belongs to the representatives of the first husband.[4]

That such marriages are considered very inferior is clear from the social status accorded to a *Pat* widow. It is the custom among the castes that allow *Pat* marriages, that women forming *Pat* are excluded from preparing food at sacrifices and festivals, and from being present at the marriages even of their own children.[5] Though subject to these disabi-

---

[1] Steele, p. 169.

[2] Steele, p. 169 ; West and Bühler, p. 99 ; Hurkoonwar *v.* Rutton Baee, 1 Borradaile, 431 ; Treekumjee *v.* Mt. Laro, 2 Borradaile, 361.

[3] Murugayi *v.* Viromakali, I. L. R., 1 Mad., 226.

[4] Steele, p. 169.

[5] Steele, p. 169.

LECTURE V. lities, the children of *Pat* widows are never considered illegitimate. They are legitimate equally with those by their first marriage.

Causes of extinction of title to property.

I shall now explain to you the causes that will operate as an extinction of the widow's title to property. They are, as in the case of any other owner or holder of property, the following :—

1. By death.
2. By degradation.
3. By quitting the order of a householder.[1]

Causes of degradation.

A person is said to incur degradation (पातित्य) if he commits one of the five offences which are enumerated as great sins (महापातक),[2] *viz.* :—

1. Killing a Brahmin.
2. Drinking forbidden liquor.
3. Stealing gold from a priest.
4. Adultery with the wife of a father, natural or spiritual.
5. Association with such as commit any one of the above four offences.[3]

A person is said to quit the order of a householder, when he enters either the third or the fourth stage of a man's existence,—that is, when he becomes a *Vanaprashtha* or a *Yati*.[4]

The widow's title to the property of her husband

---

[1] Dayabhaga, Chap. I, para. 31.

[2] Brahma Purana, quoted in Digest, Book V, Chap. V. Sec. i, v. 323.

[3] Menu, Chap. XI, v. 55.

[4] Menu, Chap. VI.

would, I think, be extinguished by either of those three contingencies. In a case which is reported in Macnaghten's Hindu Law, Vol. II, p. 130, the following question was put to the Pundits :— LECTURE V. —

A person dies, leaving a widow and two sons of his brother ; the widow is living, but has quitted the order of a housekeeper, and retired from the world ; she had not executed any deed, either of gift or sale, in favor of her husband's nephews. In this case, are they entitled to the property by reason of the extinction of her temporal affections ?

To which the Pundits returned the following answer :—

If the widow has really relinquished her right to her husband's property, and quitted the order of a householder, her husband's brother's sons become entitled to the property left by her, notwithstanding the fact of her not having made any provision in their favor.

How far degradation from caste would be a ground for the extinction of the widow's title to property, is now a somewhat open question. Reg. VII of 1832 was passed, among other objects, for the purpose of determining the law that shall be applicable to suits between persons of the Hindu and Mahomedan persuasions respectively. Degradation will not extinguish title to property.

Sec. 9 of the Regulation enacted as follows :—

"IX. It is hereby declared, however, that the above rules are intended, and shall be held, to apply to such Sec. 9. Reg. VII of 1832.

LECTURE V. persons only as shall be *boná fide* professors of those religions at the time of the application of the law to the case, and were designed for the protection of the rights of such persons, not for the deprivation of the rights of others. Whenever, therefore, in any civil suit, the parties to such suit may be of different persuasions, when one party shall be of the Hindu, and the other of the Mahomedan persuasion, or where one or more of the parties to the suit shall not be either of the Mahomedan or Hindu persuasions, the laws of those religions shall not be permitted to operate to deprive such party or parties of any property to which but for the operation of such laws they would have been entitled. In all such cases the decision shall be governed by the principles of justice, equity, and good conscience; it being clearly understood, however, that this provision shall not be considered as justifying the introduction of the English, or any foreign law, or the application to such cases of any rules not sanctioned by those principles."

That Regulation was expressly ordained for the Presidency of Fort William. The Legislature, however, thought, that the principle contained in Sec. 9 of that Regulation, embodying a rule of toleration, ought to be extended over the whole of British India. The result of this conviction is embodied in Act XXI of 1850, which enacts (Sec. 1) as follows :—

Act XXI of 1850.

"I. So much of any law or usage now in force within the territories subject to the Government of the East India Company, as inflicts on any person forfeiture of rights of property, or may be held in any way to impair or affect any right of inheritance, by reason of his or her renouncing, or having been excluded from the communion of any religion, or being deprived of caste, shall cease to be enforced as law in the Courts of the East India Company, and in the Courts established by Royal Charter within the said territories."

Conflicting opinions have been expressed, as I have mentioned before,[1] as to the construction of this Act. The Bengal Sudder Court held,[2] that this Act only applied to the cases of loss of caste owing to change of religion. But that the forfeiture will not be saved if the loss of caste was owing to any other cause than a change of religion. Sir Barnes Peacock held a contrary opinion.[3] He thought that the forfeiture would be saved in all cases whether the loss of caste was owing to a change of religion or from any other cause. Peacock, C.J., followed the interpretation of the Act as given by Peel, C.J., in *Sornomoyee Dossee* v. *Nemy Churn Doss.*[4] Sir C. Scotland seems apparently to have put the same construction upon this Act.[5]

The current of authorities, therefore, is in favor of the proposition that the forfeiture of property will be saved whether the loss of caste is owing to a change of religion or from any other cause.

---

[1] See *ante*, p. 162.

[2] Rajkumaree Dosee *v.* Golabee Dosee, Sud. Dec. for 1858, p. 1895.

[3] Matunginy Debee *v.* Joykali Debee, 14 W. R., 31, A. O. J.

[4] 2 Taylor and Bell, 300.

[5] Pandaiya Telaver *v.* Puli Telaver, 1 Stokes, p. 482.

LECTURE V.

This protection from forfeiture, based upon Act XXI of 1850, was applied to the case of the Hindu widow by Sir Barnes Peacock, expressly dissenting from the decision[1] of Justice Markby, who held that the Hindu widow may forfeit the widow's estate on account of degradation or loss of caste for a sin which has not been expiated. The Full Bench, in the case of *Kerry Kolitany*, however, expressed no opinion as to the effect of Act XXI of 1850 upon the widow's estate in case she was held liable to forfeit the same on account of unchastity.

[1] Matunginy Debee *v.* Joykali Debee, 14 W. R., 23, A. O. J.

LECTURE VI.

THE NATURE AND EXTENT OF THE WIDOW'S ESTATE.

Widow's estate, its nature and extent—The authorities generally silent on this point—The Mitacshara—The Vivada Chintamoni—The Dayabhaga—Reported cases—*Kasinath Bysack* v. *Hurrosundery Dossee*—Widow entitled to possession—Of moveable and immoveable property of her husband—Her power of alienation—Conclusion—Sir F. Macnaghten's remarks on the judgment—Effect of the judgment as regards moveable property—The widow's power over moveable property in Mithila absolute—*Sree Narain Roy* v. *Bhya Jha*—Erroneous application of English law terms to Hindu law—Widow's estate is not the English-law life-estate—Form of decree declaring the widow's estate—The widow fully represents the estate—The *Sivagunge* case—*Nobin Chunder Chuckerbutty* v. *Issur Chunder Chuckerbutty*—What bars the widow also bars the reversioner—*Jodoo Monee Debee* v. *Saroda Prosunno Mookerjee*—Conclusion.

Widow's estate, its nature and extent.

I SHALL now explain to you the extent of the interest which the widow possesses over the property inherited by her. I have pointed out before, that it is now settled law in all the schools that the widow succeeds to her husband's property : in Bengal, under all circumstances ; in the other schools, according to the state of the family of which her husband was a member. But the authorities are generally silent as to the nature or extent of her rights, at least the subject has not been expressly and separately discussed. This omission is remarkable, and has been the cause of a considerable conflict in the case-law on

The authorities generally silent on this point.

LECTURE VI. the subject; for the great majority of cases in our Courts for nearly three quarters of a century depended upon the extent of her rights and the limitations to be imposed upon them. The omission probably arose from a consciousness on the part of the commentators, that the widow, living under the control of her relations, will not afford much occasion to them to complain of her acts, which it was thought would not be exercised completely independent of them or of their advice. That the acts of the widow would ever be exercised in such a manner as to justify hostile criticism on the part of the next takers was not contemplated; and that they would form the subject of appeal to the Courts of the country called upon to decide between the widow or her alienee and the next taker, was considered still more remote.

Unfortunately, however, in the present times "the relations of Hindu widows with the families of their deceased husbands are not always amicable, whose personal liberty is now, it may be said, wholly unlimited, and whose enjoyment of the estate not merely defers, but often seriously impairs, the prospects of reversioners."[1] As a consequence of this state of things, probably more cases come before our Courts for discussion of widow's rights than all the other cases upon Hindu law put together.

The Mitacshara. In the Mitacshara, there is no discussion whatever of the extent of widow's rights over the property

[1] *Per* Jackson, J., in Kerry Kolitanee *v.* Moniram Kolita, 19 W. R., 401.

inherited by her from her husband, and the Privy Council had to complain of this in their judgment in the case of *Bhugwandeen Dobey* v. *Myna Baee.*[1] LECTURE VI.

The Vivada Chintamoni.

The author of the Vivada Chintamoni has disposed of the whole subject in one short sentence. He quotes from the Mahabharata the following passage :—"For women the heritage of their husbands is pronounced applicable to use, let not women on any account make waste of their husband's wealth;" and adds,—"Here waste means sale and gift at their own pleasure."[2]

The Dayabhaga.

The author of the Dayabhaga is probably the only writer who has discussed the subject with anything like fullness. The subject occurs in Chap. XI, Sec. i, paras. 56 to 66. After establishing the proposition that the widow is entitled to succeed, he goes on to consider the extent of her interest over property inherited by her. He says :—

Para. 56.—"But the wife must only enjoy her husband's estate after his demise. She is not entitled to make a gift, mortgage, or sale of it. Thus Katyayana says,—'Let the childless widow, preserving unsullied the bed of her lord, and abiding with her venerable protector, enjoy with moderation the property until her death; after her let the heirs take it.'

Para. 57.—"Abiding with her venerable protector, that is, with her father-in-law or others of her husband's family, let her enjoy her husband's estate during her life;

---

[1] 11 Moore's I. A., 486. [2] Page 292.

LECTURE VI. and not, as with her separate property, make a gift, mortgage, or sale of it at her pleasure. But when she dies, the daughters or others who would be regularly heirs in default of the wife take the estate; not the kinsmen, since these being inferior to the daughter and the rest ought not to exclude those heirs; for the widow debars them of the succession; and the obstacle being equally removed if her right cease or never take effect, it can be no bar to their claim.

Para. 58.—"Nor shall the heirs of the woman's separate property as her brothers, &c., take the succession, on failure of daughters and daughter's sons to the exclusion of her husband's heirs; for the right of those persons whose succession is declared under that head is relative to the property of a woman other than that which is inherited by her. Katyayana has propounded by separate texts the heirs of a woman's property, and his text declaratory of the succession to heritage would be tautology; consequently heritage is not ranked with woman's peculiar property.

Para. 59.—"Therefore, those persons who are exhibited in a passage above cited as the next heirs on failure of prior claimants, shall, in like manner, as they would have succeeded if the widow's right had never taken effect, equally succeed to the residue of the estate remaining after her use of it upon the demise of the widow in whom the succession had vested. At such time when the widow dies or when her right ceases, the succession of daughters and the rest is proper, since they confer greater benefits on the deceased by the oblations presented by them than other claimants, such as the *sapindas* above mentioned.

Para. 60.—"Thus in the Mahabharata, in the chapter

entitled *Danadharma*, it is said,—'for women, heritage of their husbands is pronounced applicable to use. Let not women on any account make waste of their husband's wealth.'

Para. 61.—"Even use should not be by wearing delicate apparel and similar luxuries: but since a widow benefits her husband by the preservation of her person, the use of property sufficient for that purpose is authorised. In like manner, since the benefit of the husband is to be consulted even a gift or other alienation is permitted for the completion of her husband's funeral rites. Accordingly the author says, 'let not women make waste.' Here 'waste' intends expenditure not useful to the owner of the property.

Para. 62.—"Hence, if she be unable to subsist otherwise, she is authorised to mortgage the property; or, if still unable, she may sell or otherwise alien it; for the same reason is equally applicable.

Para. 63.—"Let her give to the paternal uncles and other relatives of her husband, presents in proportion to the wealth at her husband's funeral rites. Vrihaspati directs it, saying 'with presents offered to his manes and by pious liberality, let her honor the paternal uncles of her husband, his spiritual parents and daughter's sons, the children of his sisters, his maternal uncles, and also ancient and unprotected persons, guests, and females of the family.' The term 'paternal uncle' intends any *sapinda* of her husband; 'daughter's sons,' the descendants of her husband's daughter; 'children of his sister,' the progeny of her husband's sister's son; 'maternal uncles,' her husband's mother's family. To these and to the rest, let her give presents, and not to the family of her own father,

LECTURE VI. while such persons are forthcoming; for the specific mention of paternal uncles and the rest would be superfluous.

Para. 64.—"With their consent, however, she may bestow gifts on the kindred of her own father and mother. Thus Nareda says,—'when the husband is deceased, his kin are the guardians of his childless widow. In the disposal of the property and care of herself, as well as in her maintenance, they have full power. But if the husband's family be extinct, or contain no male, or be helpless, the kin of her own father are the guardians of the widow, if there be no relatives of her husband within the degree of a *sapinda*. In the disposal of property by gift or otherwise, she is subject to the control of her husband's family, after his decease, and in default of sons.

Para. 65.—"In like manner if the succession have devolved on a daughter, those persons who would have been heirs of her father's property in her default as her son, her paternal grandfather, &c., take the succession on her death; not the heirs of the daughter's property as her daughter's son, &c.

Para. 66.—"The widow should give to an unmarried daughter a fourth part out of her husband's estate, to defray the expenses of the damsel's marriage. Since sons are required to give that allotment, much more should the wife or any other successor give a like portion."

From the above passages the following propositions may be considered as established :—

1. The widow must enjoy the estate during her life.

2. The enjoyment must be by a moderate use of it.

3. The use should not be by wearing delicate apparel and similar luxuries.

4. She is not entitled to make a gift, mortgage, or sale of it.

5. But a gift or other alienation is permitted for the completion of her husband's funeral rites.

6. If the widow is unable to subsist otherwise, she is authorised to mortgage, sell, or otherwise alien it.

7. The widow is permitted to make presents to the *sapindas* and other relatives of her husband at his funeral rites.

8. With the consent of her husband's relatives, she may bestow gifts on the kindred of her own father and mother.

9. The widow is enjoined to give to an unmarried daughter a fourth part out of her husband's estate to defray the marriage expenses of the girl.

10. On the death of the widow the property goes to the heirs of her husband, and not to the heirs to her *stridhan*.

11. The property inherited by the widow dces not become her *stridhan*.

In the Viramitrodaya, you will find this subject discussed[1] at some length in Chap. III, Part I, Section 3; and the conclusion at which the author has arrived is thus stated:

"Therefore, it is established that in making gifts for

[1] Golap Chunder Sarkar's translation, pp. 136-141.

LECTURE VI.

spiritual purpose as well as in making sale or mortgage for the purpose of performing what is necessary in a spiritual or temporal point of view, the widow's right does certainly extend to the entire estate of her husband; the restriction, however, is intended to prohibit gifts to players, dancers, and the like, as well as sale or mortgage without necessity. Accordingly, the term 'being moderate' is inserted; the meaning is, that, on obtaining the property, she shall not uselessly spend the property. The passage in the Mahabharata on the religious merit of gifts, however, strongly supports our view, for it begins thus: 'It is ordained that the property of the husband, when devolving on wives, has enjoyment for its use.' Here enjoyment *(upabhoga)* signifies enjoyment allied to religious duty, not however vicious enjoyment; 'ordained,' *i. e.*, declared by Menu and others. In the latter half (of the passage) the very same thing is expressed, namely, 'women shall not waste,'—*i.e.*, uselessly expend the property of their husband; by the phrase 'on any account' it is intimated, that waste is, under all circumstances, reprehensible; *apahára* (waste) is theft,—making useless gifts to dancers, players, and the like, and the wearing of delicate apparel, &c., the tasting of rich food, &c., and the like, also being improper for a widow who is enjoined to restrain her passions, are equal to theft: thus the term *apahâra* (waste) is used in a secondary sense. But gifts and the like for religious purposes are not so, and consequently cannot be included under the term *apahára* or waste. Therefore everything is consistent."

Reported cases.

The reported cases on the subject have developed the law in almost all its branches; the development has been to an extent probably not contemplated by the ancient legislators. I propose now to consider the effect of the case-law in the development of the widow's rights. LECTURE VI.

The earliest, and probably the most important, case in which the nature and extent of the widow's interest came to be discussed, is the case of *Kasinauth Bysack and another* v. *Hurrosundery Dossee.*[1] In that case the plaintiff Hurrosunderi Dossee, as the widow of Bishwanath Bysack, sued her husband's brothers to recover possession of her husband's property, moveable as well as immoveable, from the hands of the defendants. The late Supreme Court held (East, C. J., presiding), that Bishwanath Bysack having died without issue, the plaintiff, as his widow, was, by the Hindu law, entitled to an interest for her life in the whole of his immoveable estate, and to an absolute interest in the whole of his moveable or personal estate. A bill of revivor was afterwards filed by the defendants, and the Supreme Court amended its decree by declaring "that the respondent Hurrosunderi Dossee is entitled to the real and personal estate of her husband, to be possessed, used, and enjoyed by her as a widow of a Hindu husband dying without issue, in the manner prescribed by the Hindu law." *Kasinath Bysack v. Hurrosundery Dossee.*

Against this decree of the Supreme Court, the defendants appealed to His Majesty in Council and the judgment was delivered by Lord Gifford. On the question of possession of the property, whether **Widow entitled to possession.**

[1] Montriou's Cases, p. 495.

LECTURE VI.

it shall be with the widow or with the next takers of the estate, his Lordship held thus :—"Whether we refer to them (books of law), or to the opinion delivered by the Pundits, I say, all of these authorities concur in the proposition, that whatever may be the extent of power and control over the moveable and immoveable property of the deceased husband, she is entitled to the possession of both, and cannot be deprived of it by the husband's relations."

Of moveable and immoveable property of her husband.

Referring to the distinction between moveable and immoveable property, His Lordship relied upon the opinion of the Pundit, which was this :—" According to the Dayabhaga and other *Shasters* prevalent in Bengal, there is no distinction in this instance between moveable and immoveable property; the widow has a life-interest in both; she has not an absolute interest in such property; and that she has a right to the possession of such property subject to the control of her husband's relations." His Lordship, accordingly, held, that, as regards " that part of the personal property in question which was in the Supreme Court, and which principally occasioned the litigation, instead of being there, had been in the hands of the widow, the appellants, as it seems, according to the Hindu law, could not have taken it from her."

The argument on the part of the reversioners objecting to the widow's possession as prejudicing their ulterior interests is thus answered by His Lordship:—"It has been argued, however, that if she have a limited interest in the personalty, she ought not to have the possession; but that it ought to be secured for those who may become entitled to it after her death, or what may remain of it, after having disposed of any part of that property in the way she is authorized to do by the Hindu law. But the answer to this argument appears to be this,—that is not the Hindu law, but, on the contrary, the widow of the deceased husband is the person who, by the law, is entrusted with the possession of that property without restriction; and no case has been produced to show that the right has ever been interfered with according to the Hindu law, or any attempt to dispute it in any Court of Judicature. We think, therefore, that the Hindu widow, by the Hindu law, is entitled to the absolute possession of the property."

Her power of alienation.

Regarding the power of alienation by the widow, the judgment proceeded to state as the result of these different opinions of the Pundits, that the widow "has, for certain purposes, a clear authority to dispose of her husband's property; she may do it for religious purposes, including dowry to a daughter, and making gifts and donations to the husband's family; but the Pundits differ in this: the Court Pundits say, that if she alienates the property for other purposes, without the consent of the husband's relations, it would be invalid; the others say, that though she would incur moral blame, if applied for

LECTURE VI. purposes not allowed, yet the act would be valid as against the relations of the husband; in that respect, the four Pundits differ from the Pundits of the Court, founding their opinion upon the doctrines contained in the *Ratnakara* and *Chintamoni*, not overruled by the *Dayabhaga* and *Dayatattwa*." I may observe here that the law on the subject as it has been held since by our Courts, makes the opinion of the Court Pundits correct, and that of the other Pundits incorrect.

Conclusion. The conclusion at which the Privy Council arrived in the case is thus stated in the judgment: "That the principle on which the Supreme Court of Judicature at Bengal has proceeded is the right principle, being that, in the contest for the possession of the property between her and the relations of her husband, she is entitled to the possession of the property; but that she is only entitled to enjoy it according to the rights of a Hindu widow, which rights, it appears to me to be absolutely impossible to define—I mean the extent and limit of her power of disposing of it; because it must depend upon the circumstances of that disposition whenever such disposition shall be made, and must be consistent with the law regulating such dispositions. Under these circumstances, therefore, we are of opinion, that the decree appealed against ought to be affirmed, resting upon the principle I have stated, which, as it appears to us, is the proper principle to be adopted in deciding this appeal."

As regards moveable property there will be considerable difficulty on the part of the reversioners in protecting their contingent interests against wasteful expenditure on the part of the widow. The property being in the widow's hands, which may be cash, it will be difficult, if not impossible, for the reversioners to follow it in the hands of third persons, to whom it may be secretly conveyed by the widow. Besides, the scale of her expenditure cannot be regulated except by her own choice and discretion, and moveable property may be consumed by such wasteful expenditure to which no limit can be prescribed, or restraint imposed, by the reversioners. The interests of the next takers are liable to be seriously prejudiced by intentional waste by the widow, or careless and extravagant expenditure causing waste. The case of immoveable property is essentially different; beyond the enjoyment of the usufruct, the widow cannot touch or otherwise affect it to the detriment of the reversioners, unless it be for allowable causes; and the next takers can easily pursue it in the hands of the alienees, and put them to the strict proof of the alienation being within the limited powers of the widow. LECTURE VI.

Soon after the judgment of the Privy Council in the case of *Kasinath Bysack* v. *Hurrosundery Dossee* was known, Sir Francis Macnaghten, in his Considerations on Hindu Law, pointed out the probable effects of committing moveable property to the custody of Sir F. Macnaghten's remarks on the judgment.

LECTURE VI. the widow in which she has only a life-interest. He observed :[1]—" If these females have life-interest only in moveable property, the probable consequences of committing it to their custody ought to be seriously considered . . . . Possession will enable her to do all the mischief before any restraint can be applied. . . . . Formerly a widow lived with the relations of her husband, with the very persons entitled to the property after her death. This was an effectual control over the expenditure, and a sufficient security for the expectants. We are still told that the family-house is her proper abode; that she ought to live with her husband's relations; but that she may live elsewhere without penalty, provided she does not change her residence for unchaste purposes. . . . . . If one be entitled to the immediate, and another to the ultimate, enjoyment of property, it is surely reasonable and just that they should have equal protection according to their several rights. It is admitted that the widow has a right for life to the *produce* of her husband's property. Supposing that property to consist of money, the question is, has she or has she not a right to possession of the principal ? Let us say that she has. It then becomes us to look back to the time when this right was conferred, and to consider the effect of the law by which it was accompanied. If we do so we may be satisfied

[1] Considerations on Hindu Law, pp. 93—97.

that the right was but nominal; that the possessor was under control; and that the expectant was invested with a power sufficient for his own security. One party being deprived of his security, is it consistent with reason or justice that the right, which was given subject to such security, should still be retained? In what respect is the widow aggrieved by a denial of possession? Without possession she will receive all she can lawfully use, but will be prevented from dissipating that which is lawfully to devolve upon another. By possession her right is not enlarged. It will give her the power of doing irreparable wrong. The reversioner's right is as well founded as that of the widow; and I think it will be admitted that the law ought to be so administered as to render it consistent with the preservation of both. . . . .

"Everything considered, it is not only reasonable, but indispensable, to the maintenance of right that these expenditures should be under some control; and where can this control be so properly placed as in Courts of Justice? Those who administer the Hindu law, ought to cast off their own prejudices, and attend to the usages which they are bound to regard. If they act in this temper, looking upon disbursements for religious purposes as necessary, and taking care that the next in remainder shall not be defrauded under a pretext of their performance, the rights and privileges of all will remain uninvaded.

LECTURE VI.

The reversioner must submit to all proper deductions; and simplicity will no longer be wrought upon by imposture to his prejudice. I admit, and in considering this subject I am bound to admit, that the purposes for which a widow may expend the wealth of her husband are religious. My own sentiments and opinions are quite out of the question; but if it be not denied that the interest of him in remainder is as well worthy of the law's protection as the interest of him in possession; if the right of both to their several interests be equal, they surely ought to be equally secured. It is impossible that rights can be contrary and opposite to each other; and to say that one has a right to a thing which another has a right to deprive him of, is absolute nonsense in itself, and in terms a downright contradiction."

The principal objection of Sir Francis that possession should not be made over to the widow seems reasonable and consistent with the maintenance of the rights both of the widow and of the next takers; but it seems to have been answered by Lord Gifford in the judgment, where he said that the objection cannot be supported in Hindu law by which the possession of the property is entrusted to the widow without restriction. The practical effect of the decision, however, has been to give a certain amount of unrestrained liberty to the widow in the enjoyment of moveable property. Conscious of the difficulty that there is in the way of the reversioners in impeach-

Effect of the judgment as regards moveable property.

ing acts of waste, the widow often secretly, but sometimes openly, disposes of moveable property in a wasteful manner; and the reversioners seldom or never interfere, by legal means, to impeach the widow's acts of waste regarding moveable property either during her lifetime or after her death. The result is, that actions by reversioners to follow moveable property in the hands of the assignees of the widow are very rare; and a conviction has almost sprung up, supposed to be founded upon Hindu law, that the widow has absolute interest in moveable property. As pointed out, however, in the judgment, in *Bengal*, there is no difference in the widow's powers over moveable as distinguished from immoveable property; in both kinds of property the widow's interest is the same.

The widow's power over moveable property in Mithila absolute.

In the country governed by the doctrines of the Mithila school, a distinction obtains—the widow is held there to have absolute powers of disposal over moveable property, and to possess a qualified interest over immoveable property. This doctrine is laid down in the *Vivada Ratnakara* and in the *Vivada Chintamoni*.

***Sree Narain Roy* v. *Bhya Jha*.**

In the case of *Sree Narain Roy and another* v. *Bhya Jha*,[1] amongst other points of considerable importance in Hindu law, the power of a Hindu widow over the property inherited by her from her

[1] 2 Sel. Rep., p. 29.

LECTURE VI.

husband was discussed. The Pundits of the Sudder Dewany Adawlut were consulted as to the legal competency of a Hindu widow "to make a donation of the estate, moveable and immoveable, which devolved on her on the death of her husband, of the profits of that estate during her possession, and of any landed property purchased by her out of such profits." The Pundits answered, that "the widow was not competent to make a donation of any landed property without the express consent in writing of her husband's heirs and relations; but that she might make a gift, without their consent, of moveable property of every description excepting slaves; but that in all gifts it is made a condition, that half the husband's property be reserved for the due performance of his periodical obsequies." A further question was put to the Pundits as to "whether the Ranee, who is stated to have been competent to make a donation of the moveable property inherited from her husband and the moveable property arising from the profits of her husband's landed estate, equally competent to make a bequest of such property in favor of Bhya Jha, to take effect after her death?" To this the Pundits returned the following answer, *viz.*:—"That the bequest of the Ranee would be valid to convey to Bhya Jha all the moveable property possessed by her and all her *stridhan*; but not the immoveable property, except what might be hers peculiarly. For the Ranee was not authorised to transfer such immoveable property by gift, and although there is no text in which the case of a bequest is expressly mentioned, yet the same rule applies to bequests as to gifts; every person who has authority while in health to transfer property to another, possesses the same authority of bequeathing it." LECTURE VI.

Sir E. Hyde East, in delivering the judgment in the case of *Hurrosundery Dossee* v. *Kasinath Bysack*, in 1819, says, that he has seen the judgment of the Sudder Dewany Adawlut in the case of *Bhya Jha*, from which he quotes as follows:—"From these passages of most undoubted authority (quoted from the *Ratnakara* and the *Chintamoni*) it is evident that the widow has power to consume, or to give or to sell in her lifetime, the moveables which may have devolved upon her by the death of her husband, but has no power over the immoveables beyond a moderate and frugal enjoyment of them; after her death the estate which she enjoyed frugally during her lifetime shall pass to the heirs of her husband."[1]

The case of *Bhya Jha* arose in that part of the country which is governed by the doctrines of the Mithila school, and the judgment in that case was expressly put upon the authorities current in Mithila; this decision, therefore, is no authority for Bengal Proper.

The widow is entitled to enjoy the property in-

[1] Shama Churn Sircar's Vyavastha Durpun, 2nd Edition, p. 91.

herited by her during the period of her natural life, and the enjoyment is limited to the appropriation by her of the usufruct of that property. The widow's estate has, accordingly, been usually called a life-estate, and she a life-tenant, comparing her estate to the estate of a tenant for life in English law. No doubt, there is some analogy between the English law estate of a tenant for life and the Hindu widow's estate; the analogy consisting in this, *viz.*, that both are enjoyable for a certain life, and determinable at the end of that life; but the analogy stops here, and the incidents attaching to the two estates are widely different. The use, therefore, of English law expressions to denote estates in Hindu law, and particularly the widow's estate, is apt to create confusion and to give rise to misconceptions in the mind of those who are unacquainted with the nature and incidents of the English law estate.

Erroneous application of English law terms to Hindu law.

This source of error has been pointed out in several judgments both of the Privy Council and of the Courts in this country. In the case of *The Collector of Masulipatam* v. *C. V. Narainapah*[1] their Lordships of the Privy Council said as follows :—" It was justly observed in the course of the argument with reference to those authorities which speak of the widow's interest as a life-estate, that great confusion arises from applying analogies derived from the

[1] 8 Moore's I. A., p. 529; the quotation is from p. 550.

English law of real property to the Hindu law of inheritance; and that when so applied, the terms by which we describe estates in land under the English law are more likely to mislead than to direct the judgment aright. It may, however, be doubted whether the argument on behalf of the respondent does not really require some such process of reasoning to support it. The Hindu widow, it was urged, has an estate of inheritance, not a life-estate; the original estate, it is said, devolves on her in a course of succession derived from the husband, who had in him an estate of inheritance, which she takes as heir. Yet what is this in effect, but to apply the English law regulating the descent of lands in fee-simple from ancestor to heir?

"It is clear that, under the Hindu law, the widow, though she takes as heir, takes a special and qualified estate. Compared with any estate that passes under the English law by inheritance it is an anomalous estate. It is a qualified proprietorship, and it is only by the principle of the Hindu law that the extent and nature of the qualification can be determined."

In the case of *Tagore* v. *Tagore*[1] the caution has been extended further; and error is considered likely to be the result by adopting English law *notions*, and making them applicable directly or indirectly to conceptions arising under the Hindu law. Their

[1] 18 W. R., 359.

LECTURE VI. Lordships observed :[1]—" The questions presented by this case must be dealt with and decided according to the Hindu law prevailing in Bengal, to which alone the property in question is subject. Little or no assistance can be derived from English rules touching the transfer of property or the right of inheritance or succession thereto. Various complicated rules which have been established in England, are wholly inapplicable to the Hindu system in which property, whether moveable or immoveable, is, in general, subject to the same rule of gift or will, or to the same course of inheritance. The law of England, in the absence of custom, adopts the law of primogeniture as to inheritable freeholds, and a distribution amongst the nearest of kin as to personalty, a distinction not known in Hindu law. The only trace of religion in the history of the law of succession in England, is the trust formerly reposed in the church to administer personal property (*Tyler* v. *Walford*, 5 Moore, P. C., 304). In the Hindu law of inheritance, on the contrary, the heir or heirs are selected who are most capable of exercising those religious rites which are considered to be beneficial to the deceased." Two systems of law that are derived from, or have come into existence under, a widely different set of antecedents, intended for races essentially different from each

[1] 18 W. R., p. 364.

other, and originating at times widely remote from each other, can hardly possess many conceptions in common between themselves. Such is Hindu law as compared with English law.

In the case of *Goluck Money Debee* v. *Digumber Dey*,[1] the question, whether the widow takes, in the property of her husband, a mere life-estate or an estate of inheritance, was very much discussed. It was held in that case that the widow's estate cannot be properly compared to either of those estates; it was in fact an anomalous estate, the creation of Hindu law. The whole law on this subject is exhaustively discussed in the judgment of Peel, C. J., which has furnished the law in all the subsequent cases in which this point has been raised and decided. Peel, C. J., said :—"It was contended by Mr. Theobald, that the estate of the Hindu widow, when she takes as heir, is a life-estate; he asserted that this has been laid down or decided by authorities which the Court is bound to follow. There is always danger of error in proceeding upon rules or terms of one body of law whilst applying a different law. If by life-estate is meant an estate of the same nature and involving the same consequence as the life-estate known to the English law, then it is clear that the estate of a Hindu widow taking as heir is not that estate, and differs impor-

Widow's estate is not the English-law life-estate.

[1] 2 Boulnois' Rep., 193.

LECTURE VI. tantly from it. If the argument means not that, it in no way affects the decision of this question. It is perfectly true that, in several treatises of learning, and in some decisions of this Court as well as of the Sudder Dewany Adawlut, and that in some former decrees of this Court, the estate of a Hindu female is termed a life-estate. This description, though not strictly correct, is sufficiently so for the purposes for which it has from time to time been made. Neither in those treatises, nor in those decisions or decrees, was it necessary to consider or decide as to the exact value of that estate, nor whether it strictly resembled a life-estate by the English law. The phrase was used with relation to the limits on the power of alienation. It is, undoubtedly, true that her heirs as such have no capacity to inherit the estate; but if they succeed to it at all, they succeed as heirs of the immediately prior owner to whom she succeeded as heir, and in this view the estate is not in all fours with one of inheritance, and more, so far as this want of capacity goes, resembles some cases under the English law, where the party takes a life-estate by Act of law, or where, by some after circumstances, one becomes substantially a tenant for life, who had the inheritance in him, but from whom heirs can no longer proceed. It is obvious that the mere inability to convey away an estate is not repugnant to its being an estate of inheritance. I need only refer to estates-tail till the power of unfettering them was overruled, to show that there is no such repugnancy. But the want, as it were, of heritable blood in the widow, the owner, to use a phrase of the English law, in other words, the quality in the estate in the hands of such owner, that it will not go to any heir as heir of her, prevents it from being viewed as an estate corresponding to an estate of inheritance under the English law; whilst her ability to convey an estate or interest equivalent to a fee-simple, and as fully as any fully-capacitated owner can convey, makes it larger than and dissimilar to the estates to which I have before referred; which either in their original nature or by subsequent events were reduced to life-estates in substance. It is in truth an anomalous estate."

The Chief Justice, quoting the case of *Kasinath Bysack* v. *Hurrosundery Dossee*, further pointed out that the first decree of the Court was, that the widow took an *interest for her life* in the immoveable property of her husband, and an absolute interest in the moveable; that on rehearing, the previous decree was expressly rectified, and the declaration made in the following manner:—that "she should be declared entitled to the real and personal estate of her husband, to be possessed, used, and enjoyed by her as a widow of a Hindu husband, dying without issue, in the manner prescribed by the Hindu law." This decree, as I have mentioned before, was confirmed by the Privy Council. Since that decision the decrees of

Form of decree declaring the widow's estate.

the late Supreme Court and of the present High Court in its Original Civil Jurisdiction, in which it is necessary to declare what interest the widow takes, have been in conformity to it.

The widow fully represents the estate.

The Chief Justice further observed : "The course of proceeding as to parties has been in strict conformity to it, for it has been invariably considered, for many years, that the widow fully represents the estate; and it is also the settled law that adverse possession which bars her, bars the heir after her, which would not be the case if she were a mere tenant for life as known to the English law: on the contrary, if such were her estate, her heir would have twenty years after her death for making his entry, which would be a most mischievous rule to establish."

In the case of *Phool Ch. Dutt* v. *Rughoobhun Suhoye*,[1] Peacock, C.J., said :—"The widow takes a widow's estate by inheritance from her husband. It is not an absolute estate for all purposes, and it is not merely an estate for life, but she takes the estate of her husband for the benefit of her deceased husband, which includes her own maintenance and the performance of her religious duties, rather than for the benefit of those who may become the heirs of her husband upon her death."

The Sivagunga case.

In the case of *Katama Natchiar* v. *The Rajah of Sivagunga*,[2] it became necessary, among other things,

[1] 9 W. R., 108. [2] 9 Moore, 539.

to determine the effect upon the reversionary heirs of a decree obtained against the widow. In that case the widow of the Rajah had brought a suit for possession of her husband's zemindary, and had died during the prosecution of the appeal. The appellant in the case, one of the daughters of the Rajah, applied to be substituted in the appeal in the place of the deceased appellant. Her application was refused, the appeal was struck off, and she was directed to bring a fresh suit to establish her rights. She, accordingly, brought a new suit, and the defendant pleaded the former judgment in appeal as a bar. Both the Courts in India held, that the previous judgment in appeal, which was struck off, was a bar; and the plaintiff, accordingly, appealed to the Privy Council. On this point their Lordships are reported to have said as follows:[1]—"It seems, however, to be necessary, in order to determine the mode in which this appeal ought to be disposed of, to consider the question whether the decree of 1847, if it had become final in Unga Motoo Natchiar's lifetime, would have bound those claiming the zemindary in succession to her. And their Lordships are of opinion that, unless it could be shown that there had not been a fair trial of the right in that suit, or in other words, unless that decree could have been successfully impeached on some special grounds, it would have been

[1] 9 Moore, 603.

LECTURE VI. an effectual bar to any new suit in the Zillah Court by any person claiming in succession to Unga Motoo Natchiar. For, assuming her to be entitled to the zemindary at all, the whole estate would, for the time, be vested in her absolutely for some purposes, though in some respects, for a qualified interest ; and until her death it could not be ascertained who would be entitled to succeed. The same principle which has prevailed in the Courts of this country as to tenants-in-tail representing the inheritance, would seem to apply to the case of a Hindu widow, and it is obvious that there would be the greatest possible inconvenience in holding that the succeeding heirs were not bound by a decree fairly and properly obtained against the widow."

Their Lordships in this judgment maintained the same principle that was decided by Sir Lawrence Peel in the case of *Goluck Monee Debee* v. *Digumber Day, viz.*, that a Hindu widow fully represents the estate of her husband in her hands, and that whatever act would bar the widow, would also bar the reversioners in succession to her.

Nobin Chunder Chuckerbutty v. *Issur Chunder Chuckerbutty.*

In the case of *Nobin Chunder Chuckerbutty* v. *Issur Chunder Chuckerbutty*,[1] the facts were these : During the lifetime of the widow, a stranger had taken possession of the property, and the widow never recovered possession. The widow died in 1266, and the

[1] 9 W. R., 505.

reversioner brought a suit for possession against the stranger, basing his cause of action from the widow's death in 1266. It was contended for the defendant that the cause of action would date from the date of dispossession of the widow, and limitation would commence to run from that date against the reversioner as it would against the widow. Peacock, C.J., relying upon the case of *Goluck Monee Debee* v. *Digumber Day* and the *Sivagunga* case, came to the conclusion, that limitation would count against the reversioner from the date of dispossession of the widow, and that he would have no new cause of action from the date of the widow's death. He held, that whatever would bar the widow would also bar the reversioner. The Chief Justice further said :[1]—"If, then, in the *Sivagunga* case the widow was like a tenant-in-tail, and the reversionary heirs were like the issue-in-tail, and the same likeness exists in the present case, the reversionary heirs would be barred by limitation which ran against the female heir. If the female heir in the present case had sued the wrong-doer, and without fraud or collusion had failed to make out her case to turn him out of possession, the reversionary heirs would have been bound by the decision. I am assuming that they are not claiming through the female heir."

"For instance, if the female heir had sued the

[1] 9 W. R., 507.

LECTURE VI.

wrong-doer and he had set up a purchase from the ancestor, and had succeeded in that defence at the suit of the female heir, the reversionary heirs would be barred by the decision in the absence of fraud or collusion."

What bars the widow also bars the reversioner.

And the conclusion of the Chief Justice is thus stated :[1]— "These considerations lead me to the conclusion that a reversionary heir, who is bound by a decision against the widow respecting the subject-matter of inheritance, is also barred by limitation, if without fraud or collusion the widow is barred by limitation."[2] This view of the law was confirmed by their Lordships of the Privy Council in two recent cases.[3]

The result of this decision is, that although the reversioner has no right of possession during the widow's lifetime, he may be barred, nevertheless, during that period, if the widow lived for twelve years or more after the date of dispossession. This would be very unjust as against the reversioners, if without the possibility of a remedy their rights were likely to be barred. Accordingly, it is necessary to determine whether the reversioners can bring a suit against the widow and the adverse holder to reduce

---

[1] 9 W. R., 508.

[2] The judgment in this case expressly overrules the decision of the late Supreme Court in the case of Kally Doss Bose *v.* Deb Narain Kobiraj, Fulton's Rep., 329.

[3] Amrito Loll Bose *v.* Rojoni Kant Mitter, 23 W. R., 214, and Mussamut Bhogbuti Daye *v.* Chowdry Bhola Nath Takoor and others, 24 W. R., 168.

the estate into possession during the widow's lifetime. The Chief Justice saw that the necessary consequence of holding that the reversioner would be barred during the widow's lifetime, would be to declare that a suit like the above would be maintainable at his instance, and he accordingly said :—"But reversionary heirs presumptive have a right, although they may never succeed to the estate, to prevent the widow from committing waste; and I have no doubt if a proper case were made out, reversionary heirs would have a sufficient interest as well as creditors of the ancestor by suit against the widow and the adverse holder, to have the estate reduced into possession so as to prevent their rights from becoming barred by limitation."

Now, before the decision in this case, it does not appear that it was ever held in any case that the reversioners could bring a suit like the one suggested by the Chief Justice, and the general opinion was that such a suit was not maintainable; and it appears that the other members of the Full Bench did not assent to all the observations of the Chief Justice, but simply concurred in the answer which was given to the question referred to the Full Bench for decision; and I believe the observation of the Chief Justice with reference to the suit by the reversioner as suggested by him, was one of those to which the other Judges constituting the Full Bench did not like to pledge themselves expressly. Whatever may be the

LECTURE VI.

reservations with which the other Judges of the Full Bench may have answered the question put to them, it is clear that after this case it must be held that the reversioner possesses the right of bringing an action of the kind suggested by the Chief Justice.

This dictum of the Chief Justice was followed by the High Court in the case of *Radhamohun Dhur* v. *Ramdoss Dey*,[1] where it was held, that the reversioner had the right of bringing a suit against the widow and the adverse holder for the purpose of having the estate reduced into proper possession. The High Court directed that the possession of the property so recovered shall not be given to the reversioner: but that a manager appointed by the Court shall take charge of the property, who shall account, to the Court, for all the rents and profits, and the Court shall hold the same for the benefit of the heirs who may happen to succeed on the death of the widow.

Jodoo Monee Debee v. *Saroda Prosunno Mukerjee.*

In the case of *Jodoo Monee Debee* v. *Saroda Prosunno Mukerjee* and others,[2] the nature and extent of the widow's interest was the subject of much discussion. Colvile, C. J., said :—" But the estate of a Hindu widow is very different from a mere life-estate. The case of *Kasinath Bysack* v. *Hurosundery Dossee*, which has long given the law to this Court, and since it is a decision of the Privy Council, ought to have given, if it has not given, the law to the Courts of

---

[1] 3 B. L. R., 362.

[2] 1 Boulnois, 129.

the East India Company, establishes that the estate of a widow is something higher than a life-estate; that it entitles her to the possession of the property without restriction, and that she has a qualified power of disposition in it, the limits of which it is difficult, if not impossible, exactly to define further than by saying that the propriety of any particular exercise of that power must depend upon the circumstances in which it is made, and must be consistent with the general principles of Hindu law regarding such dispositions. The cases of *Oojulmonee Dossee* v. *Sagormonee Dossee*[1] and *Hurrydoss Dutt* v. *Rungunmonee Dossee*,[2] which have established in this Court the right of the reversionary heirs, though their interest is only contingent, to maintain a suit to restrain waste by the widows, are quite consistent with what I have stated. In the latter case, Sir Lawrence Peel says: "The estate, though sometimes so expressed to be, is not an estate for life; when a widow alienates, she does so by virtue of her interest, not of a power, and she passes the absolute interest which she could not do if she had but a life-estate."

Where a Hindu testator by his will simply declared his widow and his only son to be masters of his estate without any further limitation, the late Supreme Court held that the widow, by such a bequest in her favor, takes no more than a widow's estate, *i.e.*, "an estate for life of a moiety of the estate bequeathed

[1] Taylor and Bell, 370. [2] Vyavastha Durpun, Eng. Ed., p. 124.

LECTURE VI. to her by the will, with the full permission of enjoying and disposing of the rents, issues, and profits thereof during her life, and with liberty to break into the principal sum for pious uses or other purposes with the express permission of this Court or with the consent of her grandson, after he shall come of age."[1]

Conclusion. The conclusion, on an examination of the above authorities, may be thus stated,—

1. That the widow completely represents the estate.

2. That generally whatever bars the widow would also bar the reversioners.

3. That by her alienations she conveys an absolute interest under certain circumstances.

4. That the circumstances under which she conveys an absolute interest, it is very difficult generically to define.

5. She is not a mere life-tenant.

6. The extent of her interest over moveable and immoveable property is, in Bengal, the same.

---

[1] Dialchund Addy *v.* Kissoree Dossee, Montriou's Hindu Law Cases, p. 371.

LECTURE VII.

THE NATURE AND EXTENT OF THE WIDOW'S ESTATE.—(*Contd.*)

The widow not a trustee—The incidents of trusteeship do not belong to her estate—Widow's powers over the income of the estate—Limited—Contrary opinion of Glover, J.—Questioned by Mitter, J.—Opinion of the Privy Council—*Bhugobuty Daee* v. *Chowdry Bholanath*—Accumulations follow the *corpus*—Recent cases on the subject of accumulations—Their result—Widows succeed together—With right of survivorship—Not destroyed by partition—Partition at the instance of the widow discretionary—The Benares and the Bengal schools agree as regards the incidents to the widow's estate—Self-acquired property and family property distinguished for purposes of inheritance under the Mitacshara—In Bengal the widow's powers over moveable and immoveable property are the same—In Benares they are also same—The widow's estate among Jains—Hindu law applicable to Jains—Estate of a female as devisee.

THE widow's estate has sometimes been called a trust-estate, and the widow, a trustee. In the case of *Mussamut Noomurto* v. *Mussamut Doorga Koonwar*,[1] the widow had sued for possession of her husband's share of the property by setting aside a *Razeenamah*, which she had executed in favor of the next heirs of her husband, by which possession of her husband's share of the property was made over

[1] S. D. R. for 1850, p. 245; see Bungseedhur Hajrah *v.* Thakur Pryag Sing, 7 Sel. Rep., p. 114; Radhabinode Misser *v.* Sheikh Mushnut-ullah, 7 Sel. Rep., p. 350.

LECTURE VII.

to them. The Court declared that the widow was bound by the *Razeenamah*, and further stated, that the widows are heirs for the time, that is, during life, and trustees for the ultimate heirs. This case, however, is hardly an authority on the point, for it does not seem to have been directly raised in the case, and the matter passed without any discussion.

The widow not a trustee.

It is not strictly correct to say that the widow is a trustee and her estate a trust-estate. By the Hindu law, the widow holds the estate for her own benefit. She is entitled to enjoy the usufruct of the property during her life, and the alienations of the property by her, in some cases stand good and pass an absolute interest to the alienee. If the widow was a trustee, who is the beneficiary or the *cestui que trust?* No one occupies that position with respect to the widow, not the reversioners, because their right of present enjoyment of the proceeds of the property is never admitted. Further, all trustees are liable to render an account of the administration of the trust by them ; and they are liable to be sued for a breach of trust. But no such suit will, I presume, lie against a widow ; and she is not liable to render an account of the administration of the property.

Sir Thomas Strange, speaking of the widow and her duties, says:[1]—" Her duty with regard to what she may have inherited from her husband, is to

[1] Vol. I, p. 244.

regard herself as little more than its tenant for life, and trustee, for the next heirs, of the property to which she has so succeeded, together with its accumulated savings; being restricted from alienating it, by her own sole act, unless for necessary subsistence or pious purposes beneficial to the deceased." Sir W. Macnaghten thinks,[1] that the widow "can be considered in no other light than as a holder in trust for certain uses, so much so that should she make waste, they who have the reversionary interest have clearly a right to restrain her from so doing." It seems, that these authorities were not using very accurate language; the existence of a very slender analogy induced them to use the expression. It does not appear that all the incidents of trusteeship were considered applicable to the widow's estate; and it must be admitted that, at the time when those authorities wrote, the widow's estate had not been considered in all its bearings with that completeness which has marked the decisions of the Courts since.

The incidents of trusteeship do not belong to her estate.

This question was much considered in the case of *Kerry Kolitanee* v. *Moniram Kolita*,[2] which has been quoted before. Mitter, J., was of opinion that the widow is "nothing more than a trustee for her life for the soul of her deceased husband, if we may use the expression." The widow is considered as trustee for the *soul* of her husband, and not for the *heirs* of her husband, *viz.*, the reversioners, as was held in

[1] Vol. I, p. 19, Ed. of 1829.

[2] 19 W. R., 367.

LECTURE VII. the Sudder Dewany case quoted before. Further on, in the same case, the same learned Judge has observed, "whether the word 'trustee' is applicable to the widow in the strict sense in which that word is used in works on English law, is a question which I need not pause to determine. But I think I have conclusively shown, in the order of reference, that the only right which the widow acquires in the property of her husband is the right of using that property for the benefit of his soul and for no other purpose whatever, and such a right, I apprehend, is nothing more than that of a trustee."[1]

In the same case, Chief Justice Couch, delivering the judgment of the Full Bench, has combated this view of the law, and, I think, successfully. He says,[2] that, "in truth, the word 'trustee' ought not to be used, at least in the sense which is ordinarily attributed to it, and if used in any other, it proves nothing. A widow is not a trustee. She has the usufruct as well as the property in the thing inherited from her husband;" and this opinion is based upon a text of Vyasa, which says,—'For women the property of their husbands is intended only for use; let them not make waste of it on any account;' and upon the well-known text of Katyayana,—'Let the childless widow, keeping unsullied the bed of her lord, and abiding with her venerable protector, enjoy

---

[1] 19 W. R., 392.

[2] *Ibid*, 407.

with moderation the property until her death. After her, let the heirs take it.' Lecture VII.

The Chief Justice then tries to combat the following proposition, that if the widow is no longer in a position to fulfil her duties as such trustee, the trust-property must be taken away from her. As a proposition of Hindu law, observes the Chief Justice, there is no authority in support of it. "As a doctrine of the Courts of Equity in England, it is not correct. The remedies for a breach of trust are stated in a work of high authority (Lewin on Trusts, c. 27); but the taking away the trust-property is not among them, and it has been found necessary to provide for the disability of a trustee by infancy or lunacy by Acts of Parliament. There appears to me to be a fallacy in the above proposition. The possession of the trust-property is not essential to the performance of the duties. If the widow had sufficient property of her own to maintain herself, she might alienate the whole of her husband's property for her life, and still perform all her duties for the benefit of her husband's soul. In fact, there is no trust attached to the property. It is a personal obligation on the widow, and the proposition really is, that if she does not fulfil it, she shall be deprived of her estate. We must see whether that is a received doctrine in the Bengal school of Hindu law."[1] The Chief Justice then, after examining the authorities

[1] 19 W. R., 409.

LECTURE VII.

on Hindu law, comes to the conclusion that there is no real trust in this case.

I think the question may be considered as conclusively settled by the authority of this case, that the widow is not a trustee for anybody, and that her estate is not a trust-estate.[1]

Widow's powers over the income of the estate.

The question regarding the widow's powers over the income of the property which she has inherited from her husband, is one of some difficulty. Supposing the widow inherited property from her husband, the income of which is a *lac* of rupees a year : Is the widow competent to spend the whole of this income according to her own pleasure and choice? Supposing the whole of this income is not necessary for the legitimate expenses of the widow as authorised in the *Shasters:* Is the widow competent to use the surplus income for other expenses not authorised by the *Shasters?* The author of the Dayabhaga has answered this question in the negative. He says, "let not women make waste. Here 'waste' intends expenditure not useful to the owner of the property."[2] By the word '*useful*' the author means *conducive to the spiritual welfare of the late owner.* Hence any expenditure which is beyond the authorised limits is *waste,* and the widow is incompetent to spend the income for such purposes.

Limited.

There is, however, a practical difficulty in deter-

[1] *See* Muteeram Kunwar *v.* Gopal Sahoo, 20 W. R., 187.

[2] Chap. XI, Sec. i, para. 61.

mining the extent of this authorised expenditure; the *class* or *classes* of expenses which are authorised may be determined, but the *amount* of such expenses is a matter of the greatest difficulty to determine, and must, I take it, depend upon the circumstances of each case. The practical difficulty must still remain whether, in a particular religious ceremony, *ten* or *one thousand* rupees ought to be spent; because, according to the Hindu religion, the religious efficacy of an act does not always depend upon the *amount* of money spent upon it. LECTURE VII.

Contrary opinion of Glover, J.

A different view of the law appears to have been laid down in the case of *Chundrabulee Debia* v. *Brody*.[1] It was held by Glover, J., that "a Hindu widow with a life-interest in her deceased husband's estate, would be entitled to make the fullest use of the usufruct of that estate; and it seems doubtful, under the late rulings of the Privy Council, whether she could be in any way restrained, however wasteful her expenditure, so long as she kept within the limits of her income and made no attempt at alienation. If, on the contrary, she chooses to economise, she can, during her lifetime, give away her savings to any one she pleases." In another case,[2] there is a dictum of Justice Macpherson, where he says:—"There is no doubt that the income and profits arising from the husband's estate may be used by the widow at

[1] 9 W. R., p. 584.

[2] Grose *v.* Omirtomoyee Dossee, 12 W. R., p. 13, A. O. J.

LECTURE VII. her discretion, and the reversioner cannot interfere with her in the exercise of that discretion." This, however, is a mere dictum of one of the Judges, and not the judgment of the Appellate Bench, and the Chief Justice does not share in that opinion.

In another case,[1] Sir Lawrence Peel held, that the widow can spend all the income at her pleasure, and the reversioners cannot question it. The case does not appear in any of the authorised reports, but is given in the *Englishman* of the 2nd July, 1853, and is quoted by Justice Macpherson in his judgment in the previous case.

Sir Lawrence Peel in that case said:—"The Hindu authorities say, that a widow ought to live a chaste and retired life; and her duty may be to spend no more than is necessary for her support in a state of seclusion. But if, instead of living strictly as she should, she lives freely and expensively, her disposition cannot be questioned. As to the *corpus* of her husband's property, she cannot alienate it, but the income of it during her life forms no part of the husband's estate. If she received and spent it all, no one could call her in question. So, if she has money in hand, she may dispose of it as she pleases. Money in hand and accumulations are not the same thing. We do not decide on the question as to whether the accumulations belong to the husband's

[1] In the goods of Hurrender Narain Ghose, Kosheenath Ghose *v.* Bissonath Biswas.

representative. We only decide that the promovent has a sufficient interest, on the face of the proceedings."

LECTURE VII.

Questioned by Mitter, J.

The authority of the case decided by Glover, J., was questioned by Mitter, J., in his judgment in the case of *Kerry Kolitanee* v. *Moniram Kolita.* It was pointed out that the portion of the judgment referring to the widow's powers over the usufruct of the property was a mere *obiter dictum*, inasmuch as the point before the Court was whether the accumulations left by a Hindu widow were liable to be seized in execution of a personal decree against her, or would they belong to the heirs of her husband after her death as part of the estate of her husband. Justice Mitter further observed, in the same case, that there is no distinction between the *corpus* of the estate which the widow inherited and its income; that her powers over both were the same; and that there is no authority for the proposition of Hindu law, that the widow is at liberty to use the income of the property she had inherited in any manner she thought proper. The learned Judge was further of opinion that if the widow was about to spend a large sum of money derived by her from the profits of the estate for a purpose not authorised by the *Shasters*, the reversioners can sue for an injunction commanding her not to spend it for that purpose, and the Court would be bound to grant such an injunction.

Opinion of the Privy Council.

In a recent case,[1] the Privy Council held, that a

[1] Mussamut Bhugbuty Daee v. Chowdry Bholanath, 24 W. R., p. 168.

LECTURE VII. Hindu widow has no power to alienate the profits of the estate which she had inherited from her husband; and that any property which she may purchase from such profits would become an increment to the estate which she had inherited, and would follow that estate in its devolution. That case also is an authority for the important distinction between the *widow's estate* and an ordinary *life-estate*. The proprietor, one Odam Thakoor, had, by a deed executed during his lifetime, but shortly before his death, placed his wife in possession of all his property, moveable and immoveable, "to be enjoyed during her lifetime, in order that she may hold possession of all the properties and *milkiut* possessed by me, the declarant, during her lifetime, and, by the payment of the Government revenue, appropriate the profits derived therefrom, but that she should not, by any means, transfer the *milkiut* estates and the slaves; that, after the death of my aforesaid wife, the *milkiut* and household furniture shall devolve on my adopted son (Giridhari Thakoor), and that no objection thereto raised by any one shall ever be held valid."

Bhugbuty Daee v. Chowdry Bholanath.

It was contended on behalf of the plaintiffs, who were the reversionary heirs, that the estate of a Hindu widow was by this deed conferred on his wife Chunderbutti by Odam Thakoor, and that, consequently, properties purchased by her from the profits of the estate became an increment to that estate, and therefore devolved with that estate on the plaintiffs.

For the defendant, who was the grand-daughter of Chunderbutti, and therefore her heir, it was contended, that the widow, by the deed, obtained a life-estate; and therefore the properties purchased by her from the profits would be hers, and would devolve on the defendant who represents her. LECTURE VII.

The Privy Council construed the document, that it was in the nature of a family settlement, giving to Chunderbutti an estate for life, with a power to appropriate the profits; and to Giridhari, what would be termed in the phraseology of English law, a vested remainder on her death. According to this construction she would have the power of making whatever use she chose of the proceeds of her estates; and if she bought land or personal property with them, the land and that property would be hers, and would devolve on her heirs, and not on the heirs of her husband.

In the course of this judgment the Privy Council thus pointed out the incidents belonging to the widow's estate:—"If she took the estate only of a Hindu widow, one consequence, no doubt, would be, that she would be unable to alienate the profits, or that at all events whatever she purchased out of them would be an increment to her husband's estate, and the plaintiffs would be entitled to recover possession of all such property, real and personal. But, on the other hand, she would have certain rights as a Hindu widow; for example, she would have the right, under

LECTURE VII. certain circumstances, if the estate were insufficient to defray the funeral expenses, or her maintenance, to alienate it altogether. She certainly would have the power of selling her own estate; and it would further follow that Giridhari would not be possessed, in any sense, of a vested remainder, but merely a contingent one. It would also follow that she would completely represent the estate, and under certain circumstances the Statute of Limitations might run against the heirs to the estate, whoever they might be."

In another case,[1] however, the Privy Council construed a document, which, on the face of it, purported to convey certain moveable property for "the sole absolute use and benefit" of the widow, as conveying only a widow's interest in that property. The deed was a release executed by the widow in behalf of her husband's brothers, whereby, in consideration of a sum of Rs. 59,000 paid to her, she waived all her rights to the estate of her husband, of which she was heiress, and it was agreed between all the parties, that the said sum of Rs. 59,000 was to be the sole and exclusive property of the widow "for her own absolute and separate use." The late Supreme Court held, that, by the deed, the sum of Rs. 59,000 became the absolute property of the widow, and it was never intended that the money paid should vest in her only as the widow and representative of her husband,

[1] Rabutty Dosee v. Shib Chunder Mullic, 6 Moore, p. 1.

and as part of his estate. The Privy Council, however, reversed the judgment of the Supreme Court, and held that, looking to the circumstances under which the deed was executed, the several parties to it, and their respective claims, the sum in question was intended to represent the amount of her husband's estate, which was made over to her to be used by her separately as distinguished from the joint family; that the words "to her separate use" are not used in the sense in which they are used in the Courts of Equity in England, but to her separate use as distinguished from the joint estate, dividing that which was joint into separate estate. LECTURE VII.

I shall now consider the subject of accumulations as being closely connected with the subject of our present enquiry. Supposing the widow, out of the profits of the estate which she had inherited from her husband, were to purchase certain properties, does she acquire absolute rights over such property, and does it descend to her heirs on her death? or does it become part of her husband's estate, and follow the devolution of that estate? The present state of authorities inclines to the view, that these accumulations follow the *corpus*; that they become part of the husband's estate, and are liable to all the incidents belonging to that estate.[1] Accumulations follow the *corpus*.

In the case of *Grose* v. *Omirtomoyee*,[2] which has been quoted before, the assignee of the widow claimed

[1] 2 Macnaghten, p. 259.

[2] 12 W R., 13, A. O. J.

LECTURE VII. the accumulations, and contended that the reversioner's interest did not extend beyond the *corpus* of the estate. On this Macpherson, J., observed:—"There is no doubt that the income and profits arising from the husband's estate may be used by the widow at her discretion, and the reversioner cannot interfere with her in the exercise of that discretion. But accumulations are not the same as income, and in no case that I am aware of, has it been decided that accumulations can be dealt with by her as income or otherwise than as the *corpus* may be dealt with."

"No doubt there is in fact a very substantial difference between mere income and accumulations. In the present case, almost simultaneously with the recovery of the *corpus* of her husband's estate, the widow gets a considerably larger sum, being accumulations accrued due since his death. Although the theory of the Hindu law is, that the income of the husband's estate shall go to the widow for her maintenance and for the performance of the pious duties, that theory, by no means, necessarily embraces a large lump sum of accumulations. According to all the older authorities on Hindu law, accumulations should be treated in the same way as *corpus*; and I think they should be so treated now in the absence of any distinct authority to the contrary."

In the case of *Bhugbuty Daee*[1] quoted before, the Privy Council expressed the same view regarding

[1] 24 W. R., 168.

the accumulations. Their Lordships held, that whatever the widow might purchase from the profits of her husband's estate would be an increment to that estate, and the reversioners, after the widow's death, will be entitled to recover such property, whether moveable or immoveable.

It would seem from the above authorities that, according to the Hindu law, the increment or accumulations would follow the principal of which they constitute the increments or accumulations; and that the same rule which governs the devolution of the principal would also govern the devolution of the increments or the accumulations to such principal.

This principle seems to have been departed from by the Privy Council in the case of *Sreemutty Soorjeemoney Dosee* v. *Denobundoo Mullic.*[1] That case, however, depended upon the construction of the will of a Hindu testator bequeathing his property to his sons in a particular manner. The testator had five sons, and by his will declared that all his property would belong in equal shares to his five sons. The will further directed,[2] "that should any of my five sons die not leaving any son from his loins, nor any son's son, in that event, neither his widow, nor his daughter, nor daughter's son, nor any of them, will get any share out of the share that he has obtained of the immoveables and moveables of my said estate. In that event, of the said property such of my sons and

[1] 6 Moore, 526. [2] Page 529.

LECTURE VII. sons' sons as shall then be alive, they will receive that wealth according to their respective shares. However, if any sonless son shall leave a widow, in that event she will only receive Rs. 10,000 for her food and raiment."

It happened in this case that there were considerable accumulations of property arising from the savings of unspent income. The appellant, who was the widow of one of the sons, claimed, as his heiress, a right to a share of these accumulations; she urged that the gift over to the surviving sons was intended to cover the share of the principal, the estate of the testator; and that the will did not dispose of the accumulations which, on the death of the sons, descended to their heirs under the Hindu law. For the respondent it was contended that the accumulations followed the *corpus* by a well-known principle of Hindu law, and that the testator having disposed of the *corpus*, the accumulations would follow the devolution of the *corpus*, and therefore would belong, according to the terms of the will, to the surviving sons, and not to the widow of the deceased son.

The Privy Council held, that the testator intended to give absolutely to the sons a share in the estate of the testator, and that the enjoyment by the sons could not be less than the enjoyment of the income of their shares. These accumulations are nothing more than the unspent income, and was not affected by the gift of the *corpus*. The Privy Council held, that the increment did not go over with the principal, but passed to the natural heirs.

You will observe how the Privy Council excepted this case from the rule of Hindu law, which directs that accumulations follow the *corpus* of the estate. On this point their Lordships observed as follows: "Then as to the rule of the Hindu law that the increment follows the principal where the parties are joint in estate, it is not necessary for us to give any opinion upon the extent and limits of this rule, and we desire not to be understood as intimating any opinion upon those points. The question in this case, as we view it, is, whether the rule is properly applicable to the case before us; and we are of opinion that it is not."

In another case[1] the Privy Council had to construe another will similar to the one, in its terms, that was the subject of discussion in the case of *Surjeemoney Dossee.* The testator had provided that neither the widow, nor the daughter, nor the daughter's sons of any of his sons, shall succeed to his share; but there was no provision of a gift over to his surviving sons as in the case of *Surjeemoney Dossee.* The claim of the widow was confined to the accumulations, and the Privy Council, following the judgment in the case of *Surjeemoney Dossee*, decreed the same.

Recent cases on the subject of accumulations.

The law relating to accumulations has received much consideration in some recent cases. In the

[1] Bissonath Chunder *v.* Bama Sundery Dossee.

LECTURE VII. case of *Gonda Koer* v. *Kooer Oodey Singh*,[1] the Privy Council seemed to have introduced a new element in the consideration of these cases, *viz.*, what was the intention of the widow when she made the purchases out of the profits of her estate? Was it her intention to appropriate the properties so purchased to herself and to sever the same from the bulk of her husband's estate, or did she intend the same to form part of her husband's estate? The Privy Council inclined to the view that a clear intention and action on the part of the widow to sever properties purchased by her from the bulk of her husband's estate, would have the effect of rendering them her absolute property, and they would form no part of her husband's estate. In the particular case in question, the Privy Council held the properties purchased by the widow to form part of her husband's estate, inasmuch as there was no intention on her part to sever the same from the bulk of her husband's estate; on the contray, she has treated the same as forming part of her husband's estate.

This, you will observe, involves a departure from the law on the subject as previously established. If the property was purchased by the widow from the profits of her husband's estate, it became part of that estate, and followed the same in all its incidents. That *was* the law on the subject. The Privy Council, in the case of *Gonda Koer*, now says that the *intention*

[1] 14 B. L. R., 159.

and *action* of the widow is to be the test whether the properties purchased by her from the profits of her husband's estate shall form part of that estate, or shall be her absolute property. If she treats it as part of her husband's estate, it becomes part of the same estate: on the other hand, if she treats it as her own property, it becomes, for that, her own exclusive property.

In a still more recent case,[1] the Bengal High Court laid down some principles which went to modify the law on the subject. Jackson, J., held, that as regards the current income the widow is at liberty to spend the same in any manner she thought proper. "If she had squandered the whole amount on frivolous pleasures, or bestowed it on her father's relatives, the heirs would, according to a current of modern decisions, have had nothing to complain of." If the widow purchased real property from the current income of the estate then lying in her hands, she would be afterwards competent, said the learned Judge, to alienate the same in whole or in part, to reconvert it into money and spend it in any manner she chose.

The same learned Judge in this case attempted to draw a distinction between accumulations and income, following the decision of Macpherson, J., in the case of *Grose* v. *Omirtomoyee Dossee*.[2] He observed:—

[1] Sreemutty Puddomonee Dossee *v.* Dwarkanath Biswas, 25 W. R., 335.

[2] 12 W. R., 13, A. O. J.

LECTURE VII.

"But what are accumulations in the view of these cases? Not surely the accidental balances of one or two years of the widow's income, but a fund distinct and tangible. There is nothing whatever in this case to indicate that any such fund ever had been formed or had existed, and we see no reason to suppose that accumulations had ever arisen, except that the widow may have spent in some years more, in others less; and in that sense the savings of the less costly year might be an accumulation to meet the charges of the next."

This mode of distinguishing accumulation from income seems to have been questioned in the most recent case[1] on the subject. Ainslie, J., observed: "If a distinction is to be drawn from current income and accumulations, where is the line to be drawn? When does the surplus cease to be part of the current income? There is no rule requiring a widow to make up her accounts at stated intervals and carry unexpended balances to the credit of her husband's estate. How are we to say that up to 31st December she is free to spend as she chooses the money in hand, but on the 1st January it lapses like an unexpended assignment of public money at the close of the financial year. Who is to audit her accounts?"

The learned Judge was of opinion that the question of the widow's power to alienate property acquired out of savings from the income of her

[1] Musst. Hunsbuti Koerain v. Ishri Dutt Koer, 4 Calc. Rep., 511.

husband's estate was still unsettled and had not been concluded by authority. He was of opinion that she had such a power, because if it is within the widow's power to dispose of the surplus profits from her husband's estate remaining after due provision has been made for the duties which the widow is bound to perform, it must be equally within her power to do so, whether she does it at once as the profits reach her, or whether she allows them to accumulate. LECTURE VII.

The state of the law is thus somewhat uncertain on the authorities. The result, however, of these decisions may be thus summed up— Their result.

1. The widow has full power to spend the current income in any manner she thinks proper.
2. If property is purchased from those profits, it is doubtful whether she has the absolute power to alienate it.
3. If she leaves property so purchased undisposed of at her death, it will form part of her husband's estate and follow the same in its devolution.

In the present age intermarriages between the four classes being prohibited, a man's wives must necessarily be of the same class with him; and consequently, in matters of succession, no rule of preference among the several widows of different classes does now obtain. If a man, therefore, dies leaving more widows than one, all his widows succeed to his estate together;[1] the estate to which they succeed is Widows succeed together.

[1] Bhugbuty Raur v. Radhakissen Mookerjee, Montriou's Cases, 314.

LECTURE VII.

With right of survivorship.

one estate in law, with the right of survivorship attached to it; so that, on the death of one widow, her interest survives to the surviving widows, and does not descend to the other heirs of her husband. So long, therefore, as a single widow is alive, no portion of the husband's estate can descend to the other heirs of her husband.

Not destroyed by partition.

It has been held in the case of *Bhugwandeen Dobey* v. *Myna Baee*,[1] that if two widows effect, among themselves, a partition of their husband's estate, by such partition the right of survivorship is not destroyed. The right of survivorship is so strong that the survivor takes the whole property to the exclusion of the daughters of the deceased widow. They are, therefore, in the strictest sense coparceners, and between undivided coparceners there can be no alienation by one without the consent of the other. Even with such consent, one widow cannot alienate her share so as to convey a good title to the alienee in the absence of legal necessity.

Partition at the instance of the widow discretionary.

The above case is authority for the proposition that, among widows, partition is allowed. How far a widow can claim partition by metes and bounds from the coparceners of her husband may sometimes be a question. The point seems to have been expressly raised in a recent case,[2] in which the Court ruled that it was discretionary with the Court to order a

---

[1] 11 Moore, 487.

[2] Soudaminy Dossee v. Jogesh Dutt, I. L. R., 2 Calc., 262.

partition at the suit of the widow. If the widow was childless and her share small, probably the Court will not order a partition, as the defendants themselves in such cases are usually the reversioners of the widow. But where the widow's share is large, and she has children, in such cases partition will be ordered. In the case in question partition was ordered.

The Benares and the Bengal schools agree as regards the incidents to the widow's estate.

I have already pointed out before that the Benares and the Bengal schools differ from each other as regards the widow's right of succession. The Bengal school confers the inheritance on the widow under all circumstances, the Benares school recognises her right, only when her husband was living, after partition, separate from his co-sharers. Whatever difference there might exist, as regards the widow's right to succeed, between the two schools, there is none as regards the incidents to be attached to the widow's estate when the widow does succeed to the property of her husband.

In the case of *Than Sing and another* v. *Mussamut Jeetoo*,[1] which arose in the District Court of Agra, the plaintiff, Mussamut Jeetoo, sued for possession of the moiety of a village which was granted to her husband and her husband's brother, who was one of the defendants. The Zillah Judge referred the point for the opinion of the Pundit of the Court, who answered as follows :—

" If the acquirer of real property die childless, even

[1] 2 Sel. Rep., 411.

LECTURE VII.

though he were at the time in family partnership with his brothers, his property will go to his widow, and not to his brothers. The widow cannot, however, alienate it by gift or sale: she will enjoy possession thereof during her lifetime, and after her death it will go to her husband's heirs." And the authorities for the answer are declared to be Menu and Yajnawalkya.

The Zillah Judge, accordingly, gave a decree to the plaintiff, which was confirmed by the Provincial Court in appeal.

On the matter coming up in special appeal to the Sudder Dewany Adawlut, a further reference was made to the Pundits of the Court "to state the law according to the Mitacshara as received in the district of Agra." This opinion being similar to that which was given by the Pundit of the Zillah Court, the Sudder Dewany Adawlut passed a decree in favor of the plaintiff, "awarding to her possession of a moiety of the village during her lifetime, and declaring that she was not authorised to alienate it; and that, on her death, the heirs of her deceased husband should succeed thereto." I may observe here that these in substance are the main incidents belonging to the widow's estate according to the Bengal authorities.

Self-acquired property and family property distinguished for purposes of inheritance under the

In an undivided family according to the Mitacshara, the self-acquired property of one co-sharer will, on his death, devolve on his widow if he has no male issue; but the joint family property will go to his male coparceners. The interest of a widow so succeeding to her husband's estate is similar to that of a tenant-in-tail by the English law as representing the inheritance. An important principle is here established, *viz.*, the distinction between the self-acquired property and the joint family property in an undivided family governed by the Mitacshara, the former will descend to the widow, but the latter will go to the undivided coparceners.[1]

In the case of *Pakhnarain and others* v. *Mussamut Seesphool*,[2] which arose in the District Court of Tirhoot, the plaintiff, as the heiress of her husband, claimed his share of the property; the plaintiff's husband had survived his brother, whose grandson (daughter's son) was the defendant. The plaintiff claimed only half the estate, and not the whole which belonged jointly to her husband and his brother. The Court put the following question to the Pundits:—"Should the property of Ramdyal devolve on his widow Mussamut Seesphool, whether she possessed the power of alienating it by gift, sale, or otherwise, or whether she had only a life-interest in it." The Pundits gave as their opinion that, as the plaintiff's husband's estate was separate, she, as his widow, was entitled to the entire property left by her husband, to be enjoyed by her during her lifetime, but not to be alienated except for the special purpose of securing spiritual benefit to her deceased husband; and

---

[1] Katama Natchier *v.* The Raja of Sivagunga, 9 Moore's I. A., 539.

[2] 3 Sel. Rep., 152.

LECTURE VII. that, after her death, in the event of there being no heir of her husband in existence from the daughter down to the spiritual teacher, the property should devolve on the ruling power.

The matter coming up in appeal before the Sudder Dewany Adawlut, that Court declared, "that Mussamut Seesphool has a right to the possession of the estate left by her husband during her lifetime; that she may make such disbursements as are necessary for the spiritual welfare of her deceased husband; that she is not at liberty to make any other description of alienation; and that, after her death, in the event of there not being in existence any heir of her husband from his daughter down to his spiritual teacher, the property which had so devolved on the widow should escheat to the ruling power." The decree of the Provincial Court was, accordingly, amended, and it was declared that Mussamut Seesphool shall have a life-interest in one moiety of the landed property left by her deceased husband, which property shall be sequestered to the use of Government in the event of there not being at the time of her death any surviving heir of her husband from the daughter down to the spiritual preceptor.

The decision in this case was expressly put upon the authorities current in Mithila, and the opinion of the Pundits was based upon those authorities. This, therefore, must be considered as a decision according to the doctrines of the Mitacshara, which is the ruling authority in Mithila followed by such works as the Vivada Ratnakara and the Vivada Chintamoni. LECTURE VII.

In the case of *Paunchcowree Mahtoon and others* v. *Kalee Churn and others*,[1] which arose in the District Court of Patna, it was contended for the appellants that, according to the Mitacshara, the estate taken by the widow was not a restricted estate, such as that of a widow under the Hindu law current in Bengal. It was also contended, that a widow, under the law of the Mitacshara, takes an absolute interest in her deceased husband's estate, and may dispose of it as she pleases ; at least, as regards property which is not proved to have come to her husband as ancestral property. On this the High Court observed : "We, however, declined to hear any argument on these points, there being no sort of doubt that, according to a long series of decisions of the Courts of this country, which are in accordance with the decisions of the Privy Council, a childless widow under the Mitacshara law takes only a limited interest in her husband's estate, similar to that taken by a widow under the law of the Bengal school."

In Bengal the widow's powers over moveable and immoveable property are the same.

The important point as regards the incidents attaching to the widow's estate is as to the power which the widow possesses of alienating the property which she had inherited from her husband, and as to any difference, if any, between the moveable and the immoveable portions of the estate so inherit-

[1] 9 W. R., 490.

LECTURE VII.

ed. As I have already shown,[1] in Bengal, there is no difference between the moveable and the immoveable property inherited by the widow; and her powers of alienation as regards both are restricted within very narrow limits.

The question in the Mitacshara country as to the widow's powers of alienation over moveable property inherited from her husband was the subject of discussion in the case of *Bhugwandeen Dobey* v. *Myna Baee.*[2] On that point the Privy Council thus observed: "The reasons for the restrictions which the Hindu law imposes on the widow's dominion over her inheritance from her husband, whether founded on her natural dependence on others, her duty to lead an ascetic life, or on the impolicy of allowing the wealth of one family to pass to another, are as applicable to personal property invested so as to yield an income as they are to land. The more ancient texts importing the restriction are general. It lies on those who assert that moveable property is not subject to the restriction, to establish that exception to the generality of the rule. The diversity of opinion among the Benares Pundits is sufficient to show that the supposed distinction between moveable and immoveable property is anything but well established in that school."

In Benares they are also same.

"Their Lordships, therefore, have come to the con-

[1] *See* Kasinath Bysack *v.* Hurrosoondery Dossee, Montriou's Cases, 495.
[2] 11 Moore, 487.

clusion that, according to the law of the Benares school, notwithstanding the ambiguous passage in the Mitacshara, no part of her husband's estate, whether moveable or immoveable, to which a Hindu woman succeeds by inheritance, forms part of her *stridhan*, or particular property; and that the text of Katyayana, which is general in its terms, and of which the authority is undoubted, must be taken to determine—*first*, that her power of disposition over both is limited to certain purposes; and *secondly*, that on her death both pass to the next heir of her husband."

In another case, however, *Mussamut Thacoor Daee* v. *Rai Baluck Ram*,[1] the Privy Council expressed an opinion somewhat different from that which was laid down in the case of *Bhugwandeen Dobey*. Their Lordships said: "The result of the authorities seems to be that, although, according to the law of the Western schools, the widow may have a power of disposing of moveable property inherited from her husband, which she has not under the law of Bengal, she is, by the one law as by the other, restricted from alienating any immoveable property which she has so inherited, and that on her death the immoveable property and the moveable, if she has not otherwise disposed of it, pass to the next heirs of her husband." Their Lordships, however, considered it unnecessary to decide the point as to whether the widow had

[1] 11 Moore, 139.

LECTURE VII. power of disposition over the moveable property inherited by her from her husband.

The ruling in the case of *Bhugwandeen Dobey* overrules the decision of the Bengal High Court in the case of *Goburdhun Nath* v. *Onoop Roy*,[1] where it was held, that moveable property inherited by a widow became her *stridhan*, over which she had absolute power of disposition.

The result, on an examination of the authorities, seems to be that, as regards the nature of, and the incidents attaching to, the widow's estate, the Bengal and the Benares schools both agree. Therefore, any decision arrived at regarding the incidents belonging to the widow's estate in any of the schools must be considered as an authority in all the other schools.

The widow's estate among Jains.

In the case of persons belonging to particular sects of Hindus, the widow's estate, like the other branches of their law, is determined by custom governing that class, rather than by ordinary Hindu law. For instance, the *Jains*, who are dissenters from Hinduism, are governed by their own customs, which materially differ from ordinary Hindu law. The sonless widow of a *Saraogi Agarwala Jain* takes an absolute interest in the self-acquired property of her husband. She can adopt a son without permission from her husband or his heirs. She can adopt her daughter's son, who will take the place of a begotten

---

[1] 3 W. R., 105.

son.[1] These are incidents which materially differ from those of ordinary Hindu law.

Hindu law applicable to Jains.

The Privy Council, however, in a later case,[2] held, that the law applicable to the Jains is the ordinary Hindu law. But that where, in any particular case among them, any special custom is pleaded, that must be proved by evidence. If the custom is not proved or not pleaded, the ordinary Hindu law will be applicable to them.

It was further held in this case, that the estate of a daughter, inherited from her father, is, under the Mitacshara, like that of a widow, a limited and restricted estate; and does not, on her death, pass as *stridhan* to her heirs, but reverts to the heirs of her father.

Estate of a female as devisee.

The nature of the estate which a Hindu widow takes under a devise from her husband, is sometimes a question of some difficulty to determine, inasmuch as it depends upon the particular words of the devise; and, therefore, no general rule can be laid down for determination of the same. Where a testator in his will used such terms as these—"I give, devise, and bequeath unto my wife and her heirs and assigns, for ever, all my real and personal estates and effects, and do appoint my said wife sole executrix of this will," it was held, that the testator intended his wife to be something more than a trustee or manager for the

---

[1] Sheo Sing Rai *v.* Musst. Dakho and another, 2 Cal. Rep., 193.

[2] Chotay Lall *v.* Chunnoo Lall, I. L. R., 4 Calc., 744.

LECTURE VII. — infant heirs, and that she took absolutely all the property of the testator.[1]

In case of gifts *inter vivos* by the husband to the wife, generally the wife does not take an absolute estate in immoveable property, she takes it only for life; but as regards moveables, when thus given away, she takes absolutely. A gift under a will has been held to be governed by the same rule. It was held in a recent case,[2] "that a Hindu wife takes by a will of her husband no more absolute right over the property bequeathed than she would take over such property if conferred upon her by gift during the lifetime of her husband; and that, whether in respect of a gift or a will, it would be necessary for the husband to give her, in express terms, a heritable right or power of alienation." In this case, the testator gave to his two grandsons and to his wife, by the same clause in the will, certain properties; and the Court held, that although the grandsons had an absolute estate in the subject of the devise, the wife had only a life-interest in the same.

The proposition of law, as stated in the previous judgment without any qualification, seems to be somewhat questionable; and as regards the rule of interpretation adopted in that case, you will find a contrary rule laid down in a still more recent case[3]

---

[1] Taruck Nath Sircar *v.* Prosonno Kumar Ghose, 19 W. R., 48.
[2] Koonj Behary Dhur *v.* Prem Chand Dutt, 5 Cal. Law Rep., 561.
[3] Chunder Money Dossee *v.* Hurry Doss Mitter, 5 Cal. Law Rep., 557.

in construing a similar devise. There was a devise of certain property, in the same clause of the will, to eleven persons, of whom nine were male and two female, and the testator gave the property to them in equal shares.

The first Court held, that the two female devisees took the qualified estate of females under the Hindu law, and the male devisees took an absolute estate. The Appellate Court, overruling the decision of the first Court, held, that the female devisees also took an absolute estate in their shares in the same way as the male devisees. The Court was also of opinion, that "the rule of Hindu law, by which widows take only a qualified estate in their husband's property, has no application to a devise of this kind to married women under a will."

LECTURE VIII.

THE ALIENATIONS BY THE WIDOW.

Alienation by the widow—Her power in this respect limited—The widow's powers of alienation in the Mithila school—Widow incompetent to alienate—Except for legal necessity—Legal necessity defined—Widow's maintenance justifies alienation—According to the Dayabhaga—According to the Dayakrama Sangraha—According to the Digest—Not, if the reversioner agrees to maintain—Widow bound to maintain her husband's family—Alienation for that purpose allowed—Daughter's marriage to be performed by the widow—Alienation allowed for the spiritual welfare of the husband—For the husband's *sraddha*—For other religious acts—Which benefit the husband—For pilgrimage to Gya—For payment of husband's debts—Widow bound to pay husband's debts—Widow's personal debts do not justify alienation—Widow's interest saleable—Husband's debt must be proved—Alienation for payment of revenue justified—The purchaser not bound to see to the appropriation—Money borrowed to carry on litigation will not be a charge on the estate—A good charge if for the benefit of the estate—Advances for widow's maintenance and for the costs of recovering the estate a good charge—*Grose* v. *Omertomoyee*—Gifts to husband's relations allowed—Not to her father's family.

Alienation by the widow.

I SHALL now consider the Hindu widow's power of disposition over the property inherited by her from her husband. The author of the Dayabhaga says :[1]—"The wife must only enjoy her husband's estate after his demise ; she is not entitled to make a gift, sale, or mortgage of it." And in another place

[1] Chap. XI, sec. i, para. 56.

it is stated, "she has no power, as with her separate property, to make a gift, mortgage, or sale of it at her pleasure."[1] LECTURE VIII.

The reported cases on the subject have laid down the law in accordance with the ancient authorities.

In the case of *Mukhoda* v. *Kulleani*,[2] the plaintiff claimed the property on two grounds :—

1*st*,—under a deed of gift from the widow ;

2*nd*,—as next heir to her husband.

The Sudder Dewany Adawlut held, that the gift by the widow would not avail, and the plaintiff's case was decreed, on the ground that he was the next heir to the widow's husband. The important question as to the effect of an alienation to the next heir of the husband was not considered in the case ; and the opinion of the Pundits, who were consulted, did not directly refer to this point. The opinion was in these words :—"If the widow, calling plaintiff her heir, made a gift, in his favour, of the talook left by her husband, such gift, in the event of there being an heir of the husband, cannot avail. The *Shaster* declares, that a gift by a widow of the whole estate of her husband is invalid ; but that a gift of a moderate portion of his property made by the widow, with a view to his spiritual benefit, may be valid. If the plaintiff were the heir of the widow's husband, and there were no other heir, the plaintiff, at the widow's death, would take the talook left by

[1] See Smriti Chandrika, p. 169, paras. 28 to 31.

[2] 1 Sel. Rep., 82.

LECTURE VIII.

her husband. If the plaintiff were not the heir, and there were no heir, the talook would escheat to the ruling power." It is clear from this, that the effect of the gift by the widow to the next heir of the husband was not considered by the Pundits; they rested their opinion rather upon the limited power that the widow possessed over her husband's property.

Her power in this respect limited.

In the case of *Mussamut Bejoya Debee* v. *Mussamut Unnopoorna Debee*,[1] the widow of the last owner had made a gift of the property to the son of her second daughter. The plaintiff, who was the eldest daughter of the widow, claimed a moiety of the estate which belonged to her father. The defence was, that the gift was made by the widow to her daughter's son, "as a charitable donation enjoined by the maxims of religion, and calculated to benefit the soul of her departed husband." The Pundits of the Zillah Courts were of opinion, that the gift was good in law, on the ground of its being "a charitable donation by the widow beneficial to the soul of her husband." The Zillah Court, accordingly, upheld the gift, and dismissed the plaintiff's suit.

The case came up in appeal before the Sudder Court: the Pundits of that Court were consulted, who gave it as their opinion, that "a woman succeeding to the possession of property in right of her

[1] 1 Sel. Rep., 215.

husband or of her adopted son, is not at liberty to alienate it without the consent of the legal heirs; or to settle it on one heir, while there is a possibility that a co-heir may be subsequently born." On the authority of this opinion, the Court held, that the gift by the widow was void; and that the appellant, as one of the two daughters of the last owner, was entitled to the moiety which she claimed.

In another case[1] the plaintiff, who was the mother of the last owner, for herself and in behalf of her grand-daughter (the daughter of the last owner), sued for possession of certain property which had belonged to her son. The defence was, that the last owner had made over the property verbally to the defendant on account of a debt due to the defendant, and that his widow had subsequently executed, in favor of the defendant, a deed of relinquishment (*ladavee*) confirming the act of her husband and acknowledging the proprietary right of the defendant to the property in suit.

The Provincial Court decreed the plaintiff's claim, holding that there was no sufficient evidence of the debt of the husband, and the widow, therefore, was not competent to alienate the property to the prejudice of the next heirs. The Court also ordered that the plaintiff shall obtain possession of the property.

---

[1] Hem Chunder Mozoomdar *v.* Mussamut Taramonee and Mussamut Raimonee, 1 Sel. Rep., 481.

LECTURE VIII.

On appeal to the Sudder Dewany Adawlut, the question was referred for the opinion of the Pundits, who answered as follows:—"If the proprietor of a landed estate die, leaving a grandmother, mother, stepmother, wife, unmarried daughter, and son of his father's uncle, his wife succeeds to the sole possession of the estate: but she cannot, without sufficient cause, or the consent of the abovementioned relations, transfer the property by gift or sale. The widow may transfer the real and personal estate of her deceased husband in discharge of his debts, if the amount of the debt exceed or equal the value of the estate: but if the value of the estate exceed the amount of the debt, the widow is only entitled to sell such part as may suffice to cover the debt. If, in the present case, the widow has transferred her husband's estate in payment of his just debts, and the creditor under such sale obtain possession of the estate, the other heirs of the deceased are not entitled to set aside the sale by payment of the debt."

The Sudder Dewany Adawlut held, that there was no sufficient proof of the debt on which the deed of relinquishment (*ladavee*) was grounded. The decree of the Provincial Court was confirmed with this amendment, that, as the widow of the last owner was alive, the plaintiff as his mother was not entitled to the possession of the property during the lifetime of the widow; and it was further provided that, after the death of Soorujmonee (the widow), the deed of relinquishment, executed by her, should not operate to preclude the right of the other surviving heirs of the deceased.[1]

LECTURE VIII.

The widow's powers of alienation in the Mithila school.

In the Mithila school a somewhat peculiar doctrine obtains as to the widow's powers of alienation. That school maintains that an heir taking property must reserve at least a moiety of the estate for the performance of the monthly and other obsequies of the deceased person. If, however, any other person than the widow executed a gift of the whole of the property in opposition to this injunction of law, it was held, that the gift will not be void in consequence of the neglect of this single obligation; thus recognising the doctrine of *factum valet*, which obtains in the Bengal school. But if the widow made a gift or other alienation of more than half the estate, such gift or alienation would be void except under special circumstances. This point was determined in the case of *Sreenarain Rai* v. *Bhya Jha*, which has been quoted before. It does not appear to have been held in that case, that under no circumstances the widow can alienate more than half or the whole of the estate; probably in that respect the doctrine accords with what obtains in Bengal, *viz.*, that for reasons warranted by the Hindu law, the widow is competent effectually to alienate the whole of the estate

[1] See Nund Coomar Rai *v.* Rajinder Narain Rai, 1 Sel. Rep., 349; Mussamut Bhuwani Munee *v.* Mussamut Soolukhuna, 1 Sel. Rep., 431.

LECTURE VIII.

which she has inherited from her husband. Another point which the case did not determine is, whether the widow can make an alienation of less than half of the estate unimpeachable by the next heirs, although no ground justifying an alienation under the Hindu law might exist. The inference, which can be drawn from the answer of the Pundits, is that when half the property is reserved for satisfying the spiritual necessities of the deceased, the widow was at liberty to alienate the other half, according to her own choice and pleasure, and that such alienation could not be impeached by the next heirs.

The Privy Council, however, in the case of *Keerut Sing* v. *Koolahul Sing*,[1] held, that the widow cannot alienate any portion of her husband's estate. In that case the defendant claimed possession of a *raj* by virtue of a *wusseyutnameh* (or deed operating as a will) from the widow of a deceased zemindar, who died without issue, leaving collateral heirs. The Judicial Committee refused to decide on the genuineness of the instrument devising the *raj*, being of opinion that the Ranee was incompetent by law to execute such an instrument to the prejudice of her deceased husband's heirs. The Judicial Committee further held, that the widow has no power to alienate or devise any portion of her husband's estate which on her death devolves to his legal heirs. The same view of the law was laid down in the case of *Rajen-*

[1] 2 Moore, 331.

LECTURE VIII.

der Narain Rai v. *Bijai Govind Sing*,[1] decided by the Privy Council. This case was in appeal from the judgment of the Sudder Dewany Adawlut in the case of *Sree Narain Rai* v. *Bhya Jha*,[1] which has been quoted before.

Widow incompetent to alienate.

The general rule of Hindu law therefore is, that as regards the property inherited by the widow from her husband she is incompetent to alienate it. This rule, however, is subject to one important exception, and I will now proceed to consider the same. The exception is, that alienations by the Hindu widow are valid if made for a *legal necessity*. The expression *legal necessity* does not occur in the original works on Hindu law. It has been coined by English lawyers who administered justice in this country in the latter end of the last century: but it concisely expresses the notion, in a generalised form, of the grounds which, in Hindu law, render the alienations by the widow valid.

Except for legal necessity.

The Privy Council observed in the case of *The Collector of Masulipatam* v. *Cavaly Vencata Narainapah*:[2]—"It is admitted on all hands that, if there be collateral heirs of the husband, the widow cannot of her own will alien the property except for special purposes. For religious or charitable purposes, or those which are supposed to conduce to the spiritual welfare of her husband, she has a larger power of disposition than that which she possesses for purely

[1] 2 Moore, 181.

[2] 8 Moore's I. A., 529.

LECTURE VIII.

worldly purposes. To support an alienation for the last, she must show necessity."

Legal necessity defined.

According to Jimutavahana any expenditure incurred which is useful to the late owner would come within the category of legal necessity, and would justify the widow's alienation.[1] The spiritual welfare of the late owner is here meant, or acts beneficial to the soul of the deceased in the next world. It must be here observed that extravagant and wasteful expenditure in the performance of acts conducive to the spiritual welfare of the deceased, will not probably be protected under the category of legal necessity. If a widow, therefore, having a considerable income from the estate of her husband, were to spend the whole of that income, and in addition to incur debts, I presume that an alienation of any part of the husband's estate to satisfy such debts will not be valid in law.[2] Of course the amount of expenses that the widow may incur for such purposes cannot be precisely laid down. It will be a complicated question of fact depending upon many circumstances which it is impossible generally to define; each case of this nature arising must be determined upon its own merits.

This, however, is settled law that when the nature and extent of the estate is such that an alienation

---

[1] Dayabhaga., Chap. XI, sec. i, para. 61.

[2] *Doe dem* Rajchunder Pramanick *v.* Bulloram Biswas, Fulton's Rep., 133.

either of a part or of the whole is absolutely necessary for the performance of those acts of religion which are conducive to the spiritual welfare of the deceased, then an alienation will be protected. The spirit of the Hindu religion is, that religious acts can be performed with very little expense; and the religious efficacy of an act is never enhanced by larger expenditure being incurred on account of it. Hence alienations, which are attempted to be justified on this ground, must be rather rare, for the nature and extent of the husband's estate must be very small, indeed, before such a defence can be set up. In practice, however, the majority of cases in which the widow's alienations are in question, are attempted to be justified on this ground; and the tendency of our Courts having been to disfavor claims on the part of the reversioners, such defences succeed remarkably. If, however, the Hindu law was strictly administered in our Courts, one might say, that many of the claims of the reversioners which are now thrown out would have been recognised.

Widow's maintenance justifies alienation.

The first case of legal necessity justifying alienation by the widow is her own maintenance. If the income of her husband's estate is so inconsiderable that it is not sufficient to maintain her, then the widow is justified in alienating a *portion* of the estate; or if that is insufficient, to alienate the *whole* of it.[1] The maintenance here contemplated, however,

[1] Dayabhaga, Chap. XI, sec. i, para. 62.

LECTURE VIII.

is a bare maintenance sufficient to keep the widow alive, and not an indulgence in the good things and luxuries of life; for, as I have before observed, the strict mode of life which the widow is enjoined to follow, by the *Shasters*, renders an indulgence in the luxuries of life highly improper. A reasonable expenditure for the performance of religious ceremonies is perhaps to be allowed, and might be counted as a legal necessity, though even this seems to be somewhat doubtful according to the original authorities.

According to the Dayabhaga.

The author of the Dayabhaga says,[1] that because a widow benefits her husband by the preservation of her person, the use of property sufficient for that purpose is authorised. Hence, if she be unable to subsist otherwise, she is authorised to mortgage the property, or, if still unable, she may sell or otherwise alienate it.

Raghunandana, in his Dayatattwa, does not discuss this question at all. The power of a widow over the estate inherited by her from her husband is not at all considered. After establishing the widow's right to succeed, he passes on to consider as to who shall succeed in default of the widow.[2]

According to the Dayakrama Sangraha.

In the Dayakrama Sangraha, Sree Krisna Tarkalankar, following Jimutavahana, has laid down, that a widow can use her husband's property for her own maintenance. The use here permitted is not to be an indulgence in the luxuries of life; "but since a

[1] Chap. XI, sec. i, paras. 61 and 62.

[2] Chap. XI, §§ 1—24.

widow benefits her husband by the preservation of her body, the use of property for the attainment of this object is permitted."[1] Again, "if the widow be unable to subsist otherwise, she may mortgage the property; and, if even then unable, she may sell it."[2]

According to the Digest.

Jagannatha Turkapunchanun quotes the following passage from the Mahabharata :—"Simple enjoyment is declared to be the fruit which women gather from the heritage of their lords : on no account should they waste the estate of their husbands."[3] Commenting on this passage the learned compiler says: "But such use [by the widow] only is approved which is requisite for the welfare of her body, because she confers a benefit on her lord by the preservation of her person. Accordingly, the legislator says, women should not waste the estate of their husbands; and the dissipation of it consists in expenses not necessary for the owner of the estate. Hence, if she cannot otherwise subsist, hypothecation is permitted; if she cannot even thus maintain herself, sale is also permitted : for reason shows no distinction."

From the above authorities it is clear that a widow is required in the first instance to resort to a mortgage of the property; if that is not sufficient, then to alienate it. And the distinction here made is very obvious. If it is a mortgage, it is redeemable by the reversioner on the payment of the mortgage

---

[1] Chap. I, sec. ii, para. 5. [2] Para. 6. [3] Dig., Vol. IV, v. ccccii.

LECTURE VIII.

debt; but if it is a sale, there is no option of redemption. One would have expected that, administering the law strictly, our Courts would have held that an alienation out-and-out is invalid as against the reversioners when a mortgage would have been sufficient. But it has been held in some cases, that although the widow sells where she ought to have mortgaged, the sale will nevertheless be valid.[1]

In the case of *Dowlut Sing* v. *Buktiar Singh*,[2] which was decided in 1808, the question proposed for the opinion of the Pundits was as follow:— "There were three uterine brothers who held their patrimonial lands in joint tenancy. Two of the brothers died, each leaving a widow and the other brother still survives. The estate is jointly held by these individuals. The widows being much distressed for the means of maintenance, sold a part of their husbands' shares of the joint landed estate without the consent of their husbands' brother and appropriated the purchase-money to their own use. In this case is the sale good and valid?"

The Pundits, after quoting the text of Vrihaspati cited in the Dayabhaga, answered as follows:—"The widow of a person dying without male issue takes his entire heritage, even though his father and brother be living, because she confers benefit on her deceased husband by preserving her life with the

[1] Phoolchund Lal *v.* Rughoobuns Sahoy, 9 W. R., 108.

[2] 2 Macnaghten, 304.

LECTURE VIII.

enjoyment of his wealth, and by offering oblations to his manes: and if she, having become indigent, defile her chastity, then hell becomes her husband's portion. Under these circumstances, the preservation of her chastity and life is absolutely necessary. If with the produce of their husbands' estate their maintenance cannot be supplied, they (the widows), for the purpose of acquring the means of subsistence, may mortgage or sell a portion of their husbands' landed estate, and the sale in such case is legal and valid." On the authority of this opinion the sale in question was upheld.[1]

Not, if the reversioner agrees to maintain.

By the sale the widow prejudices the rights of the reversioners. If, however, the reversioners for the time being provide the widow with her maintenance, there is no necessity for the widow to sell either the whole or a portion of the estate inherited by her. A sale by the widow under such circumstances will therefore be invalid, the necessity justifying a sale being wanting. It was accordingly stated by the Pundits in an early case,[2] which opinion, I presume, was acted upon by the Court that,—"If the daughter's son supply the widow with maintenance, she cannot alienate without his consent, and if she had actually sold the property, the sale is null; but in a case where the daughter's son declines to support

[1] See *Doe dem* Bissonath Dutt *v.* Doorgaprosad Day, Easts' Notes; 2 Morley, App., 49; *Doe dem* Rajchunder Pramanick *v.* Bulloram Biswas, Fulton, p. 133.

[2] 2 Macnaghten, p. 211.

her, she may sell such portion as may be necessary to her maintenance without his consent, and the sale should be considered legal and valid." The daughter's son in this case was, I presume, the next reversioner.

Widow bound to maintain her husband's family.

The maintenance of the family of her husband is an obligation imposed upon the widow. The authorities have laid down this principle that the Hindu widow is bound to maintain those members of her husband's family whom the husband during his lifetime was bound to maintain. Who these relatives are who are entitled to be maintained out of the estate of the husband, it is somewhat difficult to enumerate exhaustively.[1] The unmarried daughter and the childless widowed daughter, who has no provision for her maintenance out of the estate of her husband or in the family of her husband, are entitled to be maintained.[2] The mother and grandmother of the late proprietor are also entitled to be maintained by the widow, inasmuch as the late owner was bound to maintain them. The maintenance here means the maintenance by the supply of food and raiment to them and by providing them with residence in the family dwelling-house. It is somewhat doubtful whether these persons who are entitled to be maintained can at their option, or on account of disagreement, claim a money-allowance from the widow on account of their maintenance. I think, however, it is clear from the spirit of the Hindu law

[1] See Menu, quoted in 3 Dig., 406.

[2] 2 Macnaghten, 118.

bearing upon the point, that the ancient sages did not contemplate separate residence and separate maintenance for these persons : what was intended was that these persons should reside in the family dwelling-house with the widow and be maintained there ; that they should form members of her family, and in all respects conform to the family discipline which is very essential to the maintenance of peace and harmony in the family. If, then, any of those persons refuse to reside with the widow and be maintained there, he or she will not be entitled to claim a money-allowance from her on account of maintenance. The same principle was followed in the case of a son's widow claiming a money-allowance for her maintenance from her father-in-law. The Court held, that as she refused to reside at the house of her father-in-law and be maintained there, her claim to a money-allowance cannot be allowed.[1]

Alienation for that purpose allowed.

If the income of the husband's estate is insufficient to maintain those persons whom the widow is bound to maintain, then the widow will be justified in alienating a portion of such estate to defray the expenses of such maintenance, and the sale taking place under those circumstances will stand good and cannot be impeached by the reversioners.

The widow is also bound to perform the initiatory rites of those members of the family for whom those rites have not been performed. It was a duty

[1] Khetra Moni Dosi v. Kasi Nath Doss, 10 W. R., 89.

LECTURE VIII. incumbent upon the late owner to perform the initiatory rites of his children, and if he has died without performing them, his widow will be bound to perform those rites; since if the ceremonies remain unperformed, the spiritual welfare of the late owner is, to some extent, jeopardised. In the case of the widow, however, the only members of the family whose initiatory rites the widow, out of her own estate, is bound to perform are the daughters; and that only when they are unmarried, because the only initiatory rite necessary for a female belonging to any of the four ancient classes, is marriage. The widow is accordingly bound to provide for the marriage expenses of the unmarried daughters of the late owner. "The widow should give to an unmarried daughter a fourth part out of her husband's estate to defray the expenses of the damsel's marriage. Since sons are required to give that allotment, much more should the wife or any other successor give a like portion."[1]

Daughter's marriage to be performed by the widow.

The marriage of the daughter is an imperative obligation on the widow; for should the girl attain to puberty without being married, the future salvation of the ancestors is forfeited. "Should the maiden arrive at puberty unmarried through poverty, her father and the rest would fall to a region of punishment, as declared by holy writ."[2]

---

[1] Dayabhaga, Chap. XI, sec. i, para. 66.
[2] Dayabhaga, Chap. XI, sec. ii, para. 6.

Jimutavahana has further observed, that the father and the rest are saved from hell by sufficient property becoming applicable to the charges of the daughter's marriage ; and after marriage she confers benefits on her father by means of her son.[1]

Devala has also ordained, "to maidens should be given a nuptial portion out of the father's estate."[2]

The "fourth part out of her husband's estate," which the widow is required to give for the marriage expenses of the daughter, is not to be taken in its literal sense; for a widow having four unmarried daughters, by no means an improbable event, will have nothing left for her own support, not to mention her other obligations, if a literal compliance with the text is exacted from her. We accordingly find Jimutavahana, speaking of the obligation of the sons to give a fourth part of their shares for the marriage of their unmarried sisters, lays down: "Thus, since the daughter takes not in right of inheritance, if the wealth be great, funds sufficient for the nuptials should be allotted. *It is not an indispensable* rule that a fourth part shall be assigned."[3] Therefore, a fourth part of the estate which the widow is required to give for the daughter's marriage, means funds sufficient for the nuptials, and no more.

---

[1] Dayabhaga, Chap. XI, sec. ii, § 7.

[2] Quoted in the Dayabhaga, Chap. XI, sec. ii, § 5.

[3] Dayabhaga, Chap. III, sec. ii, para. 39.

LECTURE VIII.

If the estate of the husband be very small, so that from its income the marriage expenses cannot be met, the widow will be justified in selling a portion of the estate to defray such expenses, and a debt contracted for this purpose will be a charge upon the estate binding the reversioners. "The marriage of unmarried daughters is one of the objects for which the Hindu law allows the widow to alienate a portion of her deceased husband's estate; consequently a debt contracted for this purpose should be a charge on the estate of the deceased, and not on the widow personally."[1]

Alienation allowed for the spiritual welfare of the husband.

But the most important case in which the widow is allowed to alienate the property is for the purpose of conferring spiritual benefits on her late husband. The Hindu law, and particularly the Dayabhaga, considers the deceased husband of the widow as still the proprietor, and the widow holds the property for the benefit of the late owner.[2] Expenditure not useful to the owner of the property is considered by the Dayabhaga as *waste:* and the widow is strictly forbidden to incur such expenditure. "Since the benefit of the husband is to be consulted, even a gift or other alienation is permitted for the completion of her husband's funeral rites."[3] Even the maintenance of the widow and other relatives,

---

[1] Preagnarain *v.* Ajodhya Prosad, 7 Sel. Rep., 602.

[2] Judgment of Mitter, J., in Kerry Kolitanee *v.* Moniram Kolita, 19 W. R., 367.

[3] Dayabhaga, Chap. XI, sec. i, para. 61.

and the marriage of the daughter, are considered as necessities justifying the widow's alienations, only because they benefit the late owner either directly or indirectly; on no other ground, as I have shown before, are the alienations in such cases maintained. Lecture VIII.

In the case of *Ramchunder Surmah* v. *Gunga Govind Bunhoojiah*,[1] the plaintiff claimed to recover possession of a share in certain villages which belonged to one Prannath, the half-brother of the plaintiff. There were two defendants,—the first claimed to hold the seven annas of the property under a deed of sale from the widow of Prannath, and out of the consideration-money, "she paid the expenses of the *sraddhas* and her husband's debts, and obtained the means of her own subsistence." The second defendant, who was the brother of the widow, claimed to hold the nine annas of the estate under a deed of gift from that lady.

The Pundits who were consulted, submitted the following *vyavastha*:—"A widow having succeeded to the property of her deceased husband, has the power of alienating by sale so much of such property (and no more) as may be necessary for the payment of debts contracted by him, for the support of his family, for her own maintenance, and for the performance of his exequial rites. She may likewise make a gift, proportioned to the extent of her late husband's property, for the benefit of his soul; and

[1] 4 Sel. Rep., 147.

LECTURE VIII.

if these objects (*viz.*, payment of debts, expenses of *sraddha*, &c.) cannot be effected without the sale of all the property, she has the power of disposing of the whole of it. But she is not permitted to alienate by gift or sale the whole or even a part of the property solely at the suggestion of her own will and pleasure."

The Sudder Court, according to this opinion, held the sale by the widow valid, but declared the gift invalid.

You will see that the opinion of the Pundits given in the above case is a very valuable one, inasmuch as it concisely lays down almost all the cases in which the widow's alienations are declared valid by the Hindu law. You will also find, on referring to the report of the whole case, that the opinion was expressly based upon the authorities current in Bengal.[1]

For the husband's *sraddha*.

For performing her husband's *sraddha*, the widow, therefore, is entitled to alienate either a portion or the whole of the inheritance, and the alienation is allowed whether it be for performing the *ekodista sraddha* (that is, the first *sraddha* performed on the eleventh day after death among Brahmins, and on the thirty-first day after death among Sudras), or the other *sraddhas* of the deceased that are performed six-monthly or annually or at stated days in the year. These ceremonies performed, directly benefit

[1] See Jairam Dhami *v.* Musan Dhami, 5 Sel. Rep., 3.

the deceased, and the widow is, therefore, bound to perform them. LECTURE VIII.

For other religious acts.

For performing the other obligations of religion, it would appear that the widow is allowed to alienate a small portion of the inheritance.[1] In the case of *Mukhoda* v. *Kulleani*, which has been quoted before,[2] the Pundits declared, "that a gift by the widow of the whole estate of her husband is invalid; but that a gift of a moderate portion of his property, made by the widow with a view to his spiritual benefit, may be valid." The same principle was accepted by Mr. Macnaghten in his note to the case of *Bijoya Debee* v. *Unnopoorna Debee*, which has been quoted before.[3]

The difficulty, however, in the practical application of this principle, is as to what constitutes a "moderate portion" or "a small portion" of the inheritance. In the case of *Ramchunder Surmah* v. *Bejoygobind Banerjee*, which has been quoted before,[4] the Pundits declared as their opinion that the widow has the power of alienating from one to three-sixteenths of her husband's property for the benefit of his soul; and the Court (S. D. A.) seemed to acquiesce in that view. The gift of nine annas of the property was, therefore, declared illegal. I presume the question must, in every case, be one of *fact*, rather than one of *law*, as to what specific portion of the inheritance the widow is at liberty to alienate.

---

[1] Mussamut Gyankunwar and another v. Dookhuru Sing and another, 4 Sel. Rep., 420. This is a Mithila case.

[2] *Ante*, p. 289. [3] *Ante*, p. 290. [4] *Ante*, p. 307.

LECTURE VIII.

Religious acts performed by a Hindu widow may have a double effect. They may contribute to the religious merits of the lady herself, or they may tend to promote the spiritual welfare of her late husband; and I think it is generally recognised by the Hindus, that between these two classes of acts there is no *necessary* connection. Acts of religion highly meritorious on the part of the widow may have no effect on the spiritual welfare of her late husband. Suppose, for instance, the widow establishes an idol in her own name, and endows it with considerable property, and the poor and the helpless are maintained from this *sheba*, as a religious and a pious act it is considered highly meritorious for the widow, but it does not add to the spiritual welfare of her deceased husband. Therefore, it has been held, that such acts, of which the religious efficacy benefits the widow and not the husband, will not justify an alienation of the property inherited by the widow. Hence it was held, that a widow could not endow an idol with her husband's property to the detriment of the reversioners. "The fulfilment of the moral and religious duties of the deceased are those by which he is to be raised to a region of bliss, and not a dedication by the widow of the nature of that under which the special appellant claims, which, under any circumstances, could only be supposed to conduce to the spiritual benefit of the widow herself (who made the gift without her husband's consent), and is accom-

Which benefit the husband.

panied by a temporal benefit to the special appellant to which he is not entitled."[1] LECTURE VIII.

It was held in another case that a pilgrimage to Benares, undertaken by the widow, is not a legal necessity so as to justify an alienation by her of her husband's estate.[2]

Again, digging a tank, and appropriating the same to the use of the public, is not considered a sufficient legal necessity to justify the widow in alienating the property, though such an act is considered in the light of a religious duty, and in itself a highly meritorious one.[3] "The digging of a tank would be a meritorious act and a great convenience to the public, but it would not be a legal necessity for which a widow could make away with property which was only left to her for her life."[4]

For pilgrimage to Gya.

A pilgrimage to Gya, however, for the purpose of performing the husband's *sradh* there, is considered a legal necessity justifying the alienation by the widow. It was held that, "according to Hindu ideas, the performance of a deceased husband's *sradh* at Gya would be a very proper and reasonable necessity, inasmuch as the soul of the deceased is supposed to be greatly benefited thereby. Such a pilgrimage would, undoubtedly, be a religious purpose, supposed to conduce to the spiritual welfare of her husband, which would give a widow

---

[1] Kartic Chunder Chuckerbutty *v.* Gourmohun Roy, 1 W. R., 48.

[2] Huromohun Adhikari *v.* Aluckmoney Dosee, 1 W. R., 252.

[3] Mitacshara, Chap. II, sec. i, para. 24.

[4] Runjeetram Koolal *v.* Mahomed Waris, 21 W. R., 49.

LECTURE VIII. a larger power of alienation than she would ordinarily have. But I do not understand that the *sradh* pilgrimage to Gya can be put any higher than a very necessary and meritorious performance. A widow ought, perhaps, to perform it: but she is not absolutely bound to do so. It is, I should say, one of those ceremonies for the due performance of which a widow might fairly and properly alienate a moderate portion of her late husband's estate, but that she would not be justified in disposing of the entire property for that object."[1]

In this case the performance of the Gya *sradh* is considered as an *optional* ceremony which the widow is at liberty either to perform or not to perform. That, I think, is not a correct view of the question. If it is once admitted that the ceremony is optional, the performance of it will be no ground for incurring debts encumbering the estate or for alienating the same. The reversioner will say that as the ceremony is optional, if there are sufficient means from the current income, let the widow perform it; otherwise let her leave it unperformed and not touch the *corpus* of the estate for the purpose of performing the same. I think by treating this ceremony only as a *necessary* one which the widow is bound to perform that an alienation on account of it can be justified.

For payment of — The payment of the husband's debts is another

[1] Mahomed Ashruf v. Brijessuree Dosee, 19 W. R., 426.

LECTURE VIII.

instance of necessity justifying the widow's alienation of her husband's property. It is also put upon the ground of conferring spiritual benefits on the deceased. The Hindu law considers the payment of debts as a religious obligation. If a Hindu fails to pay his debts in this world, his spiritual welfare hereafter is sacrificed. Hence the obligation of the heirs of a deceased Hindu to pay his debts. The son is bound to pay the debts of his father with interest; and the grandson is bound to pay the principal only of his grandfather's debts, but not the interest;[1] and this whether the ancestor left assets or not. The Hindu law does not consider the relation between the ancestor and the heir as a mere commercial one, that the heir shall pay the debts when he has inherited property from the ancestor and not otherwise; it takes a spiritual view of that relation, and renders it obligatory on the heir to pay the debts independent of any pecuniary consideration. This principle of Hindu law, however, is not enforced by the Courts of this country, and the principle of English law, which lays down that the heir is bound to pay the debts of the ancestor to the extent of the assets inherited by him, is administered.

husband's debts.

Widow bound to pay husband's debts.

The widow, therefore, in pursuance with this principle of Hindu law, is declared bound to pay her husband's debts: for otherwise the spiritual welfare of the husband is thereby sacrificed. Here the

[1] Vrihaspati quoted in 1 Dig., 273.

LECTURE VIII. widow is bound to pay the debts from the property inherited by her from her husband, and not from any other property which she may happen to possess; and if the widow sells the whole of the property or a part of it to pay such debts, such a sale cannot be impeached by the next takers. It must be here observed that a creditor of the husband taking out execution against his property in the hands of his widow is entitled to sell it; and the sale will pass to the purchaser full title as against the widow and the reversioners.

In the case of *Rani Krishnamoni* v. *Raja Udmunt Sing and another*,[1] one of the points for consideration was, whether a conditional sale executed by the widow to pay off a mortgage debt of her husband shall be declared valid. The Sudder Dewanny Adawlut held, that as the conditional sale was executed to pay off her husband's debts, the alienation was good according to the Hindu law. The Court held, "that the conditional sale by the widow of her husband's landed estate was valid, inasmuch as both the law-officers agreed in declaring that the transaction would be legal, supposing a sufficient case of necessity to have been made out, and as it must be admitted that when the period fixed for the foreclosure of the original mortgage drew nigh, there did exist a sufficient case of distress to justify recourse to this measure. The conditional sale was executed to

[1] 3 Sel. Rep., 304.

prevent the foreclosure of the mortgage, whereby the interests of the son about to be adopted by the widow would, doubtless, be best consulted; and although the measure had not the effect of saving the estate ultimately from alienation, yet it put off the evil day, and steps might have been taken in the interval to avert the loss altogether." The sale by the widow was accordingly upheld.[1]

In the case of *Uma Chowdhrani and another* v. *Mussamut Indramoni Chowdhrani*,[2] the widow had sold certain estates belonging to her husband to satisfy a decree which the vendee had obtained against him. The following question was proposed to the Pundits: "Have Hindu widows the power to alienate the whole of the landed property inherited from their husbands for payment of their husbands' debts, without the consent of the next heirs to the said property, relatives of the husband?"

To which the Pundit answered: "A Hindu woman who has inherited the property left by her husband may alienate the whole of it to pay his debts, because so inheriting her husband's property she is bound to pay his debts."

The Pundit referred for his authority to Nared Munee as stated in the Digest of Jagannatha, and to be found in Colebrooke's Translation (pp. 315-316, Vol. I): "If the assets of the husband have been

---

[1] See also Ramchunder Surma v. Gungagobind Banerjee, 4 Sel. Rep. 147.
[2] 7 Sel. Rep., 420.

LECTURE VIII.

received by the wife, she must pay the debt;" and again, "and so must a debt be paid by a childless widow who has accepted the care of the assets, even though she have not accepted the burden of the debts, for she is successor to the estate."

According to this opinion the sale by the widow to the plaintiff was declared valid.[1]

Widow's personal debts do not justify alienation.

The widow, however, is not justified in alienating the property for the payment of her personal debts, unless those debts were the consequence of prior debts owing by her husband. As for instance, where the widow executes a bond for the payment of her husband's debts, or in renewal of a bond due from him. In such cases the liability of the widow is not personal; the estate of the husband is liable, and property sold for such debts by the widow will be valid as against the reversioner. The widow will convey a good title to the alienee.

If, however, the debts were the widow's own debts, and not incurred for satisfying her legal necessity, the alienation under them will not pass a complete title to the alienee; it will pass only the widow's estate, good during her lifetime, and liable to be impeached on the death of the widow, by the reversioner, who will be entitled to enter upon the property on that contingency.

---

[1] See Haris Chunder Roy *v.* Nandalal Dutt and another, S. D. A. Dec. for 1862. Goonomonee Debee *v.* Bhugbuty Dosee, S. D. Rep. for 1845, p. 299.

In the same way a decree obtained against the widow personally will not bind the estate of her late husband, and the execution-creditor cannot follow the property in the hands of the reversioner. In the case of *Prasanna Kumar Majumdar and another* v. *Kali Chunder Chowdhry*,[1] the Court held, that the decree was against the widow (Ranee) personally; and at the time of her death she was in possession of the property, now sought to be sold under the decree, with a life-interest. After her death the property has passed to the minor, who was the reversioner, and now forms part of his estate. The Court held, that the property could not be sold in execution of the personal decree against the Ranee.

In another case[2] the contention on the part of the appellant, who was the purchaser of the decree against the widow, was, that the interest of the widow was saleable, and should be sold in satisfaction of the decree against her, even on the supposition that the decree is a personal one; but that, in fact, the decree is against the estate of her husband, and any property belonging to it should be sold.

The Court held, that "the decree against the widow did not bind the estate of her husband, but was only a personal one against her, and there can be no doubt that she is entitled to the possession

---

[1] S. D. A. Dec. for 1860, p. 250.

[2] Shahzadah Mahomed Rabiuddin *v.* Rani Prosonno Moye Debi, S. D. A. Dec., 1860, p. 358.

LECTURE VIII.

and beneficial interest in all her husband's property during her lifetime. Such being the case, and admitting, for argument's sake, that the property attached was property of that nature, we think, in accordance with the ruling of this Court in the case of *Kali Kanta Lahuri* v. *Golak Chunder Chowdhry*, that the interest belonging to her is not of a saleable nature under Hindu law, but that if the purchaser of the decree desires to realise his money from profits of the property, he should move the Court for the sequestration of the same under the rules for that purpose."

The judgment in the above case held, that the estate which the Hindu widow has in the property of her husband is not saleable in execution of a decree against her. This point has been differently decided in later cases, where it has been held, that the widow's interest is saleable in execution;[1] and it is a common practice in our Courts for the decree-holders to attach the property in the possession of the widow, in which she has only a widow's interest, in execution of a personal decree against her. Of course, by such a sale the purchaser acquires the widow's interest only,—that is, an estate determinable with the widow's life, and on her death the reversioner is entitled to enter, ousting the purchaser from possession of the same.

Widow's interest saleable.

[1] *In re* Joynarain Bose, 4 Sev., p. 781; *In re* Rashbehary Bose, 5 Sev., 537.

There is some difficulty in the determination of this question as to whether the widow's interest is saleable in execution or not. If, however, it be held that the widow can voluntarily alienate property without the existence of any one of those grounds that justify widow's alienations under the Hindu law, and that by such a sale the purchaser acquires a good title to the property during the widow's life, then I think it must be held that the widow's interest in her husband's property is saleable in execution of a decree against her ; mere consistency would inevitably lead to that conclusion. But I venture to think that the true spirit of Hindu law was departed from when the Courts held that the widow's alienations shall be good during her lifetime, although none of the grounds justifying alienation by the widow did exist. By the Hindu law, absolute ownership in the property of her husband does not vest in the widow ; she is only entitled to hold it during her life and enjoy its profits, preserving the property intact ; and she will hold it for certain purposes which are clearly defined in the Hindu law. She has no power to alienate it, or any portion of it ; and it is only when certain causes exist that her alienation is declared to be valid. That clearly is an exceptional case, and the Hindu legislators intended that the widows should not ordinarily alienate the property, and that it was not to be in their hands an ordinarily marketable commodity. The Hindu legislators did not

LECTURE VIII.

merely impose a restraint upon alienations, but declared that the alienations shall be generally void. It is only when the exceptional cause exists that the alienation is declared to be valid. It seems to me that the true spirit of the law would have been better preserved by declaring that, in the absence of the exceptional cause, the alienation was void, and that it will be open to any person interested in contesting the matter to have it set aside and to recover the property from the hands of the purchaser, for the benefit of the widow or of some other person who may be otherwise entitled to the possession of it.

In the case of *Mussamut Phool Koer* v. *Dabeepersaud*[1] the Court held, that the widow's interest could not be accepted as a sufficient security for mesne profits and costs of an appeal to the Privy Council. The Court observed, that the security is not a permanent one: the widow might die at any time, and if the appeal to the Privy Council failed, what would become of the security. It could not be a burden on the property which would go to the reversionary heir intact, the widow having no power of alienation.

In another case[2] the Court held, that a widow in possession of the widow's estate in her husband's property is *personally* liable under a decree for ancestral debts. The facts of this case were shortly these. The decree-holder obtained a decree against the

---

[1] 12 W. R., 187.

[2] Sitaram Dey and another v. Ranee Prosonnomoyee Debee, 4 W. R., 38.

widow Rashmonee on a mortgage that was executed by her late husband, Rajah Bejoy Kissen. The suit was brought by the respondent as the guardian of her minor adopted son, who was the grandson (adopted son's adopted son) of Rajah Bejoy Kissen. The suit was for a declaration of the minor's right in the property, and that it was not liable to be sold in execution of the decree against the widow Ranee Rashmonee.

The decree-holder defendant contended, that the decree under which the properties were attached was not a personal one to the Ranee Rashmonee ; the debts were ancestral, having been incurred by the late husband of the Ranee, Rajah Bejoy Kissen, and that, consequently, the estate, as derived from Bejoy Kissen, should be liable.

The Court held, that "the case turns simply on the liability or otherwise of Rashmonee alone, and on the nature of a decree ; and both in law and in equity we think the defendants can only have their remedy against the Ranee, and hold that the lower Court came to a right conclusion that the decree should be executed against her, and that the property of the minor was not liable."

This decision, I venture to think, lays down a somewhat questionable law. The decree was passed on account of debts incurred by the late owner. At the time when the suit was brought the widow was representing her husband, and the decree was given

LECTURE VIII. against her not *personally*, but in her capacity as *representative* of her husband. That being so, clearly the decree was available against the estate of her husband, and the heir succeeding to it could not resist the decree-holder's claim to take that property in satisfaction of his decree. This case is a departure from the principle that, for the debts of the husband, the estate in the hands of the widow or of other heir is liable.

Where, however, a decree is obtained against the widow for her own default, that will be a personal decree against the widow, and at a sale in execution of the same the widow's interest will only pass, and not the estate of her husband. On the death of the widow the estate would descend to the reversionary heir of her husband.[1]

If a decree is obtained against a widow in her own right and as guardian of her minor son, for a debt contracted by the widow and her husband jointly, then the widow is entitled to sell the property of her husband to satisfy this decree. The decree-holder was entitled to execute this decree against the minor as the representative of his father, and could sell the property of the minor's father. The widow, therefore, was entitled to sell the minor's father's property to satisfy this decree, and the purchaser from the widow has a good title against the son in respect of the property so purchased.[2]

---

[1] Baijun Dobey *v.* Brijbhookhun Lal, 24 W. R., 306.

[2] Goluck Chunder Paul *v.* Mahomed Rohim, 9 W. R., 316.

LECTURE VIII.

Husband's debt must be proved.

To justify an alienation by the widow on account of her husband's debts, the existence of those debts must be proved; a mere declaration or an acknowledgment by the widow that the debt is owing will not be sufficient proof of the husband's indebtedness; the debt must be proved by documentary evidence or by the testimony of witnesses.[1] In fact, the debt must be proved like any other fact regarding which there may be a contest in the case. A mere confession by the widow of a debt of the husband is not evidence that the debt really was the debt of the husband. The purchaser must prove that it is so.[2] In the same way a mere declaration by the widow of the existence of the necessity is not sufficient to justify the purchaser in proceeding to buy. He must by enquiry satisfy himself of the existence of the necessity.[3] Again, a mere recital in the deed of sale itself that the property was sold for the liquidation of her husband's debts is not sufficient of itself to prove that the property was sold for the purpose stated; but that it was on the party seeking to uphold the sale to prove by evidence that the property was sold for that purpose.[4]

The widow, however, it has been held, is not justified in selling her husband's property to pay a debt,

---

[1] Hemchunder Mozumdar v. Musst. Taramoni, 1 Sel. Rep., 481.

[2] Munshi Coseemuddin Ahmed v. Ramdass Gossain, 2 W. R., 170.

[3] Gungagobind Bose and others v. S. M. Dhunee and another, 1 W. R., 59.

[4] Raj Lukhee Debee v. Gocool Chunder Chowdhry, 12 W. R., p. 47, P. C. R.

LECTURE VIII. due from her husband, which has been barred by the Statute of Limitations. The payment of such a debt is not a legal necessity, and a sale on account of it is not justifiable.[1]

Debts incurred by the widow for preserving the estate, and the payment of such debts, would warrant an alienation of a portion of the estate, and would be treated as a legal necessity. Payment of revenue due to Government will justify an alienation when the same cannot be met from other sources. If the resources of the estate failed in any particular year, and the arrear was occasioned by natural causes injurious to the estate, such as drought, inundation, &c., and not owing to any waste or extravagance on the part of the widow, it was held to be a sufficient case of necessity justifying an alienation.[2]

Alienation for payment of revenue justified.

In a later case,[3] however, the Sudder Dewany Adawlut held, that whether the arrear was caused by waste or neglect on the part of the widow, need not be enquired into. If there was an arrear, and the alienation took place on account of it, the purchaser is protected, and the alienation is good. Raikes, J., observed:—"Doubtless, for obvious reasons, the Hindu law could not specifically provide for a case of Government sale: but it is not consistent with Hindu law that the widow should passively allow the estate

---

[1] Melgirappa v. Shevappa, 6 Bom. Rep., 270.

[2] Shekh Mulcoolah v. Radhabinode Misser, S. D. R. for 1856.

[3] Sreenath Roy v. Ruttunmala Chowdhrain, S. D. R. for 1859, p. 421.

of her husband to be swept away when the sacrifice of a small portion of it would preserve the greater part; and the act of sale or mortgage would apparently come within the line of secular duty imposed upon her, and render valid any such alienation independent of the precedent mismanagement which may have caused the necessity. If, then, the alienation be in proportion to the Government demand, and the lender be able to show that he used due caution in ascertaining the apparent truth of the representations made to him regarding the jeopardy of the estate, there seems nothing in the spirit of the Hindu law to prevent the recognition of his rights against the successors to the property; and certainly public policy seems to require that such legitimate means of staying a sale should be available to the widow."

In the same case, Loch, J., observed:—"The chief point to be looked to in all those cases appears to be the necessity under which the sale is alleged to have been made, and the conduct of the purchaser. Necessity justifying sale cannot, I think, be restricted to conditions prescribed by Hindu law, which are very limited, but must be extended under the existing state of things and under a new system of law materially affecting the rights of property introduced subsequently to the Hindu system. The private sale or mortgage by a widow of part of an estate to save the remainder from a

LECTURE VIII. revenue sale for arrears to Government, is an act not contemplated by the Hindu law; but it is admitted that, under certain circumstances, the widow is justified in making such a sale. In the present case we find that the Judge considers that a necessity which justified the sale did exist. From the evidence before him, he finds that the late proprietor died in embarrassed circumstances; that the plaintiff, when he came of age, was, owing to his embarrassed circumstances, also obliged to contract a loan, showing thereby that the resources of the estate were insufficient for the support of the family, or had been diverted into other channels, such as the payment of debts. He finds that the danger to the estate by Government sale, which was advertised to take place on a date close at hand, was imminent; and that, owing to this private sale of a part of the property, the remainder of the estate was saved, the arrears of Government revenue having been paid up from the purchase-money obtained from the vendee. There is nothing illegal in this finding, nor has the Judge, as alleged by the special appellant, thrown the burden of proof on the wrong party. I would, therefore, confirm the order of the lower Court." The lower Court, I may observe here, had upheld the sale by the widow.

In a later case[1] the widow borrowed a sum of money on the mortgage of her husband's property,

[1] Gopal Chunder Manna v. Gour Monee Dossee, 6 W. R., 52.

and having failed to pay the amount the mortgagee sued and obtained a decree and possession. The Court held, that the monies were borrowed for a legal necessity, *viz.*, the payment of the Government revenue; and this necessity is recited in the mortgage bond. The borrower was not bound to see how the money borrowed was appropriated, and the decree against the widow, which has not been shown to be collusive, is clearly binding upon the reversioner.

The purchaser not bound to see to the appropriation.

In another case,[1] where the widow had borrowed a larger sum than was necessary for the payment of Government revenue, it was held by the Court, that "the vendee was not bound to enquire into the exact amount necessary to be borrowed. It was sufficient that he did satisfy himself of the existence of a necessity to justify him in looking to the estate for repayment."

The principle, therefore, seems well established that if a widow sells her husband's property to pay an arrear of Government revenue, and if revenue be actually due, the sale is protected. Whether from the sale-proceeds the widow paid the arrears of revenue or not the purchaser is not bound to see. It may, therefore, so happen, that a property may be sold for the express purpose of paying the arrears of Government revenue due on the estate, and the widow may not pay up the arrears, and the consequence will be

[1] Nuffer Chunder Banerjee v. Gudadhur Mundle, 3 W. R., 122.

LECTURE VIII.

that the estate will be sold for arrears of revenue. The private sale will stand good, because it took place for the payment of arrears of revenue, and the revenue sale will stand good because the arrears were not paid ; and this result takes place because our Courts have held that the purchaser is not bound to see to the appropriation of the purchase-money by the widow. The interest of the reversioner is doubly sacrificed by the private sale, from which no benefit accrues to the estate, and by the revenue sale, which may be the consequence of the widow's wilful default.

Again, if the mere existence of the arrears is a sufficient justification for the lender to advance money, and it were treated as a case of necessity, it will be the easiest thing for the Hindu widow to *create* such necessities. Wilful default would produce it, and antecedent mismanagement or extravagance may lead to it ; and the interests of the reversioners will be perfectly unprotected.

Money borrowed to carry on litigation will not be a charge on the estate

How far the widow is justified in borrowing money to carry on a litigation is a much more difficult question to answer. In the case of *Mussamut Phool Koer* v. *Debee Persaud*[1] which has been quoted before, the widow offered her husband's property inherited by her as security for the costs and mesne profits of an appeal to the Privy Council which was preferred by her late husband. It was contended on behalf of the widow, that the widow's action being one of

[1] *Ante*, p. 320, 12 W. R., 187.

necessity, the Hindu law would allow her to bind the estate, so as to conclude the reversioner, for the purpose of raising the necessary funds. The Court held, "that the necessity is not such an one as is contemplated by the provisions of Hindu law, the appellant being under no necessity and under no moral obligation to take her husband's case before the Privy Council. In the next place, she is not doing it for the benefit of the estate, seeing that the reversionary heir happens to be the other co-sharer in the estate and the respondent in the appeal to the Privy Council now proposed to be made." LECTURE VIII.

If the litigation is not for the benefit of the estate, there will be no warrant for charging it with money borrowed for carrying on the litigation. But then it becomes a very difficult question to say beforehand,—*i.e.*, at the time of the loan,—whether the litigation is for the benefit of the estate or not. The ultimate result will, probably, alone determine the question. If the litigation is successful, there will be no question but that the estate will be bound by the loan: but if the litigation is unsuccessful, it will be doubtful whether the estate will be charged with the advances made to the widow. I think, however, the proper test will be to see whether the litigation was undertaken *bonâ fide* for the benefit of the estate. If it appears that it was so undertaken, I think the estate will be bound by the widow's loan, whether the litigation ultimately succeeded or not. The A good charge if for the benefit of the estate.

LECTURE VIII.

lender will be protected if he satisfied himself on enquiry that there was a real necessity for the widow to fight out the matter.[1] If, on the other hand, the litigation was a gambling or speculative one, or was otherwise unjust, there will be no justification for the lender in advancing money to the widow under such circumstances, and consequently the estate will not be bound.

I have before[2] pointed out that a decree against the widow will bind the estate, so as to conclude the reversioners. That means that the decree must be obtained in a suit the subject-matter of which involves property which the widow had inherited, and not founded upon any obligation which the widow may have personally incurred. For instance, if the decree be had upon a bond or upon a mortgage executed by the widow, it will not bind the estate. But if the suit be by or against the widow for her husband's property, independent of any obligation incurred by the widow herself, the decree obtained in such a case will bind the estate.

Advances for widow's maintenance and for the costs of recovering the estate a good charge.

Advances made to the widow for her own maintenance and for the costs of carrying on a litigation to recover the estate of her husband have been held to be legitimate charges on the estate, which will bind the reversioner. The case of *Grose* v. *Omertomoyee*

Grose v. *Omertomoyee.*

Dosee,[3] which has been quoted before, is an authority

---

[1] Grose *v.* Omertomoyee, 12 W. R., 12, O. J. A.

[2] *Ante*, p. 248 *et seq.*

[3] 12 W. R., 12, O. J. A.

in point. In that case the widow Bamasunduree, being in want of funds for the purpose of carrying on proceedings to recover certain monies due to her as the widow and heiress of her deceased husband, applied to the defendant Grose and executed a deed in his favor. By that deed Grose agreed with due diligence and to the best of his ability to carry on the law-suit in behalf of Bamasunduree, to find all the funds necessary for prosecuting the same, and to pay her Rs. 16 a month for her maintenance. In consideration of the same, the widow assigned to Grose all her interest as such widow in the estate and property of her deceased husband, and in the profits and accumulations thereof, to hold the same upon the following terms :— LECTURE VIII. —

1*st.*—That Grose should retain an eight-anna share thereof for his own absolute use for his trouble and labour in the conduct and management of those proceedings.

2*nd.*—That out of the remaining eight annas of the estate, Grose should reimburse himself all monies which he should advance and pay for the maintenance of the widow, and all sums and expenses which he might advance or incur in conducting the said suit in behalf of the widow, with interest upon such sums at the rate of 12 per cent. per annum.

Peacock, C. J., on appeal, held, that the first condition "by which the eight-anna share of the property to be recovered was assigned to Grose and his assigns

LECTURE VIII. for his and their own use as remuneration for their trouble and labour to be bestowed in the conduct and management of the suits, was not binding upon the reversionary heirs, if not upon the ground of champerty, upon the ground that it was an unconscionable bargain and a speculative, if not a gambling, contract."

As regards the second condition, the Chief Justice held, "that the assignment of the eight-anna share as security for the advances and expenses which Grose or his assigns might reasonably and properly make or incur for the maintenance of the said widow, for carrying on the necessary proceedings to enforce her rights, with 12 per cent. interest on such advances, was not void; but that it created a charge upon that eight annas of the property which was binding upon the reversionary heirs of Mudoosoodun (the husband of the widow) to the extent of such advances and expenses."

Further, "the widow, under the circumstances, had a right to charge the property, which might be recovered, with the amount of all such advances and expenses as might be necessarily made or incurred for the purpose of conducting the suits and realising the estate of her husband, and for her own maintenance in the meantime. If there was a necessity to procure advances for the purpose of realising the estate of her husband, I think she was justified in charging the *corpus* of that portion of the estate, as well as the accumulations in respect of it, with the amount of such advances and expenses, and a reasonable amount of interest." LECTURE VIII.

In the same case Macpherson, J., observed :— "The facts are, that there was no real enquiry by Grose as to there being any necessity for Bamasunduree entering into such an agreement, no attempt by him, or by any one on his behalf, to ascertain or calculate what her rights were or were worth, and that it was a mere speculation of Grose's, by which, in the best result, one-half of the whole of Mudoosudun's estate *must* be lost to his heirs, while the other half remained charged with all the costs and other sums advanced by Grose. An alienation, such as this, of the estate of her deceased husband by a childless widow, is, in my opinion, not valid as against the reversioners, except so far as it may be held merely to create a charge on the estate by way of security for the costs incurred and monies properly advanced, with interest."

Further, "I do not doubt that Bamasunduree might properly have carried on her suit by means of advances from Grose, and have given him a portion of the estate recovered as security for the repayment of the monies advanced by him. So, perhaps, she might have raised the necessary funds by absolutely assigning to Grose a portion of what might be recovered. But she could have done this, so as to bind the reversioners only if the transaction was a fair and *bonâ fide* and reasonable transaction, both on her part and on Grose's, entered into after due consideration of Bamasunduree's position as representing her husband's estate. In no event can it be right, or in accordance with Hindu law, for a widow to resign her whole position as representing her husband, and to assign her whole estate to a stranger, and appoint him her irrevocable attorney, for the purpose of realising and dealing with the estate, subject only to the repayment by him to her of such residue of a moiety as he shall consider to be payable to her after he shall have deducted out of that moiety all his own costs and charges."

This case, therefore, is an authority for the proposition that if money is advanced to a widow, after due and proper enquiry, for carrying on a litigation to realise her husband's estate, the amount so advanced shall be a charge upon the estate binding on the reversioners.

Gifts to husband's relations allowed.

The widow is authorised to make gifts to her husband's relatives at his funeral obsequies; and this for the purpose of securing his spiritual welfare, the gifts being in proportion to the estate of her husband. "With presents offered to his manes and by pious liberality, let her honor the paternal uncles of her husband, his spiritual parents and daughter's sons, the children of his sisters, his maternal uncles, and also ancient and unprotected persons, guests and females of the family."[1]

[1] Vrihaspati quoted in the Dayabhaga, Chap. XI, sec. i, para. 63.

The author of the Dayabhaga thus defines the relations who are referred to in the text of Vrihaspati: "The term 'paternal uncle' intends any *sapinda* of her husband; 'daughter's sons,' the descendants of her husband's daughter; 'children of his sister,' the progeny of her husband's sister's sons; 'maternal uncles,' her husband's mother's family. To these and to the rest, let her give presents, and not to the family of her own father, while such persons are forthcoming, for the specific mention of paternal uncles and the rest would be superfluous."[1]

LECTURE VIII.

The definition given by Jimutavahana of the persons to whom gifts can be made is very comprehensive, and it would seem to warrant gifts to any relations of the husband, however remote. The limitation, however, that the gifts must be in proportion to the husband's wealth, places a wholesome check on the widow's extravagance and wasteful expenditure; the limits to her discretion, however, not being precise, the circumstances of each case must be looked into for determining the propriety or otherwise of gifts by the widow.

Not to her father's family.

The widow, however, as a rule, is precluded from making gifts to the family of her own father. There is an evident anxiety on the part of the ancient sages to prevent the property of her husband from passing into the family of her father; and this

[1] Dayabhaga, Chap. XI, sec. i, para. 63.

LECTURE VIII.

because there is a natural inclination and after anxiety on the part of the widow to benefit her father's family rather than her husband's, from the estate which she inherits as a Hindu widow. The author of the Dayabhaga, however, has laid down that, with the consent of her husband's relatives, the widow may bestow gifts on the kindred of her own father and mother.[1]

[1] Dayabhaga, Chap. XI, sec. i, para. 64.

LECTURE IX.

THE ALIENATIONS BY THE WIDOW.—*(Continued.)*

Unjustifiable alienations—Purchaser entitled to possession—Good during widow's life—Purchaser's obligations—He must show good faith—Purchaser to show that the sale is within the widow's limited powers—Not bound to see to appropriation of purchase-money—*Hunooman Persaud Pandey* v. *Mussamut Babooe Munraj Koonwer*—Sale in execution against the widow—Decree against the widow as representative will pass the whole estate—Not in a Mitacshara family—Modified by recent decisions—Sale on a decree for rent against the widow passes the tenure—A contrary doctrine held by the Privy Council—Which is followed by the Bengal High Court—Other kinds of properties of the widow—That acquired by herself—Her *stridhun*—Inherited property not *stridhun*.

I HAVE, up to this moment, considered the cases in which the widow's alienations are good absolutely; *i. e.*, good as against the reversioner also. Supposing the widow alienates for other than allowable causes, what are the rights of the purchaser in such a case? Generally he is entitled to possession of the property purchased, and to acquire in the property all the rights which the widow possessed; and the alienation shall stand good during the period of the widow's natural life.[1] Again it was held, that the pur-

Unjustifiable alienations.

[1] Mayaram Bhakram *v.* Motiram Gobindram, 2 Bomb. H. C. Rep., 331; Tariny Churn Banerjee *v.* Nund Coomar Banerjee, 1 W. R., 47.

LECTURE IX.

chaser from the Hindu widow is entitled to possession, when the widow is living, whether there was any necessity for the widow's sale or not.[1] In fact, a purchaser from the widow suing for possession during the widow's lifetime is entitled to a decree on proof of sale, although it be proved that there was no necessity for the widow's sale.

Purchaser entitled to possession.

A different doctrine was maintained on this subject at one time. Sir F. Macnaghten maintained[2] that such an alienation was void *ab initio*. But the current of decisions since, both in Bengal and in the other presidencies, have been the other way ; it has been repeatedly held that it stands good for her life.[3] This point was expressly laid down in the very important case of *Gobind Monee Dossee* v. *Shamloll Bysack*,[4] in which all the authorities were quoted and considered.

Good during widow's life.

A lease granted by the widow for the period of her own life was held good.[5] In the same way a *putnee* or a mocuraree or a lease in perpetuity that may be granted by the widow will stand good for the period of her natural life.[6] On her death the reversioner will have a right to enter, subject to the purchaser's right to defeat the reversioner's claim by

---

[1] Bogooa Jha *v.* Lall Doss, 6 W. R., 36.
[2] Considerations on Hindu Law, p. 24.
[3] Ranee Prosonno Moyee *v.* Ram Sunder Sen, S. D. R. for 1859, p. 163.
[4] W. R., Sp. No., p 165.
[5] Lall Sunder Doss *v.* Haree Kissen Doss, 1 Marshall, 113.
[6] Considerations on Hindu Law, p. 20.

showing that the alienation was for a justifiable necessity. LECTURE IX.

Purchaser's obligations.

I shall now consider the obligations which the Hindu law imposes upon a purchaser from the Hindu widow. Generally, it may be said, that a purchaser from the Hindu widow does not occupy the same position as any other purchaser in whose favor certain presumptions will be raised under ordinary circumstances. A purchaser from the Hindu widow has an exceptional and onerous position. He must show strict good faith in his dealings with her. By law the widow has a limited power of alienation over the property inherited by her; her disability is general, her ability exceptional; and the presumption of good faith will not, therefore, be raised in favor of the purchaser, who must prove the same when it is questioned. Peel, C. J., observed in the case of *Goluckmoney Debee* v. *Digumber Dey*,[1]—"Mr. Welch quoted a dictum of mine in a decision in this Court, in which I am reported to have said that a purchaser from such a Hindu female must look to the necessity for the sale, and that his title depends on it. I think so still, and adhere to what I said in that case." "The first duty of a purchaser from a Hindu childless widow is to satisfy himself, as an ordinary prudent man would do, as to her right to sell. If he does not do so, he does not act with due care or attention in the matter, and, therefore, cannot

[1] 2 Boulnois, p. 201.

LECTURE IX.

He must show good faith.

be said to have acted legally or in good faith, although he may, in fact, fully believe or take it for granted that all is right."

In the case of *Grose* v. *Omerto Moyee*,[1] which has been quoted before, Macpherson, J., held that, unless the purchaser from the Hindu widow makes careful enquiry as to the circumstances of the widow and her necessity to sell, and satisfies himself on these points, such a purchase will not be good. The same learned Judge observed that in this case "there was no real enquiry by Grose, as to there being any necessity for Bamasunduree entering into such an agreement; no attempt by him, or by any one on his behalf, to ascertain or calculate what her rights were or were worth, and that it was a mere speculation on the part of Grose." Such an alienation was held to be void as against the reversioners. It can only be valid against them "if the transaction was a fair and *bonâ fide* and reasonable transaction both on her part and on Grose's, entered into after due consideration of Bamasunduree's position as representing her husband's estate."

Purchaser to show that the sale is within the widow's limited powers.

When a sale by a Hindu widow is questioned, the purchaser is bound to show that the transaction is within her limited powers.[2] Where the legal necessity is questioned, its existence must be shown by

---

[1] 12 W. R., 12, A. O. J.

[2] The Collector of Masulipatam *v.* Cavaly Vencata Narainapah, 8 Moore's I. A., p. 529.

the person standing on the conveyance.[1] In the case of *Mahomed Ashruff* v. *Brijessuree Dossee*, which has been quoted before, Glover, J., speaking of the widow's sale, observed :—" All purchasers from a Hindu widow know or ought to know by this time the extreme risk of such a transaction, and if they choose to run it, and to buy without consulting the next heirs or without taking such further steps as would enable them at some future time, should necessity arise, to prove that they made diligent and careful enquiry as to the existence of a legal necessity before buying, they must take the consequences."

In another case (*Gobind Monee Dossee* v. *Shamloll Bysack*,[2]) the Court observed that " though a purchaser for value is not bound to prove the antecedent economy or good conduct of the widow who alienates a portion of her husband's estate, or to account for the due appropriation of the purchase-money, he is bound to use due diligence in ascertaining that there is some legal necessity for the loan ; and he may be reasonably expected to prove the circumstances connected with his own particular loan. The purchasers are setting up sales made by a party whose title to alienate they must necessarily have known to be

---

[1] Bissonath Roy *v.* Lall Bahadur, 1 W. R., 247 ; Doe dem Rajchunder Pramanic *v.* Bulloram Biswas. 1 Fulton's Rep., 133 ; Rajlukhee Debee *v.* Gocool Chunder Chowdry, 12 W. R., 47, P. C. R.

[2] Gap. No., W. R., p. 153.

LECTURE IX.

limited and qualified, and they may, therefore, be reasonably expected to prove the needs of the estate and the motives influencing the transaction."

Not bound to see to appropriation of purchase-money.

Though the purchaser is bonnd to prove the existence of a legal necessity when the widow's sale is questioned, he is not bound to look to the actual appropriation of the purchase-money by the widow.[1] If the purchaser is satisfied on a fair and reasonable enquiry that a legal necessity for the widow's alienation exists, that will be a sufficient warrant for his purchase. Where the necessity for the widow's sale is proved, and the vendee pays a fair price for the property sold, and otherwise acts *bonâ fide*, the mere fact of the whole of the purchase-money not being paid to the creditors will be no ground for invalidating the sale, because the purchaser is not bound to see to the application of the purchase-money.[2] But whether the purchase-money is adequate, is for the purchaser to prove. The sale being questioned on this ground, the purchaser is bound to show that the consideration-money paid by him represents a fair value of the property purchased.[3]

Hunooman Persand Pandey v. Mussamut

The law regarding the rights and obligations of a purchaser or mortgagee from a Hindu widow has

[1] Gunga Gobind Bose *v.* S. M. Dhunee, 1 W. R., 59; Nuffur Chunder Banerjee *v.* Gudadhur Mundle, 3 W. R., 122; Gopal Chunder Manna *v.* Gourmonee Dossee, 6 W. R., 52.

[2] Ram Gopal Ghose *v.* Bullodeb Bose, Gap. No., W. R., 385.

[3] Jodu Nath Sircar *v.* S. M. Soramony Dossee, Wyman's Rep., 70.

Babooe Munraj Koonwer.

been considerably derived from the well known case of *Hunooman Persaud Pandey* v. *Mussamut Babooe Munraj Koonwer.*[1] That case, however, referred to the powers of the manager for an infant heir to charge an estate not his own, but which belonged to the infant. It had no reference to the power of a Hindu widow to alienate or charge her husband's estate, or the rights and obligations of a purchaser or mortgagee from her. But the decisions[2] since of the Sudder Dewany Adawlut, and of the High Court of Bengal, have followed the principles laid down by the Privy Council in that case in determining the law applicable to a purchaser from the Hindu widow. The Privy Council held, that the charge created by a manager of the infant's property will be good, if the lender, before he advanced the money, made inquiries into the necessities for the loan, and satisfied himself as well as he could that the manager is acting for the benefit of the estate; but beyond this he is not bound to see to the application of the money, for their Lordships observed—"the purposes for which a loan is wanted are often future, as respects the actual application, and a lender can rarely have, unless he enters on the management, the means of controlling and rightly directing the actual application." Their Lordships, accordingly, observed, that

---

[1] 6 Moore's I. A., p. 393.

[2] See Sree Nath Roy *v.* Ruttun Money Chowdrain, S. D. R. for 1859, p. 421; Ram Gopal Ghose *v.* Bullodeb Bose, Gap No., W. R., 385.

LECTURE IX. a *bonâ fide* creditor should not suffer when he has acted honestly and with due caution, but is himself deceived.

There is some danger in applying the law relating to a guardian to the case of the Hindu widow: the analogy between the two is very slender. The one is the development of a notion originating in very recent times, being the expression of one of the necessities of modern society; the other is founded upon a system of ancient law existing in a stereotype form from the very earliest times. The Hindu law confers on the widow the right of enjoyment of her husband's estate, and further declares that she is not entitled to make a gift, sale, or mortgage of it.[1] Then it is laid down that, for certain exceptional purposes, she can make a valid alienation, and the purpose for which this is allowed is stated to be the benefit of her late husband.[2] It does not authorise the alienation for the benefit of the *estate*. But our Courts have held, having regard to the rights of the reversioners, that an alienation of a part of or a charge upon the estate, for the purpose of preserving the whole estate will be valid as against the reversioners, because by such an act the widow benefits the reversioners.

Now, it was never intended by the ancient sages that the *mere existence* of a necessity would be a ground for rendering the alienation valid; what they

[1] Dayabhaga, Chap. XI. Sec. i, para. 56.
[2] *Ibid*, para. 61.

intended was, that the necessity must *exist*, and that it must be *satisfied* by the alienation of the widow. In fact, the *existence* of the necessity and of its being *satisfied* must constitute a condition precedent to the validity of the exercise of that exceptional power by the widow. Our Courts, however, by holding that the purchaser is not bound to look to the application of the money, have failed to consider one most important element in this branch of the law; and I take it that the Hindu law has not, in this respect, been correctly administered.

The effect of this view of the law upon the rights of the reversioners is also a serious one. Real necessity existing may furnish ground for more than one loan, and the money so raised may not be ultimately applied to satisfying the necessity, but may be appropriated to some selfish expenses of the widow. The loans existing will be a valid charge upon the estate, and the necessity unsatisfied may sweep away a portion of the estate. The estate will thus come into the hands of the reversioners seriously impaired, and seriously encumbered. The interests of the reversioners are altogether overlooked, and their rights extremely unprotected by such an interpretation of the law.

Sale in execution against the widow.

I have, to some extent, considered before the effect of decrees against the widow in binding the estate of her husband. I shall now explain to you the effect of sales in execution of decrees against the

LECTURE IX.

widow. In these cases the first thing to be observed is as to the nature of the obligation on which the decree is founded :—

1*st.*—Whether it was on account of a personal liability of the widow for which the estate of her husband will not, under the Hindu law, be bound.

2*nd.*—Whether the personal liability of the widow is such as to bind the estate.

3*rd.*—Whether the decree was obtained against the widow as *representative* of her husband,—*i.e.*, on account of an obligation of her husband, and not on account of her own obligation.

When the widow incurs a liability, and it is incurred not for satisfying a legal necessity, but on any other account, a decree obtained against the widow on the basis of such an obligation will not bind the estate of her husband, and the sale under it will be a sale of her life-interest.[1] On the other hand, if the debt was incurred for a legal necessity, the whole estate would pass upon a sale in execution of such a decree. In discussing this question the Court observed:—" Whether the plaintiff (reversioner) had or had not a cause of action on account of the execution-sale, would depend entirely upon whether the widow had, at the time she incurred the debt which burdened her husband's estate, such necessity for incurring that debt as the Hindu law contemplates. If she had, and if such necessity had been

[1] Kisto Moyee Dosee *v.* Prosunno Narain Chowdry, 6 W. R., 303.

established, her right and interest would have included the entire estate which would have passed under the decree to the purchaser in execution; whilst if she had sold without such necessity, then all that would have passed under the sale would have been her life-interest."[1]

Decree against the widow as representative will pass the whole estate.

If, however, the decree is obtained against the widow in her representative character, either as the representative of her husband or as the guardian of her minor son, the sale under it will pass the whole estate.[2] In the case of *Grish Chunder Lahoory* v. *Ramlal Sircar*,[3] a decree was obtained against the widow as the guardian of her minor adopted son for contributions on account of the payment of Government revenue. The Court observed:—"The action against Tarasunduree (the widow) was brought after the adoption, and as mother of the adopted son. She was then holding the estate on his account as his guardian. The payments made by the decreeholders were clearly for the benefit of the estate, and preserved it from sale for arrears of revenue. We think, in this case, that the decree was not against the widow personally but as guardian of the adopted son, and not for a personal debt but for payments made by co-sharers of Government revenue on account of the adopted son, as represented by Tarasunduree, to preserve their joint property; and to recover the

[1] Bistoo Behary Sahoy v. Lalla Byjnath Persad, 16 W. R., 49.
[2] Goluck Chunder Paul v. Mahomed Rohim, 9 W. R., 316.
[3] 1 W. R., 145.

LECTURE IX. money so paid, they are entitled to look to the estate which has benefited by such payments. We think, therefore, that the sale must be good as against the adopted son."[1]

In the same case there was another decree against the widow, and the sale upon it. The Court held, "that this was a personal debt of Tarasunduree for which she and not the estate is liable. The suit was on a bond for money lent to Tarasunduree, on the allegation that it was required for the payment of Government revenue; and certain petitions to the Collector, to show that the money borrowed had been so applied, were produced in support of the plea. We cannot admit this evidence. It is easily concocted, and the mere recital in the bond of the purpose for which the money was required, is no sufficient proof that such was the case. In the absence, therefore, of all satisfactory proof that the debt is other than personal to Tarasunduree, we reverse the sale."

If the decree is obtained against the widow as representative of her husband,—*i.e.*, on account of a debt due from her late husband,—the estate of the husband will pass to the purchaser, and not the mere life-interest of the widow; and this although the sale-notification might state that the interest of the judgment-debtor, *viz.*, the widow, was sold.[2] In

---

[1] See also S. D. A. Reports for 1859, p. 515.

[2] Kalee Churn Mitter *v.* Sheebdyal Tewaree, S. D. A. for 1859, p. 996; Buksh Ali *v.* Eshan Chunder Mitter, W. R., Sp. No., 119.

such a case what property was actually sold is to be seen, and not the form of the sale-notification; and as the debts were the debts of the former owner, the husband of the widow, the sale will pass the rights of the former owner.[1]

Not in a Mitacshara family.

In a family governed by the Mitacshara law, the above principle will not hold good. There, if a member of the joint family died entitled to an undivided share in such property, and leaving widows surviving him; after his death his widows were sued in their representative capacity in respect of debts incurred by him in his lifetime on his own account, and not for the benefit of the joint family, and decrees were obtained against the widows in that capacity. In execution of these decrees, an interest in certain portions of the joint family property, to the extent of the share to which the deceased was entitled in his lifetime, was sold. On a question raised as to what interest passed to the purchaser by such a sale, a Full Bench of the Bengal High Court held,[2] that the purchaser took only the rights and interests of the widows; that as the property seized did not belong to the widows or to the heirs of the deceased, but under the Hindu law passed to the survivors, it could not be made available under a decree against the widows in their representative

[1] General Manager of the Raj Durbhungah v. Moharaj Coomar Romaput Sing, 14 Moore's I. A., 605.

[2] Subaburt Prosad Sahoo v. Foolbash Koer, 12 W. R., F. B., p. 1.

LECTURE IX.

character, but could be made liable only in a suit properly laid against the survivors.

This principle is in accordance with the doctrine of the Mitacshara, which lays down that a member of the joint Hindu family has no authority to mortgage his undivided share in a portion of the joint family property for the purpose of raising money on his own account and not for the benefit of the joint family.

Modified by recent decisions.

The principle laid down in the Full Bench decision of the Bengal High Court, in the case of *Sudaburt Prosaud Sahoo*, which, as I have said, is in accordance with the doctrines of the Mitacshara, seems to have been considerably modified by two recent decisions. The first is the case of *Deendyal* v. *Jugdeep Narain*,[1] decided by the Privy Council, in which it was held that, for debts contracted by the father in a Mitacshara family not for the use of the family but for his own personal use, his interest in the family property can be sold in execution, and the execution-purchaser is entitled to obtain possession by partition of the share purchased. The principle of this decision was extended in a later case[2] by the Bengal High Court, in the case of a son in an undivided Mitacshara family, which in effect held, that the interest of any member of a joint Mitacshara family can be sold on account of his personal debts,

[1] I. L. R., 3 Calc., 198.

[2] Rai Narain Doss v. Nowuit Lal, I. L. R., 4 Calc., 809.

and the execution-purchaser is entitled to obtain possession by partition.

You will see that the above decisions really break up the cohesion of Mitacshara families. The correct principle of Hindu law according to the Mitacshara is departed from, and the protection of joint family property from the improvident acts of its members is completely lost. The preservation of family property for the benefit of unborn members of the family, and for keeping up the family worship which forms the keystone of the Mitacshara law relating to joint family property, is thus seriously impaired.

A very different doctrine prevails in the Bengal school. In Bengal, a member of an undivided family can raise money, on the mortgage of his own share in the joint property, for his own personal use; and the mortgagee will have a title to this undivided share of his mortgagor, which cannot be defeated by his (the mortgagor's) co-sharers. Hence the Bengal doctrine, by which a decree against the widow as representative of her husband passes the whole estate.

Sale on a decree for rent against the widow passes the tenure.

Where a decree is obtained against the widow for rent, and in execution of that decree the zemindar put up certain property to sale, it was held, that the sale did not transfer to the purchaser merely the life-interest of the widow, but passed the whole estate to him. In that case[1] Mitter, J., observed :—" The rent

[1] Tiluck Chunder Chuckerbutty v. Mudun Mohun Jogee, 12 W. R., 504.

due to the zemindar cannot, under any circumstances, be treated as a personal debt of the widow; and if the zemindar thought it proper to put up the properties now in dispute for sale for the realisation of that rent, after having obtained a decree for it in due course of law, the reversionary heir can have no right to come in after the death of the widow, and take back those properties from the hands of the purchaser. If the widow had contracted a debt to meet the zemindar's demand for rent, and then alienated a part of the husband's estate for the satisfaction of that debt, the alienation would have been good and valid in law; and we do not see any reason why less effect is to be given to a decree passed by a Court of competent jurisdiction, in execution of which decree certain properties belonging to the estate of the widow's husband were brought to sale and purchased by the special appellant's vendor."

The judgment in the above case does not state whether the rent, on account of which the decree was obtained, was due from the husband or from the widow,—*i. e.*, whether it became due after the death of the husband or before that period. If it become due from the widow,—*i. e.*, during the time when the widow was in possession as heiress,—it is somewhat questionable whether a decree on account of it would bind the estate; for it is on account of the widow's default that the decree was had. To hold that a decree for rent due from a widow and against her personally can, from the mere fact of its being a decree for rent, and without any other evidence, be considered as a decree for a necessary debt (the suit in which it is obtained being one to which the reversioner is not a party, and therefore has never had an opportunity of contesting whether the debt was a necessary one) is laying down, I presume, a somewhat questionable law. The Privy Council in the case of *Nogender Ghose* v. *Kaminee Dosee*,[1] held a contrary doctrine. In that case a decree having been obtained against a widow in respect of a charge which she had made, it was held that it could only be enforced against such interest in her deceased husband's estate as she possessed. The Privy Council pointed out that, if the person obtaining the decree had a right to such a decree as would affect the estate of the husband, and be anything more than a decree against the widow personally, the suit ought to have been one to enforce the mortgage and to make it a charge upon the estate. Their Lordships observed, that it was impossible for them to upset the decision of the High Court, which in substance only affirmed that an action brought under sec. 9, Act I of 1845, is only a personal action, and that in an action which was personal against Kaminee Dosee as the possessor of the tolook, only her property and her interest in the tolook can be affected; and that an equity which the plaintiff

A contrary doctrine held by the Privy Council.

[1] 11 Moore's I. A., 241.

LECTURE IX. possessed, and which he might have enforced against the owners in reversion also, cannot be enforced against them in a suit brought to extend and enforce a personal decree against the possession of the limited interest.[1]

Which is followed by the Bengal High Court.

The same principle was affirmed by the Bengal High Court in the case of *Mohima Chunder Roy Chowdry* v. *Ram Kissore Acharjee Chowdry.*[2] There, Couch, C. J., observed :—"The result of the authorities appears to be, that where the debt has not accrued in the lifetime of the husband, and is not his debt, so that the widow is sued as his representative, the decree against her in a suit to which the reversioner is not a party, can only be considered as a personal decree against her, and be enforced by the sale of her interest only, except where the proceeding is one which authorises the sale of the tenure under Act VIII (B.C.) of 1869. Here, the plaintiff, who sued for arrears of rent, did not take the course which he might have adopted, and ask to have the tenure sold for arrears due in respect of it. He sought and obtained something different from that; and under his decree he sold other tenures. It is found that what was sold was not merely the tenure in respect of which the rent accrued, but others. In fact, having obtained a personal decree against the widow, he executed it against any property of hers which he

[1] *See* Sitaram Dey *v.* Ranee Prosunno Moyee, 4 W. R., 38.

[2] 23 W. R., 174.

thought fit. We think the Courts were wrong in treating this as a sale in execution of a decree for a necessary debt, and in holding that the plaintiff is not entitled to recover." LECTURE IX.

In a somewhat similar case[1] the Privy Council held, that where the mother of a deceased Hindu brought a suit against his widow for arrears of maintenance, obtained a decree, and in execution of that decree sold the judgment-debtor's rights and interests in her husband's estate; by such a sale only the widow's life-interest passed, which determined on her death. Their Lordships observed:—"That the debt was a personal debt of the widow, and there is nothing to show that the estate of Mudun Mohun was charged by the decree. The sale against her in discharge of her personal liability was of the interest which belonged to her, and not of the estate which belonged to her husband. It was the widow's property only that was liable to be sold, or was sold in discharge of her personal debt." "What was intended to be sold was the widow's interest only, and not the absolute estate in the lot; and that, consequently, upon the death of the widow, the lot descended to the plaintiff as the reversionary heir of her husband, and that the purchaser did not obtain the absolute estate, but only the widow's interest in it, which continued only so long as the widow lived."

The above case of *Mohima Chunder Roy Chow-*

---

[1] Baijun Dobey v. Brijo Bhookhun Lall, 24 W. R., 306.

LECTURE IX. *dry* is also authority for the proposition that when a decree for rent is obtained against a widow as the possessor of tolook, and in execution of that decree the defaulting tenure was sold, the effect of such a sale will be to pass to the purchaser not merely the life-interest of the widow, but the whole tenure.[1] This is because the zemindar has the right, either by express agreement or by law, in case of a default in the payment of rent, to sell the tenure as constituted at the time of its creation, irrespective of the rights of the holder of the tenure for the time being. Hence it was held, that the purchaser at a sale in execution of a decree for rent against the widow, by which the *tenure* passed, was entitled to question leases granted by the widow during her incumbency. Norman, C. J., observed:—" The plaintiffs, as purchasers in execution of a decree for rent, obtained against Ruttun Monee (the widow) under Act VIII of 1838, acquired the whole tenure or territorial rights which were formerly vested in Ruttun Monee's husband, which she, for the purposes of that suit, fully represented; and having acquired the ownership in the estate by the sale in execution, was fully entitled to question the validity of all encumbrances created by any prior owner, either as being created in excess of her power as a Hindu widow, or as invalid for any other reason."[2]

---

[1] Anund Moyee Dossee *v.* Mohender Narain Doss, 15 W. R., 264.

[2] Rajkissen Sircar *v.* Chowdry Jaheerul Huq, Gap No., W. R., 351.

Lecture IX.

There is a slight vagueness in the judgment in the above case. The purchaser at the sale having purchased the *tenure*, is for that reason entitled to question the encumbrances that may have been created by the defaulting holder of the tenure, and not because the decree was obtained against the widow, who fully represented the estate of her husband; and further the leases will be avoided not because they were granted by the Hindu widow in excess of her powers as *Hindu widow*, but because they were granted by the holder of the tenure in excess of his powers created by the lease.

Other kinds of properties of the widow.

Up to this moment I have been considering the property of a *Hindu widow*,—*i.e.*, property which she has obtained as the heiress of her husband; and her powers of alienation over such property. This constitutes by far the most important branch of the law relating to the Hindu widow. I shall now very shortly consider other kinds of property which a Hindu widow may possess.

That acquired by herself.

First.—Property which the widow herself acquires by purchase or otherwise. If it is acquired by the widow from the income of her husband's property, it becomes an accumulation or increment to that property, and follows the *corpus* in its devolution.[1] The law, therefore, that governs the alienation of the *corpus* will also govern the alienation of this kind of property. If, however, the property was acquired

[1] See *ante*, p. 267.

by the widow from other sources, it becomes her property over which she has rights of ownership, and she has absolute powers of disposing of the same in any manner she thinks proper. In this respect her powers are not limited : she possesses the same powers as an ordinary owner of property possesses over it. In a case reported in Macnaghten[1] the question turned upon a gift by a fisherman's widow of the whole of her self-acquired estate, consisting of immoveable property, to two Brahmins. The Pundits answered, that the widow having acquired some wealth by her personal exertions, and having purchased the house with such acquisitions, made a gift of the same to the Brahmins. By the gift her property over it became extinct, and on the extinction of her right the donees' title accrued. The answer was put upon the authority of texts bearing upon the *stridhun* property of a woman. The Pundits treated this as one of the various classes of *stridhun*.

Her *stridhun*.

The subject of *stridhun* does not come within the legitimate limits of the present course of lectures. It is not an incident peculiar to the Hindu *widow*, and therefore does not exclusively belong to a discussion of the law relating to the Hindu widow. A Hindu woman, widow or not, may possess *stridhun*, and no separate incidents belong to it from the fact of the woman being a widow.

Inherited property

In Bengal, there was no doubt entertained at any

[1] 2 Macnaghten, p. 239.

time that the property inherited by a woman from her husband does *not* become her *stridhun*. The authorities are clear upon that point. In Benares, this question was involved in some doubts; and contention was raised that the property inherited by a woman also become her *stridhun*. The substance of the argument was, that *succession* was one of the modes of acquisition of *stridhun*, and therefore property *inherited* also became the woman's *stridhun*. This point now must be considered as settled on the authority of the case of *Bhugwandeen Dobey* v. *Meyna Bai*,[1] which has been quoted before; where the Privy Council observed, as follows:—

Widow's estate not *stridhun*.

"Their Lordships, therefore, have come to the conclusion, that, according to the law of the Benares school, notwithstanding the ambiguous passage in the Mitacshara, no part of her husband's estate, whether moveable or immoveable, to which a Hindu woman succeeds by inheritance, forms part of her *stridhun* or *particular* property; and that the text of Katyayana, which is general in its terms, and of which the authority is undoubted, must be taken to determine, first, that her power of disposition over both is limited to certain purposes; and, secondly, that, on her death, both pass to the next heir of her husband."

[1] 11 Moore's I. A., p. 487.

LECTURE X.

THE RIGHTS OF THE REVERSIONERS.

The rights of reversioners—Reversioners defined—Application to Hindu law not accurate—On the widow's death the heirs of the last male owner succeed—According to the Dayabhaga—Not the heirs to the widow's *stridhun*—King is the last heir, except of Brahmins—*The Collector of Musulipatam* v. *Cavaly Vencata Narainapah*—Held the contrary—Consent of reversioner—Renders alienations valid—Consent of all possible reversioners necessary—*Mohun Lal Khan* v. *Ranee Siromonee*—A contrary rule laid down by the Supreme Court—Consent of reversioner binds his heir—Reversioner's consent presumes necessity—Consent how given—By attestation—Not conclusive—Reversioner's *approval* of the widow's alienation conveys his interest—Also when he joins in the conveyance—Surrender of the widow's estate—Passes an absolute title—Presumes reversioner's consent—*Jadumoni Debi* v. *Saroda Prosonno Mukerjee*.

The rights of reversioners.

IN the previous lecture I have placed before you the law relating to the alienations by the Hindu widow; and I have considered at some length the cases in which they are valid, and those in which they are invalid. There is one important class of alienations which I have omitted to consider in the previous lecture, and which I propose to consider in this,—*viz.*, those in which the alienation by the widow is sanctioned or authorised or consented to by a class of relatives who are called the reversioners to the estate of the Hindu widow. I propose, therefore, to consider in this lecture the rights and obligations of this class of persons in the matter of the widow's alienations. LECTURE X.

I shall consider this subject under the following heads :

I.—Who are the reversioners.

II.—The consent of the reversioners as affecting the widow's alienations.

III.—Suits by the reversioners.

IV.—Removal of the widow from possession of the estate.

Reversioners defined.

Those who take the property after the widow's death are called *reversioners*, and the interest which they possess in the estate during the continuance of the widow's estate is called a *reversion*. The words *reversioner* and *reversion* are well known in the real property laws of England; and the English lawyers, who presided over our Courts in the latter end of the last century, and in the beginning of this, applied those terms to analogical conceptions in Hindu law. The word *reversion* in English law means the ulterior estate in fee-simple, which a tenant in fee-simple reserves to himself after having granted away a particular estate either for years or for life or in tail.[1] You will observe from this definition that the residue of the estate which remains in the *grantor*, after he has carved out the particular estate, is called

[1] Williams on Real Property, 7th Ed., p. 222.

LECTURE X. the *reversion*, and he himself, as the owner of that residue, is called the *reversioner*.

Application to Hindu law not accurate.

Now, in Hindu law, those who take the estate after the widow's death, were not the owners of the fee-simple, and the widow's estate was not created by grant from those persons. Therefore, it is not accurate to say that the interest of the next takers is an estate in reversion, and the widow's estate a life-estate. The only analogy between the English law term and the Hindu law conception is, that, in both cases, the estate is in the possession of one person, in which another person has an ulterior or expectant interest. Even in this slender analogy there is an important difference. In English law, I understand, generally no act of the particular tenant can defeat or destroy the ulterior or expectant interest; but in Hindu law, the widow, the holder of the estate in possession, can, under certain circumstances, validly convey away the estate so as altogether to defeat or destroy the expectant interest. Finding, however, that there was no other word in the English language which would fully and accurately convey the Hindu law conception, the English lawyers borrowed the somewhat cognate expression of English law to convey that meaning.

You will observe from the foregoing remarks that the terms *reversion* and *reversioner*, when applied to convey the Hindu law notions, are not very accurate. Still, however, those expressions have been used for nearly a century, in the law literature of this country, to denote those notions ; and they have, in the course of this long usage, acquired a meaning quite their own, independent of the English law, from which they are derived. A departure from current phraseology which has prescription on its side, even when that phraseology is inaccurate, is not proper. Such a proceeding is apt to mislead and to create confusion. I have, therefore, for these reasons, made no apology for using those expressions in the course of these lectures. If you remember the caution I have conveyed, you will not be misled by your knowledge of the English law meaning of those terms.

On the widow's death the heirs of the last male owner succeed.

I have before explained to you the events that cause a determination of the widow's estate. When that estate actually determines, the property does not go to the heirs of the widow, but to the heirs of the last male owner from whom she, or her predecessor in estate, if a female, succeeded. This is a departure from the ordinary rules governing succession in Hindu law. When a male owner of property dies, on his death, the property will go to *his* heirs, and not to the heirs of any *previous* holder of the property. In the case of a female it is not so, because a female inheriting does not acquire the proprietorship in the property ; she has only a right of possession during her life. The widow's estate is the type of all estates which other female heirs under the Hindu law have in the property inherited by them.[1] Generally, if not always, the

[1] Chotay Lall *v.* Chunnoo Lall, I. L. R., 4 Calc., 744.

LECTURE X. heirs of the female holder and the heirs of the last male owner are different, consequently there is a wide difference between the rule which lays down that the property shall go to the heirs of the last male owner and the one which ordains that it shall be inherited by the heirs of the last female holder.

According to the Dayabhaga. The author of the Dayabhaga[1] has laid down on this subject thus :—" When she (the widow) dies, the daughters or others who would regularly be heirs in default of the wife, take the estate; not the kinsmen, since these being inferior to the daughter and the rest, ought not to exclude those heirs; and the obstacle being equally removed if her right cease or never take effect, it can be no bar to their claim."

" Therefore, those persons who are exhibited in a passage above cited (the wife, daughters also, both parents, &c.) as the next heirs on failure of prior claimants, shall, in like manner as they would have succeeded if the widow's right had never taken effect, equally succeed to the residue of the estate remaining after her use of it, upon the demise of the widow in whom the succession had vested. At such time the succession of daughters and the rest is proper, since they confer greater benefits on the deceased by the oblations presented by them than other claimants, such as the *sapindas* above-mentioned."[2]

---

[1] Chap. XI, Sec. i, para. 57.

[2] Para. 59.

LECTURE X.

This is authority for the proposition that, on the death of the widow, the heirs of the last male owner, who would have succeeded in default of the widow, take the inheritance.

Not the heirs to the widow's *stridhun*.

The heirs of the widow, or those who would have succeeded to her *stridhun*, do not succeed to the property on the widow's death. "Nor[1] shall the heirs of the woman's separate property take the succession, on failure of daughters and daughters' sons to the exclusion of her husband's heirs; for the right of those persons is relative to the property of a woman other than that which is inherited by her. Katyayana has propounded, by separate texts, the heirs of a woman's property, and his text, declaratory of the succession to heritage, would be tautology, consequently heritage is not ranked with woman's peculiar property."

The reported cases on the subject have been in accordance with the above principles. The widow is never treated as the last full owner, but her husband is considered as such, to whom the right of succession is to be traced. In the case of *Rooder Chunder Chowdry* v. *Shombhoo Chunder Chowdry*,[2] the Court observed, that property which had devolved on the widow by the death of her husband goes to the heirs of her husband, and their right begins to accrue from the date of the death of the widow, and not from the date of the death of her husband.

---

[1] Dayabhaga, Chap. XI, Sec. i, para. 58. [2] 3 Sel. Rep., 142.

LECTURE X. Consequently it was held, that the husband's younger brother was entitled to succeed in preference to the nephew of her husband, whose father had died during the widow's lifetime.

The case of *Lukhi Narain Sing* v. *Tulsi Narain Sing*[1] is also an authority in point. It was there held, that the reversionary heirs to the estate of a sonless Hindu (vacated by the widow's death), are *his* heirs surviving at the time of the death of the widow: so that, of several kinsmen of equal degree, who would have jointly succeeded but for the widow, if any die in the interim between the deaths of the husband and widow, his heirs are excluded by the surviving kinsmen. The same principle was also affirmed in the case of *Bhyrobee Dasee* v. *Nobokissen Bose.*[2] The facts of that case were as follows :—A Hindu at his demise left two widows, a son by one of them, and the son of a paternal uncle. The son succeeded to his entire estate. On the son's death before marriage, his mother succeeded. On her death it was held, that the property will go to the heir of her son, who in this case was the son of the paternal uncle of his father, and not the childless widow of his father ; she is the heiress, of *his father*, but not *his* heiress, for, under the Hindu law, the step-mother never succeeds to the step-son. The last full owner being the son, his heir obtained the property.

The Privy Council also affirmed this doctrine in the

[1] 5 Sel. Rep., 330.

[2] 6 Sel. Rep., 61.

famous *Sivagunga* case.[1] Speaking of those persons who would succeed to the estate on the widow's death, their Lordships observed,—" those persons obviously were not *her* heirs, but the next heirs of *her husband* according to the canon of Hindu law, which defines the successions to separate estate."

King is the last heir,

It is thus clear from the above authorities, that, on the death of the widow, those relatives who would succeed to the estate of the deceased owner in default of the widow, succeed in order. Now the *last* heir in the list is the *king*, who, it is stated, shall succeed to the property of all classes excepting that of Brahmins : " Excepting the property of a Brahmin, let the king take the wealth on failure of heirs. So Manu directs,—' The property of a Brahmin shall never be taken by the king : this is a fixed law.' But the wealth of the other classes, on failure of all heirs, the king may take."[2]

except of Brahmins.

The same doctrine is laid down in the Mitacshara relative to the king's succession to the property of a Brahmin : " Never shall a king take the wealth of a priest : for the text of Manu forbids it. ' The property of a Brahmin shall never be taken by the king : this is a fixed law.' It is also declared by Nareda,—' If there be no heir of a Brahmin's wealth, on his demise it must be given to a Brahmin, otherwise the king is tainted with sin.' "[3]

" But the king, and not a priest, may take the estate

[1] Katama Nauchear *v.* The Rajah of Sivagunga, 2 W. R., 31, P. C. R.; the quotation is from p. 36.

[2] Dayabhaga, Chap. XI, Sec. vi, para. 34.

[3] Chap. II, Sec. vii, para. 5.

LECTURE X.

of a *Kshetrya*, or other person of an inferior tribe, on failure of heirs down to the fellow student. So Manu ordains: 'but the wealth of the other classes, on failure of all heirs, the king may take.'"[1]

The Collector of Masulipatam v. Cavaly Vencata Narainapah.

These provisions of Hindu law have received a remarkable interpretation by their Lordships of the Privy Council in the case of *The Collector of Masulipatam* v. *Cavaly Vencata Narainapah.*[2] In that case, on the death of the widow of a Brahmin zemindar (who had inherited the property of her husband) without any heirs, the Collector, as representing the Government, seized the property as an escheat. The Sudder Dewany Adawlut at Madras held, that, as the property belonged to a Brahmin owner, the right of the crown to take the property by escheat was barred by the texts of Hindu law which have been quoted before.

On appeal to the Privy Council their Lordships held, that the question should be considered both as a matter of Hindu law and as a matter of "general or universal law." Referring to the Hindu law view of the question, their Lordships observed:[3]— "That the passage quoted by the Mitacshara from Nareda, in the very section which cites the prohibition of Manu, shows what the law in its utmost strictness was. That passage is—'If there be no heir of a Brahmin's wealth, on his demise, it must be given to

---

[1] Mitacshara, Chap. II, Sec. vii, para. 6.
[2] 8 Moore's I. A., p. 500.
[3] Page 523.

a Brahmin, otherwise the king is tainted with sin.' In other words, the king is to take the property, but to take it subject to the duty which he cannot neglect without sin, of disposing of it at his discretion amongst Brahmins of the kind contemplated by the preceding texts.

"If this be so, it appears to their Lordships, that, according to Hindu law, the title of the king by escheat to the property of a Brahmin dying without heirs ought, as in any other case, to prevail against any claimant who cannot show a better title; and that the only question that arises upon the authorities is, whether Brahminical property so taken is, in the hands of the king, subject to a trust in favor of Brahmins. In this suit, where the issue is between the Government claiming the property (whether subject to a trust or not) by escheat, and a party claiming by an adverse title, it is unnecessary to decide whether the duty imposed upon the king is one of imperfect obligation, or a positive trust affecting the property in his hands, or whether, if a trust it is or is not one incapable of enforcement by reason of the uncertainty of its objects. It is also unnecessary to decide on the arguments addressed to us concerning a distinction or supposed distinction between Brahmins who have been called 'sacerdotal Brahmins,' and the ordinary members of the caste. For, assuming that the appellants' title is to be governed by Hindu law, and assuming that there is no valid distinction in this matter between sacerdotal and other Brahmins, their Lordships, for the reasons above stated, would be unable to concur in the judgment under review."

Their Lordships also were of opinion, that the question in this case ought not to be considered as one wholly and merely determinable by Hindu law, and that the title in this case may rest on grounds of general or universal law. Their Lordships observed[1]— "According to the law administered by the Provincial Courts of British India, on the death of any owner, being absolute owner, any question touching the inheritance from him of his property, is determinable in a manner personal to the last owner. This system is made the rule for Hindus and Mahomedans by positive regulation: in other cases it rests upon the course of judicial decisions. But when it is made out clearly that, by the law applicable to the last owner, there is a total failure of heirs, then the claim to the land ceases (we apprehend) to be subject to any such personal law; and as all property not dedicated to certain religious trusts must have some legal owner, and there can be, legally speaking, no unowned property, the law of escheat intervenes and prevails, and is adopted generally in all the Courts of the country alike. Private ownership not existing, the State must be owner as ultimate lord. Consequently, the claim of the Government in the present instance

[1] Page 525.

might have been considered with reference to this principle. LECTURE X.

"In the present case if the Hindu law had expressly provided that, upon the death of a Brahmin without heirs, ordinarily so-called, his property should pass to some definite person or class of persons: if, for instance, it admitted, in the case of a Brahminical succession, collaterals more remote than it would admit in the case of succession to a *Sudra*, there would be ground for excluding the title of the crown, because there would, by Hindu law, be some person in the nature of an heir capable of succeeding: but here the Sudder Dewany Adawlut rests its decision on what it terms 'the primary declaration of Manu, that the property of a Brahmin shall never be taken by the king.' That declaration is contained in an article (see Manu, Chap. IX, art. 189) which, assuming a complete failure of heirs, negatives the king's right to Brahminical property, whilst it affirms his title to the wealth of all other classes in such circumstances. In so dealing with the question, the Sudder Court was, we think, applying the actual or supposed Hindu law in derogation of the general right of the British sovereignty.

Held the contrary.

"Their Lordships' opinion is in favor of the general right of the crown to take by escheat the land of a Hindu subject, though a Brahmin, dying without heirs; and they think that the claim of the appellant (the Collector) to the zemindary in question (subject or not subject to a trust) ought to prevail, unless it has been absolutely, or to the extent of a valid and subsisting charge, defeated by the acts of the widow, Lutchmi Davamah, in her lifetime. In the latter case the Government will, of course, be entitled to the property subject to the charge."

The exposition of the texts of Manu and Nareda, as given in the foregoing judgment, seems to be opposed to the interpretation of those texts by Vijnaneswara and Jimutavahana. These authorities understand those texts as meaning, not that the king shall take the property subject to a trust, but that the king shall *not* take that property *at all*. The words in the text of Nareda, "must be given to a Brahmin," do not, I apprehend, mean that the king shall *first take* and then *give* to Brahmins; but that the king shall *adjudge* such property to a Brahmin in case of a dispute arising regarding such property between a Brahmin and any other claimant who is not a preferable *heir*.

From the above decision it follows that the king is the last reversioner to the estate of a Brahmin widow.

Consent of reversioner

I shall now consider the effect of the reversioner's consent on the alienations by the widow. The persons whose interests are affected by the widow's alienations being the reversioners, it is reasonable to hold that, if they give their consent to such alienations, the alienations will be valid; and this, for two reasons—

first, because the consent of the reversioner will be evidence of the existence of necessity justifying alienation; and *second*, because the reversioner, by giving his consent to the alienation, will be estopped from questioning its validity afterwards. Therefore, independent of the question of legal necessity, the widow's alienations will be absolutely valid if the reversioners have given their consent to such transactions. It was accordingly held in the case of *Gocul Chund Chuckerburtee* v. *Musst. Rajranee and another*,[1] that an alienation by a Hindu widow will be valid if it is made with the sanction of her husband's heirs on whom the estate will devolve on her demise.[2] The same doctrine was maintained in a later case.[3]

LECTURE X.

Renders alienations valid.

In the case of *Rajlukhee Debee* v. *Gocool Chunder Chowdry*,[4] the Privy Council affirmed this doctrine, which they considered as well established. In the judgment it was observed :—"Their Lordships do not mean to impugn those authorities which lay down that a transaction of this kind may become valid by the consent of the husband's kindred; but the kindred in such case must generally be understood to be all those who are likely to be interested in disputing the transaction. At all events, there should be such

---

[1] 2 Sel. Rep., 213.

[2] See also Hem Chunder Mozoomdar *v.* Musst. Taramunee, 1 Sel. Rep., 481.

[3] Brindabun Chunder Rai *v.* Bishun Chund Rai, 4 Sel. Rep., 180; see also Musst. Bejoya Debee *v.* Musst. Unnopoorna Debee, Note, 1 Sel. Rep., 215.

[4] 12 W. R., 47, P. C. R.

LECTURE X.

a concurrence of the members of the family as suffices to raise a presumption that the transaction was a fair one, and one justified by Hindu law."

Consent of all possible reversioners necessary.

This last case introduced one important principle, *viz.*, that the consent of *all* the kindred of the husband must be given to render the alienation valid ; and that, therefore, the consent of *one* only or *some* only of the reversioners will not have that effect. This, of course, is reasonable, because the question of validity being founded on the ground of estoppel, those persons must give their consent who are to be estopped from questioning the alienation hereafter. The Privy Council however, did not definitely lay down as to who are the persons whose consent must be obtained to render the alienation valid. It was generally observed that the consent of all those persons who are likely to be interested in disputing the transaction must be obtained. I shall afterwards show that such a condition is extremely difficult, if not impossible, to fulfil.

Mohun Lal Khan v. *Ranee Siromonee.*

The point as to who are the persons whose consent must be obtained to render the widow's alienation valid was expressly raised and decided in the case of *Mohun Lal Khan* v. *Ranee Siromonee.*[1] This case was decided so early as 1812 by the Sudder Dewany Adawlut. The appellant, Mohun Lal Khan, held possession of certain zemindaries under a deed of gift from Rance Siromonee, who had inherited the same

[1] 2 Sel. Rep., 40.

from her husband. It further appeared in the case, that the deed of gift had received the consent of three maternal first cousins of the deceased Rajah, the husband of the Ranee. It also appeared in evidence that the following relations of the deceased Rajah were living at the time of the gift by his widow.

1. Five sons of the Rajah's maternal uncle.
2. The descendants of Lukhun Sing, the great grandfather of the great grandfather of the Rajah.
3. The descendants of Lukhun Sing's brother.

Two questions were referred to the Pundits for answer :

1*st.*—Among the relations above mentioned, who would be the next heirs of the Rajah on the demise of his widow ?

2*nd.*—Whether the deed of gift was valid ; if not, whose consent was necessary to render it valid ?

The answer of the Pundits was as follows :—

1*st.*—On the death of the Ranee, the next heirs will be the maternal first cousins of the Rajah, should they survive the Ranee.

2*nd.*—The deed of gift in this case is not valid, because the consent of *all* the maternal first cousins has not been obtained to this deed ; only three out of the five having acquiesced in it. And also because it does not contain the permission of the Rajah's paternal kindred, who were then and are still living.

It was further held in the case, that an alienation by the widow to be valid, must bear the assent of the

LECTURE X. next heirs and the paternal kindred of the widow's husband. In another case,[1] in which the subject-matter of litigation was the same property as in the previous case, the Pundits on a reference answered :—"If there be no *sapindas* of Rajah Ajeet Sing (the Ranee's husband) within three degrees, the *sakulyas*, or remoter relations from three to ten degrees, may succeed to the property on the death of the Ranee. If any such survive, the Ranee has no power to give away the estate without their consent. If the Ranee have made a gift without their consent, it is invalid."

The case of *Ranee Sreemutty Debee* v. *Ranee Koondlutee and others*[2] is an important case as bearing upon the question of the alienation by the widow with the reversioner's consent. The subject-matter of the suit was that involved in the case of *Mohun Lal Khan* v. *Ranee Siromonee*, quoted above, and the points raised were the same. The facts were as follows—Kundurp Sing, the husband of Ranee Sreemutty, claimed the zemindary on two grounds :—

1*st.*—As next heir to Rajah Ajeet Sing, the husband of Ranee Siromonee, being seventh in remove from him.

2*nd.*—By the strength of an *ekrar* executed by Ranee Siromonee on his behalf before her death.

The defendant Mohun Lal Khan claimed to hold the zemindary on the strength of a deed of gift in his

---

[1] Roop Churn Mahopatro *v.* Anind Lal Khan, 2 Sel. Rep., 45.
[2] 4 Moore's I. A., p. 292.

favor by Ranee Siromonee. In the course of the case a point was raised as to whether the family shall be governed by the doctrines of the Mitacshara, which were current in Midnapore, where the property was situated and the family was residing, or by the doctrines of the Dayabhaga, which were current in Bengal, from which the family had migrated. It being found that the family had been performing their religious ceremonies according to the doctrines of Bengal, and otherwise conformed to the Bengal *shasters*, the Court held, that the rules of the Dayabhaga shall govern this litigation.

The Provincial Court which tried the case in the first instance held, that the *ekrar* relied upon by the plaintiff was not genuine. The Court also held, that it was invalid, because, as an alienation by the Hindu widow, it had not received the consent of the next heirs, who were the sons of the maternal uncle of Rajah Ajeet Sing, the husband of the widow. Further that, as the family was governed by the Dayabhaga, the mother's brother's sons of Rajah Ajeet Sing, who were alive, were entitled to succeed in preference to the plaintiff. On all these grounds the Court dismissed the plaintiff's suit.

The Sudder Court having confirmed the decision of the Provincial Court, the case was appealed to the Privy Council, which dismissed the appeal on the ground, that, as the family was governed by the Dayabhaga, and as the next heirs of Rajah Ajeet Sing are

LECTURE X. the sons of his maternal uncle who have not consented to the deed in favor of Kundurp Sing, the said deed on which the plaintiff, appellant, relies is not valid.

The Privy Council dismissed the plaintiff's suit without expressing any opinion as to the title of the defendant Mohan Lal Khan. Their Lordships also seemed to have approved of the decision in the earlier case of *Mohun Lal Khan* v. *Ranee Siromonee*[1] quoted before, for their Lordships observed, that "the decision in favor of the Ranee in the case in 2 Sel. Rep. was founded expressly on the ground that the deed then in question was executed without the concurrence of the descendants in the male line, who (though they were not heirs) were guardians or protectors of the widow."

The decision in the case of *Mohun Lal Khan* v. *Ranee Siromonee* is still good law,—*viz.*, that an alienation by a Hindu widow, unless it has received the consent of all the possible heirs, immediate or remote, is not valid.[2]

The case of *Hafuzunissa Begum* v. *Radha Binode Misser*[3] is also an authority in point. One of the points in that case was, whether a deed of sale by a Hindu widow, with the consent of the *first* reversioner, but without the consent of the second reversioner,

[1] 2 Sel. Rep., 40.

[2] See Raj Lukhee Debee *v.* Gocool Chunder Chowdry, 12 W. R., 47, P. C. R., where the Privy Council laid down the same principle.

[3] Sudder Dewany Decisions for 1856, p. 595.

was valid under the Hindu law. The Court observed :—"We are of opinion from the authorities cited in the margin, that, in order to render a sale by a Hindu widow of her husband's property valid, it must be signed or attested by all the heirs of her husband then living, the execution or attestation by the *nearest heirs alone* is insufficient. Under this view of the law, the deeds of sale propounded by the appellant in this case, on which the signature of the plaintiff, an heir in expectancy, does not appear, are invalid."[1]

A contrary rule laid down by the Supreme Court.

A somewhat different rule was laid down by the late Supreme Court. Speaking of the validity of the widow's alienation with the consent of the reversioners, Jackson, J., observed as follows:—"The consent of the heirs is all that is required by the old authorities (see Dayabhaga). If the true meaning of the word 'heirs' be all the persons living who might by possibility be heirs at the subsequent death of the widow, and it be meant that the consent of all these persons is necessary, the widow would seldom or never be able to convey, for, among so large a class of heirs, all of them would scarcely ever be competent or willing to consent. But I do not think that this is the correct meaning of the word 'heirs,' and that the term is used in the old authorities to designate that class of persons only who would immediately succeed to the estate, if the widow's interest was determined, rather

[1] See Nundo Coomar Rai v. Rajender Narain, 1 Sel. Rep., 349 ; Bhowani Munee v. Musst. Soolukhuna, 1 Sel. Rep., 431.

LECTURE X. than all the persons who might, by possibility, become heirs on the happening of that event."[1]

The point, however, that distinguishes this case from that of *Mohun Lal Khan* v. *Ranee Siromonee* is, that, in the former, the gift was to the *next heir*, whereas, in the latter, it was in favor of a *stranger*. As an assignment to the next heirs, the former case is in consonance with the current of authorities, and it was treated as such by the Court deciding it.

In a recent case[2] before the Bengal High Court, it was held, that the reversioner who gave his consent to the widow's alienation will be bound by such alienation; and that any other reversioner will not be bound by such an alienation, although the said alienation might have been consented to by the nearest reversioner existing at the time of the alienation.

A contrary rule was laid down in a very recent case.[3] There it was held, that a grant by a Hindu widow, with the sanction and concurrence of the next reversioner, is valid, and creates a title which cannot be impeached on the death of the widow by the person who, but for such grant, would be entitled as heir of her husband.

The law on this subject seems to be unsettled.

---

[1] S. M. Jadumani Debi *v.* Saroda Prosonno Mukerjee and others, 1 Boulnois' Rep., p. 120.

[2] Second Appeal, No. 1197 of 1878, Morris and Prinsep, JJ.

[3] Raj Bullub Sen *v.* Omesh Chunder Rooz, I. L. R., 5 Calc., 44.

The earlier cases require that the consent of *all* the reversioners existing at the time of the alienation should be obtained to the deed of alienation to pass a complete title. This, however, is impossible, when it is remembered that the reversioners to the estate of a Hindu widow are all those persons who are enumerated as heirs from the *daughter* down to the *king*. This list includes all the *sapindas*, *sakulyas*, *samonodacas*, &c., and it is almost impossible that any person could hope to obtain the consent of all these numerous relatives and some strangers (who are also heirs) to a proposed alienation. Practically, therefore, the fulfilment of such a condition is impossible, simply from the *number* of persons who are to be consulted and whose ultimate consent is to be obtained.

The later cases incline to the view that the consent of the *next* reversioner or reversioners at the time of the alienation will be sufficient. How far this is correct law may well be questioned, for it will have the effect of concluding a person's right by the acts of another, between whom and the former no sort of privity obtains. The *next* reversioner at the time of the alienation may die during the widow's lifetime, and another person, totally unconnected with him, may be entitled to succeed on the widow's death; and the effect of the ruling is, that this latter person will be concluded by the acts of the *then* next reversioner. There does not seem to be any warrant for such a proposition in Hindu law.

LECTURE X.

Consent of reversioner binds his heir.

It has been held in some cases[1] that, if a revlity, be-er gave his consent to an alienation, and died du[illegible] the widow's lifetime, his heirs will be bound by such consent ; and will be precluded from questioning the alienation hereafter, on the principle that the act of the ancestor will bind the heir. This proposition, when carefully examined, will, I apprehend, be one of questionable soundness. Let us suppose that the widow has the following relations living : *A*, the brother of her husband; *B*, the son of *A* ; and *C*, the son of another brother of her husband, who is dead. *A* gives his consent to an alienation by the widow, and dies during her lifetime. The persons who succeed to the estate on the death of the widow are *B* and *C*. It has been held, that *B* is estopped from questioning the alienation by the widow, inasmuch as the same was consented to by his father *A* ; but that *C* is not so precluded. Now why should *B* be estopped; if he took the property on the principle of representation from *A*, he ought to be bound by *A's* acts; but it is clear that he does not so take the property : it is not as representing *A* that he takes the property[2] on the demise of the widow (for in that case he ought to exclude *C*, which he does not), but he takes the property, inasmuch as he is the *grandson*

---

[1] Runjeetram Koolal *v.* Mahomed Waris, 21 W. R., 49 ; See also Cally Chand Dutt *v.* John Moore, 1 Fulton, p. 73.

[2] See the judgment of Colvile, C. J., in S. M. Jadumani Debi *v.* Saroda Prosonno Mukerji and others, where this principle was affirmed. 1 Boulnois' Rep., p. 120.

of the *widow's husband's father*. A slight variation in the above illustration will make the principle abundantly clear. Suppose, instead of a son, *A* had left a great grandson *D*. If the succession was by the principle of representation, *D*, as representing *A*, ought to succeed. But it is clear that *D* will not succeed, because he is the great great grandson of the widow's husband's father, from whom the succession is to be traced. *D not* being a *sapinda* will be postponed to other *sapindas* of the widow's husband, both in the paternal as well as in the maternal line. I presume, therefore, that the correct view of the law is, that he who gives his consent will be bound by it ; and that nobody else will be bound by such consent, although he may stand in certain degree of relationship to the person who may have given his consent.

Reversioner's consent presumes necessity.

The doctrine of consent is founded upon the presumption that, when the reversioner gives his consent to the widow's alienation, he has satisfied himself that the transaction was one which the widow was, under the circumstances, justified in entering into ; in other words, that it was not a wanton act on the part of the widow, but that it was one for which there was legal necessity.[1]

In practice, however, we often find it to be otherwise. A reversioner does not give his consent from the honest conviction that the alienation is one which it

---

[1] Kali Mohun Deb *v.* Dhunonjoy Saho, 6 W. R., 51 ; The Collector of Masulipatam *v.* C. V. Narainapah, 8 Moore's I. A., 529, 550.

LECTURE X. is necessary for the widow to effect, or that it is one which, under her present circumstances, she is justified by law in effecting; but he gives his consent because a certain portion of the consideration-money for the widow's alienation finds its way into his pocket;—in other words, he is bribed to give his consent. Such being the mode in which the reversioner's consent is usually obtained, it is hardly fair to draw from it the inference that the transaction was a fair one, or was one within the limited powers of the Hindu widow. Our Courts ought, therefore, to give little weight to the fact of one reversioner's consent as against other reversioners beyond binding him who has given his consent. By this, however, I am not at all to be understood to say that there may not be cases where there is such a concurrence of the members of the family as to raise the presumption that the transaction was a fair one, and one justified by Hindu law. Such cases, however, are extremely rare.

Consent how given. The consent of the reversioner to the widow's alienation may be given in various ways. In the case of *Mohun Lal Khan* v. *Ranee Siromonee*,[1] a separate instrument was put forward by which the reversioners consented to the widow's alienation. That was considered by the Court sufficient, provided the instrument purporting to convey the consent of the reversioners was well proved. In that case it was, however, suggested that the reversioners should

[1] See *ante*, p. 374. 2 Sel. Rep., 40.

attest the deed of alienation by the widow as evidence of their consent. LECTURE X.

By attestation.

The attestation of the widow's deed of alienation by the reversioners has been held to be sufficient evidence of their consent so as to preclude them from questioning the alienation afterwards.[1] If the next heir attests the deed of alienation, it is not *conclusive in law* as to the necessity for the sale, and cannot preclude further enquiry on that point, "though, as a question of fact, the circumstance of persons most interested in contesting such a sale being called in to attest the deed is the strongest possible proof of good faith on the part of the purchaser."[2] Remembering the circumstances under which the attestations of reversioners are usually obtained, I think, the law, as above laid down, has been laid down a little too strongly.

Not conclusive.

The Privy Council,[3] however, has refused to consider the attestation by a reversioner as conclusive evidence of his consent. Their Lordships think there ought to be evidence, in addition to the signature, to show the circumstances under which the reversioner signed the document. Referring to the attestation of the instrument by the reversioner, their Lordships observed :—"That the learned Judges have attached to that circumstance a weight which it really does

---

[1] Gopal Chunder Manna *v.* Gour Monee Dossee, 6 W. R., 52.

[2] Madub Chunder Hazra *v.* Gobind Chunder Banerjee, 9 W. R., 350.

[3] Raj Lukhee Debee *v.* Gocool Chunder Chowdhry, 12 W. R., 47, P. C. R.

LECTURE X. not possess. Their Lordships do not mean to impugn those authorities which lay down that a transaction of this kind may become valid by the consent of the husband's kindred, but the kindred in such case must generally be understood to be all those who are likely to be interested in disputing the transaction. At all events, there should be such a concurrence of the members of the family as suffices to raise a presumption that the transaction was a fair one, and one justified by Hindu law. That it can be a presumption of law in the sense of *presumptio juris et de jure* their Lordships do not think. It is no doubt an element to be taken into consideration, and deserving of considerable weight in the estimation of all the evidence of the transaction. And one of the difficulties of allowing the present decree to stand is, that this point, which was raised at the last moment, was decided upon the mere proof, by the production of the deed, that Juggutram was an attesting witness to it. The point had never been raised before. The opposite party has had no opportunity of examining Juggutram as to the circumstances under which he became an attesting witness, or what his understanding of the transaction really was. The utmost that the Judges ought to have done, in that state of things, was to remand the case to be retried for the full consideration of that question.

"Their Lordships cannot affirm the proposition that the mere attestation of such an instrument by to the defendantrily imports concurrence. It might, (the widow shown by other evidence that, when he contemn attesting witness, he fully understood what the transaction was, and that he was a concurring party to it; but from the mere subscription of his name that inference does not necessarily arise."

The Calcutta Sudder Dewany Adawlut had taken the same view of the question in an earlier case.[1] The Court held, that "on a sale of property by a Hindu widow, if the deed of sale be signed or attested by all the heirs living at the time of the execution of the same, the consent of the subscribing parties to the act set forth in the deed is by Hindu law presumed therefrom. This presumption is not, however, conclusive, but is rebuttable. It is competent to an heir whose name is upon a deed to show that it is there for some other purpose than that which the law presumes."

The Madras Sudder Court,[2] however, held, that when an heir countersigned a deed of sale by a widow, he must be taken to have consented to it. Unless a distinction is drawn between the *countersignature* of the heir and his *attestation* to the deed, the Madras case seems opposed to the ruling of the Privy Council.

If the deed of sale by the widow is signed by the Reversion-

---

[1] Hafizunissa Begum *v.* Radha Binode Misser, Sudder Dewany Decisions for 1856, p. 595.

[2] Jagudunda Pillay *v.* Kamachemma, Rep. for 1858, p. 241.

LECTURE X.

er's *approval* of the widow's alienation conveys his interest.

heir, not as merely *attesting* it, but a... mean to impugn of by him, it was held that this will ha... transaction of making the conveyance a joint conveyanc... the widow and the next heir, and not as a mere convey ance by the widow alone with the approval of the next heirs. This point was expressly raised and decided in the case of *Doe dem Madhusudan Doss* v. *Mohendro Lal Khan.*[1] There the deed of gift, executed by the widow, had been signed by Ajodhyaram and his five brothers (who were entitled to succeed on the death of the widow) with the word "approved" added to their signatures. The question raised in the case was, whether, by the signature of Ajodhyaram to this deed, any interest of Ajodhyaram passed to the donee ? The Court observed that, looking at the deed as the act of the widow alone, irrespective of its approval by Ajodhyaram, the donees could take nothing under it after the death of the widow.

In consequence, however, of the approval of Ajodhyaram written on the instrument itself, it has a more extended operation. The Court refused to consider the heir's approval as having the effect of giving the widow the power of disposing of this property absolutely by her deed: for in that case it will be necessary that the heir's approval, treating it as a conveyance, must precede the widow's alienation. The Court observed :—" In the present case the arrangement is effected by one deed of gift

[1] 2 Boulnois' Rep., 40.

to the defendants, and the conveyance of Sankara Deyi (the widow) and the approval of Ajodhyaram are contemporaneous acts forming one transaction. There was no evidence showing an intention on the part of Ajodhyaram to convey any power or interest to the widow, and the purport of the deed of gift does not support such a theory. But, whether you consider the deed as a transfer by Ajodhyaram to the defendants (the donees) or to the widow for the benefit of the defendants (which seems to be unfounded in fact), or as the joint conveyance of the widow and the party having the contingent interest, yet it is equally clear that Ajodhyaram, by the deed in question, deprived himself of all right as heir, and transferred from himself to the defendants that which the widow alone could not convey to them. We think the correct view of such a transaction is, that it is a joint conveyance by parties entitled to the restrained estate and the contingent interest."

Also when he joins in the conveyance.

If the next heir joins the widow in the conveyance, the question is, whether it will have the effect of passing an absolute indefeasible title to the alienee. In the case of *Mohunt Kissen Geer* v. *Busjeet Roy and others*,[1] Markby, J., held, that it will have that effect. The learned Judge observed :—" It was also contended that *Gooroo* being only the possible next taker, his joining in the conveyance would not make the title good. But I think that, even if the property did not

[1] 14 W. R., 379.

LECTURE X. eventually at Teeluk Chand's (widow's) death become vested in *Gooroo*, still, according to the rule of Hindu law, which has been adopted by this Court, the title of the alienee is complete. To hold otherwise would only necessitate the adding of two or three words to the conveyance, because the widow may at any time surrender the property to the apparent next taker, who will then become absolute owner. But that is not necessary. The two joining in one conveyance can make a complete title."

How far the above is a correct view of the law on the subject may well be questioned. If the conveyance of the widow and the *then* next heir has the effect of passing an indefeasible title to the alienee, a title which the *actual* next heir on the death of the widow is precluded from questioning, then, I submit, a conveyance by the widow with the consent of the *then next* heir ought to have a similar effect. But it has been held, that the consent of the next heir to the conveyance binds him only, and does not bind anybody else. If that is so, one does not see why the apparent next taker joining in the widow's conveyance will be enabled to bind all the other persons who may happen actually to succeed to the estate on the death of the widow. Perhaps it may be said that the next taker joining in the conveyance conveys his own contingent interest. That may be true: but that will not pass the absolute title, for between the widow and the apparent next taker the absolute title to the property is not complete. This was clearly pointed out in the case of *Madhusudun Doss* v. *Mohendro Lal Khan*,[1] which has been quoted above. One of the arguments in that case was, that if the next heir had conveyed his contingent interest to the widow first, then the widow would be competent to convey the full title to the alienee. The Court, however, negatived such a view of the law, observing, that "even in that case the widow would not have been able to convey the estate absolutely, or do more than convey her own estate, and what Ajodhyaram (the next taker) had conveyed to her." The Court further held, that it will be "a joint conveyance by parties entitled to the restrained estate and the contingent interest."

The correct view, therefore, of a conveyance by the widow and the apparent next taker is, that it is a joint conveyance of the widow's estate and the contingent interest of the next taker; that it passes the interest of the next taker who has joined in the conveyance, and cannot bind those who have not joined in the conveyance, and who happen to be the next heirs to the estate on the death of the widow. The law on this subject, I apprehend, is similar to the doctrine of consent. He who has joined in the widow's conveyance will be bound by it just as he who has given his consent to it will be bound by it. And he who has not joined in the conveyance will not be bound by it in the same way as he who has not given

[1] 2 Boulnois' Rep., p. 40.

LECTURE X. his consent will not be bound by it, although another person may have joined in the conveyance or may have consented to it.

Surrender of the widow's estate.

As intimately connected with our present subject, I shall consider the law relating to the surrender of the widow's estate in favor of the next takers. The widow is in possession of her estate, she is anxious to determine her estate, and she can do it by surrendering her estate to the next takers. The surrender must be in favor of *all* those persons who stand in the position of next takers to her. If the surrender is in favor of some of the next takers to the exclusion of others of the same class, such an act will not be valid, because the excluded person will be entitled to complain, and as against him the alienation will not be good. But if the surrender is in favor of the *second* reversioner with the consent of the *first* reversioner, it passes an absolute title.[1]

Passes an absolute title.

The effect of a surrender by the widow is to determine her present interest and to convert the contingent interest of the next takers into an estate in possession, and the widow's surrender usually takes the form either of a conveyance or a deed of gift, or a deed of trust in favor of next takers, by which the widow relinquishes her possession; and the next takers, by the effect of the widow's deed, enter into possession as absolute owners. Generally the widow relinquishes in favor of persons who stand

[1] Protap Chunder Roy v. S. M. Joymony Debee, 1 W. R., 98.

in close relationship to her or to her husband. She relinquishes either in favor of her daughters, or her daughter's sons, or her husband's brothers, or her husband's nephews, and similar near relations; and the motive for her relinquishment is, as usually stated, her incapacity to manage the property, or her anxiety for peace and pious repose; and the person in whose favor she relinquishes her present interest generally gives her a competence, or secures her a respectable maintenance to the end of her life. LECTURE X.

Presumes reversioner's consent.

The principle on which the validity of the widow's surrender is based is the assumption that the alienation being in favor of the next takers is supposed to have their consent. They are supposed to give their consent to an alienation in their own behalf; and as the consent of all the reversioners has the effect of passing an absolute title to the alienee, the surrender by the widow, it is assumed, has that effect. There is some inconsistency in this reasoning, which I must point out to you. I have before explained to you the proposition, that unless *all* the reversioners consent to the widow's alienation, the title does not pass absolutely. If any one has not given his consent, and he happens to be the next heir on the death of the widow, the alienation as against him is not valid, although it may have been consented to by persons who, at the time of the alienation, were, in the line of succession, preferable to him. Let us apply this to the law of surrender.

LECTURE X. The widow relinquishes in favor of the then apparent heirs. The deed is assumed to have their consent. If they survive the widow there is no difficulty. In this case the heirs at the time of the widow's death had consented to the widow's act; and the act therefore is valid. But let us suppose the person in whose favor the relinquishment was made dies during the widow's lifetime, and another person, on the widow's death, becomes the heir to the estate; he might say, that he did not consent to the widow's act of relinquishment or surrender, and that, therefore, he should not be bound by it, and that he should, therefore, be allowed to question it. Strictly speaking, the widow's relinquishment in favor of the then next heirs ought not to have been held to pass an absolute and indefeasible title to the alienee. The relinquishment by the widow in favor of the then next takers is substantially an act of alienation, and ought to be dealt with as such. The Hindu law lays down that, on the death of the widow, the next heir shall take the property. By this relinquishment, the person actually entitled,—*i. e.*, the survivor,—is deprived of his just rights, and the property goes to the descendants of another person, who had not the slightest chance of getting it; and all this because the widow has been guilty of a wanton act of waste by conveying the property in favor of some near relative.

I shall make my meaning clear by an illustration. Supposing the next heir of the widow is her husband's brother *A*, and the widow relinquishes her estate in favor of *A*. During the widow's lifetime, *A* dies, leaving a grandson *B*; and when the widow dies the person entitled to succeed to the estate is a nephew of her husband, *viz.*, *C*. Now the relinquishment having taken place, *C* does not get the property. It is enjoyed by *B*, as successor of *A*. If the relinquishment had not been made, *C* would have obtained the property to the exclusion of *B*. But in this case, *C* is deprived of his just rights by a wanton act of waste on the part of the widow. This is certainly opposed to the clear principles of Hindu law, which lay down, that the property shall go to the next heirs *at the time of the widow's death*, unless the property has previously passed into the hands of an alienee by a valid alienation; and a valid alienation is effected when the widow transfers the property for a legal necessity. Such an anticipation of interest, as the relinquishment leads to, or the defeasance of ulterior interests by intermediate or premature acts on the part of the widow, was never, I think, contemplated by Hindu law, and is wholly opposed to its spirit.

Whatever may be the correct view of Hindu law on the subject, a long course of decisions[1] has, however, established the proposition that a widow, by relinquishing her estate in favor of the apparent next

[1] Jadumoni Debi *v.* Saroda Prosonno Mukerjee, 1 Boulnois' Rep., 120; Protap Chunder Chowdhry *v.* S. M. Joymonee Debee, 1 W. R., 98; Shama Sundaree *v.* Surut Chunder Dutt, 8 W. R., 500; Kaleecoomar Nag *v.* Kashee Chunder Nag, 2 Wym, 212; Rojonikant Mitter *v.* Pranchand Bose, Marshall, 241; See *contra* Musst. Radha *v.* Musst. Kour, W. R. Gap. No., 148.

LECTURE X. takers, can convey an absolute title to the alienee, unimpeachable by any other reversioner. It is now, therefore, too late to raise the question ; accurate or inaccurate, it has been the law for a long course of years. That state of the law, therefore, should not be lightly disturbed.

The chief authority for the proposition on which all the later cases are based, is to be found in the note by Mr. Colebrooke to the case of *Mahoda* v. *Kuleani*. The note runs thus :—" It has been declared by the law-officers of the Courts in other suits, that the widow's gift of the estate to the next heir is good in law, though she be restrained from making any other alienation of it. This opinion, though not founded on any express passages to that effect in books of authority, seems reasonable, as such a gift is a mere relinquishment of her temporary interest in favor of the next heir. It may, however, happen that the person who would have been entitled to take the inheritance at her decease, may be different from the one who obtained it under the gift or relinquishment to him as presumptive heir ; and if the title of that person be either preferable or equal, it may invalidate such gift in whole or in part."

The case of *Beer Inder Narain Chowdhry* v. *Satyabhama Debi and others*[1] can be supported on the principle that the widow *relinquished* her rights in favor of the next heir, her daughter.

---

[1] 6 Sel. Rep., 42.

In that case the widow had made a gift of the whole of her husband's estate to her daughter and son-in-law.

The Pundit whose opinion was asked, justified the gift upon three grounds :—

1*st.*—As a gift by the widow with the consent of the next heir.

2*nd.*—As a gift to a Brahmin.

3*rd.*—Non-opposition to the deed, at the time of its execution, by the heirs of the widow's husband.

All these three grounds are erroneous and insufficient to support the conclusion that the gift was valid. As a gift or alienation it is not valid unless it has the consent of *all* the heirs living at the time, and the consent of the *next heir alone* is insufficient. As a gift to a Brahmin, it will not, I think, be contended as valid on that ground, for I do not think it was seriously contended at any time that a widow could make a valid gift of *all* her husband's property to a Brahmin. As for the ground of estoppel, I do not think it can be contended that a mere want of opposition on the part of heirs at the time of the execution of the deed, would bar their right of questioning the deed hereafter. Of course, a long acquiescence for such a period as to bar their right under the ordinary law of limitation will have that effect. The only ground, therefore, on which that decision can be supported is, that the deed operated as a surrender or relinquishment of her estate by the

LECTURE X. widow in favor of the next apparent taker, so as to pass to the latter an absolute title.

I ought, also, to point out to you here a distinction between the relinquishment or surrender in favor of the *daughter* and the relinquishment in favor of the next male heir. The male heir, if he survives the widow, will take the estate *absolutely;* but the daughter will only take a *life-interest* in it. Further, the title of the *male* heir can *never* be defeated if he survives the widow; but the daughter, although she may survive the widow, may be disqualified to inherit by being a barren wife or a childless widow. Whether a surrender, therefore, of the widow's estate in favor of one, who at best only takes a *life*-estate, can have the effect of vesting an *absolute* estate in the latter, may well be questioned. The surrender only *anticipates* the expectant interest, and cannot, I think, *enlarge* it. I think, therefore, that the widow, by surrendering her estate in favor of the daughter, gives to the latter only a *life*-estate, determinable on her death. I am not, however, aware at present of any case in which the point has been decided according to the view I hold in the matter.

I have said that the surrender by the widow passes an absolute title to the next reversioners. The converse doctrine was held to be good law by the late Supreme Court.[1] The next reversioners had conveyed their contingent interest to the widow in fee: and thereupon the widow had conveyed. The

[1] Kali Churn Dutt *v.* John Moore and others, 1 Fulton, 73.

question in the case was, whether the sons of these reversioners can set aside this conveyance of the widow. Ryan, C. J., held, that they cannot, as they are bound by their ancestor's acts through whom they claim; and that they have no reversionary interests independent of their fathers. The Court, however, did not expressly rule in this case whether the conveyance by the next reversioners to the widow had the effect of passing an *absolute* title to the widow unimpeachable by *any other* reversioner.

Jadumoni Debi v. Saroda Prosonno Mukerjee.

The case of *Srimati Jadumani Debi* v. *Saroda Prosonno Mukerjee and others* [1] is an important case as bearing upon the doctrine of assignment by the widow in favor of the *next* heir. Anindmoyi had succeeded to the estate of her son Boidonath, and she assigned over that estate to Kaliprosono, the next reversioner, in consideration of a life-annuity. The plaintiff's case was, that the assignment had not the effect of passing a complete title to Kaliprosono, but that, on the death of the widow, the heirs who survived will inherit the estate of Boidonath.

Jackson, J., referring to the validity of the deed of assignment, observed as follows :—"I think the argument for the defendant on this point is not supported to its full extent by authority, for, although it is clear that, on the occasion of the widow becoming a *byraghi*, the estate would at once descend to the nearest heirs living at the time (2 Macnaghten's

[1] 1 Boulnois' Rep., p. 120.

LECTURE X. Hindu Law, 131, 233 ; and the case of *Hafizunnissa Begum* v. *Radha Binode Misser*), yet there is no authority for the unqualified proposition that the widow can, by her surrender, vest the whole estate indefeasibly in the nearest heirs living at the time of such surrender.

"On a review of all the authorities, the correct view of the law would seem to be that a widow's conveyance of the estate to all the nearest heirs living at the time of the conveyance is valid, provided that no other heirs of equal or superior degree happen to be in existence at the time of the widow's death.

"On the whole then, applying this view of the law to the facts of the case, I think that Kaliprosonno Mukerjee was the only nearest or next heir living at the time of the execution of this deed, and that his consent to the gift in his own favor is clearly shown, and that, although Taraprosonno and Sarodaprosonno were the heirs living at the death of the widow, yet they were not heirs of superior or equal, but, on the contrary, of a remoter degree than Kaliprosonno, their father, and that, therefore, they cannot dispute the validity of the deed, which is valid according to Hindu law."

Colvile, C. J., delivered a separate judgment in the case. After reviewing all the available authorities he expressed himself more guardedly thus :—

"Upon the whole it appears to me that, although the question is not free from doubt, the balance of authorities is in favor of treating such a transaction as that which took place between Anindmoyi and Kaliprosonno Mukerjee, as a disposition which the widow was, with the implied consent of Kaliprosonno, her husband's nearest heir, competent to enter into : at all events as one which neither the sons of Kaliprosonno, nor the representatives of those sons, are entitled to impeach."

The observations of the Chief Justice as to the policy of the Hindu law in imposing restraints upon the widow's powers of alienation are very important; and the reasons why an assignment in favor of the *next heir* is distinguishable from an alienation in favor of a *stranger* are well pointed out. The Chief Justice observed:—"That the reasons for the limitations which the law sets upon the widow's interest and her disposing power afford no argument against such a disposition as that now under consideration. The policy of the Hindu law was not, I apprehend, to keep the estate as long as possible inalienable and subject to a species of entail in favor of persons unascertained, but to prevent the alienation of family property, or the alienation of a share in a joint and undivided family estate from taking place either in favor of the widow's natural heirs, who would generally be other than the heirs of her husband, or in favor of strangers, by the gift or other disposition of the widow. There is nothing contrary to such a policy in an arrangement by which the widow gives up her right of inheritance in favor of one, with whom, if

LECTURE X. he outlived her other heirs, no one could come in competition, of one who, if, as here, joint in estate with her husband, would, according to the law of some parts of India, take preferably to her. It is, in fact, but another way of doing that which in former times was continually done without violence to the letter or spirit of Hindu law."

How far the above is in strict conformity with the spirit of Hindu law is a very difficult question to determine. The Hindu law contemplates that the estate, on the death of the widow, shall go to the nearest heir living *at the time;* and that the rights of such a person should not be compromised or defeated by any act on the part of the widow not warranted by the doctrine of *necessity*. Besides, the Hindu law does not seem to display such a preponderating preference for the *next* heir over another more remote as completely to sacrifice the rights of the latter for the purpose of investing an absolute title in the former.

The *case of Jadumoney Debee,* in which all the previous cases were carefully reviewed by the eminent Judges, must now be accepted as an authority for the proposition that the assignment by the widow of the estate in favor of the next heir or next heirs is valid, and that it passes an absolute title to the alienee unimpeachable by any other reversioner.[1]

A compromise entered into by a Hindu widow, by

[1] See also Gungaprosaud Kur *v.* Shumbhoo Nath Burmun, 22 W. R., 393; Nuffer Doss Roy *v.* Modoo Sunduri Burmonia, 5 Cal. Law Rep., 551; Lalla Kundee Lall *v.* Lalla Kalee Persud, 22 W. R., 307.

which she gives up all her rights in the estate of her deceased husband, reserving only a life-interest for herself in a part of it, has been treated in the light of an ordinary alienation by the widow, and as such has been held to be not binding as against the reversioner.[1] The relinquishment in this case, I presume, was not in favor of the next heir, but in favor of a stranger ; otherwise the decision would be contrary to the current of authorities which have been quoted before. The report of the case, however, does not expressly give the facts.

Where a deed by the widow in favor of the next reversioner is in any way doubtful, its terms will be strictly construed, especially when the reversioner is the chief male member of the family, and the widow is one of its members. Such a transaction will be closely scrutinized, and unless the language clearly imports it to be a conveyance, the deed will be treated as one of management by which the widow made over the management of the property in the hands of the next heir, whose interest it is by careful management to prevent waste. In such a case all the circumstances will be considered to determine whether the instrument was intended to be a conveyance or a mere deed of management.[2]

---

[1] Musst. Indro Koomar and others v. Shekh Abdul Burkat, 14 W. R., 146.
[2] Sookyaboye Ammal v. Lutchi Ammal, 5 Madras Jurist, 183.

LECTURE XI.

SUITS BY REVERSIONERS.

Suits by reversioners—Allowed—Declaratory decrees—Discretionary—Specific Relief Act—Suit after widow's death—Cause of delay in bringing these suits—Limitation applicable to such suits—The crown can maintain such suits—*The Collector of Masulipatam* v. *C. V. Narainapah*—Suit must be by the *next* reversioner—Not by the *second* reversioner—Reversioner to refund purchase-money — Reversioner bound to redeem—Removal of the widow from possession of the estate—An extraordinary remedy—*Bolaki Bibi* v. *Nundlal Babu*—What will justify widow's removal—Positive fraud on her part—*Haridoss Dutt* v. *Rangan Moni Dosee*—Reversioner cannot sue to recover property alienated—*Gobindmoni Dossee* v. *Sham Lall Bysack*—Widow receives usufruct when removed from possession.

Suits by reversioners.

THE right of the reversioners to maintain a suit against the widow has been long established. The Hindu law declares that the widow shall not commit waste,—*i.e.*, shall not do any act which may injure the contingent interest of the reversioners. The author of the Dayabhaga, therefore, says :[1]—"The widow is not entitled to make a gift, mortgage, or sale of it," —*i.e.*, of the property which she has inherited from her husband.

Now the Hindu law does not expressly lay down any specific remedy which the reversioner is to pur-

[1] Chap. XI, sec. i, para. 56.

sue in case the widow transgresses her obligation in this respect. The Courts of this country, as Courts of Equity, have supplied the omission in accordance with the spirit of the Hindu law. The remedy prescribed does not affect the rights of the parties under that law; on the contrary, it helps to subserve those rights by protecting them from infringement. LECTURE XI.

Allowed.

The Courts of this country and also the Privy Council have, accordingly, held,[1] from a long time, that the reversionary heirs, though their interest is only contingent, have a right to maintain a suit to restrain waste by the widow. When the suit is brought during the widow's lifetime, the prayer in the plaint is to have the particular act of alienation, complained of, declared void, on the ground that it is in excess of the widow's powers; and the decree in the case does not extend beyond a mere declaration, and grants no consequential relief.

Declaratory decrees.

The declaratory decrees passed at the instance of the reversioners were based upon the provisions of Section 15, Act VIII of 1859. It was doubted at one time whether the Court could make a declaration where no consequential relief was prayed for. The subject was fully discussed in the case of *Kathama Natchiyar* v. *Dora Singa Tever*,[2] in which their Lordships put the following construction upon that sec-

[1] Uujjulmoni Dosee *v.* Sagormoni Dosee, 1 Taylor and Bell, p. 370; Haridoss Dutt *v.* Ranganmoni Dosee, Vyavastha D arpa, Eng. Ed., p. 124; Rajlukhee Debee *v.* Gocul Chunder, 13 Moore's I. A., 209, 224.

[2] I. R., 2 I. A., 169.

LECTURE XI.

tion :—" It appears, therefore, to their Lordships that the construction which must be put upon the clause in question is, that a declaratory decree cannot be made unless there be a right to consequential relief capable of being had in the same Court;" or—as laid down in the case of *Fyz Ali*[1]—in certain cases, in some other Court.

The same principle was followed in another case,[2] where it was held, that a declaratory decree cannot be made unless the plaintiff would be entitled to consequential relief if he asked for it. Their Lordships were further of opinion, that " it is not a matter of absolute right to obtain a declaratory decree. It is discretionary with the Court to grant it or not, and in every case the Court must exercise a sound judgment as to whether it is reasonable or not, under all the circumstances of the case, to grant the relief prayed for. There is so much more danger in India than here of harassing and vexatious litigation, that the Courts in India ought to be most careful that mere declaratory suits be not converted into a new and mischievous source of litigation."

In the case of *Kathama Natchiyar*, quoted before, the Privy Council, after laying down the general rule, thus provide for the exceptional class of cases, *viz.*, suits by reversioners. Their Lordships observed as follows :—" The arguments now under consideration

---

[1] Sadut Ali Khan *v.* Khajah Abdul Guny, 11 B. L. R., 203

[2] Sreenarain Mitter *v.* Kishen Soonderi Dasee, 11 B. L. R., 171.

are founded on the right of a reversioner to bring a suit to restrain a widow, or other Hindu female, in possession, from acts of waste. Although his interest during her life is future and contingent, suits of that kind form a very special class, and have been entertained by the Courts *ex necessitate rei*. It seems, however, to their Lordships, that, if such a suit as that is brought, it must be by the reversioner with that object and for that purpose alone, and that the question to be discussed is simply between him and the widow; that he cannot, by bringing such a suit, get, as between him and a third party, an adjudication of title which he cannot get without it."[1] LECTURE XI.

Discretionary.

The principle of this decision was followed in a very recent case[2] by the Bengal High Court. The widows had made a gift of their husband's property, and also of property purchased from accumulations, to the daughter. The daughter having died, leaving a minor daughter, a suit was brought by the reversionary heirs of the deceased father, against the widows and the infant grand-daughter, for a declaration that the deed executed by the widows in favor of the daughter did not and could not affect their reversionary interest. It was held in the case, that, inasmuch as no immediate relief could be granted, it was unnecessary, under the circumstances, to make a declara-

---

[1] Tekait Doorga Prosaud v. Tekaitni Doorga Kunwari, L. R., 5 I. A., 149.

[2] Hunsbuti Koerain v. Ishri Dutt Koer, 4 Cal. Law Rep., 511.

LECTURE XI. tory decree. "The Court will not, in a declaratory suit, decide intricate questions of law, when no immediate, and possibly no future, effect can be given to its decision, and when the postponement of the decision to the time when there may be before the Court some person entitled to immediate relief (if the decision is in favor of the plaintiff) will not prejudice his rights in any way."

Specific Relief Act. Section 15 of Act VIII of 1859 was repealed by the Specific Relief Act, I of 1877, which has given the sanction of positive law to suits of the description we are now considering. Section 42 of the Act runs as follows:—"Any person entitled to any legal character, or to any right as to any property, may institute a suit against any person denying, or interested to deny, his title to such character or right; and the Court may, in its discretion, make therein a declaration that he is so entitled, and the plaintiff need not in such suit ask for any further relief. Provided that no Court shall make any such declaration where the plaintiff, being able to seek further relief than a mere declaration of title, omits to do so."

You will observe that, in the case of a suit by the reversioner, the proviso of the above section will be no bar; because the reversioner, during the widow's lifetime, is not usually entitled to any other relief than a mere declaration; consequently, his omission to ask for further relief will not be prejudicial to his suit.

The illustrations to this section have expressly sanctioned such suits by reversioners:— LECTURE XI.

Illustration (*e.*)—The widow of a sonless Hindu alienates part of the property of which she is in possession as such. The person presumptively entitled to possess the property if he survive her, may, in a suit against the alienee, obtain a declaration that the alienation was without legal necessity, and, therefore, void beyond the widow's lifetime.

Illustration (*f.*)—A Hindu widow in possession of property adopts a son to her deceased husband. The person presumptively entitled to possession of the property on her death without a son may, in a suit against the adopted son, obtain a declaration that the adoption was invalid.

Section 43.—A declaration made under this chapter is binding only on the parties to the suit, persons claiming through them respectively, and, where any of the parties are trustees, on the persons for whom, if in existence at the date of the declaration, such parties would be trustees.

Suits after widow's death.

When the suit is brought after the widow's death, it takes the form of a prayer for declaration and for possession. The reversioner, now heir, prays, that it be declared that the particular act of alienation was in excess of the widow's powers, and the widow being dead, he be put in possession of the property from which he is kept out wrongfully by the defendant, the widow's assignee. The usual defence in such

LECTURE XI. suits is, that the act was within the widow's limited powers; that there was legal necessity for the alienation; or that the next heir consented to the act of alienation. There are cases where absolute rights are claimed as having vested in the widow by virtue of some deed from the last owner. In such a case the alienation is not defended as the act of the *widow*, but as the act of a person in whom was vested an estate *higher* than that of a Hindu widow; and this not by operation of law, but by the act and deed of the last owner.

Another form which these suits take is to have a declaration that an adoption by the widow is invalid. As such an act of the widow has the effect of diverting the inheritance from the reversioners, they are considered to possess sufficient interest to bring a suit of that description. Illustration (*f*) to Section 42 of the Specific Relief Act expressly authorises such suits.

When the suit is brought after the widow's death, there is always considerable difficulty in the production of evidence to show that the act of alienation was necessitated by the circumstances of the widow or the state of the property. The Hindu widows are proverbially a long-lived race of people. The alienation having taken place long before the suit, it becomes difficult to produce contemporaneous evidence of the transaction; and you must have seen the reports of cases where Judges had to complain of the paucity of evidence to prove the facts; almost all contemporaneous evidence having disappeared by lapse of time. The purchaser complains of the long lapse of time which has intervened between the date of the transaction and the date of suit, and the consequent disappearance of evidence. His complaint is accepted by the Court as reasonable, and the omissions and defects in his evidence are overlooked. It is advisable, therefore, for the reversioner to bring his suit soon after the transaction; the act of alienation being recent, fresh and full evidence will be forthcoming, and the result will be satisfactory.

Cause of delay in bringing these suits.

The reason why the reversioner does not bring his suit immediately after the wrongful act of the widow, is the uncertainty about the vesting of the ulterior interest, and the want of any immediate consequential relief. One reversioner goes to the expense and trouble of a long litigation, to establish the invalid nature of the alienations, and he happens to die during the widow's lifetime. His heir may not get the benefit of the decree, and another person, in whom the estate vests on the death of the widow, as the next surviving reversioner, derives all the benefit from the decree, without having ever contributed either his labour or his money for obtaining the same. Coupled with this is the fact, that the decree leads to no immediate relief: it ends in a barren declaration; and such a termination of the litigation appears to the litigant rather unsatisfactory.

LECTURE XI.

Limitation applicable to such suits.

The limitation applicable to such suits has been now fixed by positive enactment. Under the former law (Act XIV of 1859) there was no period fixed during which it was incumbent upon a party to bring a suit for declaration. It was held, that such a suit could be instituted at any time while the widow was alive: but that a suit for possession after the widow's death must be brought within twelve years from that event.

The next limitation law (Act IX of 1871) expressly laid down periods of limitation for both kinds of suits. It was ordained that, "suits during the life of a Hindu widow by a Hindu entitled to the possession of land on her death, to have an alienation made by the widow declared to be void, except for her life," must be brought within twelve years from the date of the alienation;[1] and that a suit for possession of immoveable property "by a Hindu entitled to the possession of immoveable property on the death of a Hindu widow," must be brought within twelve years from the date of the widow's death.[2]

The present Limitation Act, XV of 1877, contains similar provisions. It ordains, that a "suit during the life of a Hindu or Mahomedan female, by a Hindu or Mahomedan who, if the female died at the date of instituting the suit, would be entitled to the possession of land, to have an alienation of such land made by the female declared to the void, except for her life, or until her remarriage," must be brought

[1] Sched. II, art. 124.

[2] Sched. II, art. 142.

within twelve years from the date of the alienation.[1] And that a suit for possession of immoveable property, "by a Hindu or Mahomedan entitled to the possession of immoveable property, on the death of a Hindu or Mahomedan female," must be brought within twelve years from the date when the female dies.[2]

The crown can maintain such suits.

I have said before that a reversioner could bring a suit to impeach an alienation by the widow; and the point was raised in Madras, as to whether the crown, taking the property of a Hindu on failure of heirs, could question the alienations made by the widow, who was the last holder of the property. The Sudder Dewany Adawlut at Madras held, that it could not. The Court held in substance as follows:—

The Collector of Masulipatam v. C. V. Narainapah.

If the undisputed owner of the zemindary in issue had been a male, without male progeny, he could have alienated the estate at any moment before his death whether with or without consideration, and no collateral could have questioned the act. By consequence, the crown could not do so. The last owner having been a female, the power to alienate in her was placed by the law under certain special restrictions,—that is, though destitute of direct lineage, she could not alienate to the prejudice of her remotest heirs, save under their consent or under strict necessity. In the present suit, the crown claims to possess the restrictive power belonging to an heir of the female,

[1] Sched. II, art. 125.

[2] Sched. II, art. 141.

LECTURE XI. and have laid this suit to defeat her act. The Court have consulted their Pundits on the occasion, and their declaration is to the effect that the limitations under which a female is placed are exclusively for the interests of her heirs — meaning thereby her kindred, or those of her husband: that, failing all such heirs, the provision does not extend to the protection of the interests of the ruling power as coming in by escheat, and that, in regard to the ruling power, the female is absolutely free, being at liberty to alienate without seeking its consent, and irrespective of its ulterior rights. The Court held, that as the widow had alienated, and as the validity of the same could not be questioned by the crown, the claim of the crown to hold the property as an escheat must be disallowed.

On appeal to the Privy Council[1] their Lordships dissented from the doctrine laid down by the Sudder Court, and held, that the crown, taking the property by escheat, was entitled to question the widow's alienations as much as an ordinary reversioner was entitled to do. Their Lordships say as follows:—"It does not appear to their Lordships that the construction of Hindu law, which is now contended for, can be put upon the principle '*cessante ratione cessat et ipsa lex.*' It is not merely for the protection of the material interests of her husband's relations

[1] The Collector of Masulipatam *v.* Cavaly Vencata Narainapah, 8 Moore's I. A., 529.

that the fetter on the widow's power is imposed. Numberless authorities from Manu downwards may be cited to show that, according to the principles of Hindu law, the proper state of every woman is one of tutelage, that they always require protection, and are never fit for independence. Sir Thomas Strange (Hindu Law, Vol. I, p. 242), cites the authority of Manu for the proposition that, if a woman have no other controller or protector, the king should control or protect her. Again, all the authorities concur in showing that, according to the principles of Hindu law, the life of a widow is to be one of ascetic privations (2 Colebrooke's Digest, 459). Hence, probably, it gave her a power of disposition for religious, which it denied to her for other, purposes. These principles do not seem to be consistent with the doctrine that, on the failure of heirs, a widow becomes completely emancipated; perfectly uncontrolled in the disposal of her property; and free to squander her inherited wealth for the purposes of selfish enjoyment.

"Their Lordships are of opinion that the restrictions on a widow's power of alienation are inseparable from her estate, and their existence does not depend on that of heirs capable of taking on her death. It follows that, if, for want of heirs, the right to the property, so far as it has not been lawfully disposed of by her, passes to the crown, the crown must have the same power which an heir would have of protect-

LECTURE XI. ing its interests by impeaching any unauthorised alienation by the widow."

The law, therefore, is now settled, on the authority of this case, that the widow's alienations are voidable at the instance of *any one* who is entitled to take the estate on the death of the widow; and the right of impeaching alienations does not depend upon the fact of that person being a *kindred* or not.

Suit must be by the *next* reversioner. The suit for a declaration that the widow's alienation was invalid, must be brought by the *next* reversioner. A suit by the *second* reversioner during the lifetime of the *first* reversioner will not lie. The

Not by the *second* reversioner. Sudder Dewany Adawlut[1] held, that where the grandsons (daughter's sons I presume) of the last owner were living, his nephews could not object to an alienation by the widow of the son of the late owner. The Court observed :—"We find from the record that there are three grandsons of Nimananda (the last owner) still living. They are the parties whose interests are directly affected if the sale by the widow is illegal, and they are the parties who ought to sue if that sale be contrary to law; but no suit has been preferred by them. The defendants might have, on failure of certain heirs, a right to the disputed property, but it is inchoate, and until that right shall have arisen, they are not the persons entitled to sue for infraction of the Hindu law to their detriment."[2]

[1] Ramdhone Buksi *v.* Puuchanun Bose, S. D. Dec. for 1853, p. 641.

[2] See also Jadoomoni Debi *v.* Saroda Prosonno Mukerjee, *per* Jackson, J., 1 Boulnois' Rep., p. 120.

In another case,[1] the plaintiffs sued to have an adoption set aside, and also certain alienations made by the widow to be declared invalid. The plaintiffs' father was the *next* reversioner to the estate. The lower Court dismissed the suit, on the ground that, as the plaintiffs' father was alive, the plaintiffs are not competent during his life to maintain this suit.

On appeal the Sudder Court observed :—"The counsel for the appellants has been unable to show us that, under any precedent of this Court, the more distant reversioners have, during the lifetime of the immediate reversioners, a right to sue to set aside acts done by the widow; but they contend that this defect has been remedied, as the father of the appellants, who is the immediate reversioner, has filed a petition in this Court, waving his claim to the property; aud a decision of this Court, dated the 8th February 1851 (*Protap Chunder Dutt*, appellant), is quoted to show that such an application may be received even at this stage of the proceedings. We concur with the lower Courts in holding, that the suit in its present form cannot lie. We think that the immediate reversioners can alone bring an action to interfere with the acts of a widow in possession, and that the plaintiffs are reversioners in too remote a degree to entitle them to sue to set aside acts done by the widow, or to interfere with her management; and we consider that the defect of parties, which is

[1] Gogun Chunder Sen *v.* Joydurga. S. D. A. Decisions for 1859, p. 620.

LECTURE XI. apparent in the present suit, cannot now be remedied, and the decision quoted by the counsel is directly opposed to the admission of a petition such as is now sought to be filed."

In the case of *Rojonikant Mitter* v. *Prem Chand Bose*,[1] the High Court, however, was of opinion, that a petition of disclaimer filed by the *immediate* reversioner in the suit brought by the *second* reversioner will render the suit by the latter maintainable. In that case the plaintiff was the daughter's son of Ramnursing. Two maternal aunts of the plaintiff, apparently his mother's sisters, were living; and it was objected that, as the plaintiff's right to succeed is contingent on his surviving them, his suit is premature. These two ladies had, however, filed, in the record of this case, a petition, in which they acknowledged the plaintiff to be the rightful heir, disclaiming right of their own, and assented entirely to the plaintiff's suit. The question turned upon the effect of this petition of disclaimer. The District Judge was of opinion that this petition could not accelerate the plaintiff's right, and that it did not remove the defect of the suit being premature.

The High Court, on appeal, dissented from the view taken by the District Judge, and was of opinion that the effect of the petition was to vest the estate in the plaintiff, so as to entitle him to sue at once. The material portion of the judgment of the High

[1] Marshall, 241.

Court runs as follows: "Females, it has been argued, are not at liberty to do or assent to acts which may have the effect of changing the course of succession, and these two ladies' consent cannot operate to give the inheritance in this case to a person who may eventually not be the legal heir. We consider this objection untenable. A Hindu widow, it has been ruled, is competent to alienate, with the consent of the next heir, an estate in which she possesses only a life-interest; she has also been permitted to convey the estate to the next heir himself. It is admitted that, by retiring from the world, as by becoming a *Byraghin*, she might immediately cause the succession to devolve on the plaintiff; and we think that when the plaintiff raises a particular question of title with the defendants, which clearly his aunts will be fully entitled to raise, and he next after them, and when they expressly give up their right in his favor and assent to his suit, the defendants cannot be permitted to object that plaintiff cannot sue until after their death."

The distinction between this case and the previous one of *Gogun Chunder Sen* consists in this. In the case of *Gogun Chunder Sen* the Court held, that the *second* reversioner could not sue to set aside alienations made by the widow when the *first* reversioner was living; and the suit was brought during the widow's lifetime. In the other case, the widows, the aunts of the plaintiff, were entitled to the posses-

LECTURE XI. sion of the estate; and the plaintiff was held competent to sue for possession in his own right when the widows had, by petition, surrendered their interest in favor of the plaintiff, who was the next heir.

How far a disclaimer in the course of a suit may complete the plaintiff's right to sue seems questionable. The plaintiff, when he comes into Court, must have his title complete. If an assignment of rights or consent of any party is necessary to perfect the plaintiff's title, that assignment, or that consent, must be obtained *before* the plaintiff files his plaint. The defendant may justly say, that he objects to the plaintiff's right or status as existing at the date of suit, and that the plaintiff ought not to be allowed to perfect an otherwise defective title by acts or events happening *subsequent* to the institution of the suit. This is reasonable, because the decree in a suit and other proceedings therein have reference retrospectively to the date when the suit was instituted.

Reversioner to refund purchase-money.

There are cases in which it was held, that the suit of the reversioner will not succeed unless he is prepared to refund the purchase-money or a portion of the purchase-money to the purchaser. Supposing the widow had alienated a part of the estate for a certain sum of money, and it appeared, on examination, that a part of the consideration-money was appropriated to the payment of some *necessary* expenses which the Hindu law allows, and the rest of the consideration-money was appropriated by the widow to her own use,—the alienation, so far as it was to pay *necessary* expenses of the widow, is binding on the reversioner; but as regards the money which is appropriated by the widow herself, it is not binding on him. In such a case the reversioner, before he is entitled to have the sale set aside, must refund that portion of the consideration-money, which went to pay the widow's necessaries, to the purchaser.[1] The reversioner must also pay reasonable interest to the purchaser upon the said sum, and the purchaser must account to the reversioner the rents and profits of the property during the time that it was in his possession, both the interest and the account of rents and profits to run from the date of the widow's death.[2]

When the widow has sold, and the whole of the consideration-money was appropriated to the payment of necessary expenses, the sale will be *valid* as against the reversioner. But when the alienation was not necessary, and the consideration was appropriated by the widow to her own use, the sale is *invalid*, and the reversioner will be entitled to have the sale set aside without being required to refund the purchase-money. If, however, the sale was partly *necessary* and partly *unnecessary*, it will be set aside only when the reversioner agrees to refund that portion of the purchase-money which was appropriated to the necessary expenses of the widow. Such

---

[1] Phool Chand Lall *v.* Rughoobun Sahye, 9 W. R., 108.

[2] Moteeram Kumar *v.* Gopal Sahoo, 20 W. R., 187.

LECTURE XI. a principle is perfectly equitable; the reversioner's rights are protected, and the purchaser is not unnecessarily endamaged.

Reversioner bound to redeem. When the widow had mortgaged the estate, or a portion of it, for necessary expenses, the reversioner, on the widow's death, will be entitled to redeem the estate from the mortgagee. The charge created by the widow is a valid one, and the reversioner, if he wants to obtain the estate free from the incumbrance, must pay up the amount due upon the encumbrance. He is not entitled to redeem the property as the representative of the mortgagor, because he is not heir to the widow; but, as the heir of the last male owner, he succeeds to the property.

If the widow sold for legal necessity when the money could have been raised by a mortgage, it was held,[1] that the reversioner cannot set aside the sale without placing the purchaser in the same position as that in which he would have been if the widow had mortgaged instead of selling. In the same case, Peacock, C. J., expressed a doubt whether such a sale could at all be set aside. He thought that, if the widow elected to sell when it would be more beneficial to mortgage, the sale could not be set aside as against the purchaser, if the widow and the purchaser are both acting honestly; and the reason assigned for this conclusion is, that the interest of the money raised by mortgage must be paid out of

[1] Phool Chand Lall *v.* Rughoobun Sahye, 9 W. R., 108.

the estate, and thus the income of the widow would, necessarily, be reduced for the benefit of the reversionary heirs.

If there is a mortgage on the property by the last owner at the time when the widow alienates the property, the reversioner can recover the property from the hands of the purchaser only by paying the amount of the money due on the mortgage.[1]

Removal of the widow from possession of the estate.

I have already told you that when the reversioner brings a suit during the widow's lifetime, he is only entitled, if at all, to a declaration that the sale is void, and that, as a rule, the widow is not deprived of the possession of the property. I shall now explain to you the circumstances under which the reversioner will be justified in suing to remove the widow from possession and the Court will be justified in granting such a relief. I may observe generally that this remedy is an extraordinary one and will be granted only under extraordinary circumstances. It has the effect of trenching upon the rights of the widow, who is entitled by law to the possession of the property of her husband during her lifetime ; and such a trespass upon the widow's rights will not be permitted unless there is an equally serious trespass upon the reversioner's rights which it is necessary to prevent. I may observe here, that no text of Hindu law can be quoted as an authority to warrant the removal of the

An extraordinary remedy.

[1] Moulvie Mohamed Shumshool Hooda v. Shewakram, *alias* Roy Doorga Persad, 22 W. R., 409.

LECTURE XI. widow from the possession of the estate which she has inherited from her husband; but the Courts of Justice have applied this remedy to supply, what they considered, an omission in that law. When the acts of the widow become seriously injurious to the rights of the reversioners, the Courts applied this remedy. The power of the widow to commit further harm was restrained, while she was left in the enjoyment of all the substantial benefits derived from her husband's estate.

The greatest difficulty, however, arises in the application of this remedy to particular cases. What must be the nature and effect of the widow's acts which will entitle the Courts to remove her from possession, s a question of considerable difficulty, and, as will appear from the cases that will be hereafter quoted, there is not an uniformity in the decisions of the Courts in this respect. I may observe here that the authorities incline to this view of the law, that a mere alienation by the widow, which can be avoided after the widow's death, will not justify the Court in interfering with the widow's possession.

One of the earliest cases bearing upon this point is the case of *Mangal Moni* v. *Ramballab Doss*.[1] The widow in this case had sold first ten annas and then six annas of the estate to the defendant's husband, for the purpose of paying debts incurred by the widow to recover the estate of her husband; and from the

[1] S. D. A. Decisions, 12th Sept. 1848.

surplus she had purchased other property. The Principal Sudder Ameen, on the authority of the *vyavastha* of the Pundit, held, that the sales were illegal, and must be annulled. It was further observed by the Court, that as the widow had shown her readiness to injure the eventual heirs of the estate by selling it, there was no safety in putting her into possession. It was, accordingly, ordered that plaintiff, as next heir, be put into possession on condition of duly paying over to the widow, during her lifetime, all the net profits from the estate. This judgment was confirmed by the Sudder Court.

You will observe from the above decision that the wrong against the reversioner, of which the widow was guilty, is that of selling the estate without necessity; and the reversioner was allowed to recover possession as trustee for the widow. I may say that, on the present state of the authorities, such a suit will be dismissed. The sale will be held good during the widow's lifetime; and the reversioner will at best be entitled to a declaration that the sale will be void after the widow's death.[1] You will also observe that the widow in this case was not removed from possession. The possession of the estate was recovered from the purchaser, and was not made over to the widow; but the reversioner was directed to hold possession for the benefit of the widow.

---

[1] Juggut Roy v. Sahib Perlhad Sein, S. D. Decisions for 1854, p. 274.

LECTURE XI.

Bolaki Bibi v. Nundolal Babu.

The case of *Bolaki Bibi* v. *Nundolal Babu*[1] was long considered as the leading case on this point. The plaintiffs, alleging themselves to be next heirs, sued to set aside certain sales and settlements made by Bolaki Bibi, widow of the late Lala Doyal Chand Babu, as prejudicial to their rights, as also to declare a will, made by the said Bibi, null and void, and to have the estates, moveable and immoveable, placed in their possession, a suitable allowance for maintenance being awarded to the Bibi.

The Sudder Dewany Adawlut held, that an action of this kind will lie, and the Courts of Equity are bound to supply the remedy when there is an omission in the law to provide for the same. Referring to the position of a widow as trustee, removeable on account of a breach of trust, the Court observed as follows:—"The uses, however, on account of which the trust was given should be preserved, if possible; and the reasons for which the widow was selected to administer the trust should be respected. The natural course then for equity and justice to proceed upon is to remove the widow from the management of the property, and to allow her such a maintenance from the proceeds of the property as shall enable her to perform all the uses enjoined her as widow, and as much as shall uphold her respectability and rank in life, secure her from want of every kind, and leave her no pretence to disgrace her husband's family or

[1] S. D. A. Decisions, 24th July 1851, p. 351.

to pursue immoral courses. Such a procedure secures to the widow all that the law declares her right and gives her, and merely prevents her from repeating her disregard of the injunctions of that law. It, at the same time, secures to the reversionary heirs their right uninjured and unimpaired, without subjecting them to expensive and vexatious litigation to invalidate sales, and obtain possession with perhaps years of mesne profits which of itself is a sufficient answer to all arguments against hearing a suit in the lifetime of the widow."

The widow had set up an *anumati pattra* from her husband as justifying the acts complained of by the plaintiffs. The Court held, that the *anumati pattra* was not genuine. Then with reference to the hostile acts of the widow, the Court observed as follows:—"Viewing the grant of the *mokurari* tenures as acts not within the scope of a Hindu widow's authority, and regarding the late transfer of the whole of the estate by Musst. Bolaki's will to others as an act so prejudicial to the heirs, and indeed so utterly subversive of their rights, as to go far beyond any acts which could be brought under the definition of mere waste, for which the *shashtra* distinctly declares that Hindu widows to be held responsible and restrained, we think it our duty to deprive Musst. Bolaki of the future management of the property. In doing this, however, we are careful that she shall lose none of those substantial advantages to which, during her lifetime, she is entitled."

LECTURE XI.

The Court then ordered that possession of all the properties be made over to the plaintiffs, the reversioners, with the exception of the family mansion, which will remain in possession of the widow during her lifetime. The plaintiffs were further directed to pay, into the Zillah Court, the whole of the net profits of the estate for the benefit of Mussamut Bolaki during her lifetime.

You will observe that the acts complained of against the widow were:

1*st*,—the sale of a garden;

2*nd*,—the grant of *mokurari* leases of lands at inadequate *jamas;*

3*rd*,—the alienation of the whole estate by will.

The widow claimed to justify these acts on her part, on the ground of an *anumati pattra* alleged to have been executed in her favor by her husband. The Court pronounced the deed to be spurious; and the widow, therefore, was found guilty of a positive act of fraud, by which she claimed authority to alienate the property to the detriment of the reversioners. The acts complained of were also found to be beyond the scope of the widow's powers as widow.[1]

In another case,[2] the plaintiff claimed to set aside certain alienations made by the widow, on the ground that they were made for purposes not recognised

[1] See Kalee Kant Lahoory *v.* Goluck Chunder Chowdry, S. D. Decisions for 1849, p. 405.

[2] Goluk Moni Dasi *v.* Kristo Prosaud Kanoongo, S. D. A. Decisions for 1859, p. 210.

by Hindu law, and to obtain possession of the whole estate, including the portions which have been alienated, by removing the widow from possession of the same. The plaintiffs were reversioners, and the widow was living. LECTURE XI.

The Court referred to the previous case of *Bolaki Bibi* as the leading case on the subject, and held that, "on sufficient proof by the reversioners being given, that, but for the interference of the Courts, ultimate loss of the estate as to the heirs who may succeed eventually will ensue from the conduct of the tenant-in-tail in possession of the property, and with a view of remedying, or rather of preventing, such loss, this Court should step in and appoint a receiver to take charge of the estate. The proof, though inferential, must be clear and cogent; and unless the evidence lead inevitably to the conclusion that the heirs will be damnified if she be left in possession, the widow should not be divested of the possession of her husband's estate.

"The conduct of the widow may not amount to what is technically called waste; but extending the meaning of that term to any illegal act of alienation, either directly or indirectly injuriously affecting the interest of the reversioners,—alienations contrary to the nature of her estate, and therefore in the nature of waste—we think that the same course should be pursued as should also be followed in a case of technical waste."

LECTURE XI.

The Sudder Court then confirmed the decree of the lower Court, removing the widow from possession, and appointing the reversioner as receiver, on the ground that "as the Judge finds, whether rightly or wrongly, that the alienations made are so subversive of the reversioner's rights as to justify the removal of the widow from possession, in order, it would seem, to prevent future acts of the same nature."

In this case the only acts complained of against the widow were certain unauthorised alienations,—*i. e.*, alienations for purposes not recognised by Hindu law; and the Court held, that these acts on the part of the widow would justify the Court in removing her from possession; of course, the nature and character of these alienations was not before the Court, as the case was being tried in special appeal. You will, however, find from later cases which I shall presently quote, that a mere alienation by the widow for purposes not authorised by Hindu law has been held to be no warrant for the Court's action in removing the widow from possession of the estate.

In a later case,[1] Jackson, J., expressed an opinion that the precedent of Bolaki Bibi has been generally looked upon as extremely harsh, and he thought that it had been modified by the observations of the Sudder Court in the case of *Golokmoni Dasi.*

The learned Judge was of opinion that, "to justify a suit for divesting the widow of possession, there

[1] Lol Sundar Das *v.* Hurikrishun Das, Marshall, 113.

must be clear evidence of acts on her part tending to injure the property, so that interference of the Courts is necessary to prevent ultimate injury to the eventual heirs. The criterion, therefore, in this case, would be the plaintiff's success or failure in showing that ultimate loss to them would result from the widow's act." The act complained of in this case was the grant of a *patni* by the widow; and the Court held, that such an act would not warrant the removal of the widow from possession of the estate.

The present state of the authorities on this subject will not, I think, justify a Court in removing the widow from possession of the estate when she is only guilty of an alienation in excess of her powers as a Hindu widow—an alienation which is only binding during the widow's lifetime, but which is not binding on the reversioners.[1]

What will justify widow's removal.

To justify the Court in adopting this extraordinary remedy, there must be, on the part of the widow, something more than a mere alienation—some distinct act of waste—or some positive act of fraud, to injure the interest of the reversioners, must be made out. For instance, if the widow attempted to sell the property, alleging a debt of her husband which she could not otherwise pay, and it appeared that this representation of the widow was false, that there was no debt of her deceased husband to pay,

[1] Pranputty Kooer v. Futteh Bahadur, 2 Hay's Rep., 608; Brindu Chowdrain v. Peary Lal Chowdry, 9 W. R., 460.

LECTURE XI. — and that this was a mere pretence for alienating the property from the reversioners,—in such a case the widow will be removed from possession. It was clearly a fraudulent and collusive attempt on the part of the widow to create evidence which, if true, would be binding on the reversioners.[1]

In one of the recent cases,[2] decided by the Bengal High Court, this point was fully considered with reference to the existing authorities. In that case the defendant had set up a kobala alleged to have been executed by the widow's husband. The plaintiff, who is the reversioner, charged this document to be a forgery ; and he further alleged that the widow, in fraud of her husband's estate and of the reversioner's, has colluded with certain persons, to set up a forged kobala and a false case, to the effect that this property was sold by the husband himself, and never formed part of the estate to which the widow, as his heiress, become entitled on his death.

Positive fraud on her part.

The Court held, on these allegations, that "if the reversioner can make out a distinct case of waste by the widow, and of positive fraud by her on her husband's estate and the reversioner's, the latter may bring a suit to have the estate protected and to have the widow removed from the management."

The case was remanded to the lower Court to decide whether the kobala is a forgery. "If it is

---

[1] Moonshee Casimuddeen v. Ram Dass Gossain, 2 W. R., 170.
[2] Shama Sundury Chowdrain v. Jumoona Chowdrain, 24 W. R., 86.

not, there is an end of the plaintiff's suit. But if it is a forgery, and the Court finds that the widow has been a party to the setting it up, and has fraudulently abandoned her claim to the property covered by the kobala, alleging that her husband sold it in his life-time, and therefore that it never came to her hands as part of his estate, then the kobala is worthless, and passed no title whatever (not even a title good for the life of the widow), and the widow has been guilty of waste such as entitles the reversioners to ask to have her removed from the charge of her husband's estate. Of course, if the widow, claiming this property as an asset of the estate, had professed to sell it, in order to meet the necessities of the estate, the sale would, probably, have been upheld so far as the widow's life-interest was concerned, even though declared bad from her death."[1]

The above case also decided two other points, *viz.*, that if the first reversioner does not sue, the second reversioner has a right to maintain the suit, on showing that the first reversioner is implicated in the alleged fraud or waste.[2] This seems reasonable, because, if the first reversioner is party to the fraud committed by the widow, and the second reversioner is held not entitled to sue, the rights of the latter will be sacrificed without his being allowed a remedy.

---

[1] See also Radha Mohun Dhur *v.* Ramdass Dey, 3 B. L. R., 362; Gunesh Dutt *v.* Musst. Lall Muttee Kooer, 17 W. R., 11.

[2] See Kooer Golab Sing *v.* Rao Kureem Sing, 14 Moore's I. A., 193.

LECTURE XI.

The other point decided in the case is, that a reversioner cannot get a declaration that he, as next reversioner, is entitled to succeed to the property on the death of the widow, because the plaintiff may die during the widow's lifetime, and his succession may, therefore, never happen.

Haridoss Dutt v. Rangan Moni Dosee.

The principle upon which the Court will be justified in interfering with the possession of the life-tenant by injunction or receiver was pointed out by Peel, C.J., in the case of *Haridoss Dutt* v. *Rangan Moni Dosee and others.*[1] That was a case in which the reversionary heir to the estate filed a bill, alleging collusion between the defendants, and charged that their acts were in fraud of the reversioner's interests. The defendants were daughters of the last owner, and were in possession as life-tenants, and the plaintiff prayed that the defendants might be restrained from carrying out their plans or committing further alienation or waste.

The defendants objected, on the ground that the suit will not lie. The Court, overruling the demurrer, held, that such a suit will lie. Then the Court proceeded to consider whether the bill states a sufficient case of waste or misdealing analogous to waste, so as to entitle the plaintiff to the remedy sought for. On this point the Chief Justice observed as follows:—"A bill filed by the presumptive heir in succession against the immediate owner, who has

[1] Vyavastha Darpana, Eng. Edn., p. 124.

succeeded by inheritance, must show a case approaching to spoliation, must enable the Court to see that there is probable ground for apprehending that, unless an injunction be granted to restrain some threatened or impending act, ultimate loss to the heirs, who may come into possession by succession, will ensue. It is not enough to make out that some gift has been made, or some disposition taken place, or that such is about to be made or to take place which the law would not support. The estate of the female owner, her own personal estate, might be large, and adequate to repay ten times over the alleged spoliation, and there might not be the remotest prospect of loss : and the thing alienated might have no specific peculiar value."

In another case[1] the Privy Council observed that the principles which are applied in Courts of Equity in England for securing, in the public funds, any property to which one person is entitled in possession, and another is entitled in remainder, are not applicable to the case of property in India, where such property is in possession of a Hindu widow. Referring to the case of *Kasi Nath Bysack* v. *Hurosundery Dosee*, their Lordships further observed that one of the principles laid down in that case is, that "it is not sufficient to say that there is one person entitled in possession, and another entitled in remainder, in order to induce the Court to interfere to take the

[1] Haridoss Dutt v. Upoornah Dosee, 6 Moore's I. A., 445.

LECTURE XI.

property out of the hands of the individual who is in possession of it; but it is necessary to show that there is danger to the property from the mode in which the party in possession is dealing with it, in which case, and in such case only, the Court will interfere."

In this case the facts found were, that the daughter, who was the tenant for life, having a sum of money invested in Company's paper, received about Rs. 50,000 from the Company when the loan in which the money was invested was paid off by the Company: that of this sum nearly Rs. 39,000 were invested in another loan, and the remainder of the money was still in her hands uninvested, waiting for an eligible investment. Their Lordships held, that the female heir, by merely keeping in her hands a certain portion of the money, was not guilty of a devastavit; that being the ground upon which the bill was filed, and as that ground failed, the appeal was dismissed.

I have already pointed out to you that when the widow alienates property for other than allowable causes, that will be no ground for removing her from possession of the estate, because she is not guilty of any positive act of fraud which jeopardizes the interest of the reversioners. The latter can, on the widow's death, recover back the property thus unauthorisedly alienated, the alienation being good only during the widow's lifetime. But the reversioners cannot, during the widow's lifetime, bring

Reversioner cannot sue to recover property alienated.

a suit to recover the property so alienated, for themselves, or for the benefit of the widow. Lecture XI.

This point was expressly decided by the Bengal High Court in the case of *Gobind Moni Dosee* v. *Sham Lal Bysack*.[1] That was a Full Bench decision, and the question referred for the decision of the Full Bench was as follows : — " Whether a conveyance, by a Hindu widow, of immoveable property, which she takes by descent from her husband, is valid during the widow's life, if the conveyance is made for causes other than those allowed by the Hindu law ; and if not, whether the reversionary heirs of the husband can interfere by suit to cause the property to be delivered up to themselves or to the widow." *Gobind Moni Dosee v. Sham Lal Bysack*

The Full Bench answered the first question in the affirmative, and the second question in the negative. The decision of the Court is as follows :—" We are of opinion that a conveyance by a Hindu widow, for other than allowable causes, of property which has descended to her from her husband, is not an act of waste which destroys the widow's estate, and vests the property in the reversionary heirs, and that the conveyance is binding during the widow's life. The reversionary heirs are not, after her death, bound by the conveyance ; but they are not entitled, during her lifetime, to recover the property either for their own or for the use of the widow, or to compel the restoration of it to her."

---

[1] W. R., Sp. No., 165.

LECTURE XI.

Widow receives usufruct when removed from possession.

The removal of the widow from possession of the estate does not deprive her of the substantial rights of property. Beyond being deprived of possession, she is not deprived of any of the other advantages of property. She continues proprietor as before; and the Court appoints some person as manager or receiver to take charge of the property and to account for the rents and profits of the same to the Court, which it holds for the benefit of the widow, and makes over to her periodically. In these cases, however, the person who is usually appointed to take charge of the estate is the reversioner who, of all persons, is most interested in preserving the estate intact, and therefore the fittest person to take charge of it. In the case of *Bolaki Bibi* the Court made over possession of the estate to the reversioner, with the direction that he will pay over the whole of the net profits into Court, for the benefit of the widow during her lifetime. The reversioner, however, by such an appointment is never converted into an actual proprietor or a co-proprietor with the widow.[1] He remains manager just as any other manager is, and is bound to render periodical accounts, to the Court which appointed him, of his management of the property.

Reversioner's interest not saleable.

It has sometimes been a question as to whether the interest of a reversioner under the Hindu law

---

[1] Mussamut Moharanee v. Nudu Lal Misser, 10 W. R., 73.

was such an interest as could be sold in execution of a decree against him. Under the old Civil Procedure Code (Act VIII of 1859) it was held[1] that such an interest was not saleable in execution of a decree under that Act. It was a mere expectation, and in no sense a vested interest or property, and therefore was not liable to attachment or sale. LECTURE XI.

The present Code of Civil Procedure (Act X of 1877) has expressly provided that such rights are not saleable in execution. Sec. 266, cl. (*k*), lays down that "an expectancy of succession by survivorship, or other merely contingent or possible right or interest" shall not be liable to attachment or sale.

If the reversionary heir, however, voluntarily sells his reversionary right, a Court of Equity will compel him to fulfil his contract on his succeeding to the estate.[2]

---

[1] Koraj Koonwar *v.* Komul Koonwar, 6 W. R., 34. Ramchundro Tantrodoss *v.* Dhurmo Narain Chuckerbutty, 15 W. R., 17, F. B Bhoobun Mohun Banerjee *v.* Thacoor Dass Biswas, 2 Indian Jurist, N. S., 277.

[2] *Per* Phear, J., in Ramchundro Tantrodoss *v.* Dhurmo Narain Chuckerbutty, 15 W. R., 17, F. B.

LECTURE XII.

THE MAINTENANCE OF THE WIDOW.

Family property—Individual ownership—Persons entitled to maintenance—Females entitled only to maintenance—Widow entitled to maintenance—When there are assets—Not otherwise—*Musst. Lalti Kuar* v. *Gunga Bishun*—*Kasheenath Doss* v. *Khetter Money Dosee*—Unchaste widow not entitled to maintenance—The question discussed—Right of maintenance cannot be defeated by implication—Nor by express words—Nor by change of residence—Unless it be for immoral purposes—Maintenance not a charge in the hands of an alienee—Unless there is notice—Kind of notice necessary—A decree for maintenance is sufficient notice—Liability of the purchaser of part of the family property—Opinion of the Bombay High Court—Amount of maintenance—Variable—Arrears of maintenance—Widows entitled to reside in the family dwelling-house—Maintenance-grants are life-grants—Widows entitled to a share on partition—Not the childless widow—Mother's share contributed by her sons—Widow deprived of inheritance entitled to maintenance.

Family property.

ANCIENT Hindu law affords complete evidence of a state of society in which property belonged to the family, and not to any individual member of that family. The society was constituted by families, and not by individuals. Each family had a sort of corporate existence and perpetual succession. The family property was held in perpetuity by the family, and the members of the family were only entitled to maintenance out of the family property. At this time every member of the family lived on, and all his necessaries were paid out of, the proceeds of the family property, and died leaving the family property intact; no one was owner, and the management only of the family property vested in one person, the *kurta* of the family for the time being. LECTURE XII.

Individual ownership.

Gradually, however, this state of things was altered; individual ownership was evolved out of this communal holding; and then it became necessary to distinguish between the right of ownership and the mere right of maintenance. Some members of the family were entitled to ownership in the family property, and some only entitled to maintenance out of it.

Persons entitled to maintenance.

Persons who were entitled to maintenance only were generally females and certain other males who, on account of certain disabilities, were disqualified from inheriting or sharing in the family property. "Impotent persons and outcasts are excluded from a share of the heritage; and so are persons born blind and deaf, as well as mad men, idiots, the dumb, and those who have lost a sense or a limb."[1] So Yajnawalkya says,—"An outcast and his issue, an impotent person, one lame, a mad man, an idiot, a blind man, a person afflicted with an incurable disease, as well as others similarly disqualified, must be maintained, excluding them, however, from participation."[2]

---

[1] Menu, Chap. IX, v. 201.

[2] Quoted in the Dayabhaga, Chap. V, para. 10.

LECTURE XII.

In the previous passage Yajnawalkya distinctly says that all those persons who are excluded from the inheritance are entitled to maintenance, including the outcast and his issue. The author of the Dayabhaga, following the authority of Devala, holds, that the persons excluded from participation in the inheritance are entitled to be maintained "excepting, however, the outcast and his son." "When the father is dead, as well as in his lifetime, an impotent person, a leper, a mad man, an idiot, a blind man, an outcast, the offspring of an outcast, and a person wearing the token of religious mendicity are not competent to share the heritage. Food and raiment should be given to them, excepting the outcast. But the sons of such persons being free from similar defects shall obtain their father's share of the inheritance."[1] This is authority for the proposition that persons excluded from inheritance are, with the exception of the outcast and his issue, entitled to maintenance. The sons of such excluded persons, however, being free from such defects, cannot be driven to maintenance only, but are entitled to the share of their parents.

Females entitled only to maintenance.

There are distinct traces in the early Hindu law of a state of society when females were only entitled to be maintained, even after the right of ownership in *males* had been recognised. Whether the female was a widow or daughter or any other female relative, her

[1] Devala quoted in the Dayabhaga, Chap. V, para. 11.

is not did not extend to anything more than a mere maintenance. As I have pointed out elsewhere, the Hindu law silently changed and passed on to the stage when the right of a female to hold family property was recognised. This, however, was only a modification of her right of maintenance. Instead of being merely maintained, she was allowed to hold or possess property from the proceeds of which she was to secure her maintenance. Her *ownership* or *dominion* over the property, which she is to possess, is nowhere recognised. Even in Bengal, where the most advanced doctrines on the subject of female rights were recognised, the widow (the type of a female holder of property) was never considered as the *owner* or *proprietor*. She was "merely to enjoy her husband's estate after his demise. She is not entitled to make a gift, mortgage, or sale of it."[1] And the *owner* of the property was still her deceased husband.[2] The Hindu law, therefore, that is preserved to us, only recognises the right of certain females to *hold* or *possess* family property without being its *owner*. They are entitled to enjoy the profits of the same (though even that is doubtful), but are not to touch the *corpus*, except when their maintenance cannot be secured from the profits. The development of Hindu law on this point was arrested at this stage. The right of a Hindu female to inheritance was only

LECTURE XII.

---

[1] Dayabhaga, Chap. XI, sec. i, para. 56. [2] *Ibid*, para. 61.

LECTURE XII.

the modified form of her ancient right of [illegible]nance.

Widow entitled to maintenance.

The widow, when she is not an heiress, is entitled to maintenance according to all the authorities; and it is to be provided her by those persons who have inherited the property which belonged to her late husband. The obligation to maintain the widow is, therefore, not a personal one; it is a sort of a charge upon the property of her husband in the hands of the heir.[1] This, however, does not preclude the widow from obtaining a personal decree on account of her maintenance against the person who is bound to provide her with it.[2]

There are certain relations whom a man is bound to maintain, irrespective of the question of inherited property. These are the parents in their old age, a virtuous wife, and an infant son. These, according to Menu, must be maintained, although a man for that purpose is obliged to do a "hundred times that which ought not to be done."[3] A man must maintain these relations even by the commission of crime. In the same way the Mitacshara lays down that "where there may be no property, but what has been self-acquired, the only persons whose maintenance out of that property is imperative, are aged parents, wife, and minor children."[4] The obligation to maintain the widow

[1] Bhoirub Chunder Ghose *v.* Nobo Chunder Gooho, 5 W. R., 111, C. R.

[2] Baijun Dobey *v.* Brij Bhookun Lall, 24 W. R., 306.

[3] 3 Dig., 406.

[4] Mitacshara on Subtraction of Gift; Strange's Manual, § 209.

When there are assets.

is not one of this description. The obligation is dependent upon the fact of the person having inherited the property of her late husband. If he has so inherited property, he is liable, otherwise not. It is similar to the case of the heir being liable to pay the ancestor's debts only when he has inherited assets sufficient for that purpose, otherwise not. "In order to maintain the widow, the elder brother or any of the others above mentioned must have taken the property of the deceased, the duty of maintaining the widow being dependent on taking the property."[1]

In the Benares school the question of the widow's maintenance is one of frequent occurrence. There the widow inherits her husband's property under exceptional circumstances. When her husband was living, after partition, separate from his co-heirs, it is then that the widow succeeds, otherwise, in the case of undivided property, whether partible or impartible, a collateral kinsman removed in the twelfth degree or more from her husband will exclude the widow from the inheritance.[2] In the Bengal school the widow is only excluded by the son, grandson, or the great grandson, and by no other relations; consequently the widow here is more frequently an heiress than in the Benares school, and, therefore, cases of maintenance here are less frequent. In the Mitacshara

---

[1] Smriti Chandrica, Chap. XI, sec. 1, § 34.

[2] Raja Yenumula Gaouridevama Garu *v.* Raja Yenumula Rumandora Garu, 6 Mad. Rep., 93.

LECTURE XII. country, therefore, the widow is entitled to maintenance only when the family was undivided. The same rule is followed in the Mithila country.[1]

All the schools, however, agree in the proposition I have stated before, *viz.*, that the obligation to maintain the widow is not absolute, but is conditioned upon the fact of the person having obtained the property of her late husband. Accordingly it has been held in Bengal that a decree for maintenance is not generally a personal decree against the defendant, but is a decree against him, so far as he is in possession of the assets belonging to the widow's husband, and for that reason liable to satisfy the decree for maintenance.[2] Therefore, a suit brought by the widow against her husband's brother or other relations, for maintenance, must be dismissed, if it is shown that the defendant inherited no property from the husband of the widow.[3]

Not otherwise.

The same rule has been followed in Madras and Bombay in suits for maintenance brought by widows against the relations of her husband.[4]

Must. Lalti Kuar v. Gunga Bishun.

The question was raised in the High Court of the North-West Provinces as to how far the widow of a

[1] Musst. Luchee Koonwar *v.* Sheo Persaud Sing and others, 7 Sel. Rep., 26; Musst. Joraon Koonwar *v.* Chowdry Doost Domun Singh, 7 Sel. Rep., 30.

[2] Tarunginee Dosee *v.* Chowdry Dwarka Nath Musant, 20 W. R., 196; Kumulmoni Dosee *v.* Bodhunarain Mazumdar, 2 Macnaghten, 119.

[3] Khetramoni Dosee *v.* Kasi Nath Doss, 10 W. R., 89, F B.; see Sabitra Bai *v.* Luksmi Bai, I. L. R., 2 Bomb., 573.

[4] Mad. Dec. for 1859, pp. 5, 265, 272; Roma Bai *v.* Trimbuck Gonesh, 9 Bom. H. C., 283.

deceased member of a joint family could claim maintenance from her father-in-law and her brothers-in-law? It was contended on the part of the defendants that the widow could claim her maintenance from her husband's property only; and as he left none in this case, and his interest in the family property passed by survivorship to his co-parceners, the widow's claim to maintenance cannot be supported. The Court, however, overruled the objection, and decreed the claim. It held, that her husband's interest in the family property having passed to his co-parceners, they are bound to maintain her out of the property so taken by them. The Court further held, that she could not be in a worse position than the wife of a person who is himself excluded from inheritance, but whose wife is, nevertheless, entitled to maintenance; and that where she had a right to be maintained, during his lifetime, out of property in which he is interested, but from which he is excluded, the obligation to maintain her out of that property continued after his death.[1] LECTURE XII.

If the heir had taken the property of the widow's husband, he is primarily responsible, both in person and property, for the widow's maintenance. He cannot resist the widow's claim by saying, that the property out of which the widow is entitled to be maintained is no longer in his hands, but that it has been transferred and passed into some other hands. On

[1] Must. Lalti Kuar v. Gunga Bishun, 7 N. W. P. H. C., 261.

LECTURE XII. — this point it was observed by the High Court of the North-West Provinces that "the heir who takes and becomes possessed of the estate of the deceased, must be held to continue to be primarily responsible, both in person and property, for the maintenance of the widow, even though he should have fraudulently transferred that estate, or otherwise have improperly wasted it; and the widow is bound to look to the heir for her maintenance, and to claim it from him primarily, rather than from the estate transferred or wasted, which may, nevertheless, be in the last resort answerable to her claim."[1]

Kasheenath Doss v. Khetter Money Dosee.

How far the son's widow is entitled to claim a pecuniary allowance on account of her maintenance from her father-in-law was the subject of much consideration by the Bengal High Court in the case of *Kashee Nath Doss* v. *Khetter Money Dosee.*[2] In that case the plaintiff was the widow of the defendant's son, and refusing to live in the house of her father-in-law claimed a pecuniary allowance by way of maintenance. It was admitted in the case that the defendant had no ancestral property or any property upon which the plaintiff's maintenance was a charge, and that the defendant had only his separate estate which has been acquired by himself.

Two questions were raised for decision in this case: *First*, whether the widow of a Hindu refusing to live

---

[1] Ramchuwar Toraun v. Musst. Jasoda Kuar, 2 N. W. P. Rep., 134.
[2] 9 W. R., 413.

in the house of her father-in-law, can sue him for a pecuniary allowance by way of maintenance, if she leave his house without reasonable cause? *Second*, is she entitled to maintenance if she leave on account of ill-usage or other reasonable cause?

Peacock, C.J., held, that, in either case, she was not entitled to claim a pecuniary allowance by way of maintenance from her father-in-law. The learned Chief Justice put it on the ground of the distinction between the daughter-in-law's right of maintenance and the right of a wife or of a widow to maintenance from her husband or from the heirs of her husband. "A son's widow," observed the Chief Justice, "has not the same legal rights against her father-in-law as a wife has against her husband, or as a widow has against the heirs of her husband, who take his estate by inheritance. The father is not heir to his sons in preference to the son's widow. A son's widow has no right in her father-in-law's estate, and, upon partition of such estate, she is not, like a daughter, entitled to a share, even though the estate was ancestral.

"The obligation of an heir to provide, out of the estate which descends to him, maintenance for certain persons whom the ancestor was legally or morally bound to maintain, is a legal, as well as a moral, obligation, for the estate is inherited subject to the obligation of providing such maintenance. A son, who takes his father's estate by inheritance, is bound to provide maintenance for his father's widow. The

LECTURE XII. obligation is a charge upon the estate, which continues as long as the widow remains chaste, whether she continues to live in the family of the heirs or not."[1]

The authority that was chiefly relied upon in the decision of this case is the case of *Rujomonee Dosee* v. *Shib Chunder Mullick*,[2] in which it was decided that the maintenance of a son's widow is a mere moral duty on the part of her father-in-law, and that the case is distinguishable from those in which an heir takes property subject to the obligation of maintaining persons who are excluded from inheritance.

The texts of Hindu law which enjoined the head of the family to maintain the dependent members, were considered by the Court as imposing a moral obligation only, which, in case of a breach, is not enforceable in a Court of law.

The judgment in the case was appealed against.[3] The Appellate Court confined itself to the decision of the only question which was raised in the case, *viz.*,— "whether the plaintiff, not finding it agreeable to live in her father-in-law's house, can legally claim from him a money-allowance by way of maintenance to live elsewhere;" and the Court held, that she could not. The Appellate Court refused to give any opinion upon the question as to whether she could still claim a pecuniary allowance if she was compelled to leave her

[1] See Ganga Bai *v.* Sitaram, I. L. R., 1 All., 170.

[2] Hyde's Rep., 1864, p. 103.

[3] Khetramoni Dosi *v.* Kasheenath Doss, 10 W. R., 89, F. B.

father-in-law's house on account of ill-usage or other improper conduct on his part, as it thought that point was not raised in the pleadings in the case. LECTURE XII.

Another point, which was not decided by this case, is, whether the son's widow is not entitled to receive food and raiment from her father-in-law, living as a member of his family. The whole judgment, however, seems to have assumed that she is so entitled. If she is, can she, in case of a refusal, enforce her right by recourse to law ? and if she, not voluntarily, but on account of ill-usage or other improper conduct on the part of her father-in-law or other members of his family, is compelled to reside elsewhere, can she claim a money-allowance in lieu of food and raiment from her father-in-law ? These questions are not decided by the judgment in this case.

Unchaste widow not entitled to maintenance.

The widow, however, who is guilty of unchastity, is not entitled to claim maintenance from the heirs of her husband.[1] If she is guilty of unchastity during her husband's lifetime, she cannot claim maintenance after his death. As by unchastity the widow is deprived of her inheritance, much more so for the same cause will she be deprived of her right of maintenance. If the widow is guilty of improper conduct, such as having eloped from the residence of her husband, she forfeits her right to future maintenance from the heirs of her husband.[2]

[1] 2 Macnaghten, 112.

[2] Ranee Basunt Kumaree v. Ranee Kumul Kumaree, 7 Sel. Rep., 168.

LECTURE XII.

If the widow who has been receiving maintenance from the heirs of her husband becomes unchaste, it has been held that she will be deprived of her maintenance, for, as observed by Jackson, J., " a man cannot be bound to feed misconduct in his own family, or to recognise a bond of union which the widow herself has trampled under foot."[1]

The question discussed.

How far the above will be correct law after the decision of the High Court in the case of *Kerry Kolitanee* v. *Moneeram Kolita*,[2] it is difficult to say. If there is no authority for depriving the widow of her right of inheritance on account of subsequent unchastity, it is difficult to see why she should be deprived of her maintenance for the same cause. If the heirs cannot resume the inheritance from the widow for unchastity, why should they be entitled to resume her maintenance for the same cause. The widow's right of maintenance does not depend upon the discretion of the heirs ; it is a legal right enforceable in a Court. It cannot be said that the widow's right of maintenance is conditioned upon her remaining chaste, as the widow's right to hold the estate of her husband was held *not* to be conditioned upon her remaining chaste. The same authorities bear upon both these questions of Hindu law, and it does not appear that the text-writers ever intended to draw any distinction between the two cases. I shall give you an illustra-

---

[1] Kerry Kolitanee v. Moneeram Kolita, 19 W. R. The passage occurs at p. 405.

[2] 19 W. R., 367.

tion which will make the analogy more complete. Let us suppose, instead of a pecuniary allowance, the widow had certain immoveable property assigned to her for her maintenance, and she had been holding this property as and in lieu of her maintenance. The widow subsequently became unchaste. Would this fact entitle the heirs to re-enter and dispossess the widow? If she has been holding this property as heir to her husband, the heirs cannot re-enter. Why should they be entitled to re-enter if she has been holding this property in lieu of her maintenance? I must also observe here, that the widow's right of inheritance is based upon the necessity to maintain her; and the property is given to her as the safest mode of securing her a sufficient maintenance. In ancient law, the widow's right of inheritance is the next advanced step from the widow's right of maintenance. Historically the right of maintenance precedes the right of inheritance. LECTURE XII.

The Bombay High Court has ruled,[1] that a widow getting maintenance under a decree will not be deprived of it by the fact of subsequent incontinence. In this case the widow had been put out of caste; the Court, nevertheless, held, that this will not operate as a forfeiture of her right of maintenance, as forfeiture of rights of property, owing to loss of caste, will be protected under Act XXI of 1850.[2]

---

[1] Honama *v.* Turnamabhat, I. L. R., 1 Bomb., 559.

[2] Parvati *v.* Bhiku, 4 Bom. H. C. Rep., 25, A. C. J.

LECTURE XII.

Right of maintenance cannot be defeated by implication.

The right of a Hindu widow to maintenance is based upon the fact of marriage, and is an inherent right. It requires peculiar protection in the hands of the Courts, from the very helpless position of the Hindu widow both by Hindu law and the social customs of the country. This right, therefore, cannot be defeated except upon the clearest grounds, or on account of serious misconduct on her part. A nuptial or testamentary gift by the husband, with the express object of barring her right of maintenance, might have that effect, or at all events might put her to her election. Where a Hindu leaves *all* his property to his sons by will, and a partition is effected amongst them according to the terms of the will, the Court will grant maintenance to the widow after partition, and will direct each of the sharers to contribute. In such a case the right of the widow does not extend to anything beyond maintenance, and she has no right to a share of the property, in lieu of maintenance, upon a partition.[1] In the construction of the will of a Hindu, the widow's right of maintenance will not be barred by implication, although the *whole* estate might have been left to others.[2]

Nor by express words.

As the law at present stands, I think the widow's right of maintenance cannot be defeated by anything short of gross misconduct on her part, or a testamentary or a nuptial gift on the part of the husband. I

[1] Kumulmoney Dossee *v.* Romanath Bysack, Fulton, 189.

[2] Ranee Hurosundery *v.* Kowar Kistonath Roy, Fulton, 393.

think the husband cannot defeat her right of maintenance by an *express* clause in the will depriving his widow of maintenance. The widow's right of maintenance arises by marriage, it is not a matter of contract;[1] it exists during the husband's lifetime, and continues after his death. It is a legal obligation attaching upon himself personally, and upon his property after his death. He cannot free himself of this obligation during his lifetime, nor can his heir after his death, so far as he inherits his property; and I take it that a devise of the property will not authorise the devisee to hold the property free from the widow's claim to maintenance, when neither the testator nor his heir could have resisted such a claim. It has been held, that, "in Bengal, a widow has no indefeasible vested right in the property left by her husband, though she has, by virture of her marriage, a right, if all the property be willed away, to maintenance."[2]

Nor by change of residence.

I have pointed out before that the obligation of the widow to reside with her husband's family is now treated as a mere moral obligation, and that the infringement of the same by the widow does not carry with it any penalty. "Residence with the relations of the deceased husband is, after all, a moral and not a legal duty, and no forfeiture ought to be imposed on a widow who, for no immoral purpose, shows a

---

[1] Sidlingapa *v.* Sidava, I. L. R., 2 Bomb., 624.

[2] Bhoobunmoyee *v.* Ramkissore, S. D. D. of 1860, p. 489. See also Sonatun Bysack *v.* S. M. Juggut Sundaree Dossee, 8 Moore's I. A., 66.

LECTURE XII.

preference for a residence elsewhere than with her husband's family, who are bound to give her support."[1] It will follow, therefore, that if the widow leaves voluntarily the abode of her husband's family, she cannot be deprived of her maintenance, with the single exception that the change of residence shall not be for unchaste purposes. How far this exception can be enforced, according to the present state of the authorities, I have elsewhere pointed out. No doubt, there is a difference in the matter of residence between a *wife* and a *widow*. The wife is bound to live with her husband; she cannot have a freedom in the choice of her residence. It is true the same considerations do not apply to the widow: but the ancient sages were anxious that the widow should make her abode in her husband's house; *ordinarily* and *naturally* she must reside there, *exceptionally* she may reside elsewhere. Now the law, established by decisions of Courts, is just the other way; what was before an exception, is now treated as the rule.[2]

Unless it be for immoral purposes.

I have pointed out before that the widow's right

[1] Aholya Bai Debia *v.* Lukhee Monee Debia, 6 W. R., 37.

[2] See the case of Rango Vinayek *v.* Yamuna Bai, I. L. R., 3 Bomb., 44, where a contrary rule is laid down. It was there said that "a widow is not entirely her own mistress, being subject to the control of her husband's family, who might require her to return to live in her husband's house." In the absence of special circumstances necessitating her withdrawal from the family, the widow will not be entitled to separate maintenance. See also 2 Strange's Hin. Law, 401; Kastur Bai *v.* Shivajiram, I. L. R., 3 Bomb., 372.

of maintenance is a charge upon the whole of the property in the hands of the heir; and that she has a right to have a declaration of the charge upon the said property. How far the right of maintenance will be a charge upon the property in the hands of an alienee is a somewhat difficult question. The texts of Vrihaspati,[1] Katyayana,[2] Menu,[3] and of other sages, which prohibit the giving away of family property, by which the maintenance of the members of the family may be imperilled, have been treated as merely moral injunctions, and consequently their violation does not render the act invalid. The texts of the ancient sages will not, therefore, help us in this respect.

Maintenance not a charge in the hands of an alienee.

This question, however, has been, to a certain extent, settled by the decisions of our Courts. Where a person purchases property without notice of the existence of the widow's right of maintenance as a charge upon the said property, it has been held, that the property in his hands will not be liable for such maintenance. In a case[4] bearing directly upon this point, Phear, J., observed :—"I do not think, however, that, in Bengal, she has any lien on the property in respect of her maintenance against all the world irrespective of such notice. No such lien, as far as I know, has ever been established in these Courts. In truth,

Unless there is notice.

[1] 2 Digest, 131. [2] 2 Digest, 133.

[3] Quoted in the Dayabhaga, Chap. II, paras. 23, 24.

[4] Srimati Bhogoboti Dosi *v.* Kanailal Mitter, 8 B. L. R., 225.

LECTURE XII.

if the heir has any power of alienation at all, it would be most unreasonable that a *bonâ fide* purchaser for valuable consideration should be subjected to the possibility of a charge springing up at any time, though it had no definite existence when he purchased."

There is some difficulty in determining the question as to the kind of notice that will be sufficient to charge the estate in the hands of the purchaser with the widow's maintenance. I think a notice of the fact of the existence of the widow, and that she is entitled to maintenance, or has been obtaining her maintenance from the estate, will not be sufficient;[1] because such a notice is so indefinite, that the property will never fetch its proper value if it is to be encumbered by a charge created by a notice so vague and uncertain. There must be something more definite than that. The amount of maintenance must be determined beforehand, either by decree or by contract, and made a charge upon the property conveyed, before the purchaser can be made liable for it. "Lien for maintenance is a somewhat vague expression as long as the amount of maintenance is undetermined. It does not attain the character of a proprietary right, until the proper amount of maintenance is either determined, or is in the course of being determined. When the property passes into

Kind of notice necessary.

[1] A somewhat different rule was laid down by Mitter, J., in Babu Goluck Chunder Bose *v.* Ranee Ahilya Dayee, 25 W. R., 100.

the hands of a *bonâ fide* purchaser without notice, it cannot be affected by anything short of an already existing proprietary right; it cannot be subject to that which is not already a specific charge, or which does not contain all the elements necessary to its ripening into a specific charge."[1]

The same view of the law was adopted in a later case[2] by Chief Justice Couch. He observed—"Whatever may be the rights of the younger members of a family, where the estate is one of this description, and is inherited by the eldest member, until the maintenance has become a specific charge upon the property, which it might be by a decree of a Court making provision for the payment of the maintenance, and declaring that a part of the property should be a security for it, or by a contract between the parties, charging the property with a certain sum for maintenance, we do not see how it can be a charge upon the estate in the hands of a *bonâ fide* purchaser for consideration."

A decree for maintenance is sufficient notice.

Where the widow has obtained a decree fixing a certain sum as her maintenance, to be obtained out of certain property, it was held that she has a right to have this amount declared as a charge upon the property into whosesoever hands it may come.[3]

---

[1] *Per* Phear, J., in Srimati Bhogoboti Dosi *v.* Kanailal Mitter, 8 B. L. R., 225.

[2] Juggernanth Samunt *v.* Maharanee Adhiranee Narain Koomari, 20 W. R., 126.

[3] Koomari Debia *v.* Roy Lutchmeeput Sing, 23 W. R., 33.

LECTURE XII. This, I think, will be independent of any notice given to the purchaser at the time of his purchase. The charge already exists, and the purchaser must be bound by it, whether he has notice of it or not. The question of notice, therefore, becomes immaterial. If there is an existing valid charge upon the property on account of the widow's maintenance, the purchaser will be liable, whether he has notice or not. But if the charge was not in existence before the purchase, no amount of notice will have the effect of creating a charge so as to bind the purchaser. This view of the law was maintained by Phear, J., in the case already quoted.

Supposing, at the time of the purchase, no charge had been in existence, but the widow was receiving her maintenance in the shape of food and raiment, and no definite sum of money was allotted on account of it, and she gave notice to the purchaser of the existence of her right of maintenance out of this property, the question is,—Can she afterwards bring a suit against the purchaser to have her maintenance ascertained and made a charge upon the property in his hands? This case is uncovered by authorities: but I take it that, in such a suit, the widow, probably, will not succeed on account of the indefinite nature of the notice. If, however, she did *not* give a notice, she has not the slightest chance of success in such a suit.

Liability of the pur- If the purchaser has purchased a part of the family property, and a portion still remains in the hands of the heir, can the widow, whose maintenance is a charge upon the family property, proceed against the purchaser for her maintenance without proceeding in the first instance against the heir? This is an open question: but the inclination of the authorities is in favor of the proposition that, if there is, in the hands of the heir, property sufficient for the widow's maintenance, the widow will be compelled to proceed first against the heir before proceeding against the purchaser. But the Court was of opinion that the general proposition of law, that in every case the widow must proceed first against the heir before her suit against the purchaser can be maintained, is unsupported by authority.[1]

LECTURE XII.

chaser of part of the family property.

Where property was confiscated by the Crown on account of rebellion, it was held that the widow of the former owner, whose sons, the then owners of the property, were guilty of rebellion, was entitled to maintenance from Government out of the property which had been confiscated.[2] In this case, I must tell you the widow's maintenance was not an already existing charge upon the property at the time of its confiscation.

Opinion of the Bombay High Court.

The Bombay High Court has gone further than the Bengal High Court on the question as to how far the

[1] Babu Goluck Chunder Bose *v.* Ranee Ahilya Dayee, 25 W. R., 100.

[2] Mussamut Golab Koonwer *v.* The Collector of Benares, 4 Moore's I. A., 246.

LECTURE XII. widow's maintenance is a charge upon the property in the hands of the purchaser. There it was held,[1] that mere notice of a claim for maintenance will not be sufficient, although it contained, to use Justice Phear's language, "all the elements necessary for its ripening into a specific charge." There must be proof of the fact that the vendor was acting with a view to defraud the widow of her claim to maintenance, and that the purchaser had notice not only of her claim to maintenance, but of the fraud which was being practised to deprive her of it. In fact, to make the purchaser liable for her maintenance, it must be shown that he was a party to the fraud which the heir was practising upon her to deprive her of her maintenance. "If the heir sought to defraud her, he could not, indeed, by any device, in the way of parting with the estate, or changing its form, get rid of the liability which had come to him along with the advantage derived from his survivorship; and (the purchaser) Luksman—taking from him with reason to suppose that the transaction was one originating not in an honest desire to pay off debts, or satisfy claims for which the estate was justly liable, and which it could not otherwise well meet, but in a desire to shuffle off a moral and legal liability,—would, as sharing in the proposed fraud, be prevented from gaining by it; but if, though he

[1] Lakshman Ramchundra v. Satyabhama Bai, I. L. R., 2 Bomb., 494, 524.

knew of the widow's existence and her claim, he bought upon a rational and honest opinion that the sale was one that could be effected without any furtherance of wrong, he has, as against the plaintiff, acquired a title free from the claim which still subsists in full force as against the recipient of the purchase-money."

Amount of maintenance.

The amount of maintenance to which the widow is entitled is generally a question of fact. The amount of the family property is always an element in the consideration of this question; as also the number of other persons whose wants and necessities are to be met out of the family property and other obligations that there are upon the said property. The question always will be what sum will properly and reasonably meet the requirements of a widow in her position of life. Generally a person brought up in affluence will have more numerous and more expensive wants than another who is brought up in comparative poverty, and the amount of maintenance will be graduated accordingly. The life of strict and severe discipline, to which Hindu widows are obliged to conform according to the *Shasters*, will not be enforced by our Courts to reduce her maintenance;[1] at the same time there is no fixed ratio between the amount of the family property and that of the widow's maintenance, as each case must depend upon its peculiar facts. In

---

[1] Hurry Mohun Roy *v.* Sreemutty Nyantara, 25 W. R., 474.

LECTURE XII. the Mitacshara country, it may be generally said, that the widow will not be entitled, at the utmost, to a larger portion of the produce of the family property on account of her maintenance than what her husband would have been entitled to on a partition.[1]

In a very early case,[2] decided by the late Supreme Court of Calcutta, the widow had claimed maintenance from her step-son. The value of the estate was admitted to be three *lacs* of rupees, and the Court awarded Rs. 280 a month. The Court further ordered that a sum of money be secured in the hands of the Accountant-General and invested, from the interest of which the maintenance of the widow may be met. There was another widow of the late owner, who afterwards filed her bill for maintenance, and the Court awarded her Rs. 40 a month. The Court directed that this sum of Rs. 40 be paid out of the amount of Rs. 280 that has been awarded to the eldest widow.

In another case,[3] where the income of the estate was proved to be Rs. 7,000 a year, the High Court, modifying the decree of the lower Court, which had awarded Rs. 100 a month, considered a sum of Rs. 25 a month sufficient under the circumstances.[4]

---

[1] Madhavarao *v.* Ganga Bai, I. L. R., 2 Bomb., 639.

[2] Srimoti Mondadari Debi *v.* Joy Narain Pakrasi, Montriou's Hindu Law Cases, 402-412.

[3] Aholya Bai Debia *v.* Lukhee Monee Debia, 6 W. R., 37.

[4] See also Hurry Mohun Roy *v.* S. M. Nyantara, 25 W. R., 474; Jadumoni Dasi *v.* Khetra Mohun Sil, Vyavastha Darpana, Eng. Ed., 384.

The amount of maintenance that will be awarded to a *wife* will not be awarded to a *widow*, because the widow is bound to lead a life of abstinence and privation, and consequently the allowance which is sufficient for the widow will not be sufficient for the wife. In the case of *Rani Ichamoyi Dasi* v. *Rajah Apurvakrishna Bahadur*,[1] the wife of the defendant was allowed Rs. 80 a month for her maintenance, and the evidence in the case went to show that the allowance for maintenance granted to the widows of the family was only Rs. 40 per month.

Variable.

The amount of maintenance which is awarded to a widow may sometimes be varied ; as, where the family property is reduced subsequent to the date of the award of maintenance, the defendant may apply to the Court to have the amount of maintenance reduced on that ground.[2] On the same principle I take it, the widow may apply for the enhancement of the amount if the assets increased.[3]

Where a Hindu widow has received certain property as and for her maintenance, she cannot, when she has exhausted it, enforce from the relatives of her husband, or from the family estate, a further allotment or a money-allowance for maintenance.[4]

Arrears of maintenance.

How far the widow is entitled to claim arrears of maintenance in a suit declaring her right to it, has

[1] Vyavastha Darpana, Eng. Ed., 392.

[2] Ruka Bai *v.* Ganda Bai, I. L. R., 1 All., 594.

[3] Sreeram Bhuttacharjee *v.* Puddomookhee Dabee, 9 W. R., 152.

[4] Sabitri Bai *v.* Luxmi Bai, I. L. R., 2 Bomb., 573.

LECTURE XII. sometimes been raised. It is not necessary that there should be a demand and refusal to entitle her to claim arrears. Without a previous demand and refusal, she will, nevertheless, be entitled to it. A demand is not necessary to create her right to it.[1]

There may be cases in which the circumstances are such that her claim to arrears will be disallowed. Long neglect on her part to claim the same, and the fact of her being maintained by her parents or other near relatives, without her being obliged to incur any expense on account of it, will, probably, be grounds on which a Court will be justified in disallowing her claim to arrears of maintenance.[2]

Widows entitled to reside in the family dwelling-house.

In addition to her right of maintenance, the widow is entitled to reside in the family dwelling-house of her husband. The son or other heir cannot turn her out of the same without providing for her a suitable residence elsewhere : nor is the purchaser from the heir entitled to turn her out of the family residence.[3] The same principle was maintained by the Allahabad High Court, where it was held,[4] that the purchaser from the nephew was not entitled to evict the widow of his vendor's uncle from the dwelling-house, in a part of which she was living from the time of her husband.[5]

---

[1] Jivi v. Ramji, I. L. R., 3 Bomb., 207. Sukvar Bai v. Bhovanji, 1 Bom. H. C. Rep., 194. Vencapadya v. Kavari Hengasee, 2 Mad. H. C. Rep., 36.

[2] Ahollya Bai Debia v. Lukhee Monee Debia, 6 W. R., 37.

[3] Mungala Debi v. Dinonath Bose, 12 W. R., 35, A. O. J.

[4] Gauri v. Chandra Moni, I. L. R., 1 All., 262.

[5] See Bhigham Dass v. Pura, I. L. R., 2 All., 141.

LECTURE XII.

Maintenance-grants are life-grants.

As a general rule, grants of property made for the maintenance of the widow or any other person determines on the death of the grantee, and is resumable by the grantor or his heirs.[1] The question, however, would depend upon the express terms of the grant, if there is a written instrument in evidence of it; but if there is no written grant, and it is admitted that the grant was for maintenance, the presumption will be, that it is resumable by the grantor or his heirs on the death of the grantee. There is nothing, however, to prevent the grantor from making a grant in perpetuity for the maintenance of certain persons, in which case the grantee and his heirs shall be entitled to hold the property free from all claims of resumption by the grantor or his heirs.[2]

Widows entitled to a share on partition.

As connected with the present subject, I shall now explain to you the law by which the widow is entitled to a share of the family property, in case of a partition, among her sons or other heirs, of the same. The share which the widow gets is equal to that of each of her sons.[3]

She obtains it in lieu of her maintenance. By partition the joint family is disintegrated; one family is converted into a number of independent families. In the joint family, the widow mother was the res-

---

[1] Rajah Woodoy Aditto Deb *v.* Mukoond Narain Babu, 22 W. R., 225; Kishen Mohun Gosain *v.* Chutterput Sing, 1 Sel. Rep., 347.

[2] Rajah Nursing Deb *v.* Roy Kailas Nath, 9 Moore's I. A., 55.

[3] Dayabhaga, Chap. III, sec. ii, para. 29; Pran Kissen Mitter *v.* Muttosundery Dosee, Fulton, 389.

LECTURE XII.

pected head of the household, and consequently could never be in want of her maintenance. After partition she loses her accustomed position, she cannot attach herself to any one of the several families created by partition, and it is improper that she should be floating about between one family and another for the purpose of obtaining a precarious maintenance. This the ancient sages could not tolerate; and they accordingly ensured her maintenance, in case of a partition, by making her the recipient of a share, which, inalienable by her during her lifetime, would, on her death, devolve on her surviving heirs. This, I conceive, is the correct principle on which a share is granted to the mother in case of a partition of the family property among the sons.

Not the childless widow.

The *mother* is entitled to a share, not the *stepmother*.[1] Therefore, if the stepmother is childless, she will only get a maintenance. The share of the mother is contributed by *her* sons from their portion of the inheritance.[2] Where a Hindu died, leaving six sons, one of them was by his first wife, who was dead; the remaining five sons by his second wife, who was living; and a third wife, who was childless, was living. On a partition among the six sons, it was ordered that the son whose mother was dead shall get one-sixth of the estate, the remaining five-sixths to be

---

[1] Dayabhaga, Chap. III, sec. ii, para. 30.

[2] Issur Chunder Corformah v. Gobind Chunder Corformah, Macn. Cons. of Hin. Law, 74.

divided into six equal parts, of which the five sons and their mother shall get one share each. But it was further ordered, that, *before* any partition be made, the Master do enquire and report what would be a requisite sum for the purpose of securing a suitable maintenance for the childless widow, and that the said sum be, in the first instance, set apart for the purpose.[1]

On a partition, therefore, among the sons, while the widow mother is entitled to a share, the childless widow is declared entitled only to maintenance—a distinction of which it is somewhat difficult to understand the reason. Where property was divided between four sons, three of them the sons of one wife, and the fourth the son of the second wife, it was held, that the property will be divided into four equal parts, of which one share will go to the only son of the second wife, who will get no share, but will be entitled only to maintenance from her son. The remaining three shares to be again divided into four equal parts, of which the three sons and their mother shall take one share each.[2]

Mother's share contributed by her sons.

In the same way, the grandmother is entitled to a share when the partition is made between her *sons* and *grandsons*, but the right of the great grand-

---

[1] Seebchunder Bose *v.* Gooroo Prosaud Bose, Macn. Cons. of Hin. Law, 62.

[2] Srimati Jeomoney Dassee *v.* Attaram Ghose, Macn. Cons of Hin. Law, 64.

LECTURE XII. — mother to a share is nowhere admitted,[1] though she is declared entitled to maintenance.

Widow deprived of inheritance entitled to maintenance. Where, by the custom of the family, the widow of a co-sharer, in Bengal, is not entitled to succeed to her husband's share of the property, she is entitled to a sufficient maintenance out of it.[2] In the case of large zemindaries, usually designated as a *raj*, it is generally the rule to exclude the widow of the last sonless rajah from succession to the *raj*. This is sometimes the result either of a local or family custom *(kulachar)*, oftener it is the consequence of the Mitacshara law, by which, in an undivided family, the property of the last male owner does not go to his widow, but to his surviving coparceners.[3] In such cases the widow of the late rajah is entitled to a sufficient maintenance.

---

[1] Macn. Cons. of Hin. Law, 28; see also Gooro Prosaud Bose *v.* Shib Chunder Bose, Macn. Cons. of Hin. Law, 29.

[2] Tarunginee Dassee *v.* Chowdry Dwarkanath Masunt, 20 W. R., 196.

[3] Maharanee Heeranath Kooer *v.* Babu Burm Narain Singh, 17 W. R., 316. See also Naragunty Lutchmee Davamah *v.* Vengama Naidoo, 9 Moore's I. A., 66; Jawala Buksh *v.* Dhurm Singh, 10 Moore's I. A., 511; Neelkristo Deb *v.* Beer Chunder Thakoor, 12 Moore's I. A., 540; Katama Natchier *v.* The Rajah of Sivagunga, 9 Moore's I. A., 539.

INDEX.